# IN SEARCH OF HARMONY

## Metaphysics and Politics

THE AMERICAN MARITAIN ASSOCIATION

BOOK SERIES • VOLUME 29

# AMERICAN MARITAIN ASSOCIATION BOOK SERIES



Since 1988, when the American Maritain Association Book Series was founded by Anthony O. Simon, the American Maritain Association has annually published a collection of essays based largely (although not exclusively) on papers presented at its international meetings. The many volumes of the series range over the entire span of themes and problems found not only in Maritain's writings but also in those of St. Thomas Aquinas and are intended for specialists and non-specialists, alike. In Maritain we find a Thomist who is fully engaged with his times and an encouragement to do the same with our own. So encouraged, these volumes are offered in the same spirit of friendship for which Jacques and his wife, Raïssa, had so notable a genius.

# IN SEARCH OF HARMONY

## Metaphysics and Politics

EDITED BY JAMES G. HANINK

AMERICAN MARITAIN ASSOCIATION

*Distributed by*

THE CATHOLIC UNIVERSITY

OF AMERICA PRESS

*Washington, D.C.*

Manufactured in the United States of America

Distributed by the Catholic Univesity of America Press
620 Michigan Avenue, N.E., 240 Leahy Hall
Washington, D.C. 20064

Design and typeset by Kachergis Book Design

Cataloging-in-Publication Data available
from the Library of Congress
978-0-9972205-1-3

*For Elizabeth and in thanksgiving for our sons and daughter:*
*John†, Joseph, Peter, Thomas, Zoe, and Theo*

# Contents

# Acknowledgements

Warm thanks are due to Giuseppe Butera, the general editor of this series, for his encouragement, counsel, and patience in bringing this new volume to publication. Its anonymous referees deserve credit, as well, for their good judgement and helpful recommendations. The volume's scholarly contributors, I am confident, will join me in saluting the membership and friends of the American Maritain Association. We all join together in the work of deepening our understanding of the legacy of Jacques and Raïssa Maritain. It is a legacy that our weary world so much needs.

I am in debt, once more, to Anne Kachergis and her colleagues. They have again shared their creative energies to produce the cover art of this volume. For the art itself we thank the genius of Giotto di Bondone. Between 1297 and 1299, while in his early thirties, Giotto painted the *predella* scenes for the Upper Basilica of St. Francis of Assisi. In his "Dream of Innocent III," we see *Il Poverello's* right hand raising up the collapsing Church of the Lateran. History notes the sharp contrast between St. Francis and the powerful Innocent III. Yet the pontiff's dream encouraged him to recognize the new religious order that would do so much to renew the Church. We await more such dreams and the initiatives to which they give rise. Perhaps the best of them involve a blessed conspiracy of friends, and here one thinks of Raïssa Maritain's memoir *We Have Been Friends Together* (1942). Indeed, in her commentary on Dante's *Divina Commedia,* Dorothy Sayers mentions the friendship of Giotto and Dante. For his part, at *Purgatorio* XI, Dante notes the fame of the Giotto whom some now see as the father of modern painting. And it is to Giotto that the portrait of Dante in the Bargello at Florence is attributed.

JAMES G. HANINK

# Introduction

## In Search of Harmony

THE UNIFYING THEME of this new volume from the American Maritain Association is how the search for harmony in the midst of discord leads us to explore the interplay between metaphysics and politics. Many of our contemporaries will find this claim surprising, in part because of its seeming obscurity. Metaphysics, for most of even the educated public, suggests the amorphous or the grandiose. And what of politics? That same public, not without reason, seldom sees politics as more than a struggle for power. For many, the political enterprise accomplishes about what might be expected from it when it deflects our leaders from the endless wars to which we are accustomed. Nonetheless, contesting confusion and apathy, however widespread, is central to the philosopher's vocation. So, too, is taking delight in the occasional harbingers of hope. Intriguingly, and not so long ago, a leading journal of opinion headlined an essay "The Metaphysics of Democracy." Perhaps doing so was ironical. But why not see it as a "green shoot" already signaling better and wiser days?

If we do look for brighter days, we will want to reflect on the legacy of Jacques Maritain. This French philosopher and friend of America understood the tightly interwoven bonds between metaphysics and politics. For him, charting their relationship proved to be a lifelong organizing theme. How could it be otherwise if metaphysics is an ordered and dynamic reflection on the structure of the real? How could it be otherwise if politics calls us beyond the techniques of cost-benefit analysis to the ongoing renewal of the governing institutions that we construct to pursue the common good?

Three examples of the intersection of metaphysics and politics come immediately to mind. Each provokes persistent, disputed, and foundational questions. The first is the character of human rights, an issue dear to Maritain's heart. The second is the character of the State, a matter closely joined to his conviction that human rights transcend positive law. The third is the character of a culture of life, an ideal central to the teaching of St. John Paul II—who recommended Maritain as a philosophical mentor.[1]

This past year marked the seventieth anniversary of the United Nations' Universal Declaration of Human Rights (UDHR). During the time of his service in helping prepare the UDHR, Jacques Maritain was acutely aware of the conflict between those who would read the document with two competing understandings of the human person. On the first view, the person is a bearer of rights keyed to realizing his or her vocation and eternal destiny. On the second view, rights derive from the individual's role in the historic revolution of the people to which he or she belongs as a part. But now, with the fading of both Christianity and Marxism—so runs a new line of analysis—a renascent positivism sees human rights chiefly as a secular catalyst, sometimes effective but increasingly not, for progressive aspirations. This analysis is, at root, historiographical. Maritain would stoutly reject it. What is now at stake is contest between a politicized history and an enduring metaphysics. In *Existence and the Existent,* written a decade after the UDHR, he observes:

> [T]o enclose a metaphysics in a compartment of history is not a way to give evidence of a sense of history; and it is no proof of philosophic sense to think that there is nothing more in a metaphysics than the scientific imagery which, in a given era, permitted it to exemplify itself in the plane of phenomena, which plane never in fact confined it.[2]

Central to the metaphysics that cannot be reduced to an historical compartment is the reality of the human person always in relation, to be sure, but never simply relational. And why not? The reason is that the person is an incommunicable substance. Yes, we are transformed in our relationality with others and above all in our relation to the Trinity, which is itself relational. But each one of us is always the very person we have always been, with *this* soul and *this* body.

1. *Fides et Ratio,* no. 74.

2. Jacques Maritain, *Existence and the Existent: An Essay on Christian Existentialism,* translated by Lewis Galantiere and Gerald B. Phelan (Garden City, New York: Doubleday & Company, Inc., 1956), 54.

Too often, the "historical compartment" that would imprison the person is the State. Jacques Maritain, and his beloved Raïssa, experienced the totalitarianism of Communism and Fascism. His own coming of age was put in jeopardy by the "soft" totalitarianism of the liberal secular State. Totalitarianism instrumentalizes the person. Instruments are means and not ends. Instruments have no rights, though the State aims to use them efficiently. The liberal and secular State, to be sure, presents itself as the champion of freedom. By abandoning the "thick" goods of persons and communities for the "thin" goods of process and procedure, it artfully touts a liberty for each citizen to seek his or her private good. But the ensuing liberty is a merely negative freedom. Recall that Plato observed that greed brings oligarchy to self-destruction and thus ushers in democracy. If democracy collapses, he noted, it is because the worship of liberty only too soon begets libertine individualism. Without a commitment to the common good, which is so much more than merely procedural justice, a liberal secular democracy undermines the rights which freedom should honor.

In sharp contrast, Maritain develops a critical view of the State that highlights the primacy of the person. For this very reason, he also highlights the spiritual: the person, unlike the State, has an eternal destiny. The State is neither a moral person nor a bearer of rights. To be sure, the complexity of life requires sophisticated, embracing, and calibrated political organization. Moreover, at every stage the State should serve as the highest agent of the people; it remains always their representative and never their master. The rights of the person, and of persons acting politically, cannot be "transferred" to the State. In exercising its office of representation, the State evidences its dignity. The greatness of a State is not a question of power or wealth. Rather, it achieves greatness in its respect for justice and the common good.

Such a State is central to achieving a culture of life, though a culture of life includes much more. The culture of a people is a mosaic of the communities which compose it. Absent true communities, it is "inflationary" to speak of a culture. The question, then, is what we are to count as a community. It is more than a group and more than a demographic. It is not a mere advocacy group. Nor need a community be a quasi-organic *gemeinschaft*. It is not, a fortiori, an ontological "super" person. Rather, a community is the coming together of persons to pursue a common good by way of shared pursuits and shared reflection. Its unity is more than a sum of individual interactions. That we are persons, indeed, requires that we be so in community. Here we find our distinctive interplay of substantiality and relationality that illustrates Thomas's metaphysical thesis: "[A] twofold perfection is found in all things: one, by which a thing subsists in itself; another, by which it is ordered to other things" (*In III Sent.*, d. 27, q. 1, a. 4).

In a culture of life, the mosaic of communities, however varied their functions, seeks to advance the common good. Rightly understood, the common good includes the good of human life at the foundation of all the other goods. States that pursue public goods only as the summation of private interests increasingly deny the good of life to those that are the most vulnerable. Perhaps the most damning example of this disregard is the appeal to genetic health, using State supported medical initiatives, as the basis for counseling parents to abort babies with Down syndrome. The religious order of the Little Sisters of the Lamb offers a remarkable alternative to such "genetic cleansing." With the original encouragement of the eminent geneticist Jerome Lejeune, the order ministers to women with Down syndrome. Indeed, it helps them to follow a religious vocation in a single community with the support of sisters who do not have this disability. (Of course, we all have *some* disability, often self-inflicted.)

When we reflect on human rights in relation to the State and the building of a culture of life, we find, as others have, that the United Nations' UDHR is profoundly incomplete. It can offer a working basis for overcoming criticism of deep-seated wrongs. Yet it has nothing to say about the metaphysical foundation of the human dignity to which it appeals, much less the metaphysical foundation of the authentic communities that can alone shape the State. For his part, Jacques Maritain rightly appreciated the strategic worth of the UDHR. At the same time, he lamented its shortcomings. It would be badly mistaken to see him as either a contractarian or a pragmatist. Early on he wrote, "[T]he problem of human rights involves the whole structure of moral and metaphysical (or anti-metaphysical) conventions held by each of us" and, in his own voice, "I am concerned with the principles as much as, and more than, with the conclusions, and with the rational justification of human rights as much as, and more than, with a practical agreement thereon."[3] For Maritain, such anxious concern—expressed with eloquent conviction—would demand nothing less than the

3. *Human Rights: Comments and Interpretations.* A Symposium edited by UNESCO, with an Introduction by Jacques Maritain (New York: Columbia University Press, 1949), 11.

new anthropology of an incarnational humanism. The contributors to this volume, in their many and fruitful ways, can assist us to appreciate this humanism. It is time to identify, in the most preliminary fashion, how they have chosen to do so. Each of their essays repays careful reading.

In my above remarks I have, without apology, argued as a Christian. Many in academia would ask on what basis I dare to do so. Our first pair of contributors have much to offer in response to this challenge. They consider what it is to for us to be *capax dei* in God's Creation. Eleonore Stump's essay, "The God of the Bible and the God of Philosophers," addresses the charge that classical theism presents a God so unlike human beings that we cannot think of them as made in God's image. Indeed, the God of Aquinas seems altogether unlike the God of Scripture. Stump, however, thinks that the charge is unfounded; accordingly, "open theism" is a poor remedy that comes with a wrong diagnosis. The God of Aquinas the philosopher is the very God of Aquinas the biblical theologian. To illustrate this unity of his thought she draws our attention to what Aquinas teaches on the indwelling of the Holy Spirit. For Aquinas, God is a personal friend and intimately engaged with every believer. Nor does anything prevent the God of Aquinas from acting in time in his continuing conversation with human beings.

Stephen L. Brock's essay, "Aquinas the Conservationist," aims to clarify the value of persons in comparison with that of irrational creatures. Doing so is necessary to avoid both an exaggerated personalism and an extreme environmentalism. His clarification includes a perceptive gloss on ST II-II, q. 25, a. 3, "Whether Irrational Creatures Also Ought to Be Loved out of Charity?" Brock's analysis highlights Thomas's conceptions of nature, substance, and form and, especially, the asymmetry Thomas identifies between modes of being and modes of goodness. Brock's goal is to show the grounds of both human dignity and the logic of conserving the ecology in which we pursue our destiny.

Though the adage that all philosophy is a footnote to Plato is an exaggeration, a volume addressing the interplay of metaphysics and politics will welcome his legacy. Plato's *Republic* will be read as long as there are citizens who seek politicians who would be statesmen. Our second pair of contributors elucidate themes in Plato that find a place in Jacques Maritain's writing. Mark Moes's erudite essay, "Intimations in Plato's *Republic* of Some Doctrines of Maritain's *The Person and the Common Good*," argues that the doctrine that to act well requires that one see the Form of the

Good suggests Maritain's doctrine of the human person's orientation to the transcendent God. Moreover, the *Republic's* analogy between the tripartite city and the tripartite soul calls to mind Maritain's distinction between the individual and the person. In addition, the account of the decline of the tripartite city intimates Maritain's analysis of societies that neglect the common good. And what of the cultural life of society? Maritain, like Plato, explores the place of art in our shared life. Hannah Woldum Ragusa's "Plato and Maritain on the Role of Art in Society: Obscuring or Revealing the Truth?" offers a balanced discussion of how they differ and of what they both affirm. Indeed, differ they do in what they take the nature of art to be. Yet they importantly agree that the service of art to the common good depends on its relationship to the truth and that the best art can lead us to the ultimate truths.

Our next four contributors directly address Maritain's distinctive metaphysics of existence and the existent. Drawing on his familiarity with French intellectual history, John Conley's "Critical Engagement: Maritain's Encounter with Existentialism" explains why Maritain makes no compromise with Sartre's rejection of essence. Even so, he also shows that some existentialist themes can enrich our understanding of the moral act and of moral responsibility. Thus Maritain is an example of a Catholic thinker who constructively reads the signs, and philosophical movements, of the times. Denis A. Scrandis, in "The Existential Metaphysics of Maritain's *Existence and the Existent*," argues that Maritain goes beyond a critique of subjectivism to present man as a rational animal. As rational, man is able to construct a just social order. Scrandis instructively sketches Maritain's analysis of the structures of being and of knowledge—from the basic report of the senses to the intellectual intuition of being. He contends, too, that Maritain can meet the common objections to such an intuition of being.

John Froula and Heather Erb explore Maritain's metaphysics in a theological context. They focus on Christology and eschatology. Froula's closely reasoned "Maritain's Christological Metaphysics: Unity of Person, Primacy of *Esse*, Integrity of Essence" presents the core principles of the irreducibility of *esse* and essence, the primacy of esse, and the supposit as the only real subject of metaphysical principles; he then applies them to the mystery of the Incarnation. Froula also carefully explains Maritain's difficulty in giving a fully satisfactory account of Christ's human *esse*. Heather Erb's wide ranging "Existents Seeking the Kingdom of God: *Esse* and Mystical

Ascent in Maritain and Aquinas" examines the ways in which the principle of *esse* is critical in the mystical theology of both Aquinas and Maritain. She compares Aquinas's mapping of form and *esse* with Maritain's "existentialist intellectualism" and points to the problems some Thomists meet in their minimizing the role of form in both speculative and mystical theology.

The roots of our deepening political disorders are the special object of our next four contributors. Thomas L. Mammoser, in "A Metaphor Gone Mad: Jacques Maritain and Separation of Church and State," offers a well-documented diagnosis of a malignant misunderstanding that drives secularization in the United States. The supposed "separation" at issue lacks historical, much less, constitutional support. As Maritain keenly appreciated, the secularist reading of this separation violates Article 18 of the United Nations' UDHR. It is this article that recognizes a right "to manifest [one's] religion or belief in teaching, practice, worship and observance." For Maritain, the democratic state of mind, in the long run, cannot exist without the Gospel. Next comes Joshua Schulz's "Toward a More Perfect Liberalism." His essay adroitly brings Maritain's political theory into conversation with the writings of Alasdair MacIntyre and Martha Nussbaum. Both, indeed, acknowledge Maritain's influence yet disagree with him—and each other—at key junctures. MacIntyre would find Nussbaum's liberalism a symptom of modernity's failure. Nussbaum, for her part, charges that MacIntyre puts authority before reason. Yet MacIntyre, unlike Maritain, cannot make peace with the discourse of human rights. Nussbaum applauds Maritain as a believer who, out of respect for freedom, welcomes a pluralist order. Nonetheless the two disagree about the fact-value distinction, and Nussbaum allows national sovereignty to serve as a shield for moral relativism.

Both Joshua D. Brumfield and Robert Delaney discuss the connections between, on the side of theory, Maritain's political vision and, on the side of practice, the Catholic Worker Movement's witness for peace and distributist advocacy. Brumfield's "Pure Means for Yesterday and Tomorrow: The Catholic Worker's Embodiment of Maritain's Prophetic Shock-Minorities" shows how Dorothy Day and Peter Maurin's friendship with Jacques and Raïssa Maritain animated their experiments with non-violence. Rather than aligning themselves with what Day called "Holy Mother the State," they worked for the sort of social reconstruction in which, as Maurin said, "it was easier to be good." Social reconstruction, of course, remains a pressing need. Robert Delaney's "Consumerism and Secular Statism: Two Forces Opposing the Common Good" puts together a detailed indictment of both. He concludes that the two forces are disintegrating phenomena that jeopardize the common good. Is there an alternative? Though it is widely overlooked, Delaney recommends distributism as the most viable approach to building social harmony.

The competing influence of politics and culture, and which is more dominant, is a familiar and important debate. It will doubtless continue. Political disorder and cultural confusion feed on each other. Our next five contributors identify and constructively challenge a range of deep cultural confusions. James M. Jacobs, in his "Intensive Subjectivity and the Paradoxical Need for Society," distinguishes between radical autonomy and the person's full exercise of subjectivity. The former is disintegrative. The latter opens the person to community and thus the quest for the true and the good. The precepts of the natural law, Jacobs forcefully argues, grow out of this communitarian drive. Kathryn Rombs, in her insightful "Thomistic Personalists in Dialogue with Atheists: Defending the Dignity of the Human Person," shows that vigorous disputation is by no means incompatible with authentic dialogue. Despite the often haughty dismissal of dignity on the part of skeptics, believers and atheists can communicate with each other. What is necessary is that both show their commitment to reason. Real communication can enable them to make a persuasive case for dignity as the foundation of human rights, and personalists can make a distinct contribution. Communication is also central in Francisco E. Plaza's welcome "Maritain's Philosophy of Culture: A Bridge Between Metaphysics and Politics." His essay examines the anthropological basis, especially with regard to subjectivity and its structure, of Maritain's philosophy of culture. Plaza highlights, as well, the place of cultural evolution and shows how Maritain's account of culture leads to his proposals for post-modern politics.

Rose Mary Hayden Lemmons's "Unity, Diversity, and Maritain's Stages of Civilization: Reconsiderations" takes ambitious steps forward. She asks that we analyze human history in terms of what unifies civilizations. Along with others, Maritain writes of both sacral and secular stages of civilization and the weaknesses of each. Thus he points the way to how, inspired by Christian activism, we might lay the groundwork for a non-sectarian and personalist democracy. There remains, however, the "Adversarial Growth Law." Maritain recognizes that even in a culture that recognizes human rights based on natural law the struggle to realize them in human institutions does not end. Gregory Kerr's perceptive "A Faustian Bargain: Jacques Maritain, C. S. Lewis, and the Loss of Reason" reminds us of the folly of imposing misguided restrictions on reason. The supposed friends of reason can be as harmful as its foes. Kerr observes that the engineers of modernity—Descartes, Locke, Hume, and Darwin—set out to exalt reason. In the end, however, they largely diminish it. Reason becomes lifeless and mechanical; it is evacuated of any ontological significance. Our culture suffers accordingly, and its healing requires that reason, no longer blind to the soul, incorporates knowledge of the self.

To be sure, neither a State nor a society nor a culture as such can act. Social scientists might decide to quantify their institutional behaviors. But only the persons who live and breathe in such political and social environments are able to act. Only persons are moral agents who act or fail to act on conscience. In times of political disorder and cultural confusion, the right exercise of conscience is of paramount importance. Our last group of contributors examines the structure of conscience and some of its counterfeits. Alice M. Ramos, in her compelling "Shame, Honor, and Conscience," contrasts the new "shame culture" with the traditional culture of honor. In the former, fame and obloquy determine worth. Expanding her analysis, she surveys contemporary phenomenological accounts of shame and value. Ramos then turns to the contributions of classical thinkers; she highlights the connection of shame and conscience found in Richard of St. Victor. Lastly, she underscores the proper role of shame in regard to the character, self-regard, and dignity of the person. Nikolaj Zunic, in his carefully articulated "Conscience and Responsibility: Maritain *contra* Arendt," asks a pair of fundamental questions. Can we completely deaden our moral consciences? What causes us to commit evil acts? He argues that conscience as *synderesis* cannot be fully expunged, although secondary precepts of conscience are often enough compromised. Adolf Eichmann might serve as a test case. Zunic's treatment of Hannah Arendt's Eichmann inspired theme of "the banality of evil" shows that her bypassing metaphysics badly undercuts her theory of morality.

Our final essay is Mary Katerina Masek's probing "Enraptured with Being: Maritain on the Preconscious and Connatural Habits as Sources of Conscience Influencing Moral Choice in Contemporary Society." Masek explores the preconscious as pivotal in the right ordering of thought and action. She guides us along a pathway from first recognizing the preconscious as grounded in *intellectus,* then through connatural knowledge and on to habits of thought, ending finally in moral judgement. Conscience proves to be a natural aspect of the soul which we rightly form insofar as we are truthful. Without understanding conscience, we cannot make sense of either the person or the common good.

This introduction does no more than "flag" how the contributors to this new volume, in their several ways, help us to appreciate the foundations and key implications of Jacques Maritain's call for an incarnational humanism. The contributors themselves exemplify the philosophical and theological work that Maritain calls for; in doing so, they encourage us to enrich the tradition of creative Thomism.

I

# DARE WE BEGIN? ON BEING *CAPAX DEI* IN GOD'S CREATION

ELEONORE STUMP

# The Personal God of Classical Theism[1]

## I. Introduction

IT IS COMMON among contemporary theologians and philosophers to suppose that the God of the Bible is radically different from the God of the philosophers. The God of the philosophers is generally understood to be the God of classical theism, whose standard divine attributes are those paradigmatically given by the great medieval philosophers of the three monotheisms, Averroes, Maimonides, and Aquinas. Some of the current trend towards open theism among philosophers of religion has its source in the twinned convictions that there is an inconsistency between the description of God given by the Bible and the characterization of God upheld by classical theism, and that the biblical portrayal is greatly preferable to the account of God accepted by classical theism.

To see the apparent inconsistency, take first the presentation of God in the Hebrew Bible; and consider, for example, the Bible's story of Jonah in the biblical book that bears his name.[2] As that story opens, God comes to talk to Jonah, who knows God and recognizes God's voice right away. God tells Jonah to go to Nineveh and warn the people that their city will be destroyed in forty days.

1. This essay is a shortened version of my Marquette Aquinas lecture: *The God of the Bible and the God of the Philosophers, Aquinas Lecture* (Milwaukee: Marquette University Press, 2016), and it is reprinted from "The Personal God of Classical Theism," in *The Question of God's Perfection: Jewish and Christian Essays on the God of the Bible and Talmud*, edited by Yoram Hazony and Dru Johnson, Philosophy of Religion—World Religions 8 (Leiden: Brill, 2018).

2. It should be said in this connection that some thinkers take the book of Jonah as intended to be read allegorically or in some other analogical way. For my purposes, taking the story literally is appropriate, since it is the picture of God in the literal story that is opposed to the picture of God apparently given by classical theism.

Jonah not only understands what God is saying to him, but he understands that it is God who is saying it. Only Jonah does not want to do what God is asking of him, and so he reacts to God's speech by taking ship to a far country. Once Jonah is on board ship, God responds to Jonah's attempt to run away by making a violent storm that imperils everyone on the ship. When the sailors cast lots to see whose fault it is that there is a storm, God somehow brings it about that the lots come out to indicate Jonah. And when, at Jonah's urging, the sailors throw Jonah overboard in consequence, God responds to their action by calming the sea for them.

Cast overboard, Jonah begins to drown; and, as he goes down in the water, he prays to God for help. In response, God prepares a rescue for Jonah in the form of a large sea beast who saves Jonah by swallowing him whole. Inside the beast, Jonah finally prays to God a prayer accepting the task that God originally set him. Because of this prayer of Jonah's, God speaks to the beast, who hears and obeys God's voice and spits Jonah out on shore. Then Jonah does in fact go to the people of Nineveh to give them God's message that their city will be destroyed in forty days.

The result of Jonah's prophesying God's plan for the city's imminent destruction is that the whole Ninevite people repent in dust and ashes. Because they do, God responds to their repentance by abrogating the destruction of the city which he had told Jonah to announce. And this is not yet the end of the story. When Jonah is filled with anger at God's failure to follow through on the message of destruction that God told Jonah to announce to Nineveh, God teaches Jonah a lesson about mercy. He makes a fast-growing plant appear by Jonah and then quickly die. When Jonah laments the death of the plant, then in interactive conversation with Jonah God uses the example of the plant to try to get Jonah to understand God's actions towards Nineveh.

In this story, the God of the Hebrew Bible is so present to human beings that they know God and relate to God in highly personal ways. For his part, God converses with people, responds to their needs and prayers, apparently changes his mind about what he has told them, issues prophecies about them that he seems to decide not to fulfill, and in general engages with individual human persons in close and personal ways.

One might say that the God portrayed in this story and in the Hebrew Bible generally is very human. When Genesis says that human beings are made in the image of God, the stories of God in the Hebrew Bible bear out the claim. As the story of Jonah illustrates, the humanity of human persons has its correlative image in the responsive and personally present God of the Hebrew Bible. There is a rich anthropomorphism here that the stories underscore and approve.

By contrast with these biblical representations of God, to many people the God of classical theism seems unresponsive, unengaged, and entirely inhuman. That is because, on classical theism as it is often interpreted, God is immutable, eternal, and simple, devoid of all potentiality, incapable of any passivity, and inaccessible to human knowledge. So described, the God of classical theism seems very different from the God of the Bible.

In this essay, I will try to show that the God of classical theism is the engaged, personally present, responsive God of the Bible. I will focus on just one proponent of classical theism, namely, Aquinas, because Aquinas's work contains the representative classical theism that I know best. I will show that, for Aquinas, who is the most frequently invoked proponent of classical theism, an immutable, eternal, simple God is most certainly the God of the Bible, knowable, accessible, interactive with human beings, and responsive to them. As I will argue, the sense that the God of classical theism cannot be the God of the Bible is based on a mistaken understanding of the divine attributes at the heart of classical theism, at least in Aquinas's version of it.

## II. The Apparent Inconsistency

The claim that God is immutable because God has no potentiality but is pure actuality has seemed to many philosophers and theologians to imply that God cannot be responsive to human beings, since nothing that a human person does or says could effect a change in such a God. The facts about God, one might say, are set, and nothing that human beings do can alter those facts. It seems that an immutable God could not answer prayer, as Jonah's God does, because, it seems, God's decisions cannot be altered by human prayer. A fortiori, since an immutable God cannot change his mind or retract a previously made decision, it seems that an immutable God could not first decide to destroy a city and then decide not to do so because of the actions of the people in that city.

Eternity implies immutability. Consequently, many of the problems highlighted above in connection with an immutable God apply also to an eternal God. In addition, however, the claim that God is eternal has seemed to some contemporary philosophers and theologians to raise special problems of its own, because it seems to imply that God cannot engage in second-personal interaction with human beings, as, for example, conversation requires. On this view, nothing that is outside of time could engage interactively with a person inside time. An eternal God could produce timeless decrees, but such a God could not answer Jonah after Jonah has prayed to God; and, in general, such a God could not be personally engaged in conversation with a human person, as God is with Jonah in the story.

Finally, the claim that God is simple has seemed to some contemporary philosophers and theologians to imply that, at best, human beings can have no positive knowledge of God and that, at worst, God is entirely unknowable by human beings. Unlike Jonah in the story, no human being could know a simple God or be engaged in inter-personal conversation with God. The anthropomorphism of the God who talks to Jonah looks antithetical to the incomprehensibility of a simple God.

Even worse, the view of divine simplicity held by many of its adherents (and many of its detractors, too) seems to imply that God is only *being* itself, *esse* alone, and not an entity or a being (an *id quod est*) at all. But if God is not a being at all, not any kind of concrete particular, it is hard to see how a human person could have a personal relationship to God and engage in conversation with him, as Jonah does in the story.

So understood, then, the God of classical theism has seemed to many opponents of classical theism to be not only unbiblical but even religiously pernicious. Nothing that is not even an entity could enter into any kind of personal relationship with human persons. In fact, it seems that *no* standard divine attributes such as *being omniscient* or *being possessed of free will,* for example, could apply to something that is not a being. Or, to put the same point another way, it is very hard to see how something which is not a being but which is characterized only as *being* itself could be capable of knowing or loving anything.

In the biblical stories, there is a readily discernible image of God in human beings, and conversely a readily discernible divine original in God for the image of God in human beings. By contrast, there seems to be so little in common between God and human beings on the characterization of the God of classical theism as I have described it here that it is hard to imagine why anyone would suppose that human beings are made in the image of such a God.

In the Christian world, classical theism held sway for well over a millennium, in a tradition that ranges from the thought of Augustine (and earlier) to that of Aquinas (and later). Augustine and Aquinas both certainly accept the divine attributes central to the characterization of God in classical theism as I sketched it above: immutability, eternity, and simplicity. And yet it is noteworthy that each of these great thinkers also wrote biblical commentaries without giving any indication of unease at the combination of biblical stories and classical theism. What is even more noteworthy is that each of them supposes that the engaged, knowable, personally present, responsive God of the biblical stories is available to him personally. In his *Confessions*, for example, Augustine addresses God directly, in second-personal terms, and he clearly assumes that God is available and responsive to him. A similar point can be made about Aquinas. In all his works, but especially in his biblical commentaries, he shows that he expects God to be engaged with all human beings, himself included, in such a way that God is known by human beings and is personally present and responsive to them.

How is it possible that these and other philosophers and theologians in the tradition of classical theism could also have accepted the picture of God in the biblical stories? Is it so much as metaphysically possible for the God of classical theism to be the God of the biblical stories?

I want to approach these questions by what may seem a circuitous route. I will begin by sketching Aquinas's views of the Holy Spirit and his account of the gifts and fruits of the Holy Spirit when it indwells in a person of faith. On Christian doctrine, which Aquinas certainly accepts, the Holy Spirit is God; all the characteristics of God are also the characteristics of the Holy Spirit. That is, if God is immutable, so is the Holy Spirit; and the same point applies to the other attributes characterizing the God of classical theism, including eternity and simplicity. If God is eternal or simple, then so is the Holy Spirit; on the doctrine of the Trinity, it could not be that the Holy Spirit is temporal or composite while God is eternal and simple.[3] And so whatever Aquinas accepts as true of the Holy Spirit is also true of God. I will argue that, on Aquinas's views of the Holy Spirit, God is as intimately and responsively engaged with human beings, as knowable and

3. Some contemporary scholars suppose that the doctrine of the Trinity is incompatible with the doctrine of divine simplicity. For an argument that the doctrine of the Trinity *requires* the doctrine of divine simplicity, see Thomas Joseph White, OP, "Divine Simplicity and the Holy Trinity," *International Journal of Systematic Theology* 18, no. 1 (2016): 66–93, and "Nicene Orthodoxy and Trinitarian Simplicity," *American Catholic Philosophical Quarterly* (2016): 1–24.

personally present to human beings, as any proponent of the characterization of the biblical God could want. There is no difficulty in seeing that the God of the biblical story of Jonah could be the God Aquinas describes in his account of the Holy Spirit's interactions with human beings.

On the other hand, of course, in the history of Christian thought, Aquinas is one of the most influential proponents of classical theism. So in the next sections of this book, I will show why Aquinas's account of the Holy Spirit is compatible with his view of God as immutable, eternal, and simple. Contrary to some contemporary interpretations of classical theism, nothing about these divine attributes as Aquinas understands them rules out the characteristics and relations Aquinas attributes to the Holy Spirit. Consequently, both the questions above have an answer. Aquinas accepted the picture of God given in the biblical stories, because it did not contradict his own classical theist view of God. And he was right in this assessment. As I will try to show, nothing about God's immutability, eternality, or simplicity, as Aquinas interprets these divine attributes, precludes any of the characteristics of the biblical God.

## III. Aquinas on the Holy Spirit

To show the way in which Aquinas thinks of the relations between God and human beings that are mediated by the Holy Spirit, it is helpful to begin with Aquinas's exposition of the characteristics of the Holy Spirit.

The very name of the Holy Spirit, as Aquinas explains it, is indicative of Aquinas's views. When Aquinas describes the Holy Spirit in the *Summa theologiae* (ST), he says that the name of the person of the Holy Spirit is "Gift." To explain this claim, he says,

> We are said to possess what we can freely use or enjoy as we please.... A rational creature does sometimes attain to this, ... so as freely to know God truly and to love God rightly. Hence, rational creatures alone can possess the divine person. [But] this must be given to a rational creature from God, for that is said to be given to us which we have from another source. And so a divine person can be given and can be a gift.[4]

Aquinas expands on these views this way:

4. ST I, q. 38, a. 1, c. I like and therefore have used the translations from *Summa Theologica,* trans. by the Fathers of the English Dominican Province (reprinted by Christian Classics, 1981), but I have felt free to modify those translations in the few places where I felt I could do better.

God is in all things by his essence, power, and presence, according to his one common mode, as the cause existing in the effects which participate in his goodness. In addition to this common mode, however, there is one special mode belonging to the rational nature in whom God is said to be present as the object known is in the knower and the beloved in the lover. Since by its operation of knowledge and love a rational creature attains to God himself, then according to this special mode God is said not only to exist in a rational creature but also to dwell in that rational creature as in his own temple.[5]

In *Summa contra Gentiles* (SCG), Aquinas makes clear that, in his view, God himself, the whole Trinity, indwells a person of faith when that person has the indwelling Holy Spirit: "Since the love by which we love God is in us by the Holy Spirit, the Holy Spirit himself must also be in us.... Therefore, since we are made lovers of God by the Holy Spirit, and every beloved is in the lover ... by the Holy Spirit necessarily the Father and the Son dwell in us also."[6]

Aquinas holds that the divine indwelling unites a human person with God to some (no doubt limited) degree. In so doing, it makes God available to her to know, to love, and to enjoy. This is a position Aquinas maintains and develops in many places. So, for example, in commenting on Paul's wish for the Ephesians, "that you may able to comprehend, with all the saints, what is the breadth and length and height and depth [of the love of God]," Aquinas says,

It is evident from John 14:21 that God reveals himself to one who loves ... and that he shows himself to one who believes.... Now it should be noted that sometimes to comprehend means 'to enclose', and then it is necessary that the one comprehending totally contains within himself what is comprehended. But sometimes it means 'to apprehend', and then it affirms a remoteness or a distance and yet implies proximity. No created intellect can comprehend God in the first manner.... But the second kind [of comprehension] is one of the gifts [of the Holy Spirit], and this is what the Apostle means when he says [to the Ephesians] 'that you may comprehend'—namely, that you may enjoy the presence of God and know him intimately.[7]

5. ST I, q. 43, a. 3, c.

6. SCG IV, chap. 21, no. 3. I like and therefore have used the translation of Anton Pegis, but I have modified it in those few cases where I thought I could do better; Aquinas, *Summa contra Gentiles*, translated by Anton Charles Pegis (Notre Dame: Notre Dame University Press, 1975).

7. *Commentary on Ephesians*, chap. 3, lect. 5. I like and therefore have used the translations from *Commentary on Saint Paul's Epistle to the Ephesians by St. Thomas Aquinas*, translated by Matthew L. Lamb (Albany, New York: Magi Books, 1966), but I have felt free to modify those translations in the few places where I felt I could do better. Page references below are to their translation.

For Aquinas, then, the relationship between God and a human person of faith which is brought about through the indwelling of the Holy Spirit is one that is close enough and intimate enough to be thought of as a uniting in love.

Expanding on the idea that a person of faith is friends with God, Aquinas says:

> In the first place, it is proper to friendship to converse with one's friend.... It is also a property of friendship that one take delight in a friend's presence, that one rejoice in his words and deeds ... and it is especially in our sorrows that we hasten to our friends for consolation. Since then the Holy Spirit constitutes us God's friends and makes God dwell in us and us dwell in God, it follows that through the Holy Spirit we have joy in God.[8]

In fact, for Aquinas, the Holy Spirit so fills a person with a sense of the love of God and God's presence to him that joy is one of the principal effects of the Holy Spirit.[9] Aquinas says, "When [Paul] says 'the Lord is near,' he points out the cause of joy, because a person rejoices at the nearness of his friend."[10]

It is evident, then, that the God described in Aquinas's account of the Holy Spirit could deal with a person such as Jonah in the ways that the biblical story portrays. I do not see how one could make it clearer than the texts cited above do that, on Aquinas's view, God is personally present to a person of faith in maximally responsive ways, communicating, counseling, and comforting, able to share rejoicing, as one friend does with another.

But, equally, I do not see how anyone could suppose that Aquinas is guilty of so great an inconsistency as to maintain this view of God when discussing the nature and actions of the Holy Spirit and yet also to hold that God is immutable, eternal, and simple, if by these attributes Aquinas means what some contemporary philosophers and theologians, friendly or unfriendly to classical theism, suppose Aquinas to mean. If God is not an entity (an *id quod est*) but only *being* (*esse*) alone, unable to act as a concrete particular does, incomprehensible to human beings, and by nature unable to respond to them, then Aquinas's views of the indwelling Holy Spirit are so inconsistent with his views of God as to be obviously ridiculous.

8. SCG IV, chap. 23, nos. 125–26.

9. See, for example, *Commentary on Romans*, chap. 5, lect. 1.

10. *Commentary on Philippians*, chap. 4, lect. 1. For the English translation, see *Commentary on Saint Paul's First Letter to the Thessalonians and the Letter to the Philippians by St. Thomas Aquinas*, translated by F. R. Larcher and Michael Duffy (Albany, New York: Magi Books, 1969), 113.

And there really are not two Aquinas's, one who wrote the questions on the divine attributes in the Prima Pars of the *Summa* and one who wrote biblical commentaries. The same mind composed both.

In my view, the solution to the conundrum posed by seeing that Aquinas accepts both classical theism and these views of the Holy Spirit consists in recognizing that the interpretation of classical theism on the part of some contemporary philosophers and theologians is not the interpretation Aquinas himself held. For Aquinas, classical theism's view of God as immutable, eternal, and simple is not inconsistent with the view of God Aquinas presents in his discussions of the Holy Spirit's characteristics and relations with human beings.

## IV. The Doctrine of Eternity and the Biblical God of Aquinas

To begin to see the consistency of Aquinas's position, it is helpful to start with the doctrine of eternity, as Aquinas understands it.[11] Contrary to the way it is sometimes thought of, eternity is not just timelessness. The concept of eternity as Aquinas accepts it is the concept of a life without succession but with infinite atemporal persistence or atemporal duration, where "duration" is understood analogically with temporal duration. God's life consists in the duration of a present that is not limited by either future or past.[12] Nonetheless, nothing in the concept of eternity denies the reality of time or implies that temporal duration or temporal events are illusory.[13]

An analogy may help here. So consider Erwin Abbott's famous *Flatland*, a story about a two-dimensional world occupied by sentient two-dimensional creatures. In *Flatland*, one of these two-dimensional creatures, a sentient square, comes into conversation with a sentient sphere, who is an inhabitant of a three-dimensional world. The sphere has a terrible time explaining his three-dimensional world to his new friend, the

11. To avoid clumsy locutions, I will leave this qualifier out in the subsequent discussion, but it should be understood throughout.

12. For more detailed discussion of this doctrine, see my "The Openness of God: Eternity and Free Will," in *New Essays Against Open Theism*, edited by Benjamin H. Arbour and Kevin Timpe (New York: Routledge, 2018).

13. For more discussion of these and related issues, see my and Norman Kretzmann's "Eternity," *Journal of Philosophy* 78 (1981): 429–58; "Prophecy, Past Truth, and Eternity," *Philosophical Perspectives*, 5 (1991): 395–424; and "Eternity, Awareness, and Action," *Faith and Philosophy* 9 (1992): 463–82.

two-dimensional square. As *Flatland* presents things, there is more than one mode of spatial existence for sentient beings. There is both the Flatland two-dimensional mode of spatial existence and the three-dimensional mode of spatial existence. That the sentient sphere is in three-dimensional space does not mean that the sentient square of Flatland is really somehow three-dimensional or that the square's mode of spatial existence somehow really has any of the three-dimensional characteristics of the sphere's mode of existence. In the story, the two spatial modes of existence, that of Flatland and that of the sphere, are both real; and neither is reducible to the other or to any third thing.

An analogous point holds as regards temporal and eternal modes of duration. Reality includes both time and eternity as two distinct modes of duration, neither of which is reducible to the other or to any third thing. Nonetheless, it is possible for inhabitants of the differing modes of duration to interact.

To understand the nature of the interaction, it is important to see the implications of the Boethian definition of eternity.[14] Because an eternal God cannot be characterized by succession, no temporal entity or event can be past or future with respect to, or earlier or later than, the whole life of an eternal God. On the other hand, eternity is also characterized by the duration of a present that is not limited by either future or past. Because the mode of existence of an eternal God is characterized by a limitless and atemporal kind of presentness, the relation between an eternal God and anything in time has to be one of simultaneity. Of course, the presentness and simultaneity associated with an eternal God cannot be temporal presentness or temporal simultaneity.In earlier work, Norman Kretzmann and I called this special sort of simultaneity "ET-simultaneity," for "simultaneity between what is eternal and what is temporal."[15]

If Flatland were finite and linearly ordered with an absolute middle, there might be an absolute Flatland *here*, which in the Flatland world could be occupied by only one Flatlander at a time. Nonetheless, if Flatland were small enough, then from the point of view of a human observer in the three-dimensional world, all of Flatland could be *here* at once. And yet it would not follow and it would not be true that all of Flatland would be *here*

14. Boethius gives the classical definition of eternity: eternity is "the complete possession all at once of illimitable life."

15. See our "Eternity," *Journal of Philosophy* 78 (1981): 429–58.

with respect to any occupant of Flatland. So it could be the case both that only one thing in Flatland could be *here* at once (with respect to the occupants of Flatland) and also that all of Flatland could be *here* at once (with respect to the inhabitants of the three-dimensional world). The reason for this apparently paradoxical claim is that all of Flatland can be encompassed within the metaphysically bigger *here* of the three-dimensional world.

An analogous point holds with regard to the present, on the doctrine of eternity. With respect to God in the eternal present, all of time is encompassed within the eternal present, insofar as all of time is ET-simultaneous with the eternal present. The logic of the doctrine of eternity has the result that every moment of time, as that moment is *now* in time, is ET-simultaneous with the whole eternal life of God. Or, to put the same point the other way around, the whole of eternity is ET-simultaneous with each temporal event as that event is actually occurring in the temporal *now*. But it does not follow and is not true that all of time is present with respect to anything temporal at any particular temporal location.

One consequence of God's eternality is that in respect of time God can be more present with regard to a human person Paula than any other contemporary human person Jerome can be. As regards Paula, her contemporary Jerome can be present only one time slice after another. When Paula is thirty years old, for example, neither her three-year old self nor her sixty-year old self are available to Jerome. But eternal God is present at once to every time of Paula's life; none of Paula's life is ever absent or unavailable for God.

On the logic of the doctrine of eternity, it is therefore possible for an eternal God to have the kind of conversation with Jonah represented in the biblical story. In one and the same eternal now, eternal God is ET-simultaneous with every moment of Jonah's life. And in one and the same eternal act of will, God can will that he make one speech to Jonah which Jonah apprehends at time $t_1$ and another speech to Jonah which Jonah apprehends at time $t_2$. God's act of will which is in the eternal now can be for effects which are in different temporal locations. Furthermore, it is entirely possible and compatible with the doctrine of eternity that the speech God wills to introduce into time at t2 is a function of what God in the eternal now knows that Jonah says at some time between $t_1$ and $t_2$.

God's eternality therefore does not rule out God's having effects in time or God's responding to things that temporal human beings do.

Someone might object that even if God's eternality does not preclude

God's responsiveness, God's immutability does; but this is a mistaken objection. It is true that since change requires time, nothing eternal and therefore outside of time can change. An eternal God is immutable. But it does not follow that an eternal and immutable God cannot alter his plans or be responsive to human beings.

An eternal, immutable God is not changeable across times, since he does not exist at any times. At each and every time ET-simultaneous with the one eternal *now*, God is one and the same. And so an eternal immutable God cannot do anything *after* something happens in time. But such a God can certainly act *because of* something that happens in time. So, for example, in one and the same eternal *now*, God can will to introduce into time $t_1$ an announcement to the Ninevites of the destruction of their city within forty days and also will to introduce into time $t_2$ the retraction of the destruction of Nineveh, because the people repented between $t_1$ and $t_2$. In making this complex act of will, God is not changing. He is responding to what the Ninevites do, but his responsiveness does not require any alteration on his part. To generalize from the point about Jonah above, in one and the same eternal act of will, without alteration, an eternal immutable God can will to introduce different effects into different points in time because of what human beings do at other points in time.[16]

Some people, however, have supposed that the doctrine of simplicity rules out precisely any kind of responsiveness on God's part. As I explained above, on the view of such philosophers and theologians, the doctrine of simplicity implies that God is identical to *being* (*esse*) alone. On their view, God must be distinguished from a being or an object (an *id quod est*). Furthermore, since *being* is just *being* and nothing else, God has no accidents. But, then, this claim seems to entail that the only things God can do are the things God does in fact do.[17] In that case it is hard to see how God could be responsive to human beings.

16. Some philosophers suppose that even if these claims can be adequately supported, they do not suffice for the sort of engaged interaction between God and human beings that the story of Jonah illustrates. Something about God's being outside of time and immutable seems to them incompatible with God's being personally present to human beings. For a discussion of this problem, see my "Eternity, Awareness, and Action," coauthored with Norman Kretzmann, in *Faith and Philosophy* 9, no. 4 (1992): 463–82.

17. The question whether God could do what he does not do, or refrain from doing what he does, is a well-recognized problem in the tradition of rational theology. Aquinas, for instance, discusses it several times—e.g., *In Sent* I, 43.1.1–2; SCG II, chap. 23, nos. 26–27; *Quaestiones Disputatae de Potentia Dei* (QDP), q. 1, a. 5; ST I, q. 25, a. 5. For detailed examination of different interpretations of Aquinas's views on this score, see, for example, W. Matthews Grant and Mark

To see why some scholars have supposed that this conclusion follows from the doctrine of simplicity, consider that if God could do otherwise than he does, then some characteristics of God would be contingent, not necessary. But contingent features of God would be accidents in God, or so it seems. In medieval logic, an accident is just a characteristic that a thing can have or lack and still be what it is.[18] Since the doctrine of simplicity rules out accidents in God, it seems to follow that everything about God is essential to him and therefore necessary for him. And so, on this way of thinking about simplicity, God would do what God in fact does no matter what human beings do. And if that is so, it is indeed very hard to see how God could be responsive to anything human beings do.

It is perfectly clear, however, that Aquinas does hold that God *can* do other than he does. In particular, Aquinas holds that God was free to create or not to create. God's creating was not brought about in God by any necessity of nature.[19] And since this is so, with regard to creating, God could do other than he did. Not creating is therefore something that God could have done but did not do. And if it is possible for God to do other than he does, then it is possible for God to do something that God does not do in the actual world or to omit something that he does do in the actual world.

But then it is also the case that God's simplicity does not by itself rule out God's responsiveness. It could be true even of a simple God that if Jonah had not prayed to God, then God would not have saved Jonah from the sea. In that case, then in the possible world in which Jonah does not pray, God does otherwise than God does in the actual world (the actual world of the story, that is) and does not rescue Jonah. And since the doctrine of simplicity does not rule out such claims, then it also does not rule out saying that God rescues Jonah because of Jonah's prayers. In that case, we have what we need for the compatibility of divine simplicity with divine responsiveness to human beings.

Those who suppose (contrary to Aquinas) that a simple God cannot do other than God does and those who, contrary to their own views, find themselves stuck with this conclusion go wrong because they interpret Aquinas as

---

Spencer, "Activity, Identity, and God: A Tension in Aquinas and his Interpreters," *Studia Neoaristotelica* (forthcoming).

18. See, for example, *Peter of Spain* (*Petrus Hispanus Portugalensis*), *Tractatus. Afterwards Called Summule logicales*, edited by L.M. de Rijk (Assen: Van Gorcum, 1972), 23: "Accidens est quod adest et abest praeter subiecti corruptionem."

19. See, for example, SCG II, chap. 23.

holding that God is *being* alone. In fact, Aquinas's position is more nuanced and more sophisticated.[20] Aquinas explicitly takes the doctrine of simplicity to imply that God is—somehow, in some way we do not understand—both *being* itself and also a being or an entity, both *esse* and *id quod est.*

In his commentary on Boethius's *De hebdomadibus,* where he spells out his position explicitly, he says, "In simple things, in reality (*realiter*), *esse* itself and *id quod est* must be one and the same."[21] After giving an argument that there cannot be more than one thing which is both *esse* and also *id quod est,* Aquinas sums up his position by saying, "This one sublime simple is God himself."[22] And later in that same work, he says, "[in God] *esse* and *quod est* do not differ."[23]

For Aquinas, then, on the doctrine of simplicity, *being* (*esse*) and a being (an *id quod est*) are somehow the same in God. And for this reason, contrary to what some scholars have maintained about Aquinas's view, for Aquinas God is not just *being,* but rather *being* which somehow also subsists as a being or an *id quod est.* On Aquinas's view, it is right to say that God is *esse,* but this *esse* is somehow also an *id quod est.* That is, it is acceptable to say that God is *being,* provided that we understand that this claim does not rule out the claim that God is an entity, a concrete particular, an individual, an *id quod est.*

Those who take the doctrine of simplicity to imply that God is not an entity but is only *being* therefore misread Aquinas's position. In effect, their interpretation takes the doctrine of simplicity to make God metaphysically more limited than concrete things, such as composite human beings, who can do otherwise than they do. But this is to get the doctrine upside down. The doctrine of simplicity implies that at the ultimate metaphysical foundation of all reality there is *esse.* But it also implies that this *esse,*

20. For helpful discussion of related metaphysical issues, see Michael Rea, "The Problem of Material Constitution," *The Philosophical Review* 104 (1995): 525–52; "Sameness Without Identity: An Aristotelian Solution to the Problem of Material Constitution," *Ratio* 11 (1998): 316–28; "Constitution and Kind Membership," *Philosophical Studies* 97 (2000): 169–93; "Relative Identity and the Doctrine of the Trinity," *Philosophia Christi* 5 (2003): 431–46; (with Jeff Brower), "Material Constitution and the Trinity," *Faith and Philosophy* 22 (2005): 487–505; (with Jeff Brower), "Understanding the Trinity," *Logos* 8 (2005): 145–57. For a discussion of divine simplicity different from that presented here but helpful in this connection, see Jeffrey Brower, "Simplicity and Aseity," in *The Oxford Handbook to Philosophical Theology,* edited by Michael Rea and Thomas Flint (Oxford: Oxford Univeristy Press, forthcoming); "Making Sense of Divine Simplicity," *Faith and Philosophy* 25 (2008): 3–30; (with Michael Bergmann), "A Theistic Argument Against Platonism (and in Support of Truthmakers and Divine Simplicity)," *Oxford Studies in Metaphysics* 2 (2006): 357–86.

21. *In De hebd.,* II. 33.

22. *In De hebd.,* II. 35.

23. *In De hebd.,* V. 66.

without losing any of its characteristics as *esse,* is something subsistent and concrete, a particular, an individual (an *id quod est)* with more ability to act and with more freedom in its acts than any concrete composite entity has.

This interpretation of Aquinas's account of divine simplicity also serves to correct the misconstrual of Aquinas's prologue to ST I, q. 3. When Aquinas says of God that we do not know of God what he is (*quid est*), he is not espousing a radical *via negativa,* as some scholars have supposed. He is maintaining only that, on the doctrine of simplicity, what we do not know is the *quid est,* the quiddity, of God. As Aquinas explains this point elsewhere, "With regard to what God himself is (*secundum rem*), God himself is neither universal nor particular."[24]

Consequently, with regard to the quiddity of God, the best we can do is a kind of quantum metaphysics, analogous to the physics that characterizes light as both a wave and a particle. In some contexts, we can say appropriately that God is *esse;* and in other contexts, we can say appropriately that God is a being, just as in some contexts we can say appropriately that God is love and in other contexts we can say appropriately that God is loving. But neither claim rules out the other, on the doctrine of simplicity, as Aquinas interprets it. Furthermore, just as the human inability to understand fully the nature of light is compatible with a developed quantum physics, so the human inability to know the quiddity of God is compatible with a great deal of positive knowledge about God.

The doctrine of simplicity is the most fundamental and therefore also the most difficult of the standard divine attributes, and it is clear that many of the details of this interpretation of the doctrine of simplicity would benefit from further discussion in order to ward off the objection that the doctrine is just incoherent if it is interpreted in this way. But the important thing to notice is that this *is* the interpretation of divine simplicity that Aquinas, the exemplary proponent of classical theism, gives. And if we understand divine simplicity in the way Aquinas explicitly does, as perfectly compatible with the claim that God can do other than God does, then nothing about simplicity rules out God's responsiveness to human beings.

## V. Conclusion

Genesis maintains that human beings are made in the image of God. But the relation *being an image of* requires some reciprocal relation of sim-

24. ST I, q. 13, a. 9, ad 2.

ilarity. Something X is an image of something else Y only if X resembles Y in some way; but then Y must also resemble X in some way. The biblical commitment to seeing human beings as made in the image of God makes it reasonable that the biblical God so often seems so human. Anthropomorphism is wrong-headed only if it is stupid. Philosophically literate anthropomorphism is exactly what one would expect of any worldview which affirms that human beings are made in the image of God.

Classical theism has been widely interpreted as rejecting any kind of anthropomorphism and as making God totally other than anything in the created world. The God of this version of classical theism is so unlike human beings that it is false even to think of God as a being or a concrete particular. On this view, the divine attributes of simplicity, eternality, and immutability preclude God's being anything like the deity portrayed in the Bible.

In the Christian tradition, Aquinas is universally recognized as one of the main proponents of classical theism; and certainly he is committed to the view that God is simple, eternal, and immutable. But, as his views on the indwelling Holy Spirit make clear, the God Aquinas takes himself to be discussing is a God in whose image human beings are made. Aquinas's God is highly responsive to human beings and engaged with them in personal and interactive ways. He is a God who is a particular and personal friend to every person of faith. And he looks very like the biblical God. The God Aquinas describes in his biblical commentaries and in his texts about the indwelling Holy Spirit is very human.

Aquinas can accept this characterization of God even while maintaining classical theism, because there is nothing in the logic of the attributes of simplicity, eternity, or immutability, as Aquinas understands them, that rules out God's acting in time, responding to human beings, conversing with them, and altering his announced plans for them because of what they do. As Aquinas understands these divine attributes, the God of the story of Jonah could also be simple, eternal, and immutable.

And so, for that exemplary and influential proponent of classical theism, the God of the philosophers and the God of the Bible are the same God—not because the biblical God is after all a frozen and unresponsive deity, but because the God of classical theism is truly the engaged, responsive, intimately present God of the biblical stories.

STEPHEN L. BROCK

# Aquinas the Conservationist

THE TITLE OF THIS ESSAY may seem to fit well enough the general theme of this volume, namely, metaphysics and politics. Conservationism, after all, certainly has a political side to it, and Thomas Aquinas has occasionally been suspected of indulging in metaphysics. I am afraid, however, that what I actually have to say in this essay is quite one-sided. It is almost entirely metaphysical. I do not mean that has no political implications. No doubt it does. At any rate, it definitely has ethical implications. Regarding the latter, however, I would strongly recommend a superb article by Marie George, on Aquinas and environmental ethics.[1] I find myself very much in in agreement with her. But here I want to go a little more into the metaphysics of the matter. As for Jacques Maritain, I am afraid that I do not refer to his works at all. But I do have things to say about both "the existent" and "the person."

Some readers may be surprised that I use "conservationist" rather than what I gather is the more common term nowadays, "environmentalist." I have a simple textual reason, which I shall present further on, for choosing "conservationist." But I think this word is also more fitting. I say this because my sense is that it does not carry the somewhat extreme associations that "environmentalist" sometimes does. For example, Thomas does not think that the entire world is a single animal or a single organism. Nor does he regard nature itself as a sort of divinity, an object of worship, to which we ought to bow down, and against which we have sinned.

1. Marie I. George, "Aquinas on the Goodness of Creatures and Man's Place in the Universe: A Basis for the General Precepts of Environmental Ethics," *The Thomist* 76, no. 1 (2012): 73–123. My central passage, ST II-II, q. 25, a. 3, is one that she mentions but does not dwell on: see ibid., 82n22 (here cited as echoing her own main text, ST I, q. 20, a. 2, c. and ad 3); 84n27 and 89n41.

However, if Thomas is not an extreme environmentalist, neither is he what I would call an extreme personalist. For instance, he does not think that only persons are real or that only they have value. And there are also less radical sorts of personalism that do not fit his thought. One in particular comes to my mind. I heard it some years ago at a public lecture by a professor of some prestige, who wishes to be considered a follower of Saint John Paul II's personalism. During the lecture, it came out that the professor regularly tells students that non-human animals are nothing but "recycled matter." Now, I am no expert on the thought of John Paul II, but I would be very surprised if he held that view. In any case, I am sure that St Thomas does not hold it. He would not have said it even about weeds, or water, or rocks, let alone other animals.

And yet there is a genuine sense in which Thomas can be called a personalist. Although he values other natural beings very highly, the value that he assigns to persons is incomparably higher. Thus, for example, Thomas do not think that irrational animals have rights, in the proper sense of the term. That is, he does not think there is such a thing as acting justly or unjustly toward them. Indeed, he holds that, no matter how they act toward us, we can licitly kill them when doing so is truly useful for us.[2] Only rational beings, persons, can be treated justly or unjustly.

So in this essay I want to do two things. The first and main thing is to push back against the "recycled matter" outlook, by laying out the metaphysical basis of what I am calling Thomas's conservationism, and by drawing out some of its implications. I shall go so far as to suggest that for him there is, after all, something to the idea that how we treat natural things is a matter of justice, and even something to the idea that nature is divine. The second thing is to show why, despite his sort of conservationism, Thomas still has strong grounds for ascribing a special sort of dignity, in the sense of lovability or goodness, only to persons. In fact, I shall suggest that the difference which he maintains between the dignity of persons and that of other beings is even greater than that which many personalists maintain. I shall organize my remarks around a single and (I think) seldom-noticed article of the *Summa theologiae*.

2. See SCG III, chap. 112, nos. 2867–2868 (Marietti); ST II-II, q. 64, a. 1.

## I. Irrational Creatures as Unfit for Friendship, and so for Charity

The article is from the treatise on charity in the moral part of the *Summa*. It belongs to the third question on this virtue. The previous two questions were on the general nature of charity and on how it is possessed. The third is on what realities fall within charity's scope, or in other words, what its objects are. Thomas has already explained that charity is essentially friendship with God, so he does not even ask whether its objects include God. What he asks first is whether love of charity extends to one's neighbor. Not surprisingly, he says that it does. Then he asks whether charity itself is to be loved with charity. He says that it is, though only in a way. Here he invokes a distinction that will be important later in the essay, so it is worth examining it closely before going on.

Friendship, Thomas says, involves a twofold love. One, of course, is love for one's friend. Love for someone as a friend is simply called love of friendship. But to love someone as a friend is to want the good for them. And so in some way one also loves the good that one wants for one's friend. This sort of love is called love of concupiscence. We should notice that, despite the negative connotations the term "concupiscence" might have, this love is not always bad or selfish or opposed to charity. Quite the contrary. In fact, it need not even have one's own private good as its object. Elsewhere, speaking of the love that God Himself has, Thomas makes this point quite explicitly: "we desire (*concupiscimus*) something both for ourselves and for others."[3] It is in this second way, then, that one loves charity out of charity itself: with charity's love of concupiscence, as a good that one wants for one's friends. The same point, he says, applies to happiness and to other virtues. We do not love them *as* friends. We love them *for* our friends.

Next comes the article that I wish to explore in detail. It is about whether even irrational creatures are to be loved with charity. Notice that it is not asking only about the other animals. It is asking about all irrational creatures, sentient or not, living or not. You might object to lumping them all together in this way, but it is not that Thomas sees no differences among them. It is that the differences are incidental here. The considerations that he finds decisive apply to all.

3. ST I, q. 20, a. 2, ad 3; see also ST I-II, q. 26, a. 4.

Thomas's unqualified answer to the query is a flat no. The love of charity does not, and in fact cannot, extend to any irrational creature. He gives three reasons for this judgment.

Two of the reasons lead to the conclusion that we can have no friendship at all, charitable or otherwise, with irrational beings. Of these two, the first says that friends want the good for their friends, but we cannot want the good for irrational beings. This is not because they are of alien kinds. So are angels, but we can be friends with angels. It is simply because irrational beings, unlike rational beings like men and angels, cannot even *have* the good, in the relevant sense of "have." Here Thomas gives a very simple formulation of that sense. To have a good is to be "master of the use" of it. Elsewhere he puts it this way: "we are said to 'have' that which we can freely use or enjoy as we will."[4] So "having" a thing means that the thing is in one's power to dispose of as one sees fit. Only beings endowed with free decision are even capable of that kind of having. And only rational beings have free decision.

To confirm this judgment, Thomas cites a remark by Aristotle on luck.[5] Properly speaking, Aristotle says, only beings endowed with choice, beings that decide their own goals, can be termed lucky or unlucky, just as only they can be termed happy or unhappy. To be someone's friend involves desiring them to be happy, and this at least means desiring them to lead a good and fulfilling life, one that turns out well and that they themselves find satisfying.[6] But we cannot desire this for irrational beings, any more than they can desire it for themselves. They are simply not capable of having it or even conceiving it. They do not "lead" their lives at all, either satisfyingly or otherwise. They are not their own masters. That requires free choice. There can be true friendship only among free beings. And only rational beings, beings with minds, are free.

The lack of free decision in the other animals, by the way, is also why Thomas does not think that they have rights or can be treated justly or unjustly. A right, a *ius*, is what belongs or is due to some individual. It is *suum*, his or hers, the individual's own. But the other animals do not truly own anything. They do not even own the activities that they perform. They do only what they are naturally made to do. They are slavish, to be owned and

4. ST I, q. 38, a. 1.

5. Aristotle, *Physics*, 2.6, 197a36–b22.

6. See ST I, q. 26, a. 1.

used by others. Only free beings, persons, act for their own sake and by their own determinations or decisions. Only a person can be a true master, an owner, to which something belongs or is due. Hence only a person can be given his or her due, or have it withheld; that is, can be treated justly or unjustly.[7]

Thomas's second reason for holding that no friendship is possible with irrational beings is that friends somehow share their lives with each other or live together. To me this brings to mind Aristotle's justly famous definition of a friend as another self. Selfhood is a sort of unity, indeed, a unity of a very strong sort: unity in being. For living things, being is life. And obviously only living beings can be friends. To be another self, then, is to share another's life. But irrational beings, Thomas says, cannot share in human life, since it is life according to reason.[8] Thomas is no doubt thinking of Aristotle's remark in the *Nicomachean Ethics* that, for human beings, living together mostly means sharing words and thoughts and not, as for cattle, feeding in the same place.[9] Thomas does qualify this judgment slightly, saying that perhaps we can speak of being friends with irrational creatures in a metaphorical way. A dog does seem to share somewhat in its master's life. But it does not quite share in what makes that life properly human, its rationality.

The third and final reason why charity does not extend to irrational creatures specifically regards the friendship of charity. This friendship consists in sharing together, not in just any rational life, but in the life that is eternal. Irrational creatures are incapable of it. Eternal life is the life of God. Really it is God Himself. To be *capax Dei*, capable of receiving or sharing in God, is proper to intellectual or rational beings. Irrational creatures cannot relate directly to God.

The article's second objection is related to this point. It says that charity extends to things other than God insofar as they pertain to God, and that if the rational creature pertains to God, as His image, the irrational creature pertains to God, too, as His vestige. Thomas had explained this distinction earlier in the *Summa*.[10] An image is a thing whose very species, or at least

7. See, *inter alia*, ST I, q. 21, a. 1, ad 3; ST II-II, q. 57, a. 4; ST II-II, q. 64, a. 1.

8. The article's *sed contra* really makes the same point, saying that charity extends only to God and neighbor, and that the term "neighbor" does not apply to a being that cannot share in rational life.

9. Aristotle, *Nicomachean Ethics*, 8.9, 1170b11–14.

10. See ST I, q. 45, a. 7; ST I, q. 93, aa. 2 and 6.

some feature that is proper to it within its genus, makes it like what it is an image of. The name of this feature applies properly (maybe not univocally) to both the image and the original. It is proper to man, among animals, to be rational, and both man and God are rational. By contrast, a vestige is like its original only according to some generic or common feature, one that shows it to be the original's effect. In other words, whereas an image somehow displays the very form of the original, a vestige only displays its causality. Now, any creature has features that bespeak God's causality: for example, its unity and being, its determinate and intelligible form, or its order to a perfection and an end. The objection, then, is saying that these features bring a thing under the scope of charity. Thomas's reply is simply that being a vestige does not cause capacity for eternal life. Only rational or intellectual nature, with its infinite openness to universal being and goodness, makes a creature *capax Dei*.[11]

## II. Aquinas the Conservationist

Our article is not yet finished. In fact, what remains is the portion that especially interests me. Thomas says, "nevertheless, irrational creatures can be loved out of charity as goods that we want for others; to wit, inasmuch as, out of charity, we want them to be conserved (*conservari*), for the honor of God and the use of men. And God too loves them out of charity in this way."

"We want them to be conserved." This is the source of my title. Thomas's using that word is really a little surprising. Before I explain why, I should point out that, in effect, what Thomas is saying is that irrational creatures can be loved out of charity in the way that charity itself, happiness, and other virtues can: with charity's love of concupiscence. His last remark, that this is also how God loves them, provides confirmation of this point, by recalling his earlier discussion of God's love for all things. That was where he invoked the distinction between the love of friendship and the love of concupiscence. Right there he was explaining how God can love irrational creatures. God loves them "with a love as of concupiscence, inas-

11. ST I, q. 93, a. 2, ad 3; cf. ST I, q. 59, a. 1, c.; ST III, q. 4, a. 1, ad 2. Of course, friendship with God in charity does not follow immediately upon the rational creature's mere nature. A supernatural share in God's nature—grace—is also needed. But only rational nature, with its "immediate order" to God as universal cause of being, is fit for grace. See ST II-II, q. 2, a. 3.

much as He orders them to rational creatures, and even to Himself; not as though He needs them, but on account of His goodness, and for our use."[12]

But let us dwell a moment on Thomas's saying that "we want them to be conserved." His putting it this way seems a bit odd, for two reasons. First, why does he not just say that they are goods which, out of charity, we want for God's honor and man's use? Why does he focus on their being conserved? I think it is because their being conserved is nothing other than their continuing in being. Their being is their most proper and most fundamental perfection. Nothing is more a thing's own than its being, and its being is what first makes it, in itself, a good.[13] To want the conservation of irrational creatures is not to want goods that merely happen to be associated with them. It is truly to want the goods that they themselves are. In effect, Thomas is saying that irrational creatures are intrinsically valuable, just as the things that they are.

The second reason for wondering why Thomas speaks of wanting irrational creatures to be conserved arises from a point that comes out more explicitly in other places. This point is that he is talking about the conservation in being, not of individual irrational creatures, but of the natures of their species or kinds.[14] What makes this curious is that he seems to hold that the species of things are quite permanent. Marie George even says that "it did not occur to Aquinas that a species could go extinct."[15] Can it make sense to speak of wanting something to be the case, if one thinks that it cannot fail to be the case? About this I would say two things.

First, yes, Thomas thinks it can make sense. To take the extreme instance, he thinks God wants to have His own goodness.[16] This is so even though His goodness exists with absolute necessity and cannot possibly be lost. Indeed, for that very reason, His satisfaction or joy in the possession of it is utterly perfect.

Secondly, although Thomas does not think that any species will actu-

12. ST I, q. 20, a. 2, ad 3. This text is obviously pertinent. It is what allows Thomas to treat his remark about God's love in the corpus of ST II-II, q. 25, a. 3, as a sufficient answer to its first objection, which appeals to God's love of all things as grounds for holding that even irrational creatures are objects of charity.

13. See ST I, q. 5, a. 1, ad 1; ST I, q. 6, a. 3. Cf. ST I, q. 20, a. 2, c.

14. See, e.g., SCG III, chap. 112, nos. 2864–65.

15. George, "Aquinas on the Goodness of Creatures," 99. At the same time, she effectively rebuts Francisco Benzoni's claim that extinguishable species conflict with Aquinas's metaphysics; see ibid., 102–105.

16. ST I, q. 19, a. 1.

ally go extinct—I mean, before the end of the world—he also thinks that the conservation of the species requires a cause, indeed, a concurrence of many causes. And in fact, he does not think that the extinction of a species is absolutely impossible or that its survival is absolutely necessary or inevitable. He at least presents extinction as conceivable or logically possible. Thus, he says that "our intellect can grasp the essence of a lion or a horse even if all such animals were to be destroyed."[17] And I think it is clear that he also regards the possibility as real; I mean, as having a basis in the natures of the species themselves. For the way in which they are conserved in being is through the ongoing generation of new individuals of the species, by the action of individuals that already exist and that must eventually pass away.[18] None of the existing individuals is a necessary being, and the action of generating new ones is always a contingent process, able to be thwarted. Besides, I think it is clear that Thomas took the story of Noah's ark as literal truth.[19]

Notice, too, that Thomas does *not* say that we "work" for the conservation of these creatures. He speaks only of "wanting" them to be conserved. That is enough for his purpose, which is to bring them within the range of the love of charity. Love is primarily and essentially in the will itself, and only secondarily in exterior action.

Still, I think that Marie George is quite right to say that Aquinas "does not realize that we can play a role in safeguarding the integrity of nature," and that "it never crossed his mind that we could eradicate a species or that we could disrupt the harmony of nature to any significant extent either by eliminating species or by disrupting the inanimate natural environment upon which they depend."[20] I think she is also right to argue that if Thomas had known these things, he would have judged us responsible for conserving the species, as our capabilities and higher priorities allow. It would be a responsibility rooted in charity.

17. SCG I, chap. 66, no. 545. Cf. Aquinas, *In III De caelo*, lect. 8, no. 598 (Marietti).
18. See Aquinas, *In I Post. an.*, lect. 37, no. 330 [8] (Marietti).
19. See, e.g., Aquinas, *In II Polit.*, lect. 12, no. 292 (Marietti).
20. George, "Aquinas on the Goodness of Creatures," 101.

## III. First Motive for Wanting their Conservation: God's Honor

Now let us look a little more closely at why, out of charity, we want these creatures to be conserved. It is for God's honor and man's use. It seems to me that here we have something of an echo, and not by chance, of a distinction that Thomas draws between two types of good: the noble and the useful.[21] These are not two species of a genus. Rather they are two senses of the word "good." It is analogical. The noble is its primary sense. Things are called noble insofar as they "have in themselves that on account of which they are desired."[22] Their own perfections make them desirable. The useful is a derivative sense. A thing is truly useful insofar as it is conducive to some other, noble thing.[23] Nothing prevents the same thing from being both noble and useful; Thomas says that moral virtue is so, being both desirable in itself and conducive to happiness.[24] But the reason why I say our text echoes this division is simply the language that he employs. The word "use" (*utilitas*) of course points to the useful. And then there is the word "honor." Thomas's word for noble is *honestum*, which he says means "worthy of honor."[25] So, in a way, our text is basing the desire for the conservation of irrational creatures on the fact that they are goods both useful and noble.

Someone may object: according to the text, what gets the honor is not the irrational creature, but God. So the only noble good in the picture, it seems, is God. And in a sense that is right. Properly speaking, the only beings to which we give honor (or dishonor) are persons. However, we honor them for something good that they have. It is in that sense that we can speak of things that are not persons as honorable. Here, too, comparison with moral virtue helps. "Honor," Thomas says, "is a certain testimony to

21. See ST I, q. 5, a. 6. The division of the good presented here includes the pleasant, but it can be set aside; as divided against the noble and the useful, it refers to things not truly good, having only a specious desirability, by offering some sense-pleasure. They may even be base or noxious; see ibid., ad 2. But if the division is taken merely as a distinction of concepts and not of things, then they can overlap and be said of the same thing. Thus, what is noble is intrinsically pleasant, and it can also be useful for something else. See ST II-II, q. 145, a. 3.

22. ST I, q. 5, a. 6, ad 2; ST II-II, q. 145, a. 1, ad 1.

23. I say *truly* useful to distinguish it from the *speciously* useful—that which is conducive to what is only apparently an end, the merely pleasant and specious good. Again, see ST I, q. 5, a. 6.

24. ST II-II, q. 145, a. 3.

25. ST II-II, q. 145, aa. 1 and 3; a. 4, ob. 3; II-II, q. 145, a. 1, ad 2.

the virtue of him who is honored."[26] Virtue is certainly a noble good. But the nobility or honorability of virtue, and that of the virtuous person, are the same. And most properly, I suppose, it is the virtuous person, not the virtue, that is called noble and honorable, just as the person is most properly called virtuous. Virtue is a quality, a mere accident; it is only a "that by which something somehow is," not a "that which is." What it properly qualifies, and ennobles, is its subject, not itself. We honor soldiers for their courage. We honor scientists for their contributions to knowledge. And we honor God for His creatures.

Obviously irrational creatures are not accidents, and they do not inhere in God at all. But a subject can very well be denominated by an extrinsic thing, even by a substance, so long as the thing has an order to it. In this way, a man is called clothed by reason of his clothes.[27] The irrational creature is a noble thing, and it is God's. It therefore makes Him honorable.

Of course, God is also honorable, and infinitely more so, on account of His own nature. But His creatures are modeled on His nature and flow from it. And they make Him more honorable *to us*. For we do not see His nature in itself, but we do see them. Thomas even says that the forms or natures of things are "something divine," because they are shares in likenesses of the divine being.[28] So that is one way in which extreme environmentalism has something of a point.

However, I do not mean that only we are alive to the nobility or intrinsic goodness of irrational creatures. Prior to our appreciation of a creature's being is its own inclination or desire to be. This inclination, as a fitting and due order in the creature, is noble, too; and it pertains to the creature's very status as a vestige of God.[29] It is a prominent aspect of the creature's being a vestige, its conveying God's causality. In fact, I think the natural inclination in irrational things to conserve the being of their kinds is at the very core of Thomas's Fifth Way of proving that there is a God. True, this inclination is not charity. But it does have an affinity with charity. Thomas says that, in a way, all things are desiring God simply in desiring their own perfections.[30]

I said that the creature is not an accident. For Thomas, only a substance, a subsistent being, is properly called a creature. And even if all beings are

26. ST II-II, q. 63, a. 3.
27. See ST I, q. 37, a. 2.
28. Aquinas, *In I Physicorum*, lect. 15, no. 135 [7] (Marietti).
29. See ST I, q. 47, a. 2.
30. ST I, q. 6, a. 1, ad 2.

somehow like God, only subsistent beings can be a vestige of the Trinity of divine Persons.[31] But he insists that every subsistent, rational or irrational, is such a vestige. It is so insofar as it is one substance, with a certain form and species, and with a certain order and inclination toward something else.[32] Common to all creatures, for instance, is the inclination toward others of their own kind.[33]

## IV. Second Motive for Wanting their Conservation: Man's Use

Now let me say a few things about charity's other motive for wanting irrational creatures to be conserved: for the use of men.

As will be obvious to anyone at all familiar with Thomas, this use is not at all confined to bodily needs, though it certainly does include them—even to the point of allowing our killing brute animals and eating their flesh. But irrational creatures also serve our intellectual and even spiritual needs, in very basic ways.

Recall, first of all that, for Thomas, the proportionate object of the human mind, that which it first grasps and in relation to which it grasps everything else, is the quiddity or nature of bodily things. To be sure, this covers not only irrational creatures but also rational ones. Our nature, too, is the nature of a bodily thing. But the understanding of our own nature is achieved only through comparison and contrasts with others. Our minds are perfected by the knowledge of irrational natures. On Thomas's view, in Paradise this was the only way in which the other animals were useful to man. But it was so in a very important way. *Genesis* itself speaks of God's presenting the animals to Adam so that he could know and name them.[34] Moreover, according to Thomas, every kind of thing, no matter how low or humble it is, has some proper perfection of its own, found in no other kind.[35] And the principle or origin of our understanding of a bodily thing is in the thing itself. It is the thing's form, which is a sort of "intelligible light."[36] This is so even though, as existing in matter, such form is only po-

31. ST I, q. 45, a. 4; a. 7, ad 2.
32. ST I, q. 45, a. 7.
33. See, e.g., Aquinas, *In VIII Ethicorum*, lect. 1, no. 1547 (Marietti); ST I, q. 60, a. 4.
34. See ST I, q. 96, a. 3.
35. See ST I, q. 55, a. 1, ad 3.
36. See ST I-II, q. 3, a. 6. On our mind's need for sensible things, see ST I, q. 89, a. 3.

tentially intelligible and needs the intellect's work of abstraction to give it the mode of being in which it can actually manifest itself to the mind.

So bodily things perfect our mind, providing it with knowledge that it is not naturally able to get otherwise. This is knowledge not only of the things themselves but also of their divine origin. Just as each has its proper perfection, so each represents the perfection of God in a way that no other does. It is for this very reason, Thomas judges, that God chose to create a multitude of natures.[37] And not just personal natures. He teaches that the universe of creatures as a whole, though not a person and though including non-persons, is in a very real way more perfect than its intellectual part. It is so, "extensively and diffusively."[38] The perfection that is intrinsic to intellectual nature is only part of the perfection of the whole universe. This is so even though the intellectual creature has a greater likeness of the divine perfection, "intensively and collectively"; that is, insofar as he is *capax Dei*.[39] Our greatest, most ennobling property is not an absolute, self-contained item. It is entirely relative to God. Paradoxically, it is really an infinite *need*.

But we should notice that right here, in our relation to God, the irrational creature is still of use to us. It is so not only by its helping to make God known to us, but also, precisely, by its making Him honorable to us. As Thomas sees it, to honor God is the proper end, the very point, of the virtue of religion.[40] It seems quite fitting, then, that the Roman Pontiff should show concern for these creatures, just for the motive indicated in his encyclical's title: *Laudato si'*—"Be ye praised, my Lord."

Notice also that, on Thomas's account, the virtue of religion is a part of the virtue of justice. It is the virtue by which we render to God what is due to Him or what He has a right to, as far as we can. This is why I say there is something to the idea that the way in which we treat other animals, and all other natural things, is a matter of justice. To be sure, it is not justice toward the things themselves. We can no more be unfair to them than they can be to us. But Thomas says quite explicitly that to act against the natural order is to do an injustice toward God. As such, it is graver than to act against any

37. ST I, q. 47, aa. 1–2; cf. ST I, q. 65, a. 2.

38. ST I, q. 93, a. 2, ad 3.

39. Ibid.

40. See ST II-II, q. 81, aa. 2, 4, 6; q. 83, a. 3; on our need for sensible things by which to honor God, and on the honor's being only for our benefit, not His (who in Himself is "full of glory"), see ST II-II, q. 81, a. 7.

humanly instituted order, any man-made law.[41] Irrational beings may only be tools, but they are not primarily *our* tools. If their Master has put them at our disposal, it is on condition that we care for them and use them in ways that befit them.

One last remark about the irrational creature's usefulness to us. In our text's reply to the third objection, Thomas says that the friendship of charity does not extend to irrational creatures, even though the theological virtue of faith does. Faith can extend to whatever is in any way true. Faith's "formal object," in fact, is God as primary truth, principle of all truth. Faith assents only to what is revealed by God.[42] Now, revelation expresses God's own knowledge, and of course His knowledge is not taken from creatures, nor is its truth measured by them. Rather they are measured by His truth. And if there is any sense in which creatures themselves can be called true, it is by their order toward His truth, not to ours.[43] But notice that this is so even though they themselves are causes and measures of our truth—I mean, of the truth that we attain naturally, not by supernatural revelation—and even though their intrinsic intelligibility, rooted in their forms, is actualized only in us. They are not called true for this reason. For they are not ordered to our minds per se, but only *per accidens*.[44] Their relation or order to our minds is incidental to their own natures.

I find this quite striking. Irrational creatures exist for our use and are by nature subordinate to us, but our use of them is not a perfection of their natures.[45] The subordination is not, so to speak, anything *in* them. It is only in the mind of their maker. They themselves do not really care—do not depend on—whether we know them or what we think about them. This, Thomas says, is why we do not have to give them the "benefit of the doubt," as we do to persons.[46] Irrational creatures are not harmed or offended if we think of them as (say) recycled matter. Granted, such a thought could lead to acting in ways that are very bad for them and that may thereby harm human beings and dishonor God. But my point is that one of the greatest benefits that we gain from irrational creatures lies in their *not* existing merely relative to us or in function of us. They are beings in themselves.

41. ST II-II, q. 154, a. 12, ad 1.
42. See ST II-II, q. 1, a. 1.
43. ST I, q. 16, a. 1.
44. Ibid.
45. See ST I, q. 87, a. 3, ad 2.
46. See ST II-II, q. 60, a. 4, ad 2.

Each one is a substance, a very subject of being, a true "existent," to use Maritain's word. They have the nobility that is conveyed by the word "reality." And so they push us toward the consideration of truth, which is our end. That is an exquisite kind of utility.

## V. Being and Goodness, Substances and Persons

Enough has been said, I hope, to put to rest the "recycled matter" view. On that view, I dare say, the only subsistent, apart from persons, is matter; the forms in it are, at most, accidental; and there is no real inclination in nature toward conserving the being of any specific kind. This is not a Thomistic view. It is closer to some pre-Socratic reduction of all things to elements or atoms, or to the Cartesian conceptions of body as mere extension and of animals as machines. But now, in this final section, let me turn to the question whether, holding the irrational part of the world in such high estimation, Thomas can do justice to the immeasurably higher worth of the rational part, the persons. There is no question that he affirms this worth. We have already seen him saying that persons alone are properly objects of charity, that only they can be treated justly or unjustly, and so forth. But the question is whether he can explain this adequately. How much of a difference between persons and non-persons does his metaphysics succeed in establishing?

Think of his famous assertion that the term "'person' signifies what is most perfect in all of nature, namely, that which subsists in a rational nature."[47] This is something, of course, but is it sufficient? It puts persons on top of the scale of things. But it seems to put them on the *same* scale. And even if Thomas does see in intellectual nature the root of a certain infinity, in the case of created persons it is after all only a qualified infinity. It is an infinite capacity to share in the perfection of being as a whole and in its supreme cause. For Thomas, the created person, taken absolutely, is only a finite being, with a finite intrinsic perfection.[48] And the intrinsic perfection of the universe as a whole is greater. The staunch personalist may therefore feel that the true value of the person has not yet been disclosed or explained. Persons and non-persons must be shown to be, in the final analysis, incommensurable. The difference must be infinite. No amount of non-personal goods can equal the goodness of even a single person. Not even all the species of animals and

47. ST I, q. 29, a. 3.
48. See ST I, q. 7, a. 2; ST I, q. 50, a. 2, ad 4.

plants and minerals together are worth what any one human being is worth. Even if the species are to be conserved, any mere individual of a species is expendable, replaceable. One oak tree can substitute for another. But nothing and no one can substitute for a person. As some personalists actually put it, it is as though each person is a whole species of his or her own. Each one makes a unique contribution to the world. Others may add to it, but none can replace it. And at least some personalists maintain that the notions of nature, form, substance, and the like, do not suffice to account for this difference. They insist that a richer metaphysics is needed.

What would St Thomas say about that? I think he would say first of all that it rather misses the point. It does not really hit upon the dignity that is proper to persons at all. Even if it assigns greater dignity to persons than to anything else, even infinitely greater, it is still the same *kind* of dignity. It is still measuring persons and non-persons on the same scale. It is looking to the sort of *contribution* that they make to the world. Suppose a fellow were to open his heart to you and say, "You know, I have so many loves. I love my job, and I love my house, and I love my car, and I love my iPhone, and I love my dog, and I love my wife." There would be something wrong with that, would there not? There would be something wrong, even if he added that he loves his wife infinitely more than the other things. For he would still be presenting her as lovable in the same way that the others are. He would be presenting her as something that it is *good to have*. Of course, it *is* very good to have a wife, as it is very good to have a friend. But wives, and friends, and persons generally are not just goods to be had. They are what all the goods to be had are to be had *by*. That is, they are what all the good things, themselves included, are *for*.

It is just what we considered earlier, in Thomas's explanation of why irrational beings can in some sense be loved, but not as friends. They can only be loved as goods that we want for our friends. Natural things are valuable *in* themselves, but they are not *for* themselves. They are for persons. Just as only persons can be happy or unhappy, only they can truly possess their goods and relate to them as goods, knowing their goodness and using and enjoying them, and wanting others to have and use and enjoy them, too. Of course, they also know their own goodness and that of other persons, and they benefit from it and enjoy it. Their goodness is not for themselves alone. But it *is* for themselves, and that puts them on an entirely different level from that of good things that are not persons. Even though a person be only part of the world, and the world as a whole contain more perfection and goodness than that person does, that person is not just another contribution to the world. The world itself is *for* that person. Again, of course, it is not for that person alone. It is for every person. But it is not for any non-person. It is not even for itself.

In short, only persons are for their own sake. If we want a single word that encapsulates this difference between the goodness or the lovability or the dignity of persons and that of everything else, Thomas has one at hand. It is the word "freedom."[49] Most fundamentally, for him, to be free is just that: to be for one's own sake. If you treat persons as though they were only for your sake and not for their own, as well, you are treating them as tools, slaves. And while you may be kind to them, and you may like them, and you may even want them to like you, nevertheless, insofar as you treat them as slaves, you cannot be friends with them. A friend is someone you love the way you love yourself. But the point is, only persons can be loved that way.

Now I think it is true that in order to account for this, such metaphysical notions as nature, form, and substance are not sufficient. That is, the notions pertaining strictly to the explanation of a person's *being* are not sufficient. But I also think the additional metaphysical notions and principles that are needed to do the job are provided by Thomas himself. They are notions pertaining to the metaphysics of the *good*. Again, we have already caught a glimpse of them, in the distinction between what is fit to be an object of love of friendship and what is fit only to be an object of love of concupiscence.[50] Since something is lovable insofar as it is good, this amounts to a distinction between ways of being good. Much could be said about it.[51] I only want to call attention to is how strong it is.

As alone fit for love of friendship, persons are not just more lovable, not just greater goods, than other beings. Not even "infinitely greater" quite

49. See SCG I, chap. 88, no. 734.

50. I say "only"; what is lovable with love of friendship can also be, and in fact always is, lovable with love of concupiscence as well. Only personal beings can enjoy the good, and they are also the beings that can be the most enjoyable.

51. For thorough and excellent treatments of the distinction and of its relation to Thomas's notion of the person, see these studies by David M. Gallagher: "Person and Ethics in Thomas Aquinas," *Acta Philosophica* 4, no. 1 (1995): 51–71; "Desire for Beatitude and Love of Friendship in Thomas Aquinas," *Mediaeval Studies* 58 (1996): 1–47; "Thomas Aquinas on Self-Love as the Basis for Love of Others," *Acta Philosophica* 8, no. 1 (1999): 23–44. I discuss the distinction, and the point about it that I signal here, more fully in Stephen L. Brock, "Is Uniqueness at the Root of Personal Dignity? John Crosby and Thomas Aquinas," *The Thomist* 69, no. 2 (2005): 173–201, esp. 191–97.

captures it. Rather, persons are good in a different, and predominant, *sense* of the word "good." Thomas goes so far as to compare how the objects of the two loves differ, as goods, with how a subsistent thing and a merely inherent thing differ from each other, as beings. He does this in the first question on love in the *Prima secundae* of the *Summa*:

> What is loved with love of friendship is loved without qualification and for itself, while what is loved with love of concupiscence is not loved without qualification and for itself, but it is loved for another. For just as an entity (*ens*), without qualification, is that which has being (*esse*), while an entity in a qualified sense is that which is in another; so good, which converts with entity, taken without qualification is that which itself has goodness; while that which is the good of another is good in a qualified sense.[52]

Now we should not confuse what Thomas here calls being "good for another" or "of another" with being good merely as a means. A means, as such, is good only as conducive to some further result, some end. Yet even a genuine end, a noble good, can be a mere "good of another," in the sense that it is only for another to enjoy. In this sense even the very last end, happiness, is a "good of another."[53]

But the point that I mainly wish to stress is that even some of the subsistent beings, the irrational ones, are only goods of another. That is, the comparison between goods and entities is not a strict symmetry. Persons and non-persons can have a common mode of being, or be entities in the same sense—namely, in the sense of a (composite) substance—and yet they have radically different modes of goodness and are good in diverse, merely analogical senses. And the primary sense applies to persons.[54]

This may sound like an ad hoc response to the request for an account of the special value or dignity of persons. But I think it dovetails with something that Thomas explains early on in the *Prima pars*. This is that although

52. ST I-II, q. 26, a. 4. For a similar discussion, see Aquinas, *In De divinis nominibus*, chap. 4, lect. 9, no. 404 (Marietti).

53. George, "Aquinas on the Goodness of Creatures," 83–84, seems to get a bit confused on this point, speaking as if the fact that irrational creatures are noble and can never become "junk" (as mere tools can) means that they are loved with something more than love of concupiscence.

54. Another asymmetry is seen in the fact (mentioned in n. 49 above) that what is good for itself, lovable with love of friendship, can also be good for another and lovable with love of concupiscence; this is true even of God (see, e.g., ST I, q. 60, a. 5). But what subsists, at least as a complete subsistent (this rules out the human soul) cannot also inhere in another as a form in matter or in a subject. That would imply a contradiction: being in another and not being in another.

entity and good are convertible—whatever is somehow an entity is somehow good, and vice-versa—nonetheless the primary or unqualified senses of "entity" and "good" are not convertible.[55] (This is not absurd. After all, as he stresses here, the two terms are not simply synonymous.) In this text, the discussion of the good seems to be confined to how the term is used when taken strictly in relation to the nature of what it is said of; I mean, for example, when a horse is said to be a good *horse*. He is saying that what makes a horse be an entity without qualification—what makes it simply exist—is its substantial being, and this does give it some goodness; but in order for it to be an unqualifiedly good horse, it needs much more—it must be of a certain size, be healthy, be strong, etc. By contrast, I take the passage from the *Prima secundae* to be saying that even to be an unqualifiedly good horse is not the same as to be unqualifiedly good, *period*. That belongs only to what is lovable with love of friendship. And this must be a person. Persons and non-persons may be entities in the same sense.[56] But they are not good, or lovable, in the same sense. The lovability of persons is not on the same scale with that of other entities.

But what is especially typical of Thomas, it seems to me, is his not having to disparage trees in order to exalt persons—or vice-versa. We find the same thing in his treatment of other rankings: nature and grace, philosophy and theology, creature and creator. To his eyes, the non-rational part of reality is very great, fascinating, noble. But its value is in no way enhanced by merely denying that it exists for us and for its (and our) maker. For in any case, it simply cannot be loved as friends are loved. I do not say *should* not; I say *cannot*. Irrational creatures cannot be other selves to us. But they can, and should, be loved *for* us and for our friends. And if we do want their conservation, we should certainly be glad to have a Friend who can always do something about it.

55. See ST I, q. 5, a. 1, ad 1.

56. Both a human person and a tree exist through a form inhering in matter. They are divided from the potency of matter in the same way. (On division from what is merely in potency, in relation to being, see the passage cited in n. 55 above.) They are in the same real genus of substance. Angelic persons exist through, and are, forms that are entirely separate from matter. They are not in the same real genus as human persons. But a human person's form (soul) has something in common with an angel, namely, subsistence. And although it shares its being with matter, it and its being do not depend on matter in a way that lower forms do. (See ST I, q. 76, a. 1, ad 4; also Aquinas, *Quaestio disputata de anima*, a. 1, ad 5, and a. 2, ad 2, 3, etc.) In this way, I think we can say that any person's being transcends that of any non-person in a disproportionate way. But I am suggesting that the person's goodness differs even more radically.

# II

# THE LEGACY OF PLATO

MARK MOES

# Intimations in Plato's *Republic* of Some Doctrines of Maritain's *The Person and the Common Good*

PLATO'S *REPUBLIC* FORESHADOWS key Thomist doctrines of Maritain's *The Person and the Common Good.* In my essay I argue for a theistic interpretation of the Form of the Good in *Republic* 6 in order to suggest that Socrates' doctrine that anyone who is to act well must see the Form of the Good adumbrates Maritain's doctrine of the fundamental orientation of the human person to the transcendent God. I then outline Maritain's discussions of (1) the distinction between individuality and personality, (2) the nature of the common good, and (3) the types of society that disregard the common good. Next, I show that Socrates' use of the analogy between the tripartite city and the tripartite soul intimates Maritain's distinction between individuality and personality. Finally, I show that Socrates' parable of the decline of the tripartite regimes in books 8 and 9 of the *Republic* anticipates Maritain's views about societies that neglect the common good.

## I. Plato's Form of the Good and Maritain's Fundamental Orientation of the Person to God

Maritain singles out God's Trinitarian life as the ultimate human common good by showing the relation of this transcendent life to the common goods realized in human communities. In the Trinity, the Divine Essence is the *common good* of the three subsisting personal Relations. Maritain shows that in a true human society, members participate in common goods that flow back upon them. For him, the Trinitarian God is the super-analogue of the human community. Earthly societies fall on a scale between, at one extreme, those that to some extent image the Trinitarian society and, at the other extreme, animal societies, such as beehives, whose members have no common good and are utterly subservient to the proper good of the whole.[1]

At the end of book 9 of the *Republic*, Socrates says something that, on one interpretation, remarkably anticipates Maritain's doctrine. Socrates suggests that the "philosophical ruler,"[2] whose soul has been transformed by philosophy and is dedicated to serving others in the task of imitating the divine, can participate in a more divine life even if he is confined on earth in a corrupt society. At 592ab, after Glaucon avers that a truly good society exists nowhere on earth, Plato has Socrates respond: "Perhaps there is a pattern of it laid up in heaven for him who wishes to contemplate it and so beholding to constitute himself its citizen."[3] Socrates, on this interpretation, is referring back to his teaching in book 6 that a "philosophical ruler" must have a spiritual-intellectual encounter with the transcendent Form of the Good.

### 1. *What is the Form of the Good?*

Kenneth Sayre has argued that the non-hypothetical *arche* that is the final goal of inquiry in the Divided Line passage of the *Republic* is the interconnected field of eternal Forms—the totality of Forms in their natural relationships, something like a Logos or World-Plan.[4] This field of blending Forms is that upon which, according to the Eleatic Stranger in the *Sophist*, all discourse depends, in that discursive knowledge consists in articulating

1. Jacques Maritain, *The Person and the Common Good*, translated by John J. Fitzgerald (London: Geoffrey Bles, 1948), 12–22.

2. Socrates' treatment of the craft of ruling in *Republic* 1 (345b–350d) has already suggested that craft communities share common goods internal to themselves and have practitioners whose expertise consists in the service to their clients and fellow practitioners, and he suggests that political "ruling" is itself a craft that serves others.

3. Translation by Paul Shorey in Plato, *The Republic*, vol. 2, Loeb Classical Library (Cambridge, Massachusetts: Harvard University Press, 1987), 415–16.

4. See Kenneth Sayre, *Plato's Literary Garden: How to Read a Platonic Dialogue* (Notre Dame: University of Notre Dame Press, 1995), 173–81.

some Form or set of Forms in its setting within the field of Forms. On the basis of a partial vision of this field, the dialectician "proceeds downward" to the "conclusion" (or, better, to the "end" or "accomplishment" that is, the construction of true linguistic formulations), using only "pure ideas moving on through ideas to ideas and ending with ideas" (511c2–3). The interrelated status of all the Forms in the field of Forms, Sayre maintains, constitutes the "existence and being" (509b; *to einai te kai ousia*) of the Forms.

Socrates famously says of the Form of the Good:

> ... the Forms not only receive from the presence of the Good their being known, but their very existence and essence (*to einai te kai ousia*) is derived to them from it, though the Good is not essence (*ousia*) but is still beyond essence (*tes ousias*) in dignity and power (*dunamei*). (509b7–8).

How are we to interpret this dictum? How does the "existence and being" of the Forms *derive from* the "Form of the Good"? How should we translate *einai* and *ousia*? What does it mean to say that the Good is not *ousia*, and in what sense is it *beyond ousia*? How does the Form of the Good, distinct from the rest of the field, add (*proseinai*; 509b8) "existence and being" to the forms that constitute the world-order?

Sayre's answer is that the Form of the Good *explains* how the Forms can be what they are, namely normative standards. The basic requirement for Forms to serve as fixed standards is that the world be so disposed that there is such a thing as being *agathos* or good in the first place. Sayre writes:

> The role of the Good is to dispose the world in this general manner. The role of the Good, that is to say, is to *establish* what might be called a "field of being" in which there are objective distinctions between things shaped accurately and only approximately, between things done well and done poorly, between things seen correctly and things seen otherwise, etc. In any given sector of this "field of being," moreover—ethical, epistemological, ontological, etc.—there are standards by which these objective values can be measured. These standards are what Plato called Forms. What they owe to the Good is a *world* in which there are values to be measured—i.e., a world in which standards of the sort they represent have a legitimate application.[5]

5. Ibid., 185–86.

Despite his saying that the Good "establishes" the field of being, on his view it is not quite right to characterize the Good as the divine creative *productive cause* of this field as some Christian Platonists have done. For Sayre, the Form of the Good is still an abstract item—the *general* disposition or overall *plan* of the world that enables the other Forms to serve as standards in the way they do. Goodness is the most comprehensive and inclusive value, whose less inclusive species include order, proper function, justice, beauty, knowledge, and truth. What the less inclusive forms of value owe to the Good, according to Sayre, is a structured world in which any of these values might find realization.

A passage at 517c seems at first difficult to reconcile with Sayre's view that the Form of the Good is just another Form, an abstract item like the other Forms, but unlike them a Form of *overall* organization or *taxis*, a *general* disposition, a *world*-plan. Socrates says:

> . . . in the region of the known the last thing to be seen, and seen with difficulty, is the Idea of the Good, and that when seen it must needs point us to the conclusion that this is indeed the cause (*aitia*) for all things of all that is right and beautiful, *giving birth* (*tekousa*; generating or producing) *in the visible world to light and the sun*, and itself in the intelligible world being the authentic source of truth and reason, and that anyone who is to act wisely in private or public must have caught sight of this.[6]

The present participle of *tiktein* (*tekousa*) suggests that the Good is a *productive* cause, and not merely a formal cause, of physical things informed by the Forms. Socrates seems to identify the Good with a productive principle that transcends the field of the Forms. Apparently, he is hinting not only that the Good is somehow the cause both of the other forms *and of their physical instantiations* together at once, but also that man is at his best only when he has seen or encountered this transcendent source of all that is right and good. Sayre, however, reads *tekousa* here as merely metaphorical. He takes Socrates to assert only that the Good is an exalted *formal* cause (a world-plan) of all right and beautiful things (and so *a fortiori* the formal cause of "the power of knowing" and of "the power of being known").[7] Socrates is not, on Sayre's interpretation, saying that the Good

6. Italics added.

7. Socrates in the Sun passage only uses a term for causation when he says that the Idea of the Good (508e3) is the cause (*aitian*, 508e4) of the *capacity of knowing* the forms (*epistemes*) on the part of knowers and of the *truth or knowability* (*aletheias*) of the objects known (508e1–5),

is the *productive* cause of Forms and things together, in the sense that they receive their *existence* from the Good. Socrates' dictum about the Forms receiving their "existence and being" (*to einai te kai ousia*) from the Good means only that the other Forms would not *be* (*einai*) what they *are* (*ousia*)—objective norms by which things are identified and come to exhibit attributes with varying degrees of excellence—apart from the presence of this superlative higher-order Form.[8] What 509b says, according to Sayre, is that the other Forms owe their being (*ousia*) what they are (*einai*)—their being objective norms—to the presence of the Form of the Good. What they receive from the Good is not their being (existence) itself, but rather their being objective norms. Sayre is clearly treating the Form of the Good as just one more abstract Form.

Sayre's interpretation of 517c, with its conception of the Form of the Good as a super-Form or world-plan determining intra-cosmic ethical, epistemological, and ontological values, has some cogency. Many theists, however, have been attracted to an identification of the Form of the Good with the Creator God. Is the conception of the Form of the Good as just another super-Form among many Forms the only way to understand it? That the status and character of the Good should be puzzling ought not to surprise us if we are familiar with Plato's maieutic pedagogical purposes in composing the dialogues. Alasdair MacIntyre[9] emphasizes that the *Republic* is a book of ironies and apparent paradoxes, and that its central seeming paradox is that Socrates' interlocutors (and presumably many readers) lack the capacity to understand what he is trying to say. Socrates says that he must use images and diagrams to point toward realities that images and diagrams do not adequately express. His interlocutors, not yet able to use dialectical reasoning adequately, as Socrates says at 534c, cannot know the Good and are acquainted only with images of it. Since readers are among his interlocutors, Socrates' dictum suggests that any interpretation by *us* of the Good that is lucid, precise, and non-metaphorical, will probably be at

while being more beautiful than knowledge and truth. The sense of truth in question seems to be that the Forms provide objective norms to which the mind can appeal in judging the worth of other things. The Form of the Good sustains the rightness of the knower's grasp as well as the truth of the objects known, providing the "truth" that is both the bond between mind and thing and the nature of the thing the mind apprehends.

8. Sayre, *Plato's Literary Garden*, 184–88.

9. Alasdair MacIntyre, "The Form of the Good, Tradition, and Enquiry," in *Value and Understanding: Essays for Peter Winch*, edited by Raimond Gaita (London: Routledge, 1990).

least oversimplified. Socrates says puzzling things about the Form of the Good. He tells us that it is the ultimate goal of any theoretical or practical enquiry, that we can apprehend it only with difficulty, and that we should not identify it with human truth or knowledge. He seems to say that it *produces* both the Forms and the material world (509a, 517c), that it transcends the realm of *ousia* by explaining it, and that it must be seen (however inadequately) by anyone who is to act well. MacIntyre does not think that the super-Form interpretation of the Form of the Good exhausts its meaning. He does not accept that Plato intends it as merely an arrangement (*taxis*) of forms, an abstract lifeless standard of goodness.[10] He opts for a theistic interpretation of the Form of the Good. Is there any good evidence in the *Republic* or in any other dialogue for such an interpretation?

### 2. *The Form of the Good as a Power to Order the Whole Universe*

Michael Wiitala's reading of the digression on Being and non-Being in the *Sophist*[11] points toward a conception of the "Form of the Good" that makes it much more than just an abstract Form. Wiitala shows that the long digression on Being and non-Being in the *Sophist* (236c–264c) depicts attempts by the Eleatic Stranger to refute a presupposition that Theaetetus unwittingly holds: the assumption that "to be" is to be a countable *individual* item. A countable individual item, whether a physical thing or a non-physical thing such as a universal form, has some structure that identifies it as a countable unit, both numerically self-identical and numerically different from other individuals. To assume that "to be" is to be an individual thing is to assume that reality at its most fundamental level consists of individuals that are countable objects.

10. Alasdair MacIntyre, "The Form of the Good, Tradition, and Enquiry," in *Value and Understanding*, 252. MacIntyre emphasizes that Plato's Socrates means to communicate more than can be found expressed in the text and is trying to elicit a mental vision that words cannot fully express. The Good is far more than just a source of theoretical and practical knowledge; it is an obscure object of ultimate human desire. For MacIntyre, an adequate reading of the relevant parts of the *Republic* shows that Plato's Form of the Good is complex. It is not merely an organization (*taxis*) of forms or of a lifeless standard of goodness. For MacIntyre, what Aristotle's criticisms of Plato's Form of the Good amount to is that such characteristics as Plato's Socrates ascribes to the Form of the Good cannot be exhibited and discharged by a form in any ordinary sense, unless by "form" one means only "super-physical entity."

11. Michael Wiitala, "Truth and Falsehood in Plato's *Sophist*" (Ph.D. dissertation, University of Kentucky, 2014), especially 54–148.

Because Theaetetus holds this presupposition, he has problems understanding the relation between parts and wholes. The presupposition inclines him to reduce wholes to the part-things that compose them. In the *Theaetetus*, Socrates asks Theaetetus whether by a "compound whole," we mean just all the elements that compose it or one character produced by the combination of elements yet different from them. Upon examination, both options prove to be untenable. The problem is that we cannot understand ordered wholes simply in terms of the *numerically* distinct elements that compose them. A compound whole can neither be numerically identical to the elements that compose it nor numerically distinct from them. Each whole is numerically self-identical, distinct from every other whole; but no whole is numerically distinct—some different thing—from all the elements that are its parts. Since Theaetetus implicitly assumes that "to be" is to be an individual, he lacks the resources to overcome the whole/parts dilemma facing anyone who needs to make sense out of the hylomorphic structure of a compound entity.

This assumption continues to affect Theaetetus through much of the *Sophist*. As the Stranger leads him through various definitions, Theaetetus treats the forms or kinds that the Stranger is dividing and defining as individual countable things. He is not altogether wrong to do so, for both the Stranger's "method of division" and discourse presuppose that Forms or kinds are countable. Yet the Forms are not primarily countable objects, *but countable objects embedded within and organized into compound structured wholes of forms*. Forms are eidetic wholes of eidetic parts, and they are eidetic parts of other eidetic wholes. In order for Theaetetus to understand the structure of ideas or Forms, the Stranger must lead him to recognize that "to be" is not reducible to being a countable individual of any kind, be it form or formed thing. "To be" in its most basic and comprehensive sense, the Stranger contends, is the power to communicate form and existence to any and all countable compound wholes. On my interpretation, the Stranger is making a metaphysical point here: that Being itself is the one *ultimate and transcendent power* causally responsible for all Forms and things with their limited abilities to affect and/or be affected by one another. Concrete individuals all have causal powers but Being itself is a transcendent limit-case instance of unbounded causal power (not countable as a one of many, and not an "instance" or an "individual" in any but an analogous sense).

The Stranger defines Being as such a power when he says:

> *That which possesses* any sort of power—either by nature to affect anything else or to be affected even in the least by the most trivial thing, even if only once—I say that all this really is. For I set down as a definition by which to delimit the things that are, that they are *nothing other than power*" (236e).

The Stranger actually offers two closely related definitions of being. The first is that a being is any *individual thing* that *possesses* any sort of active or passive power. This definition applies both to countable material objects and to countable Forms. The second is that what is most real in things is *nothing other than power.* The second definition allows him to articulate a conception of ultimate Being as the *power which is responsible for all individual beings (in the first sense)*, for all individual beings insofar as they possess their powers in relation to other individuals.

In his treatment of the individual being of the Forms, the Stranger counsels Theaetetus to stop thinking of them as discrete individuals and to start thinking of them in terms of their ordered relations to one another. He introduces the notions of "motion" and "rest" and begins to clarify how "motion" and "rest" apply to the immaterial forms. The Stranger establishes that the most general sense of "to be moved" (*kineisthai*) is "to be causally posterior in explanation" and the most general sense of "to move" (*kinein*) is to "be causally prior in explanation." (A is *causally prior* to B if and only if A explains why B is the sort of thing B is, but B does not explain why A is the sort of thing A is.) He urges that moving and being-moved, in these most general senses, apply not only to spatial and temporal movement but also to eidetic "motion."[12] The Stranger argues that causal priority and posteriority in explanation are always involved in any sort of motion, including a-temporal motion.[13]

12. To say that eidetic wholes and parts move and are moved does not imply that ideas or forms change in quality, time, or place. The part/whole relations of the forms are a-temporal and always the same; the forms are "being moved" according to one timeless order, that order being the normative principles in terms of which the forms are structured in relation to each other.

13. Since the Stranger does not mention time discussing the motion of the forms in the *Sophist*, and, to the contrary, the Stranger argues that the forms are being moved in reference to what seems to be the divine *nous*, the text suggests a general and a-temporal sense of motion. Since, in the *Timaeus*, Timaeus describes a motion and life prior to time (*Timaeus* 37c–d), and since, in the *Laws*, motion is attributed to the a-temporal divine mind (*nous*) (*Laws* 897c–898b), it seems Plato was happy with a-temporal motion. See also Leo Sweeney SJ, *Divine Infinity in Greek and Medieval Thought* (New York: Peter Lang Publishing, 1992), 53–55. He interprets the Stranger's discussions of divine and human productive *techne* (in *Sophist* 219b ff., 248e–249b, and

The Stranger uses his notion of eidetic motion in order to underscore a conception of the Forms as constituting a *field* of interrelated beings having powers to affect and be-affected-by each other. The Stranger emphasizes that the field of Forms is an interrelated *whole* which as such cannot be merely a countable collection of individual beings; counting the forms amounts to counting *parts* of the field, which are *many*, but which form one cosmic whole which cannot be reduced to its parts. Comprising all determinate finite Forms, the noetic cosmos is not another countable *part* of the cosmos but is necessarily unique.[14] Yet Being in its most unlimited sense is not exhausted even by this whole. For according to the second definition of being as "nothing but power," Being is not reducible either to the whole of the parts of the cosmos or to a mere collection of the many parts of the cosmos. *Being in its ultimate reality is rather the power that makes the cosmic whole of parts the whole that it is.* Ultimate Being, *qua* power to structure the cosmos, is not a countable individual something.[15] Ultimate Being, causally prior to the whole field of Forms, must be the power that structures the communion of forms. It is causally prior to the whole/part compounds that it structures. The power that makes the cosmos a cosmos is "one" power, but the oneness here is not the oneness of cardinality. It is that *by virtue of which* countable individual beings are individuals and are beings. It is one in simplicity and integrity. If the ultimate power of Being is an "individual," it can only be so in an *analogous* sense.

The Stranger's account of Being enables us to solve the puzzle of the status of the Form of the Good in the *Republic*. For an upshot of the Stranger's investigations of the notion of Being as power is that Being can be approached in four ways, yielding four senses of "being": (1) *a being* is any countable individual; (2) *being* is the ordered whole of countable individuals; (3) *being* denotes the most comprehensive individual form or idea, the Idea of Being; (4) *being* is the one *ultimate power* causally responsible for all Forms and things with their limited abilities to affect and/or be affected by one another. The difference between senses (3) and (4) is

264d–260d) as pointing to the productive "movement" of divine intelligence in bringing about formed beings in the cosmos.

14. When logicians count "possible worlds," they are counting complex Forms which are "beings of reason" that are themselves parts of the universe.

15. This seems to foreshadow the scholastic dictum that God is *Ipsum Esse Subsistens*, the infinite power of being which does not have an essence as finite individuals do but is identical to its essence.

especially important, since the ultimate *power* of Being is not the same as the comprehensive *idea of being*. Now let us note that the same distinction between senses (3) and (4) of "being" can be made in respect to two senses of "goodness." The Idea of the Good, like the Idea of Being (3), is a most comprehensive individual form or idea. Goodness Itself (in a sense that corresponds to (4)) is an ultimate power causally responsible for all Forms and for all properly disposed things; it produces knowledge and truth, beauty, order, proportion, and proper functioning. Thus, it is another name for Being in the sense the Stranger works out in the *Sophist* digression—namely "nothing but power," the ultimate *causal power* which produces and structures all the countable Forms and all material things, a power to communicate normative order to compound wholes. Being in this fourth sense is indistinguishable from Socrates' Form of the Good.

Recognizing the distinction between the third and fourth senses of being enables the reader of the *Sophist* to solve the puzzle of the *Republic* about whether the Form of the Good is just another Form among Forms or whether it is a transcendent divine productive cause of the field of the Forms and of the Universe. Let us assume that the Stranger's account of Being shows, without explicitly asserting, the identity of Being with the Good. Let us further assume that Plato's Socrates understands the Good along the lines of the Stranger's conception of Being. Given these assumptions, we can suppose that in *Republic* 6–7 Socrates sometimes speaks of the Good as just another abstract Form or Idea and sometimes speaks of it as a transcendent divine entity. We can suppose that Socrates demurs from disambiguating the two senses of the Good on account of the intellectual deficiencies of his interlocutors, or on account of the limits of time in a long conversation about justice, or because Plato intends to set a puzzle for his reader.

### 3.*The Form of the Good as a* Concrete *Power Able to Produce the Universe*

The Stranger argues, as we have seen, that in an important sense Being is the ultimate power that gives being to all Forms and to all things instantiating such Forms. Being structures beings insofar as they are beings and makes the universe the whole that it is. Being is the power in which all Forms and things with the ability to affect and/or be affected by one another participate. We have suggested, in light of the Stranger's conception of ultimate Being, that it is identical to ultimate Goodness and to the

"Form of the Good" in its theistic sense. However, Christopher Shields, like Kenneth Sayre, thinks that we must consider the Form of the Good to be an *abstract* entity. Whereas Sayre thought of it as the structure of the universal world-whole, Shields thinks of it as one abstract Form among Forms, comprehensive in scope like the Forms of Unity, Simplicity, Abstractness, or Being.[16] He rejects the view of August Krohn that the Form of the Good is *not* just another intra-cosmic Form but an entity that transcends categorization. Krohn took the genitive absolute *ouk ousias ontos tou agathou* at *Republic* 509b (the Good is not *ousia*) to mean that the Form of the Good "has no *ousia* but rather is a power."[17] Shields asserts that the phrase does not say the Form of the Good *has* no *ousia*, but rather that it somehow *is* not *ousia*; the Good is an abstract Form that is not identical to the abstract Form of Being. Shields's only argument for this, however, is the assertion that Krohn's view of the Form of the Good as an ultimate power is *incoherent*, because it implies that the Form of the Good exists as nothing but a "baseless disposition" that does not "belong to anything."[18]

On our interpretation, however, based on the Stranger's exposition of Being, the Form of the Good and the Form of Being, in the theistic sense, *are* identical, two names for the ultimate power that makes individuals possible. How then can we *coherently* conceive of this ultimate power in such a way that it is not merely a "baseless disposition that does not belong to anything"? How can we coherently conceive it to be the *productive cause* of the universe? Because Being as ultimate power is not an ordinary countable individual, but rather a power responsible for the cosmos itself, it is not comparable to an ordinary *attribute* of an intra-cosmic *individual*. Such an intra-cosmic power would depend upon something else for its activation. Is the notion of an *ultimate* power even intelligible?

To fully answer these questions, we would need a summary exposition of the Thomistic-Aristotelian concept of God as *Ipsum Esse Subsistens* and a display of its coherence. (This would involve, among other things, a defense of the doctrine of analogy in the philosophy of language.)[19] Failing that, a few brief comments about *Ipsum Esse Subsistens* are not out of place. The

16. Christopher Shields, "Surpassing in Dignity and Power: The Metaphysics of Goodness in Plato's *Republic*," *Philosophical Inquiry* 30, nos. 3–4 (summer–fall, 2008): 1–17.

17. August Krohn, *Der Platonische Staat* (1876; reprinted, New York: Arno Press, 1976).

18. Shields, "Surpassing in Dignity and Power," 12.

19. Perhaps Shields is a Scotist who would reject analogy in theological discourse.

divine names do not designate countably distinct attributes or powers that belong to God in the way that such attributes belong to created entities. The particularized essences that belong to creatures *limit* their being and goodness. The Creator, as a *limit case instance* of existence and goodness, is not just one *countable instance* among other countable instances of being and goodness but rather is *unbounded* existence and goodness. "Limit-case" is an *alienens* adjective in the phrase "limit case instance," and so God is not an instance of existence or goodness in the way created things are but only in an analogous sense. Moreover, God is identical with his attributes; God is identical with his limit-case instance of unbounded existence and with his limit-case instance of unbounded Goodness. The divine attributes are not "baseless dispositions" that "do not belong to anything." They belong to God but not like attributes belong to finite subjects. A "baseless disposition" not belonging to anything would be an abstraction. To the contrary, the divine attributes, identical with the divine nature, are eminently concrete. Even in the case of finite things, property *instances* are not abstract but concrete. God is not an abstraction but rather the most concrete Being there is, so long as we remember that we speak analogously when we call God *a being* with *property instances*. Subsistent Existence is an entity to which the categories of *individual* and *property instance* are only analogously applicable. Once we understand the *concreteness* of God and understand that the Form-of-the-Good-*qua*-ultimate-power[20] is identical with God, we can grasp why Socrates in the *Republic* attributes to the Form of the Good its role as a *productive cause* of Forms and things (517c).[21]

20. Notice that "Form" has different senses only related by analogy. See MacIntyre's comment in n. 10 above.

21. For a brilliant account of God as Subsistent Existence, see Barry Miller, *A Most Unlikely God: A Philosophical Enquiry into the Nature of God* (Notre Dame: University of Notre Dame Press, 1996). See pp. 87–89 for an insightful exposition of divine omnipotence as "responsibility for *all* of any effect it produces." See pp. 129–34 for a fine account of the differences between divine causation and intra-cosmic or secondary causation. For Miller, God produces causal effects (1) without ever acting *on* anything, (2) timelessly, producing effects in time without acting in time, and (3) simply, without acting through a *multiplicity* of acts. Miller's work shows not only why Sayre, thinking of the Good as an abstract world-plan, was puzzled about how the Form of the Good could be the productive cause of Forms and things, but also why the notion of divine causality must be analogical.

### 4. *The Form of the Good as a Pure Perfection*

Josef Seifert helps us understand the monotheistic interpretation of Socrates' Form of the Good by reading Plato in the light of the Thomist doctrine of the *pure perfections.*[22] At *Parmenides* 130b, Plato depicts Parmenides teaching a very young Socrates how to think about the natures specified by different kinds of Forms. Parmenides cites the just, the beautiful, and the good as clear instances of Forms, remaining agnostic about whether there are separate Forms of natural kinds such as humanity, fire, and water. He seems to be suggesting a difference between the Forms of natural kinds of material entities, on the one hand, and, on the other hand, the Forms of the pure perfections (as they came to be called), Forms that constitute their instances as intrinsically good without requiring any limitations from material embodiment. Pure perfections find their fullest realizations in ultimate infinite being. The essence of a pure perfection is only fully realized when it is unlimited. A pure perfection does not require any material limitation. If Socrates' Form of the Good is a pure perfection, its highest exemplification is a reality infinitely and immaterially good. Pure perfections are compatible with each other, and in the divine life, they occur together. Each in its infinite exemplification includes the full perfection and unity of all the pure perfections. For example, the fullness of being must be identical with the fullness of Wisdom and of Goodness. The pure perfections are irreducibly one and simple in their ultimate limit case instantiation.[23] Hence, no *pure perfection* can fully be what it is without being at one with the Form of Goodness.

### 5. *The Form of the Good as not Really Distinct from the Demiurge*

Many scholars read the "likely story" of the *Timaeus* to indicate that the Creator-Demiurge of the universe is *subordinate* to an impersonal, lifeless, and abstract Form of the Good. This separation of the living Creator-

22. Josef Seifert, "The Idea of the Good as the sum-total of pure perfections: A new personalistic reading of *Republic* VI and VII," in *New Images of Plato: Dialogues on the Idea of the Good*, edited by Giovanni Reale and Samuel Scolnicov (Sankt Augustin: Academia Verlag, 2002), 407–424.

23. Again, see Barry Miller, *A Most Unlikely God*. See also his *From Existence to God: A Contemporary Philosophical Argument* (London: Routledge, 1992) and *The Fullness of Being: A New Paradigm for Existence* (Notre Dame: University of Notre Dame Press, 2002).

Demiurge from the Form of the Good portrays the Demiurge as Craftsman but not Creator, and it makes the Form of the Good an abstraction with its own extra-personal existence. Yet this is not the only way to read the Timaeus. The Platonic-Socratic treatment of the Form of the Good is entirely compatible with thinking of it as a transcendent pure perfection and ultimate power. If Plato's God is the living personal or super-personal limit case instance of all the pure perfections and the Creator of "all that is seen and unseen," as the preceding reflections indicate, we must adjust our interpretation of the *Timaeus*. It is plausible to interpret the separation of the Demiurge from the Form of the Good in the *Timaeus* myth as a Platonic provocation set as a test for his more astute readers.[24] Such an interpretation of the *Timaeus* harmonizes it better with our reading of the Form of the Good. It also coheres better with the conception of the Creative Cosmic Nous in *Philebus* 23c–36d, with that of the single transcendent God beyond the gods in the *Statesman* myth or in the *Theaetetus* digression, and with that of Being as *power* in the *Sophist* digression.[25] These other texts apparently refer to an Intelligence with the causal power to generate all finite Forms and their instances.

### *6. Plato and Maritain on the Fundamental Orientation of the Person to the Transcendent God.*

In *Republic* 6 Socrates characterizes a spiritual-intellectual encounter with the transcendent Form of the Good as necessary for the proper functioning of the philosopher-ruler, the model for the just human being. In the analogy of the Good with the Sun, Socrates suggests that *generosity* is one of the most salient aspects of the Good (the Sun is an inexhaustible font of light), an aspect that must be imitated by any "philosopher." At *Timaeus* 68d, Timaeus characterizes the *Demiurge* as the supreme model for human virtue. But if it is correct that the Form of the Good and the Demiurge are not really distinct, both models convey the same message: the well-functioning human has a fundamental orientation to the transcendent

24. See John Dillon, "The Riddle of the *Timaeus*: Is Plato Sowing Clues?" in *Studies in Plato and the Platonic Tradition: Essays Presented to John Whittaker*, edited by Mark Joyal (New York: Routledge, 1997), 25–42.

25. Near the end of the *Sophist* at 265de, the Stranger says that Theaetetus will be able, based on of what he has learned, to understand the divine origin of the natural world.

God, to whom he ought to be assimilated so far as possible.[26] Plato's work may seem to emphasize the equal dignity of contemplation and action, characterizing God as the maker of all and as the limit case instance of that creativity and generosity in which man can participate. To become like to the Form of the Good or to the *Demiourgos,* according to such an interpretation of the Platonic conception, would be to participate in the divine life through rational activity and not just through contemplation.

Yet Plato's emphasis on an intellectual *vision* of the Good anticipates Maritain's exposition of how the doctrine of man's supreme end in the beatific vision maintains the superiority of the speculative over the practical intellect.[27] In the beatific union the soul enters into a perfect love by which God loves his creatures "not only as the artisan loves his work but also ... as friend loves friend." Because of this union, another society forms among the blessed souls who love one another mutually in God. Because of this union, the blessed communicate in God's love with one another by all the created communications of mutual knowledge and charity that flow from the vision. Those exchanges render back to each of the blessed the created goods that they hold in common. Maritain emphasizes, following Aquinas, that beatitude pertains primarily to the speculative and not to the practical intellect, that the good of speculative union with God is greater than every created common good, and that therefore the contemplative life is pre-eminent over the political life. Yet Maritain acknowledges that it is from the speculative union with God that the works of the active life "must overflow."[28] The doctrine of the beatific union, he says, "is at the same time a doctrine of the primacy of the common good." Because the common good is the *human* common good, it includes the active service of the human person. This latter dictum leads Maritain to draw his profound distinction between *individuality* and *personality.*

26. Divinization, becoming like the God who is the font of all goodness and maker of heaven and earth (*homoiosis tou Theou*), is the ultimate human goal in Plato's thought.

27. Maritain, *Person and the Common Good,* 17–22.

28. Ibid., 20.

## III. Maritain on Individuality and Personality, the Common Good, and Societies Disregarding the Common Good

The last three chapters of *The Person and the Common Good* attempt to clarify the ways in which Aquinas's theory of the person—with its distinction between individuality and personality—stands in opposition to possessive individualism and totalitarianism. For Maritain, the human being, an embodied spiritual substance, lives between two poles: a material pole that concerns his material *individuality* and a spiritual pole that concerns his *personality*. Individuality is the narrowness of the ego forever eager to *grasp for itself*. "Evil arises," writes Maritain, "when, in our action, we give the preponderance to the individual aspect of our being."[29] Personality, on the other hand, is the metaphysical center of the human being, intelligent and free, that in loving another *gives itself* to the other by contributing to the common good. He contends that *bourgeois liberalism*, in which human beings conceive of themselves as individuals rather than as persons, inevitably ends in totalitarianism.

Maritain explicates the human common good by contrasting it with animal groups or colonies that are collective wholes of mere individuals. Unlike animals, human persons tend to *overflow into social communications* in response to the law of superabundance inscribed in their being. Such communications are more necessary for human development than are provisions for material needs. The works of reason in the arts, sciences, crafts in service of the highest values of culture and the works of love in community life, respond to the spiritual nature of human beings. They require development through character training, education, and social cooperation. Persons participating in the common goods of intellectual and moral communities receive goods that are common to all participants, each one of which is, as a person, a *mirror of the whole.* Persons in such communities indirectly conform themselves to their ultimate end and common good, the Divine Trinity. "Among the bees, there is a public good, namely the good functioning of the hive, but not a common good, that is, *a good received and communicated.*"[30] The common good of a community of persons is common to both the whole and the part. It includes the access of all persons to their liberty of personal development and to the communications of gener-

29. Ibid., 31.
30. Ibid., 35.

osity consequent upon such development. These include communications of moral and political virtues, of friendship, of material and spiritual riches, of unconsciously operative hereditary wisdom, all of which are communicable and revert to each member.

When, according to Maritain, we conceive the end of human society as the satisfaction merely of the individual goods of the members, we arrive at an *anarchic* materialism. On this view, the function of the city is to safeguard the negative liberty of its members, giving the strong sway to oppress the weak. This conception Maritain dubs *bourgeois individualism*. When we conceive, on the other hand, the end of human society as merely the proper good of the whole (like the proper good of the hive with its bees), then we arrive either at *communistic anti-individualism* or at *totalitarian-dictatorial anti-communism and anti-individualism*. All of these types of society disregard the human *person* and the *common good* and consider the material human individual alone. Bourgeois liberalism ends in a statism in which the state takes the place of the genuine community and the individual extracts from the state the satisfaction of material desires while receiving only an illusory liberty. Communism reacts against bourgeois liberalism, but it attempts to emancipate only collective man, not persons in their relation to God. Totalitarianism, in reaction to the other two types of society, incorporates man in all his being into a social whole composed of material individualities rather than persons. Each of these societies generates tragic conflicts.

## IV. The Tripartite Soul and the Parable of the Decline of the Regimes in Plato's *Republic*

Maritain's reflections on the common good, on the distinction between individuality and personality, and on the nature of and relations among societies that disregard persons and the common good recapitulate in a striking way some main themes in Plato's *Republic*. We find there intimations of the distinction between individuality and personality in Socrates' criticism of the tripartite soul in the *Republic*. We find also a tragic parable of the way in which an ancient forerunner of bourgeois liberalism is bound to decline toward totalitarianism, a parable that highlights a number of types of society that are united by their disregard of the common goods.

### 1. *The Tripartite Soul as a Model of the Individual but not of the Person*

To understand Plato's use in the *Republic* of the model of the tripartite soul, we must begin with some remarks on how to interpret a Platonic dialogue. According to Mitchell Miller, the rhetorical aim of the Platonic dialogue is to overcome obstacles in auditors and readers to the task of aspiring to the truth about the highest goods. These obstacles include ignorance, hostility to philosophy, a tendency to assent to propositions without real understanding, and limited insight. In Miller's view, Plato's dialogues anticipate these obstacles and respond to them by employing *mimetic irony*[31] within a four-part compositional structure.[32] (1) The guide elicits an opinion from the interlocutor or solicits agreement to a problematic thesis; (2) The guide pretends sympathy for the thesis while showing its problematic character. (3) Just when the interlocutor faces puzzlement and *aporia,* the guide introduces a "reorienting insight" which sets the issues at hand in a new light and provides the basis for resolving the *aporia.* (4) In the final part of the dialogue, the *exegesis,* the guide resumes the initial part of the discussion interrupted by the refutation and reassesses it with the reorienting insight. In this *exegesis,* oriented to the interlocutor's insight (or lack of it), the guide often seems to be *testing* his interlocutor to see how well he employs the reorienting insight. This testing challenges readers to apply the reorienting insight for themselves.

Keeping this structure in mind, we can understand why Socrates introduces the tripartite model in the early parts of the *Republic* in the first place—as a *problematic* thesis about the soul.[33] Projecting into the soul three agent-like parts corresponding to three classes of citizen of the *feverish* city, Socrates brings to light a model of the *feverish* soul in pursuit of external goods, of the "prudent autonomous individual" who manifests Thrasymachean selfishness. His strategy is to enable his interlocutors to achieve

31. See Mitchell Miller, *The Philosopher in Plato's Statesman* (Hague: Martinus Nijhoff Publishers, 1980), ix–xix; ——, *Plato's Parmenides: The Conversion of the Soul* (Princeton, New Jersey: Princeton University Press, 1986), 3–12.

32. For the compositional structure, Miller credits René Schaerer, *La question platonicienne: Étude sur les rapports de la pensee et de l'expression dans les Dialogues,* second edition (Neuchatel: Secretariat de l'Universite, 1969); ——, "Le mecanisme de l'ironie dans ses rapports avec la dialectique," *Revue de metaphysique et de morale* 22, no. 4 (2005): 181–209.

33. Even the contractarianism that Glaucon articulated in his devil's advocate's defense of Thrasymachus presupposed that communities derive benefit from the just behavior of their members. Socrates' initial move in book 2 is to transfer this intuition from the context of the city to that of the soul by conceiving of the soul as a "community" of soul parts along the lines of a civic community. This move gives the thesis that justice pays off for just persons most of its plausibility.

insight into themselves—into their (deficient) self-conceptions and conceptions of justice. To do so constitutes a *self-scrutiny*, a *self-diagnosis* of themselves trapped within a culture of possessive individualism.[34] Plato's plan, on another level, is that this will help those of his readers who identify with Glaucon and Adeimantus to gain a like self-knowledge. Even if the tripartite account is not an adequate account of the good and just soul, it might be appropriate for the conversational context[35] in which Socrates finds himself in the Piraeus with his interlocutors, as well as to the larger context in which Plato stands in relation to his audience.[36] In Plato's depiction, neither Glaucon nor Adeimantus ever actually sees the serious problems with the sick-city/sick-soul analogy as a means for discovering what justice is. Each is unimpressed by the fact that Socrates models the putatively "just" soul upon a city that is a violent aggressor. Plato depicts them as presuming to know from the outset what justice is, as accepting the conventional (contractarian and individualistic) notion of justice, self-restraint in one's actions toward others in pursuit of self-interest in respect of external goods.

These deficient conceptions of the just city and soul dominate the *Republic* in books 2–5. Nevertheless, after the introduction of the philosopher-ruler in the middle of book 5 and until the end of book 7, the tripartite city

34. The definition of justice in the feverish city will be "the minding of one's own business." It suggests something like individual autonomy in a form foreshadowing post-Hobbesian political theory.

35. At 372b–c, Glaucon requires Socrates to use as a model for justice in the soul not what counts as justice in a simple and healthy "city of sows" but what counts as justice in a city that is luxury-loving and feverish. In the latter city, one of the most important classes consists of warriors dedicated to territorial expansion; it is a city more in accord than the other with Glaucon's experience in Athens. The city constructed from this point up to the reorienting introduction of philosophical rule at 473b ff. mirrors *Glaucon's* ideas of political justice. It will be a city of selfish individuals which will supervise myths and stories, will require rulers to be first trained in military science, will be indoctrinated into a "Noble Lie," and will be subject to a eugenic breeding program. It will be a city that is "ideal" only under the condition that the feverish city, whose main goal is military effectiveness, is best.

36. The militarist ideal of justice and goodness worked out in terms of the tripartite city and soul represents aspects of late fifth- and early fourth-century Spartan and Athenian culture that *rival* the Socratic/Platonic way of thinking but capture the interest of the interlocutors. Socrates wants to mime certain views of his interlocutors, and Plato certain views of his readers, so that they might be held up for examination. Though Socrates pretends to agree with the interlocutors that the tripartite polis and soul are good models of the just city and soul, at points he hints at his own disagreement with them (e.g. 432b and 434d express reserve about the virtues of the feverish city; 434d–435e and 437a and 444a-e about the tripartite model of soul). These hints lure the interlocutors into self-examination, and by means of them Plato lures readers, as well.

and soul suddenly disappear! The conversation begins to focus upon the Forms and the Form of the Good and upon the content of the mathematical studies propaedeutic to dialectic. In this middle section, which in Miller's terms is the *reorientation* section, Socrates calls for a reconsideration of the virtues (hinting again that the book 4 account of the virtues is inadequate). He also offers, in the Divided Line, a non-tripartite division of the powers of the soul that we might compare with the division of pleasure and knowledge in the *Philebus*.[37]

Having disappeared from the central section of the *Republic*, the tripartite soul returns at the start of book 8. This coincides with a shift from the *reorientation* stage of the conversation to the *exegesis* stage—the stage in which Socrates returns to the question of whether justice pays. Now in the exegesis *stage the reorienting conception of philosophy as inquiry into and imitation of the true Good lies in the background* and Socrates can test the interlocutors for any insight they might have gained. In books 8–9 he suddenly speaks again in terms of the tripartite city and soul. It is as if Socrates in books 8–9 is going back down into the Cave of the sick polis of books 2–5, having briefly emerged during the discussion of Philosophy and the Good, needing when there to use the language of the Cave dwellers to be understood. All this suggests that Plato wants to associate the decline of regimes with the dis-unified state of the soul in the pre-philosophical polis and wants the parable of the decline further to expose the deficiencies of the divided tri-partite soul, at least to his best readers,[38] if not to Glaucon and Adeimantus.

37. At 434d ff., Socrates says that if he and Glaucon find that the pattern of the feverish city works as the model for the just soul, all will be well. But if something different is the pattern of the just soul, they must revise their understanding of the just city. Later, in the Divided Line *logos*, we find a model of the powers of the just soul in their relationship very different from the model of the tripartite soul. Socrates introduces a new view of the soul's nature and a new view of justice. The new view relies upon the notion that the soul is capable of insight into the generosity of the Good. From this standpoint, Socrates attempts to display Glaucon's misconceptions. This dialectical process juxtaposes the conventional *politeia* with the philosophic *politeia*.

38. On one level, Socrates addresses his leading suggestions at the exegesis stage (as in all four stages) to the interlocutor. On another, Plato addresses them to the reader/auditor. When, as often happens, the interlocutor has *not* grasped the reorienting conceptions or the ways in which they refute the errors of the first two stages, the guide reverts to pre-reorientation modes of discourse.

## 2. *The Parable of the Decline of the Regimes toward Tyranny*

To his pre-philosophic interlocutors Socrates characterizes the parable of decline only as the first of three demonstrations that justice pays and that the tyrant is miserable. On the surface, it seems that he is endorsing the aristocratic regime while bemoaning its inevitable decline. But this reading invites the question whether any "good" regime would so degenerate. Can a regime that "inevitably" falls apart have been the good regime? Socrates faults the Promethean breeding program as the thing that triggers the decline of the aristocracy into worse forms. In this he seems to be trying to show Glaucon and the others, in a way that will not anger them or violate their trust, that the aristocracy is bound to decline toward tyranny unless it is rescued and completely reoriented, by philosophy. He wants them to see that a city with a structure like that of the city of Adeimantus in books 2–5, a city with citizens whose psychology mirrors that structure, must fail.[39] It will degenerate through a series of stages into totalitarianism. Here we see that Socrates' parable of the decline of the tripartite regimes precisely foreshadows Maritain's contention that bourgeois individualism inevitably ends in totalitarianism.

Not one of the leading factions in the five polities declining toward tyranny "rules" by reason understood as inquiry into the common good. Recall that in book 4 Socrates said that the *logistikon* "rules" in the aristocratic soul without defining what this ruling consisted in, indeed suggesting that it did little more than calculate about the maximization of external goods. In books 5–7 then, while apparently abandoning the tripartite model, he examined the notion of "philosophical" rule and implied suggestions about the work of reason. If books 8–10 constitute a critical return to the structure of the pre-philosophical city, it makes sense to suppose that Socrates there employs the language of the Cave to express the importance of philosophical inquiry into goodness. He does this by recasting the *logistikon* as itself passionate for truth (for "true" pleasure) and goodness (the "best" pleasures), with the result that the other interests atrophy in the face of its all-consuming interest.[40]

39. More radically, he wants them to grasp that the true art of politics is a *craft* that serves its clients.

40. In the parable of decline, Socrates speaks of how the "whole person" hands over political power to this or that part of his soul.

Why does the rule of a philosophical reason capable of inquiring into the Good serve justice? Because this is the only rule that aims at the well-being of the whole city or the whole person in its constitution, ensuring a beneficial outcome for groups or parts by eliminating conflict. Such a ruling element rules by persuading other elements to cooperate in the pursuit of common goods.[41] A key implication of the parable of the decline is that only the philosopher's conception of happiness is just and unselfish, because the goods sought by the aristocrat, timocrat, oligarch, democrat, and tyrant are not common goods but rather zero-sum goods. Bourgeois success in the "aristocratic" way cuts one off from service to others. Striving for prestige requires the inferiority of others. Striving for unlimited wealth impoverishes others. Striving for unlimited negative freedom to satisfy disordered desires deprives others of their legitimate freedoms. Striving for tyrannical power deprives the citizen body of its freedoms. Knowledge, and the other goods internal to rational crafts, on the other hand, can be shared without being lessened, because they constitute a common good; indeed, ordinarily such goods increase by being shared.[42] Socrates began in Book 2 by promising to show selfish individuals that justice pays and injustice harms the individual agent. In books 8 and 9, however, he ends by showing that the truest goods are *common* goods achievable only in community and that the pursuit of false goods harms those who pursue them and those with whom they thereby come into conflict.

How striking an anticipation is Socrates' Parable of the Decline of the Regimes of Maritain's discussion of the nature of and relations among societies that disregard persons and the common good! Socrates shows

41. Any falling off from rule that understands the proper functions of all parts of city and soul produces injustice.

42. The analogy between city and soul has become, in *Republic* 8–9, not only a means for diagnosing sick cities but also a means for communicating to non-philosophers a moral-psychological truth: that only a philosophical life can make them happy. "Philosophic" reason, when it rules a soul, neither dominates the soul by entering into conflict with the soul's non-rational desires, as ruling political factions dominate rival factions, nor deals in zero-sum goods. Rather it works to *transform* non-rational desires into rational ones that benefit the whole soul in its own inner growth and in its community with others. Socrates' main point is that "factionalized" souls, mistakenly striving for the wrong goals, are doomed to unhappiness. If happiness resided in bourgeois success, honor, money, freedom, or coercive power, then persons would achieve happiness best where these were most available, and Thrasymachus would be right about human motivation. But perhaps the main point of the parable of the decline of the cities and souls in books 8–9 is that Thrasymachus was wrong to contend that injustice "pays" and the tyrant is the happiest of men.

how a polity based on individual gain inevitably declines toward totalitarian tyranny. Maritain shows how bourgeois liberalism generates first communist anti-individualism and then totalitarian anti-communism *and* anti-individualism. In his parable, Socrates in *Republic* 8–9 compares the members of the degenerate polities to bees in the hive. Maritain insists that a human society taking its end to be other than a common good takes it to be something like the proper good of a hive with its bees.[43] The truths expressed in *The Person and the Common Good*—the orientation of the human person toward God, the distinction between individuality and personality, the primacy of the common good, and the relations among societies that disregard persons and the common good—each finds an early expression in Plato's *Republic.*

43. Jacques Maritain, *The Person and the Common Good*, 35.

HANNAH WOLDUM RAGUSA

# Plato and Maritain on the Role of Art in Society

## Obscuring or Revealing the Truth?

### I. Introduction

IN RECENT YEARS, perhaps coming to its climax in the several months leading up to and following the election of President Donald Trump, a conspicuous public debate on the role of the media in society has occurred in the United States. Is the media—and here we might include not only the traditional news media but also new forms of social media—an aid or a hindrance to the common good? Is the media a glowing beacon of truth-telling, shedding light on our situation, despite what those in power might wish to conceal? Or is the media itself a form of propaganda, reporting on so-called "facts" in a manner that promotes its own agenda? To make matters even more interesting, both elected officials *and* members of the media have leveled charges of "fake news" and "alternative facts" against each other.

Beneath this fascinating, if also somewhat alarming, public discussion about the role of media lurk deeper questions, especially age-old questions about the role of art in society and the relationship between art and truth. Philosophical contemplation on the nature of art dates back at least as far as Plato.[1] As he realized, in order to understand the importance—and pos-

1. See Stephen Halliwell, *The Aesthetics of Mimesis: Ancient Texts and Modern Problems* (Princeton, New Jersey: Princeton University Press, 2009). Halliwell calls Plato "the 'founding father' of mimeticism" and argues that *mimesis*, often translated as "imitation" or "representation," is the "most long-lasting, widely held and intellectually accommodating of all the theories

sibly the danger—of art in society, one first must know what art is, how it relates to the truth, and what impact it has on those who encounter it. Jacques Maritain also has much to say on these topics. At first glance, it might seem strange to include Plato and Maritain in the same discussion about art. After all, Maritain is a Thomist whose heritage is considered to be Aristotelian.[2] Nevertheless, references to Plato occur fairly frequently in Maritain's writings about art. In fact, Plato is the first philosopher Maritain mentions in his *Creative Intuition in Art and Poetry*. He characterizes the very subject of this book as a response to the Platonic conception of poetic inspiration.[3] In another of his works, *The Responsibility of the Artist*, he directly considers the relationship between art and society, making explicit reference to Plato's thoughts on this subject in the *Republic*.[4] These examples suggest that Maritain sees his own aesthetic philosophy at least in part as a response to Plato's ideas about art.

Both Plato's and Maritain's thoughts about art can shed light on our own situation and our current conversations about media, even if only to identify and elucidate the philosophical issues involved. In this essay, I outline Plato's and Maritain's accounts of art—including their views on the relationship of art to truth—and discuss the ensuing implications of these views in regard to the role of art in society. I argue that despite quite different accounts of what art *is*, Plato and Maritain share, at least in part, two

---

of art in the West" (24–25). While the concept of art as *mimesis* pre-dates Plato, he was the first to explore the mimetic philosophy of art "in a theoretically extensive and probing manner" (37). Plato was also the first to question the value of art and the first to link questions of mimetic art to larger metaphysical and epistemological concerns (37). See also Christopher Janaway, *Images of Excellence: Plato's Critique of the Arts* (Oxford: Clarendon Press, 1995). Janaway agrees that Plato is the first Western philosopher to discuss the nature of art and question its value (4). Janaway also makes the important point that while there is no one Greek word in Plato's writings that translates consistently and directly to our word "art," Plato compares poetry and painting under the concept of *mimesis* and connects what we might call music, drama, and poetry under the Greek concept of *mousike* (5). Additionally, both Halliwell and Janaway agree that even though Plato is continually preoccupied with questions about *mimesis* and poetry, he offers varying perspectives on these in different dialogues, and, consequently, his views cannot be described as a systematic theory.

2. For example, see Anthony Richard Haynes, "Jacques Maritain's Definition of Art," *New Blackfriars* 96, no. 1065 (September 2015): 530–31. Haynes explains that Maritain's understanding of art as a virtue of the practical intellect relies upon the Aristotelian distinction between the speculative and practical intellect.

3. Jacques Maritain, *Creative Intuition in Art and Poetry* (Cleveland: The World Publishing Company, 1953), 3.

4. Jacques Maritain, *The Responsibility of the Artist* (New York: Charles Scribner's Sons, 1960), 73.

convictions. First, they agree that art's place in society rests upon its relationship to the truth; and second, because at least some art *can* lead those who experience it to the ultimate truths, art can play a profound and beneficial role in society. Their conclusions about the role of art in society rest upon *both* their underlying metaphysical and epistemological explanations of art *and* their views of society and the common good. Plato and Maritain teach us that our concerns about the media today are not superficial; they point to a deeper crisis in our understandings of truth and the common good.

## II. Plato's View of Art in the *Republic*

Plato discusses questions related to art—poetry (*poiesis*), *mousike*, and mimetic images (*eikones*)—in many of his dialogues, including the *Apology, Euthyphro, Ion, Republic, Sophist,* and *Laws*. But I have chosen to focus primarily on the *Republic* since it contains his most comprehensive and passionate discussion of art's relationship to truth and to the just society and the just soul. The *Republic* centers on the question of justice. In trying to pinpoint what justice is, Socrates tells Adeimantus that they must first investigate justice in the city before they can understand justice in an individual soul.[5] In books 4 and 9, Plato draws a direct comparison between the just city and the just man.[6] Both are just and therefore truly happy when they are well-ordered, when their various parts are in harmony and guided by what is highest and best in each—that part in both city and soul that loves wisdom.[7] Socrates' last words in book 9 suggest that the "just city" in which citizens may live happily and freely is not a physical place at all; it is the "city within," the city of the soul that is guided by reason and the love of wisdom.[8]

In the midst of this larger discussion about justice, Plato considers the effects of art—especially poetry, but also images—on society and the individual human soul. Plato's apparently critical account of poetry as *mimesis* or imitation and his belief that poets should not be admitted into the just

5. Plato, *Republic* 2, 368e–369a. I rely upon Allan Bloom's translation in Plato, *The Republic of Plato*, 2nd ed., translated by Allan Bloom (New York: Basic Books, 1991).

6. *Republic* 4, 435b; 9, 590e–591a and 592b.

7. *Republic* 4, 443d; 9, 580d–581c and 586e–587a.

8. *Republic* 9, 590d–591a; 592b. See also Halliwell, *The Aesthetics of Mimesis*, 49. He notes that the ideal city serves as "a large-scale paradigm for the mind, 'the city in the soul.'"

society are both well known.[9] It is important, however, to look into these views more carefully. His criticisms are not as unambiguous and sweeping as might be thought.

Books 2, 3, and 10 of the *Republic* introduce us to Plato's seemingly negative view of poetry and poets. In a discussion of the proper education for the guardians or rulers of society that takes place in book 2, Socrates argues that poets—the makers of tales—must be supervised and only approved tales can be told to children. False tales will not be allowed. Socrates offers an example of a false tale via an analogy between poetry and painting: "when a man in speech makes a bad representation of what gods and heroes are like," he acts in a way that is similar to "a painter who paints something that doesn't resemble the things whose likenesses he wished to paint."[10] The problem with the poems of Homer and Hesiod is that they sometimes misrepresent both the heroic and the divine, depicting false versions of each. In book 3, Socrates offers examples of passages in Homer that must be censored, such as those that portray noteworthy human beings or gods as being overpowered by laughter and those that portray the gods doing evil things.[11] These false tales that misrepresent both the human and the divine should not be told to children; opinions formed at a young age are difficult to change later on. For these reasons, Socrates says, "we must do everything to ensure that what they [children] hear first, with respect to virtue, be the finest told tales for them to hear."[12]

As that last passage suggests, not all poetry should be banned from the just society or from the education of the young guardians. Poetry that contains false depictions of reality and therefore promotes vice should be banned, but poetry that presents the truth and promotes virtue should be advocated and taught to children. For instance, Socrates provides several examples of passages from Homer that should be preserved because they foster the virtues of moderation or courage: "Friend, keep quiet, and obey my word" (*Iliad* 4.412) and "Endure, heart; you have endured worse be-

9. See, for instance, Morris Henry Partee, "Plato's Banishment of Poetry," *The Journal of Aesthetics and Art Criticism* 29, no. 2 (winter 1970): 209–22, and Janaway, *Images of Excellence*, 2. Despite their different interpretations regarding why and to what extent Plato is critical of poetry, Partee and Janaway take Plato's expulsion of poetry from the just city and the just soul to be in earnest.

10. *Republic* 2, 377e.

11. *Republic* 3, 389a and 391e.

12. *Republic* 2, 378e.

fore" (*Odyssey* 20.17–18).[13] Since poetry can influence children's views of the world and their behaviors, only those poets who portray "what is fine and graceful" are welcome in the city.[14]

Although the context for this discussion is the education of children who are to become guardians of the city, we can still gather from it quite a bit about Plato's critique of poetry. Poetry is not seen to be either a good in itself or an unmitigated good for society. It is subject to "ethical criteria of judgment"[15] and "subservient to moral aims."[16] Halliwell identifies a clear link between Plato's views on the education of the young guardians and his understanding of human psychology:

> What is at stake throughout [books 2 and 3], then, is the artistic projection of ideas (embodied in images of divine and human behavior) capable of shaping the souls of those exposed to them; the education of the young is a paradigm of more general processes of psychological and cultural self-formation.[17]

In short, the rubric for judging poetry presented in books 2 and 3 includes attention to its ethical dimension. Poetry is judged according to its ability to foster order in the human soul based on what it depicts. Yet Plato's description of approved tales as "fine" ones suggests a certain ambiguity in regard to the distinction between the beautiful and the ethical.[18] The approved tales are considered good and beautiful not merely because they depict virtue, but because they do so gracefully. The only poetry that belongs in the just society is that which beautifully presents the truth about the greatest things—about the great and virtuous man (i.e., the hero) and the gods.

In book 10 we encounter Plato's sternest critique of poetry as well as the clearest presentation of his reasons for it. Poetry is problematic because it is imitation, and nothing imitative should be admitted into a just society: "all such things seem to maim the thought of those who hear them and do not as a remedy have the knowledge of how they really are."[19] Socrates ad-

13. *Republic* 3, 389e; 390d.

14. *Republic* 3, 401c–402a.

15. Halliwell, *The Aesthetics of Mimesis*, 27.

16. Janaway, *Images of Excellence*, 11.

17. Halliwell, *The Aesthetics of Mimesis*, 53.

18. Ibid., 70. In footnote 76 Halliwell makes an important observation about several passages from books 2 and 3: they suggest "an ethically charged concept of beauty." He elaborates on this idea later. For Plato "beauty of form is a matter not just of appearances but of appearances that embody and convey ethical value" (132).

19. *Republic* 10, 595b.

mits that he has always had a "friendship" for Homer; but, he says, "a man must not be honored before the truth."[20] In other words, as we have seen in books 2 and 3, Plato's harshest critique of poetry has to do with its relationship to truth. And the problem with poetry—as with all imitation—is that it is "third from ... the truth" or "third from what *is*."[21]

What does it mean for poetry to be "third from the truth"? To make sense of this, we must turn to Plato's metaphysics. He is famous for his theory of the "Forms." A complete understanding of his account of the Forms would demand consideration of other of his dialogues; but even in the *Republic*, we are introduced to aspects of it. In Books 6 and 7, Plato uses the image of the "divided line" and immediately follows with the "allegory of the cave" to illustrate the different levels of reality.[22] Reality is, roughly, of two sorts: the visible world—the realm of plants, animals, humans, and the like, as well as their shadows, reflections, and images—and the intelligible world, the realm of abstract numbers, ideas, the divine, the soul, and the Forms. This second kind of reality is not physical or visible, and yet it is the most real. Although these two types of reality greatly differ from each other, there is still a relation between them. The visible world is in some way an image or reflection of the intelligible world, of what is most real.[23]

Now we are in a better place to understand Plato's charge that poetry, as imitation, is "third from the truth." In book 10 Socrates draws an analogy between poetry and painting. Using the example of a couch, Socrates explains that there are three kinds of couches: the Form of couch (what a couch *is*), the tangible couch that the carpenter produces, and lastly the painter's painting of a couch.[24] Of these, the most real is the Form of a couch. The physical couch that a carpenter makes is made according to the Form of a couch. But a painter's painting is one more step removed from the truth, for it is an imitation of the appearance of the physical couch that the carpenter made. This example of a painting of a couch serves as a humorous analogy for Socrates' larger point that poetry, too, is "third from the truth."

20. *Republic* 10, 595c.

21. *Republic* 10, 597e and 599a.

22. See *Republic* 6, 590d–511e and 7, 514a–517c.

23. See Halliwell, *The Aesthetics of Mimesis*, 71. He argues that this notion of the physical world as an image of the Forms is most fully pronounced in the *Timaeus*, 55c6. In this passage, the world itself is a "mimetic creation, wrought by a divine artist who ... is expressly visualized as a painter."

24. *Republic* 10, 597b.

The problem with poetry is that it, like painting, imitates the *appearances* of things. A painter can paint the likeness of a couch without knowing whether that couch is well-made. Similarly, a poet can describe the gods or heroes vividly without knowing what is truly good or just or beautiful. The imitator, whether poet or painter, "will imitate, although he doesn't know in what way each thing is bad or good. But as it seems, whatever *looks* to be fair to the many who don't know anything—*that* he will imitate."[25] The poet is likely to imitate what is easiest and most interesting to imitate: the "irritable and various disposition," as Socrates explains—we might say what is flashy, juicy, or titillating—and much less likely to imitate the "prudent and quiet character."[26] Plato is suggesting that the poet's skill in accurately imitating those who are overly emotional, intemperate, or unjust is not valuable in itself. As Halliwell explains, the technical accomplishment of the poet is a separate matter from the poet's knowledge of ethics: "the apparently comprehensive familiarity with the phenomenal world, with the 'surfaces' of life, exhibited in the works of Homer and others ... cannot in itself vouch for anything that deserves to be regarded as knowledge or wisdom.... [V]erisimilitude, the look of the real, should not be confused with veracity, a grasp of the real itself."[27]

Because poetry imitates appearances and has no guaranteed link to the truth, Socrates argues that the imitative poet "produces a bad regime in the soul of each private man by making phantoms that are very far removed from the truth and by gratifying the soul's foolish part."[28] For example, poetry leads those who hear it, even the best of men, to wallow in sadness they would otherwise meet with fortitude, to laugh at jokes they would never tell themselves, and to indulge in sexual desires that would otherwise be controlled. In the end, the reason that poetry does not belong in a just society is because—on account of *what it is*—it is harmful for those who seek the truth and strive to live virtuously.

Socrates' own words best convey my point: "For the contest is great, my dear Glaucon ... greater than it seems—this contest that concerns becoming good or bad—so we mustn't be tempted by honor or money or any ruling office or, for that matter, poetry, into thinking that it's worth-

25. *Republic* 10, 602b; italics added.
26. *Republic* 10, 604e.
27. Halliwell, *The Aesthetics of Mimesis*, 59.
28. *Republic* 10, 605b.

while to neglect justice and the rest of virtue."[29] The goal of life is the kind of happiness that comes only from justice, from having a well-ordered soul in which reason and the love of wisdom prevail. Poetry cannot be admitted into the just society—or into the "interior city" of the just soul—if it hinders us from becoming good.

Thus far Plato's account of art's role in society has sounded rather pessimistic. There are, however, hints in the *Republic* that some art, such as verbal images or stories, might play a more positive role in society and in the life of the just man. Socrates himself often uses metaphors and stories to convey his knowledge of higher things to those who do not yet understand. For instance, in book 6, Adeimantus asks why it will be good for philosophers to rule society, when philosophers are useless. Socrates responds that this question "needs an answer given through an image" (*eikon*).[30] Images, including reflections in mirrors or water, paintings, and so on, fall into the lowest category of reality; they imitate the physical world and are the sorts of things that painters and poets make. Yet here we find Socrates saying that he needs to answer Adeimantus with an "image."

He proceeds to tell the story of sailors on a ship who do not know that a skilled pilot must pay careful attention to the year, the seasons, the stars, and the wind. Instead the sailors fight with one another, trying to take over, and they praise those who can persuade or force the ship-owner to give them control. Because they do not understand the art of piloting, they think that the true pilot is useless. After telling this story, Socrates says, "I don't suppose you need to scrutinize the image to see that it resembles the cities in their disposition toward the true philosophers, but you understand what I mean."[31] This is not the only example of Socrates using a literary "image" to convey a deeper truth. His famous allegory of the cave in book 7 illustrates both the different levels of reality and the philosopher's intellectual journey away from shadows toward what is most real. The very end of the *Republic* consists of Socrates telling a long story about the afterlife—the Myth of Er.[32] Furthermore, the entire dialogue of the *Republic* can itself be seen as "a kind of philosophical word-picture."[33] In recount-

29. *Republic* 10, 608b.
30. *Republic* 6, 487e.
31. *Republic* 6, 489a.
32. *Republic* 10, 614b–621d.
33. Halliwell, *The Aesthetics of Mimesis*, 130. He mentions the *Timaeus* 19b-c where the *Republic* is referred to as a "painting."

ing real or imagined conversations between Socrates and various characters, some of whom themselves also repeat or craft additional myths, all of Plato's dialogues bear the form of *mimesis*.[34]

Perhaps further reflection on the allegory of the cave can provide the key to understanding why Socrates criticizes the poets for their imitation and yet does not himself hesitate to use "images." In the allegory, the philosopher is portrayed as the one who escapes from the darkness of the cave (that is, from the ignorance of one's ignorance) and emerges into the sunlight (that is, to the knowledge of what is most real and to the love of wisdom). Socrates, however, insists that the philosopher should not remain "up there," outside the cave, but should return to share his labors and honors.[35] This tale suggests an important difference between the poet and the philosopher. The poet does not know what is true, and so he or she cannot know if his imitations of appearances correctly imitate the truth. But the philosopher has already come to know *what is*; the philosopher knows the truth and loves wisdom. For this reason, the philosopher can use whatever tools are at his or her disposal—including "images"—to translate the truth into a language better understood by those who have not yet left the cave.[36]

If this kind of art—the philosopher's word-images and myths—results from the philosopher's knowledge of reality and of what is good, then it can lead those who experience it to the ultimate truth of things, too. This kind of art presents a "true image" of reality; it does not imitate appearances. We might be able to say, then, that in Plato's eyes the philosopher is in a sense the true artist, even the true poet, because his myths are true myths. Unless Plato wants to ban himself from the just society or prohibit Socrates from conversing as he does about justice and wisdom, the subtle message of the *Republic* is that the philosopher's art is not only permissible but perhaps the very best way to communicate the truth to those still inside the cave.[37]

34. Todd S. Mei, "Justice and the Banning of the Poets: The Way of Hermeneutics in Plato's Republic," *The Review of Metaphysics* 60, no. 4 (June 2007): 766.

35. *Republic* 7, 519d.

36. Both Janaway and Mei suggest something similar, that poetry is acceptable if it is subordinated to the pursuit of the true and the good. See Janaway, *Images of Excellence*, 183, and Mei, "Justice and the Banning of the Poets," 765.

37. See Halliwell, *The Aesthetics of Mimesis*, 70–71. He suggests that there is ultimately a tension in Plato's thought regarding *mimesis* and poetry. On the one hand, Plato sometimes seems to embrace a "negative theology" according to which "reality cannot adequately be spoken of, described, or modeled, only experienced in some pure, unmediated manner (by *logos*, *nous*,

## III. Maritain's View of Art

At this point, let us turn to Maritain. We have said that Maritain references Plato fairly frequently in his works that concern beauty, art, and poetry. Here I will rely primarily upon two of Maritain's later works: *Creative Intuition in Art and Poetry* (1953) and *The Responsibility of the Artist* (1960). In *Creative Intuition,* Maritain offers a definition of "art" somewhat different from Plato's. Following Thomas Aquinas and Aristotle, Maritain calls art a "virtue of the practical intellect,"[38] but at the same time he acknowledges that the fine arts (such as poetry, music, or painting) differ from the useful arts like house-building or cooking. The fine arts spring from what Maritain calls "poetic intuition"—a type of non-conceptual, connatural knowledge—and *not* from a blueprint in the artist's mind that is simply copied onto a canvas or notebook.[39]

For our purposes, we do not need to analyze the details of poetic intuition; it is enough to emphasize that it is a type of knowledge. Poetic intuition is "connatural knowledge of both self and reality (or, more specifically, a glimpse of the profound correspondence between the subjective self and objective reality), sparked by emotion below the level of consciousness and oriented toward creative expression."[40] Poetic knowledge is oriented toward the work of art created. Yet it is quite different from the conceptual knowledge of the carpenter who first conceives a plan for the table before building it. What the artist intuits through poetic intuition is not conceptualized rationally; it is *only* expressed in the work of art created and not before. As Maritain explains, "Be it a painting or a poem, this work is a made object—in it alone does poetic intuition come to objectivization."[41] The artist does *not* first form a concept in his mind that he or she then cop-

*dianoia,* or whatever)." On the other hand, passages from books 6 and 7 of the *Republic,* as well as dialogues like the *Critias,* point to the possibility that "all human thought *is* an attempt to speak about, describe, or model reality—to produce 'images' (whether visual, mental, or verbal) of the real." In the first scenario, mimetic art does not fare well. But in the second, mimetic art or representation "is all that we have, or all that we are capable of."

38. Maritain, *Creative Intuition,* 35.

39. Ibid., 55, 100–102. For a more detailed explanation of poetic intuition as a type of connatural knowledge, see also his, "On Knowledge through Connaturality," *The Review of Metaphysics* 4, no. 4 (June 1951): 477.

40. Hannah Woldum Ragusa, "Beholding the Beauty of Being: Artistic Creativity in the Thomistic Tradition," *LOGOS: A Journal of Catholic Thought and Culture* 20, no. 2 (Spring 2017): 116.

41. Maritain, *Creative Intuition,* 93.

ies into the work of fine art. Doing so would, in Maritain's words, "make art a cemetery of imitations."[42]

Already we see that Maritain's understanding of poetry—which originates in poetic intuition, a type of knowledge—appears quite different from Plato's view that poetry is "imitation" and "third from the truth." According to Plato, poetry is *mimesis*, imitation of appearances and not truth. According to Maritain, poetry is implicitly connected to reality and truth, since it is a type of knowledge. Thus there appears to be a disagreement between Plato and Maritain in regard to the nature of art. Art is imitation, according to Plato's view in the *Republic*, while Maritain explicitly says that fine art is *not* imitation. According to Maritain's understanding of fine art as something that arises only from poetic intuition, it is not likely that Socrates' word-images or even Plato's dialogues would fit the bill if they were the result of a pre-meditated attempt to translate philosophical ideas into myths.

Maritain attributes Plato's suspicion of art to his account of the "madness" of the poets. As Maritain explains, in Plato's assessment the poets such as Homer and Hesiod do not rely on reason. Their poetry originates from the inspiration of the Muses. Furthermore, Maritain explains that "although the mania of poets is divine, the only beauty they are able to provide the city with is sense-appealing beauty, moving in our earthly shadows and fond of lies, so that their mania finally makes them a nuisance for religion and morality, and for the order of the city."[43] It turns out that Maritain's disagreement with Plato concerns the origins of poetry. Maritain wants to understand artistic "inspiration" *not* as a form of divinely-given madness, as Plato described it at least in the *Ion*, but as something that is ultimately rooted in the pre-conceptual activities of the intellect. In fact, Maritain characterizes the very subject of his book *Creative Intuition in Art and Poetry* as a response to the Platonic conception of inspiration. His book attempts to have "the Platonic Muse descend into the soul of man, where she is no longer Muse but creative intuition; and Platonic inspiration descend into the intellect united with imagination, where inspiration from above the soul becomes inspiration from above conceptual reason, that is, poetic experience."[44]

42. Maritain, *Creative Intuition*, 100.

43. Ibid., 64. Despite his hint that he is referring to Plato's *Republic* here, Maritain seems to be including an explanation of the origin of poetry that belongs rather to Plato's *Ion*. In the *Ion* Socrates wonders if poetry ultimately springs from the inspiration of the Muses, since it does not result from the poet's knowledge of reality.

44. Ibid., 66.

In *The Responsibility of the Artist,* Maritain offers his thoughts about the role of art in society and, in doing so, critiques Plato's view. Maritain believes in the autonomy of art; it belongs to a different sphere than morality. As he explains, "Artistic value and moral value belong to two different realms. Artistic value relates to the work, moral value to man."[45] Because art and morality are autonomous in their own spheres, Maritain does not agree with those who advocate the idea of "art for the social group." As he explains,

> the theory of *Art for the social group* . . . simply ignores this autonomy; it makes the *social value,* or *social significance,* or *social impact* of the work into an aesthetic or artistic value, even the supreme aesthetic or artistic value. According to this theory, a good which is not the good of the work, but a certain good of human life, is made into the very object, essential and intrinsic, determining and specifying, of the very virtue or art.[46]

This approach seeks to manipulate art toward a social or political end, whereas the proper end of art is simply the good of the work itself. It is not difficult to read into this passage a critique of Plato's attitude toward art in the *Republic.*

We can begin to see why Maritain is critical of Plato's view that poetry must be censored for the moral good of society and of the soul. Maritain does not question Plato's motives, but he thinks that this course of action is ultimately self-defeating. Maritain argues that this strategy—forcing art to deliver a specific moral message or censoring art in the hope that doing so will better preserve the truth—cannot work. As he explains, a person with this mentality "believes that the work must be immediately touched and attained, in its very making, by judgments and determinations which depend not on the virtue of art but on emotions, purposes or interests of the moral or social order. . . . *Art for the social group* becomes, thus, inevitably propaganda art."[47] If art is to retain its integrity and remain a form of knowledge—if it is to preserve its connection to reality, to the truth—then it must be allowed a certain autonomy. Art that is manipulated for moral purposes by default becomes propaganda; it ceases to be itself.[48] Thus

45. Maritain, *The Responsibility of the Artist,* 29.

46. Ibid., 72; italics in original.

47. Ibid., 72–73; italics in original.

48. Maritain would reject any kind of social or political manipulation of art in terms of deliberately steering art toward a moral, social, or political end. See Jude P. Dougherty, *Jacques Maritain: An Intellectual Profile* (Washington, D.C.: The Catholic University of America Press,

Maritain says of Plato, "At least he was fair to [the poets] in expelling them from the state. He knew that poetry, as long as it remains poetry, will never and can never become an instrument of the State."[49]

Despite these criticisms of Plato, Maritain agrees with Plato that a good society should care about the effects of art and media on its citizens. After all, as Maritain says in chapter 4 of *The Person and the Common Good,* "The end of society is the good of the community, of the social body."[50] The goal of society is the common good. Consequently, as Maritain explains in *The Responsibility of the Artist,* "It is not true that every thought or artifact as such, poisonous as it may be, has, because of the mere fact that it was born of a human mind, an absolute right to be displayed in the human community."[51] He directs his attention to the specific case of the writer's art, because he believes it presents a more challenging question about the relationship between art and the common good. After all, writers do not deal in poisons or idols; they are concerned with words and ideas. In this context Maritain makes a distinction between the freedom to express *ideas* and the freedom to express *actions.* The first (expressing and imparting ideas) must be protected and guaranteed in society; the second (actions) "can be repressed if they tend to destroy the foundations of life in common."[52] For instance, ideas that are directed toward the pursuit of knowledge or the expression of creativity should not be restricted, since the freedom of thought is a fundamental right of the human mind. Conversely, the use of ideas to bring about a practical effect or to incite people to some kind of action can be restricted when the common good is endangered. Maritain identifies pornography as an example of an "incitation to action" that can be justly opposed by some appropriate means. But he admits that there is a tension here, not least because even the most

2003), 77, and James V. Schall, *Jacques Maritain: The Philosopher in Society* (Lanham, Massachusetts: Rowman and Littlefield, 1998), 28. Both make the point that for Maritain art can never be instrumentalized for moral or political purposes. See also Deal W. Hudson, "'The Ecstasy Which is Creation': The Shape of Maritain's Aesthetics," in *Understanding Maritain: Philosopher and Friend,* edited by Deal W. Hudson and Matthew J. Mancini (Macon, Georgia: Mercer University Press, 1987), 238: "Maritain's rule seems to be that in trying to become more—whether it be God, metaphysics, or politics—art invariably becomes less."

49. Maritain, *The Responsibility of the Artist,* 73–74.

50. Jacques Maritain, *The Person and the Common Good,* translated by John J. Fitzgerald (Notre Dame, Indiana: University of Notre Dame Press, 1966), 50.

51. Maritain, *The Responsibility of the Artist,* 76.

52. Ibid., 78.

abstract of ideas "are laden with a tremendous implicit power of action."[53]

While Maritain does acknowledge the right of the state to intervene in artistic matters when the common good is threatened, he believes that the state should do so only in a limited way. This view is partly due to his belief that the "social community" is better equipped than the state to undertake this work. For instance, education, public opinion, and private organizations are each ways "to confront the risks of possible drawbacks resulting from freedom of expression and freedom of art."[54] Maritain also believes that the common good is best served when the government respects intellectual values, freedom of inquiry, and "the inner energies of intelligence and conscience, which are the mainsprings of social and political life, and which cannot be coerced, but can adhere only to what they have good reasons to believe true."[55] In short, he does not believe that government coercion is respectful of human persons or the best means of safeguarding the common good.

Maritain makes the further point that the common good *requires* art: "poetry is necessary, because it brings to men a vision of reality-beyond-reality, an experience of the secret meanings of things, an obscure insight into the universe of beauty, without which men could neither live nor live morally."[56] A good society, then, is concerned not only with protecting its members from the possible dangers of art but also with fostering art. Maritain suggests that art plays a valuable role in pointing citizens toward ultimate truth and that it is relevant even for the moral good of man. While Maritain disagrees with much of Plato's account of art, perhaps this is a point on which they would find common ground. Plato, remember, makes the case that at least some poetry belongs in the moral formation of youth. Additionally, while Maritain and Plato might disagree about whether philosophical word-images are, properly speaking, art, they seem to agree at least on the possibility that some art can lead those who encounter it to the truth of things.

53. Ibid., 79.

54. Ibid., 82. See also Schall, *Jacques Maritain*, 32. Schall rightly points out that although Maritain shares Plato's concern for the common good of society, he disagrees with Plato about the manner and method of safeguarding it: "The very common good of which Maritain speaks so often and so well requires that art be itself in any well-ordered polity, that it be allowed to be what it is. In saying this, Maritain is not unmindful of Plato's worry about the political danger of the arts. But he does not see the solution of this danger to lie in the interference of the politician in the work of art."

55. Maritain, *The Responsibility of the Artist*, 81.

56. Ibid., 85.

If Maritain believes that art is generally good for society, how does he attempt to resolve the inevitable conflict that arises between the artist's autonomy and the potentially harmful consequences of his or her art? Maritain looks to Francois Mauriac's call "to purify the source" for an answer.[57] The artist cannot manipulate his art directly without ruining it. He can, however, seek to purify *himself*, and as he changes, his art will naturally follow. But, says Maritain, "with respect to that final impact on the common good of mankind of which we are now speaking, it is not the purity of the source, it is rather its depth, it is the inner depth of the experience from which it springs which is of primary importance in actual fact."[58] In other words, Maritain seems to be suggesting that even a sinful artist—one whose "source is not purified," so to speak—can still, through creative intuition, create a profound work of art that is ultimately valuable to society because it is authentic. He acknowledges that the passage of time can erase the harmful side effects that a work of art might have produced in an earlier era. For example, "the statues of Greek gods no longer wound human souls with the arrows of idolatry. They have lost their magical and bewitching power. Only beauty remains."[59] The implications here are that the common good is best served by allowing artists to work authentically, listening to creative intuition, and that fine art by its very nature is the organic expression of non-conceptual knowledge and thus always a glimpse of the truth. The scandal and cause for temptation that might accompany some works of art are merely temporary; they will not have the last word.

## IV. Conclusion

In conclusion, we see that both Plato's and Maritain's views about the role of art in society rely upon their understandings of what art *is* and how it relates, or should relate, to the truth. While Plato in the *Republic* is suspicious of poetry because it is "third from the truth," crafted by poets who lack real knowledge, and because it can lead to disharmony in the societies and the souls of those who encounter its falsehoods, Maritain understands poetry to be a type of knowledge and therefore intrinsically related to the

57. Ibid., 88. For Mauriac's account of "purifying the source," see his, *God and Mammon and What Was Lost*, translated by Raymond N. MacKenzie (Lanham, Maryland: Rowman and Littlefield, 2003).

58. Maritain, *The Responsibility of the Artist*, 88.

59. Ibid., 87.

truth. Due to these differences about the essence and origins of art, Plato and Maritain also come to different conclusions about its role in society. Plato believes that false stories and images have no place in a just society or in the life of a just man. Maritain believes that the best way to preserve the common good is to allow art its own proper autonomy, since manipulating art in order to serve a pre-determined moral purpose would be a sort of self-contradiction, an "untruth" for the sake of "truth."

At the same time, both philosophers share a real concern for art's relationship to the common good. In fact, Plato and Maritain seem to agree that the ultimate goal of the common good of society is the good of each soul.[60] We also cannot forget the caveat in the *Republic*, the possibility that the philosopher—and only the philosopher, who knows what is true and loves wisdom—can use "images" to convey the truth to others. And in this way, perhaps there is yet another similarity between Plato and Maritain. The spontaneous and non-conceptual poetic intuition of Maritain's artist is not quite like the deliberate and conscious image-making of Plato's philosopher, and yet both of them communicate the truth through images. It is here, if anywhere, that we can locate the positive role of art in society.

If we return to the questions raised at the outset, questions about the role of the media in the United States today, we can consider them anew in the light of what has been said about both Plato and Maritain. Beneath our suspicion of the media is the worry that what they present to us is false, and even purposely distorted to serve a hidden agenda. In one sense, the ideologically-influenced news of our era might be illustrative of what Maritain called "Art for the Social Group" (i.e., propaganda), or, in other words, it might highlight the dark side of Plato's well-intentioned belief that both censorship and government-crafted myths have a place in society. However, to be fair to Plato, the guardians in his ideal city were those who had gained knowledge of reality and possessed harmony in their souls; they

60. Maritain, *The Person and the Common Good*, 62. Maritain's words seem to echo Plato's view when he writes "the common good of the city or of civilization—an essentially human common good in which the whole of man is engaged—does not preserve its true nature unless it respects that which surpasses it, unless it is subordinated, not as a pure means, but as an infravalent end, to the order of eternal goods and the supra-temporal values from which human life is suspended. This intrinsic subordination refers above all to the supernatural beatitude to which the human person is directly ordained." Even if human beings as individuals are inferior to the common good of political society, political society must admit that it is subordinated to the ultimate good of these persons, that is, to their supernatural beatitude in God, since it is a society comprised of human beings who are also persons.

were lovers of wisdom. Whereas it is evident that many, even most, of today's governmental leaders and media personalities lack such qualities.

Both Plato and Maritain provide us with possible ways to make sense of art and media in our culture. Plato's appreciation of art in the *Republic,* books 2 and 3—art that portrays goodness and truth beautifully and therefore has a place in the education of the youth—gives us hope that many classic works of literature and some films and music, for instance, can inspire both children and adults to know and love the true, the good, and the beautiful. Plato's suspicion in book 10 of the poets who imitate appearances and lack knowledge of what is good and true prompts us to reflect on the originators of today's art and media. Are they people of good character whose judgments, posts, and stories we can trust? Plato's suggestion that philosophers—lovers of wisdom—are the only ones who can convey truth through images should encourage us to consider the artist before naively trusting a work of art or a news story. Following Maritain's suggestion that harmful art and media are best counteracted locally in social contexts, we might endeavor to combat morally dangerous art through the education of the youth and by using popular opinion to influence media personalities. Unfortunately, in a culture swamped with various forms of social media, popular opinion is easily swayed and not exactly a reliable source of moral instinct. Nevertheless, there have been instances when social media campaigns have been used effectively to draw apologies from celebrities and politicians for their distasteful comments or reprehensible posts. Maritain's insight that the moral and aesthetic spheres are fundamentally distinct also alerts us to stay attentive to what we encounter, because authentic art, which stems from poetic intuition, will point us to the truth in the long run, even if it also sometimes scandalizes us in the short run. Whereas Plato's approach seems to suggest that we pay special attention to the artist's character, Maritain allows that even a morally unvirtuous artist could produce authentic art that leads us to what is true. Despite these possibly contradictory insights, both Plato's and Maritain's philosophy should give us hope. Despite the false images and stories that we encounter, and despite their dangerous moral implications, art still has the potential to lead us to the truth.

# III

# THE METAPHYSICS OF EXISTENCE AND THE EXISTENT

JOHN J. CONLEY, SJ

# Critical Engagement

## Maritain's Encounter with Existentialism

CHRISTIANITY HAS LONG WRESTLED with the question of how much it can integrate into its own life schools of philosophy whose sources are foreign to Christianity itself. Never without criticism from within the church, Christianity has generated its own variants of Platonism, Aristotelianism, Stoicism, Cartesianism, Marxism, Freudianism, and even postmodernism. In *Existence and the Existent,* Jacques Maritain critically engages one of the leading philosophical movements of the 1940s: existentialism. Neither baptizing nor completely rejecting the movement, Maritain demonstrates in what sense Thomism shares the better insights of existentialism while avoiding the errors into which many of its practitioners have allegedly fallen. In so doing, Maritain not only dissects the challenge of existentialism, he provides a model for Christian engagement with the ambient philosophical movements of the moment.

### I. Critiquing Existentialism

In evaluating existentialism, Maritain rejects any strategy of simple assimilation. To claim that Thomism is true existentialism by simply draping a trendy title over it is an unworthy deception. "[This is] a verbal artifice I should be ashamed to employ, by attempting to trick out Thomas Aquinas in a costume fashionable to our day."[1] This refusal to embrace fashionable or popular philosophies is of a piece with Maritain's later admonitions against "kneeling before the world" in *The Peasant of the Garonne.*[2]

In his focused critique, Maritain rejects what he finds most pernicious in the existentialism defended by Sartre among others. This is the abolition of essence. For Maritain authentic existentialism maintains a concept of essence because an existent can only exist as a particular kind of being. But the inauthentic existentialism of Sartre and company abolishes essence, a move which not only produces chaos, but which ultimately destroys the very being it attempts to champion. "The other way is to affirm the primacy of existence, but as destroying or abolishing essences or natures and as manifesting the supreme defeat of the intellect and of intelligibility.... If you abolish essence, or that which *esse* posits, by that very act you abolish existence, or *esse.* Those two notions are correlative and inseparable. An existentialism of this sort is self-destroying."[3]

Similarly, Maritain rejects the efforts of some existentialists to substitute the notion of project for that of essence.[4] Given their emphasis on the free act, some existentialists conceive of human beings as engaged in various projects designed and executed over time. But Maritain argues that without some sense of essence, such projects are unintelligible. Human beings plan to produce a particular object or state of affairs which has a name because it has an essence. The existentialists who promote this faulty, amorphous concept of project are reflecting the distorted sense of freedom in their account of the human agent.

In demonstrating how Thomism constitutes an authentic existentialism, Maritain focuses on metaphysics. At the center of metaphysics stands Maritain's celebrated intuition of being:

1. Jacques Maritain, *Existence and the Existent,* translated by Lewis Galantiere and Gerald B. Phelan (New York: Pantheon Books, 1948), 12.

2. See Jacques Maritain, *The Peasant of the Garonne: An Old Layman Questions Himself About the Present Time,* translated by Michael Cuddihy and Elizabeth Hughes (New York: Holt, Rinehart, and Winston, 1968), 53–64.

3. Maritain, *Existence and the Existent,* 13.

4. According to Sartre, human agents determine their future by freely engaging in a *projet* which orients and consolidates their intentional actions. Especially important are political versions of *projet,* in which groups of human agents collaborate to establish the ends and means of collective action in the future. See Jean-Paul Sartre, *L'Être et le néant* (Paris: Gallimard, 1943), parts 2 and 3. For Maritain, this concept of *projet* is one of many signs of an unintelligible existentialist concept of action in which the act has been stripped of all internal final causality.

At the root of metaphysical knowledge, St. Thomas places the intellectual intuition of that most mysterious reality disguised under the most commonplace and commonly used word in the language, the word to be; a reality revealed to us as the uncircumscribable subject of a science, which the gods begrudge us when we release, in the values that appertain to it, the act of existing which is exercised by the humblest thing—that victorious thrust by which it triumphs over nothingness.[5]

According to Maritain, without this intuition of being one cannot even claim to be a philosopher. It is this intuition of being which permits the metaphysician to penetrate the nature and structure of particular types of beings. Thomism is existentialist inasmuch as its primordial impulse is this intuitive grasp of existence itself. In this sense being itself enjoys priority.

In defending the metaphysics of being, Maritain dismisses the metaphysics of becoming which had captured some members of the existentialist movement. The study of the history or evolution of a being can neither reveal the being's essence nor approach the mystery of being itself. The historicism gripping contemporary philosophy obscures philosophy's very purpose:

That idea [of development or evolution] is neither enlightening nor fertile except in the context of an ontological analysis of reality. In claiming to take the place of such an analysis, and itself become the supreme explanatory principle, it does no more, as Goethe observed, than to exercise upon thought an infinite power of dissolution. For it is not a metaphysical instrument and it does not concern the analytical explanation of being; it is an historic instrument and concerns the historical explanation of becoming.[6]

Like other moves in the existentialist community, the historicist stress on becoming not only obscures the existence of essences; it distracts the philosopher from the very intuition of being by its endless panorama of change, mutation, and evolution.

Maritain will employ a similar critique of historicist philosophies in his later criticism of the evolutionary philosophy of Teilhard de Chardin.[7] In Maritain's perspective, the analysis of the stages of development of species cannot substitute for a properly metaphysical analysis of the essence of a particular plant or animal or of the particular class of beings (species) to which it belongs. Teilhard also represents a conflation of theology, philoso-

5. Maritain, *Existence and the Existent*, 29.

6. Ibid., 54.

7. See Maritain, *Peasant of the Garonne*, 116–26.

phy, natural science, poetry, and mysticism, which Maritain finds intolerable. The degrees of knowledge have been confused with each other.

To reinforce the existentialist contours of Thomism, Maritain recasts epistemology and moral philosophy in an existentialist key. Let us look at each in turn.

The realist epistemology of Thomism contends that knowledge resides in the correspondence between a noetic agent's beliefs and the actual state of affairs in an independent existent. In this correspondence model, truth presupposes the existence of the world and the beings in them independently of the noetic agent. Claims to truth point to the real existence of such existents and are not simple inventories of the mind of the noetic agent.

Truth follows upon the existence of things, i.e., of those trans-objective subjects with which thought stands face to face. Truth is the adequation of the immanence in act of our thought with that which exists outside our thought. True knowledge consists in a spiritual super-existence by which, in a supreme vital act, I become the other as such, and which corresponds to the existence exercised or possessed by that other itself in the particular field of intelligibility which is its peculiar possession. The very act of knowledge affirms the existence of other beings who are different than I am. In the noetic act, the correspondence between myself and the external being is no longer physical in nature. In forming a concept of this being and in judging that it exists, I absorb the other into a new spiritualized kind of existence.

Maritain's recasting of Thomist moral philosophy clearly indicates a certain sympathy for the existentialist emphasis upon the act and the anguish of the acting person in matters of great consequence. He emphasizes the uniqueness of each moral act and the burden of conscientious action by each unique individual:

> The same moral case never appears twice in the world. To speak strictly, precedent does not exist. Each time, I find myself in a situation requiring me to do a new thing, to bring into existence an act that is unique in the world, an act which must be in conformity with the moral law in a manner and under conditions belonging strictly to me alone and which have never risen before. Useless to thumb through the dictionary of cases of conscience! Moral treatises will of course tell me the universal rule or rules I am bound to apply; they will not tell me how I, the unique I, am to apply them in the unique context in which I am involved.[8]

8. Maritain, *Existence and the Existent*, 60.

Maritain affirms the existence of a universal moral law; moral decision-making is not a locus of pure subjectivity. But he also stresses the painful work of conscience in applying moral principles to a unique situation. There is plenty of room here for anguish, perplexity, and the weight of personal responsibility for action which cannot be resolved by appeals to precedent or authority—all common themes in the existentialist literature of the period.

To demonstrate the irreducible uniqueness of the moral act, Maritain appeals to the witness of the saints. The saints have often engaged in acts which seem bizarre. The uniqueness of the moral act here becomes a type of blessed eccentricity:

> They [the saints] have their own kind of mean, their own kind of standards. But they are valid only for each one of them. Although their standards are higher than those of reason, it is not because of the object taken in itself that the act measured by their standards is better than an act measured by the mere moral virtues; rather, it is so by the inner impetus which the saints receive from the spirit of God in the depths of their incommunicable subjectivity, which impetus goes beyond the measure of reason to a higher good discerned by them alone, and to which they are called to bear witness.[9]

Animated by charity, the moral lives of the saints point to the originality and unpredictability of a moral life bathed in grace. They are also living contradictions of the Kantian thesis that moral laws must be universalizable. The saints engage in many acts which are proper for them alone and which are not to be imitated by others.

Similarly, Maritain's presentation of philosophical theology takes into account common existentialist objections. In discussing God's omniscience and omnipotence, he counters the atheist existentialist objection that God's existence is incompatible with human freedom. God's eternal plan for the world includes the existence of free existents who can say yes or no to God by their choices. Rather than being the enemy of human freedom, God is its author:

> The divine plan is not a scenario prepared in advance, in which free subjects would play parts and act as performers. We must purge our thought of any idea of a play written in advance, at a time prior to time—a play in which time unfolds, and the characters of time read the parts. On the contrary, everything is improvised, under the eternal and immutable direction of the almighty Stage Manager.[10]

9. Ibid., 64.
10. Ibid., 122–23.

Human beings have the power to assent to or to refuse the divine will. This play of freedom is part of the divine design of creation, not its contradiction.

Maritain recognizes that in the concert of existentialism there are theistic as well as atheistic voices. Among Christian existentialists Kierkegaard enjoys pride of place. In his writings he reveals the spiritual anguish tied to the Christian dialectic of sin and salvation. Maritain recognizes the importance of the introduction of such theological themes into the self-enclosed rationalism of modern philosophy. "It must be said that by way of a spiritually crucifying existence, Kierkegaard revealed to modern philosophy a truth which undoubtedly was always known to the saints and was always more or less scrutinized by theologians, but which went far beyond philosophy; a truth which modern philosophy was unable to understand and which has disorganized it."[11] The thought of Kierkegaard and his descendants is a powerful cry of anguish before the mystery of salvation and the suffering of the world.

Nonetheless, Maritain criticizes such Christian existentialism for violating the frontier between philosophy and theology. For all its theological verve, it cannot serve as the basis for a Christian philosophy. The distinction between philosophy and theology must be maintained:

> It is non-sense to think of making the bearing or posture of Jacob in the night of his combat with the angel the attitude of metaphysics, with its special way of coming to grips with the law of things. It is non-sense to think of making the bearing or posture of Minerva in her search for causes the attitude of faith, with its special manner of tackling the dialogue with the God of faith. We do not philosophize in the posture of dramatic singularity; we do not save our souls in the posture of universality and detachment from self for the purpose of knowing.[12]

Moreover, for all its theological and moral depth, Christian existentialism does not construct a metaphysics built upon the primacy of the act of existence itself. As such, it does not constitute a species of authentic existentialism. "I do not believe that [Christian existentialism] can ever develop into a metaphysic properly so called, any more than any other philosophy which refuses to admit the intellectual intuition of being. It cannot father a metaphysis that is comprehensive, articulated, founded upon reason, and

11. Ibid., 129.
12. Ibid., 131.

capable of exercising the functions of wisdom as well as of knowledge."[13] Maritain's censure of Christian existentialism echoes the still-simmering debate over "Christian philosophy" during this period.[14] The admixture of philosophy and theology ultimately destroys the integrity of each discipline. Ironically, many richly Christian schools of thought can fail to qualify as a Christian philosophy due to their metaphysical impoverishment. The critique also echoes Maritain's enduring intellectualism. It is the intellectual intuition of being, the sine qua non of an authentic metaphysician, which must palpably guide a work for Maritain to consider it an authentic work of Christian philosophy.

## II. Philosophical Irenicism

What does Maritain's encounter with existentialism have to say to us, contemporary Christian philosophers, who are struggling here below with gusts of postmodernism, environmentalism, post-structuralism, and the like?

First, it indicates that any such engagement must recognize the differences within a movement. Kierkegaard is not Sartre. If Maritain critiques both philosophers, the ground of the critique of each is significantly different. Refusal to recognize such difference as one critically analyzes a movement can only yield caricatures. Within the concert of postmodernism, the philosophy of Lyotard, which designates postmodernity as the collapse of the great, comprehensive narratives (such as Marxism), diverges from the philosophy of Foucault, in which all claims to truth are reduced to assertions of power.[15] As Maritain's critique of existentialism indicates, the criticism of contemporary philosophical movements must transcend the limits of a lament against a broadly construed "ism." The particulars of the brief against a specific author, work, or thesis must be present if the critique is to be a fair philosophical one, one which generates insight rather than simple polemic.

Second, it suggests how one's own philosophical convictions can be

13. Ibid., 135.

14. For a comprehensive but somewhat anti-Thomist analysis of the debate over "Christian philosophy" which roiled the Francophone Catholic philosophy community at mid-century, see Maurice Nédoncelle, *Existe-t-il une philosophie chrétienne?* (Paris: Fayard, 1956).

15. See Jean-François Lyotard, *La condition postmodern* (Paris: Editions de Minuit, 1979) and Michel Foucault, *L'archéologie du savoir* (Paris: Gallimard, 1969).

enhanced by critical engagement with non-Christian schools of thought. Maritain's theory of the uniqueness of each moral act, while drawn from the traditional natural-law category of conscience, is clearly flavored by the existentialist discussions of the nature of the "free act." His account of moral decision making transcends the limits of traditional casuistry, which often reduces the uniqueness of the moral act to an application of universal principles to a new set of facts, executed with the logical rigor of a syllogism. Maritain's account of the subjective anguish inherent in the moral act carries an existentialist stamp. The encounter with existentialism is not only the occasion for refutation of error; it is also the opportunity to recover or enhance certain themes in his own Thomistic philosophy and to present these themes with new accents. Similarly, the current encounter of Catholic philosophy with the various strands of postmodernism is more than an occasion to contest the relativism ambient in many postmodern thinkers; it invites Catholic philosophers to attend to the narrative embedded within our philosophical arguments and to attend to the narrative in which these arguments are embedded.

Third, the critique of foreign philosophical movements must be literally a radical one, that is, it must go to the roots of the movement's errors. Strikingly, Maritain's critique of Sartre does not focus primarily on his atheism or even mention his supine Stalinism; it focuses on his abolition of essence. Such metaphysical criticism is precisely the work of the philosopher. Maritain has long and rightly been acclaimed as the model of a public intellectual, of a philosopher who publishes essays and gives lectures to a broad, educated public and does not confine his publications to the monograph and the academic journal. But Maritain's treatment of controversial political issues regularly goes beyond the surface controversies to the underlying metaphysical, anthropological, and epistemological issues. His metaphysical critique of Sartre can guide contemporary Catholic philosophers who attempt to offer social criticism as public intellectuals in the media and the blogosphere. Interventions in the debate over euthanasia should probe the concepts of autonomy undergirding the debate. The philosopher should make explicit the concepts of the common good and social justice surrounding the political controversies over health care. The critique of postmodernity must challenge the "end of metaphysics" championed by many postmodern thinkers and demonstrate why metaphysical reflection is necessary and what type of metaphysical reflection is true.

Simply spotting the contradictions or the political inanity of a given postmodern philosopher is insufficient.

Fourth, Maritain's critique of Sartrean existentialism is a warning on the danger of succumbing to trends or fads within the arena of philosophy itself. The discipline of philosophy often—and rightly—prides itself on its capacity to take a critical distance from majority opinion or popular beliefs in the ambient culture. The Socratic project of philosophical dialogue in ancient Greece emerged as a skeptical critique of religious beliefs, political ideals, and concepts of virtue held by the majority or by powerful elites. *Existence and the Existent* is a gauntlet thrown down at the feet of a philosophical trend that in the 1940s had captivated the Left Bank and then the entire academic and artistic world. One of Maritain's intellectual tasks was to demonstrate that the philosophical emperor had no clothes and that the gauzy Sartrean appeals to *projet* and *angoisse* did not constitute a substantial argument. In doing so, he continued his work as a critic of modern philosophical trends already present in his early critique of Lutheranism, Cartesianism, and Rousseauism (*Three Reformers*, 1925) and in his later dismissal of Teilhardian evolutionism (*The Peasant of the Garonne*, 1966). For contemporary philosophers, the peril remains. Critical engagement with contemporary philosophical movements cannot entail a surrender to the concepts and rhetoric of the latest movement to dominate the conference programs of the American Philosophical Association. Stern and reasoned resistance to the trends of the moment, even when one is confined to the status of an unpopular minority, must remain the mark of the vigilant philosopher.

Finally, Maritain argues that a Christian philosophical critique of non-Christian philosophies must be purely philosophical. It must refuse to use theological tools and to import the data of revelation into its argument. This is perhaps the most questionable of Maritain's guidelines for philosophical engagement. It carries echoes of the rationalist Thomism to which he was introduced by Dominican mentors after his conversion to Catholicism.[16] Strikingly, Maritain himself often violates the border between philosophy and theology. He published works on the biblical book of Job

16. Under the influence of Humbert Clerissac and other French Dominicans, Maritain read extensively in the works of Renaissance commentators on Aquinas, especially Cajetan and John of St. Thomas. Their rationalist effort to construct a purely philosophical Thomism, freed from theological references to revelation, clearly influences Maritain throughout his philosophical career.

and Song of Songs, on the liturgy, on Christology, and on ecclesiology.[17] Theological preoccupations became so prominent in his later works that Ralph McInerny claims that "Maritain was a philosopher who metamorphosed into a theologian in his last years."[18] The very metaphysics of being Maritain attempts to defend had been deeply shaped over the centuries by the biblical doctrine of the divine name (especially God's self-revelation as "I am the one who is" in the burning-bush epiphany of Exodus; Ex 3:1–7) and of creation ex nihilo. Fideism has been a perennial but minor temptation for Catholic philosophy. And simple appeals to biblical and ecclesiastical authority carry no weight in a properly philosophical demonstration. Nonetheless, no philosophy—and certainly no Catholic philosophy—emerges in isolation from religious convictions rooted in faith, revelation, and worship.

Maritain's critical encounter with existentialism models a path of critical discernment for contemporary Catholic philosophers engaged in combat with analogous movements today. They should not shy away from polemical refutation of error, but this refutation should dive to the metaphysical roots of error and not settle for criticism of secondary issues or surface symptoms. No matter how convincing the refutation is, the philosophy defended by the critic of error will be altered by the encounter. The commonplace use of the term "alienation" to designate evil or sin by contemporary Christian philosophers is the residue of a decades-long combat against Marxism and Freudianism. In a media sea of blanket condemnations and facile brandings by public intellectuals, the philosophical critique of ideas must struggle for specificity. It is the particular theses in particular passages by particular authors that should be the object of criticism. Accuracy, precision, and depth should mark the gladiators engaged in a genuinely philosophical quarrel.

17. See Jacques Maritain, *Liturgie et Contemplation* (Paris: Desclée de Brouwer, 1960); *De la grâce et de l'humanité de Jésus* (Paris: Desclée de Brouwer, 1967); ——, *Approches sans entraves* (Paris: Fayard, 1973); ——, *L'Église du Chris, la personne de l'Église et son personnel* (Paris: Desclée de Brouwer, 1973).

18. Ralph McInerny, *The Very Rich Hours of Jacques Maritain* (Notre Dame, Indiana: University of Notre Dame Press, 2003), 3.

DENIS A. SCRANDIS

# The Existential Metaphysics of Maritain's *Existence and the Existent*

## I. Introduction

JACQUES MARITAIN WROTE *Existence and the Existent*[1] as Western civilization emerged from the ravages of World War II. It is an essay intended to aid the intellectual recovery of the West from the philosophical errors that he believed had driven Western cultures and nations to their catastrophic conflicts. The powerful errors at issue trace back to Enlightenment attacks on religion and philosophy that launched Europe in the direction of modernity.

René Descartes had sought to replace Aristotelian philosophy. The ensuing rationalist and empiricist philosophies attacked traditional notions of knowledge and belief. Subjectivism in metaphysics and epistemology led to subjectivism in anthropology, political thought, ethics, and humanism. Western culture was toxic by the twentieth century. Some post-war proponents of the new subjectivism called themselves existentialists and their philosophies "existentialism." Like their predecessors, they abolished the notion of essence and conceived of man as lacking the human nature upon which rest the natural law, human rights, and a truly human social order. Maritain engaged this complex environment of contrary and contradictory philosophies.[2] He lectured and wrote about Christian humanism,

1. Jacques Maritain, *Existence and the Existent*, translated by Lewis Galantiere and Gerald B. Phelan (Garden City, New York: Image Books, 1957).

2. See ibid., 17.

natural law, human rights, and the principles of democratic government. At the start of the post-war reconstruction of France, he served in government.

Maritain had embraced St. Thomas Aquinas's metaphysical analysis of being, which recognizes the primacy of existence. He considered Thomas's metaphysics to be an authentic existentialism, unlike the existentialist theories of Heidegger and Sartre. This is not to say that Maritain either said or implied that Aquinas had personally taught a doctrine of existentialism. But, Maritain did elaborate in *Existence and the Existent* an analysis of being and knowledge that used Thomistic principles and showed the primacy of existence (*esse*) in both being and knowledge.

Maritain also believed that every culture has a metaphysical foundation and teleology, whether its participants know it or not. Armed with a true metaphysics, Maritain believed that post-modern man could create a culture that would nurture human development and rescue him from his own culture, which is still failing because it still lacks a true understanding of being, knowledge, and human nature. This essay explains the basic themes of Maritain's existential metaphysics with an eye to its role in this all-important rescue.

## II. Basic Principles of Being: Essence and Existence and the Primacy of Existence

Aristotelian-Thomistic philosophy nourishes itself on the intelligibility of the world. The things that populate the world are actually sensible but potentially intelligible. For this reason, we have knowledge of the world both by means of sensible objects (by way of our senses) and by means of sense-derived, intelligible objects (thanks to our senses and an active intellectual power).

The natural philosopher examines natural things in terms of the actions that flow from their intrinsic capacities. Such actions, faculties, and their underlying basis or nature provide intelligible objects. For example, we take the property "eats meat" from observing an animal's eating habits or "produces fruit" from observing a plant's lifecycle. The functional nature or essence is named a quiddity or "whatness" and is expressed in a definition. The essential definition itself is expressed in terms of formal and material co-principles. Natural or material being is sensible, but its constituent principles of being, especially its essence and existence, while not sensible, are potentially intelligible.

Now, Aquinas and Maritain taught that essence provides a being with its "whatness" but not its existence and for this reason is not a sufficient principle of a complete being. Essence needs existence. Existence exercises efficient causality and actualizes essence's potentiality to exist in a being and thus has primacy over essence in the structure of being. For this reason, this metaphysics (that of *Existence and the Existent*) is an existentialism.

## III. The Intelligibility of Essence and the Super-Intelligibility of Existence

In his inquiries, Maritain works to discover the truth. But he wants more. He wants to know the reasons why something is true. We see this in his metaphysical investigations in *Existence and the Existent.* He is not satisfied only with showing the structure of being, which would respond to phenomenological existentialism's challenge; he wants to elaborate further how the human cognitive capacities and operations come to know being, its principles, and its parts—especially nature and existence.

Human knowledge begins in the senses and the higher integrative imagination. Maritain says that sensible being exists outside of cognition and that sense delivers sensible being to the intellect, thus giving to the intellect a potentially intelligible treasure that sense itself does not know to be intelligible.[3] The sense's report is commonly referred to as the sensible species. For example, upon the observation of a red rose, this species (image or phantasm) contains sensible rose determinations but not actually intelligible forms, i.e., it contains neither the "quality called red" nor the "nature called rose" nor the "being called rose." However, these ontological features are latent within the sensible species, which the agent intellect has not yet rendered intelligible. The senses, Maritain says, also "attain existence in act without . . . knowing that it is existence."[4]

The intellect's operation of simple apprehension or abstraction disengages intelligible features from sensible species. Yet, we also know beings, not just essences. The act of judgment restores the unity severed by simple

3. See ibid., 21.
4. Ibid.

apprehension even as it restores essence to the existential state. Judgment transposes the mind from the order of simple objects to the order of subjects possessing existence, actually or possibly. Moreover, Maritain says that the intellect, when judging, "performs" or "lives" by means of an act proper to itself, the same act of existing that the thing exercises outside cognition.[5] Now, the judgment's performed act of existing is more than a mere positing of an "empty" cognitive operation, that is, it is more than an operation without a content or intelligible value of its own. The judgment's content, an act of existing, is also the same act of existing that the thing exercises. Maritain calls this content the completion in mind "of intelligibility in act," since the operation restores existence's actuation of the intelligible essence. Maritain says it (the restorative intellection) is "act or energy par excellence,"[6] which expresses the efficient causality of existence. He believes that the intelligibility of existence here discussed is of monumental significance:

> The intelligibility with which judgment deals is more mysterious than that which notions or ideas conveyed to us; it is not expressed in a concept but in the very act of affirming or denying. It is the super-intelligibility ... of the act of existing itself, either possible or actually given. And it is on this super-intelligibility of existence that St. Thomas hangs the whole life of the intellect.[7]

Has Maritain found something of value? On the one hand, we are told that the judgment operates on a being's native existence, say on a cat's existence, when it says, "the cat exists." On the other hand, this singular existence, when the intellect utters "the cat exists," manifests an extraordinary intelligibility: a super-intelligibility. When Maritain said that St. Thomas hung the whole life of the intellect upon the super-intelligibility of existence, he meant that the super-intelligibility of existence powers the intelligibility of the world and illuminates all the works of intellect.

## IV. How the Concept of Existence Is Formed

A problem for Maritain in *Existence and the Existent* is to account for the genesis of a concept of existence. He warns that the notions of exis-

5. Ibid., 25–27.

6. Ibid., 27.

7. Ibid., 28. Here Maritain is quoting a passage from his earlier monograph, *De Bergson à Thomas d'Aquin* (1944).

tence and essence cannot be detached from one another, since existence and essence relate to each other as act and potency.[8] This caution is helpful, because Maritain's own discussions frequently treat these co-principles separately to avoid cumbersome locutions. Another caution warns that this analysis frequently discusses cognitive operations in terms of their active, causal principle without explicit identification of its underlying basis. The principle may for example be an intellectual virtue, which in turn is an accident of a power, which in turn is an accident of a knower. In this situation the virtue's act is also the faculty's act, which is also and ultimately the knower's act, even if these details pass unnoticed.

So far, the treatment of intellectual operations has stated that apprehension comprehends concepts and that judgment "lives" or "performs" acts of existence; but neither operation forms a concept of existence, say, of the "essence of existence." Maritain finds a paradox here. Although simple apprehension does not abstract existence from a sensible species in the way in which it abstracts essence from sensible species (that is, by illuminating a sensible species), the intellect nevertheless comes to have a concept of existence.[9] How does Maritain account for a valid concept of existence? In judgmentally affirming the act of existence (say in affirming "the canary exists"), the intellect takes hold from the sensible species, not of an idea of existence but, of the very act of existing in order to perform or live that act of existing itself, which—as was observed before—is a super-intelligible object. It is at this point, that is, while the intellect judgmentally operates on its super-intelligible object, that the intellect in-act is itself intelligible in-act. Coincident with the intelligibility of the immaterial intellect, the intellect's operation and its operation's object (that contains existence) are also intelligible and thus available for apprehension and conceptualization. Simple apprehension can form at this moment and in this way a concept of existence and a concept of being.[10]

## V. The Intuition of Analogous Being

To this point, we have seen that intellect grasps essence with abstraction and affirms being and existence in judgment. Yet neither of these op-

8. Maritain, *Existence and the Existent,* 34.
9. See ibid., 32–33.
10. See ibid., 35–37n13.

erations disengages or releases the distinctive object of the metaphysician, namely, the object known as *ens in quantum ens* (being inasmuch as being) or *ens qua ens* (being as being). This object, unlike the essence "mouse" and like the transcendental "good," has a content that is not limited to a single nature or analogate. This object is neither univocal nor equivocal; rather, it has a distinctive intelligibility that includes what Maritain describes as "an infinity of analogates."[11] This object is released by the operation of an intellectual habit or virtue[12] in a kind of intuition.[13] Maritain describes this analogous object:

> It is being disengaged for its own sake, in the values and resources appertaining to its own intelligibility and reality; which is to say, in that richness, that analogical and transcendental amplitude which is *inviscerated* in the imperfect and multiple unity of its concept and which allows it to cover the infinitude of its analogates and causes it to overflow or super-abound in transcendental values and in dynamic values of propensity through which the idea of being transgresses itself.[14]

Maritain compresses in this sentence a description of the content of the analogous concept, *ens in quantum ens*. He had elaborated at length this content a decade earlier in his work *A Preface to Metaphysics*.[15] Nevertheless, he suggests here that the object contains a collection of analogates and causes, including perhaps all created being, all causes, and all transcendentals. This idea of being contains in some way not just the cat-being or the dog-being whose *esse* occasions the intuition but every other actual or possible act of contingent existing. Maritain believes also that the intellect that once intuits this object is changed forever, since the object, as a principle of act, actualizes an intellectual virtue and makes the man a metaphysician of being. Consider how he describes the encounter with *ens in quantum ens*:

> What counts is to take the leap, to release, in one authentic intellectual intuition, the sense of being, the sense of the value of the implications that lie in the act of existing. What counts is to have seen that existence is not a simple empirical fact but a primitive datum for the mind itself, opening to the mind an infinite supra-observable field—in a word, the primary and super-intelligible source of intelligibility.[16]

11. Ibid., 29.
12. See ibid., 30.
13. See ibid., 28.
14. Ibid., 29; italics in original.
15. Jacques Maritain, *A Preface to Metaphysics* (New York: Mentor Omega, 1962).
16. Maritain, *Existence and the Existent*, 31.

In real being, existence actualizes essence. In knowledge, judgmentally released existence, which is a super-intelligible object, is the source of the intelligibility of the intuited object and its analogous contents, that is, of the "analogical and transcendental amplitude" which covers "the infinitude of its analogates and causes it to overflow in transcendental values."[17] Super-intelligible existence exudes the intelligibility of the analogates and is the source both of the existence of extra-mental being and of the intelligibility of the known reality.

## VI. The Foundation of Maritain's Metaphysics: The Intuition of Being

Maritain's metaphysics may eventually be fully articulated and published in book-form with self-evident first principles and demonstrations. But it is described in *Existence and the Existent* in terms of a direct intellectual seeing or way of intellectually grasping reality in terms of a specifically defined kind of intelligibility. A highly refined insight scrutinizes things (or their species), without being halted or deflected by material and quantitative characteristics, and searches for non-material intelligibility,[18] such as the intelligibility of *essence, ens,* and the other metaphysical principles. Being as being, includes such principles.[19]

Now, Maritain's metaphysical vision is famously characterized as an intellectual intuition, namely, the intellectual intuition of being. He says:

> [There is a] higher intuition [in which] the intellect disengages being from knowledge of the sensible in which it is immersed, in order to make of it the object or rather the subject of metaphysics; when, in a word, it conceptualizes the metaphysical intuition of being (seen now in the light of all the values proper to it, in its typical and primordial intelligible density), what the intellect releases into that same light is, here again, first and foremost, the act of existing.[20]

The object of metaphysics described in this quotation is the act of existing seen "in the typical and primordial intelligible density," that is, the act of existing seen as existing or able to exist without matter and seen "in the light of all the values proper to it," that is, seen in reference to the tran-

17. Ibid., 29.
18. See ibid., 42.
19. See ibid., 40.
20. Ibid., 35.

scendentals (*bonum, res,* etc.) and first principles of being (*essentia, esse,* as well as the principles of identity, sufficient reason, and finality). When the metaphysician affirms that "this tree exists," his or her consciousness contains more than just tree-essence and tree-existence. The analogous concept being as being is there also for the alert observer. The foundation of metaphysics seems to be a very special object, one that is immaterial and analogous; an object that is conceived by the operation of a special intellectual virtue in an act of intellectual judgment upon the act of existing of any, if not every, sensible being.

## VII. Some Twentieth Century Criticisms of Maritain's Metaphysics

Some twentieth-century Thomists have debated the "starting point" of Thomistic metaphysics. For Maritain, the intuition of being deserves the title of starting point, since it is in that act that the intellect and its habit jointly receive the judgmentally released *esse* and together conceive being as being, that is, the subject of metaphysics. Here both the super-intelligible *esse* (a principle of act) and a corresponding cognitive capacity (a principle of potency) come together in the conception of being as being. Maritain describes in *Existence and the Existent* the origin of the concept of being as being in a footnote: "It is in a judgment declaring that being is *not* necessarily linked to matter nor to any of its conditions that the intellect abstracts being from all matter and makes for itself the metaphysical concept of being as being."[21] Maritain says that the intellectual operation that releases being as being is a negative judgment that denies that being itself (even if taken from a sensible or material species) is tied by definition or existential circumstance to matter of any sort. Some of these critics offer alternative points of departure. John F. X. Knasas thinks that Maritain's position is fatally flawed.[22] While he acknowledges that the subject of Thomistic metaphysics includes both material and immaterial beings, Knasas thinks that Maritain's intuitive grasp of a sensible being's *esse* delivers a so-called "material *esse*" (and never an "immaterial *esse*"), since a sensible phantasm (the grasped *esse*'s origin) is a material source. Knasas says:

21. Ibid, 38–39n14.

22. See John F. X. Knasas, *Being and Some Twentieth-Century Thomists* (New York: Fordham University Press, 2003), 61–65.

The difficulty in Maritain's presentation of the entry into Thomistic metaphysics has long been noted. Maritain's approach claims more from experience than experience can give. From a number of judgments, I can see that *esse* is an act that need not actuate this body or that body. Nevertheless, in every case, *esse* is still presented as the act of some body. From the data, no indication yet exists that *esse* possesses an ability to actuate more than bodies. From judgmentally grasped *esse*, Maritain draws an object too great for the data to bear. In general, the apprehension of a transphysical commonality presupposes some knowledge of an immaterial being.[23]

Knasas, accepting that the judgment's operation releases *esse* from a sensible and material source, reasons that this abstracted *esse* is necessarily material *esse*. He thinks that a judgment bearing upon an immaterial being, such as a conclusion affirming the existence of the immaterial human soul, is needed to provide the intuition of being with an immaterial being from which immaterial *esse* can be drawn.[24] Are these remarks telling against Maritain's position?

Can Maritain obtain immaterial *esse* from a sensible source? Yes, Maritain in an earlier writing, and Thomas in his commentary on the Aristotle's *Metaphysics*, pointed out that the metaphysical objects are immaterial objects regardless of their source. The *Preface to Metaphysics* discussed metaphysical objects in terms of their definitions (they are defined without matter of any sort) and their mode of being (they may exist in material or immaterial beings):

At the degree of metaphysical knowledge, the mind abstracts from matter of any kind, that knowledge of the object is wholly emancipated from matter. There is neither "intelligible" nor "sensible" nor "individual matter." We are in the world of

23. John F. X. Knasas, "How Thomistic is the Intuition of Being?" in *Jacques Maritain: The Man and his Metaphysics*, edited by John F. X. Knasas (Mishawaka, Indiana: American Maritain Association, 1988), 86.

24. Writing years later (see *Being and Some Twentieth-Century Thomists*, 64–65), Knasas cited Étienne Gilson's last argument concerning the abstraction of existence. Since the human intellect does not think without an image (a sensible object) and since there is no image of existence (because existence is a non-sensible, constituent part of a sensible being), there can be no abstraction of an immaterial (or "pure intelligible") concept of existence. Yet, Aquinas reminds us (*In VI Metaph.*, n. 1165) that metaphysical objects are "separate from matter and motion in being and in their intelligible structure [or definition]," and that the metaphysician also studies sensible beings "inasmuch as they are beings." Existence is "itself" immaterial. If it were to activate an essence that is a material nature (consisting of matter and form), making a material being, existence would remain "separate from matter in its intelligible structure" although not separate "in being." See Conclusions (below) for further discussion of this criticism.

being as such, of the transcendentals, of act and potency, of substance and accident, or intellect and will, all of them realities which can exist in immaterial as well as in material objects. Now the intellect sees in material objects realities capable of existing not only in the objects in which it sees them, but also in immaterial subjects themselves, and finally in the transcendent Cause of all things whom the transcendental notions, being, unity, truth, intellect, will, and the like are realized in a super-eminent unity.[25]

Metaphysical realities are defined immaterially or without matter, and they may exist in both material and immaterial subjects. Metaphysical realities are not rendered (or redefined as) material by existence in material beings.

Thomas's commentary on Aristotle's *Metaphysics* says that first philosophy (or metaphysics) studies immaterial objects as well as material beings inasmuch as they are beings:

However, we must remember that even though things which are separate from matter and motion in being and in their intelligible structure [or definition] belong to the study of first philosophy, still the philosopher not only investigates these but also sensible things inasmuch as they are beings.[26]

Thomas's first philosopher investigates things separate from matter and motion in being and definition such as angels or separated substances.[27] The philosopher or metaphysician also studies sensible beings (not as mobile or changeable) but as constituted in existence (not in kind) by principles (such as essence and existence), which are defined without matter, and inasmuch as they exercise existence or are beings.

## VIII. Conclusions

Maritain's purpose in writing *Existence and the Existent* was to sketch a metaphysics that would defend truth. This metaphysics would protect

25. Maritain, *A Preface to Metaphysics*, 84. Maritain has in mind here that Thomistic speculative theology uses "transcendental notions" to study the "transcendental Cause" or God.

26. Thomas Aquinas, *Commentary on the Metaphysics of Aristotle*, translated by John P. Rowan (Chicago: Henry Regnery, 1961), 6.1, n. 1165.

27. It is instructive to compare Aristotelian physics and metaphysics. The natural philosopher studies, for example, the cat and finds that it is a composed of form and matter. The metaphysician studies the cat and finds that it is constituted by essence and existence. Thus, the cat is a natural being knowable in terms of physical concepts and overlapping but non-physical or metaphysical concepts.

true anthropology, ethics, ontology, physical science, and theology from skepticism and sophistry. Such theology would combine revelation with a well-developed doctrine of being and analogy.

The things that populate the world are actually sensible and potentially intelligible. We know them by means of sensible objects and sense-derived intelligible objects, and we know that they are constituted from principles, which are potentially intelligible. According to Thomistic epistemology, simple apprehension disengages parts of being and conceptualizes them, while judgment joins or separates parts and existentially affirms or denies integral beings. Thomas's epistemology accounts in this way for the basic knowledge of every day human experience but not for the grasp of objects of the speculative sciences and especially of metaphysics.

Being as being, unlike all other objects, is analogous and contains the parts of being, the self-evident principles of being, the transcendentals, the causes, and so forth. Maritain thought from his own personal experience that being is the subject of an intellectual intuition, which is the starting point of metaphysics.

The intuition of being isn't just for metaphysicians. It provides a rich content of analogates for reference to all people. How might being as being facilitate everyday knowing? The typical or non-metaphysical person has an attenuated or limited access to being as being, enough, say, to validate "horse" (seen as an analogate of "living animal") when it is used in the judgment "This horse is a living animal." This limited access to being as being may be enough to invalidate the proposition "A unicorn is a living animal," since unicorn is not an analogate of animal, and it is thus not verifiably in being as being. On the other hand, the metaphysician's glimpse of the principle of sufficient reason (whatever exists has a sufficient reason for its existence) confirms his demonstrations of the existence of the Cause of being and the first Cause of motion.

Examination of Maritain's critics in fact strengthens Maritain's views. First, it had been said that the starting point of Maritain's metaphysics in the intuitive grasp of *esse* can only yield material *esse* (and not immaterial *esse*), since it is taken from a sensible or material species. Yet, as was concluded above, metaphysical realities are defined immaterially or without matter and may exist in both material and immaterial subjects. Metaphysical realities are not rendered material by existence in material beings and can be distinguished or separated from material species and beings as immaterial objects. The intuitive grasp of *esse* from a material species is therefore of immaterial *esse*.

Second, it had been implied by Gilson's critique that Maritain had mistakenly thought that a concept of existence could be abstracted from a sensible species. Yet, to portray the method of conceptualizing existence in the manner of abstracting a sensible accident from a substance suggests that existence is an accident of a substance rather than an active principle constitutive of a substance. Existence is not an accident, and Maritain does not treat it as one.

The metaphysician's distinctive intellectual virtue facilitates the intellect's cognitive operation at the metaphysical degree of intelligibility. That is, it facilitates apprehending concepts defined without matter of any sort (without individual matter, without sensible matter, and without intelligible matter). It facilitates grasping being (*ens*), being as being, essence, existence, substance, subsistence, act, potency, causes, first principles, and such. In other words, it facilitates grasping the subject matter of metaphysics, which I submit is no small accomplishment.

Maritain's purpose in writing *Existence and the Existent* was to provide the intellectual support needed for a new post-modern culture, and he seems to have succeeded. Yet, the task of renewing civilization involves will as well as intellect. Contemporary subjectivist culture, a tangle of sophistries and hedonism, darkens enculturated minds and holds hapless spirits enthralled. It will not be replaced until its ends have been abandoned and its grip broken. Maritain's Christian philosophy and existential metaphysics provide the intellectual tools that can support the construction of a truly human social order.

JOHN FROULA

# Maritain's Christological Metaphysics

## Unity of Person, Primacy of *Esse*, Integrity of Essence

JACQUES MARITAIN'S explanation of *esse,* essence, and subsistence provides a lucid metaphysical framework for understanding how Christ has two natures in the unity of one person. That lucidity is somewhat obscured when Maritain attempts to account for the *esse secundarium* of Christ as found in the Thomistic theological tradition. What follows is an overview of the fundamental principles of Maritain's metaphysics and an explanation of how he applies them to Christology. There follows a summary of how Maritain revises his views in part to explain Christ's humanity in terms of a secondary *esse* of Christ as received by his human nature yet exercised only by the divine supposit. The argument of this essay is that Maritain's revised Christology and its consequences obstruct or even break down his more certain earlier principles of *esse,* essence, and subsistence. However, viewed critically from the vantage point of his earlier account, his revised account does advance the discussion about *esse* as applied to the humanity of Christ insofar as it represents an attempt to avoid both Nestorianism and the view that Christ as man is nothing.[1]

1. For an overview of the medieval opinion that Christ insofar as he is man is nothing, *quod Christus nihil sit secundum quod homo,* see Clare Monagle, *Orthodoxy and Controversy in Twelfth-Century Religious Discourse: Peter Lombard's Sentences and the Development of Theology* (Turnhoult, Belgium: Brepols, 2013), 107–108.

## I. Maritain's Metaphysical Principles

In *Existence and the Existent,* with the simplicity of genius, Maritain lays out a classic account of authentic existentialism as found in St. Thomas.[2] It is an account very much in keeping which the metaphysical claims he made some fifteen years previous in *The Degrees of Knowledge,* especially in the "First Version" of Appendix IV entitled "On the Notion of Subsistence."[3] Maritain understands authentic existentialism as a philosophy of being that recognizes the primacy of existence or *esse,*[4] while still recognizing essence or nature as a real and irreducible principle.[5] Indeed, existence without essence would be a void; being would lack intelligibility. Essence and existence are dependent correlatives.[6] Existentialism, without a strong but secondary role for essence, tends at turns to support a voluntarist God who acts without wisdom, or an atheist worldview searching in vain for meaning.[7] For Maritain, then, "essence and existence belong to

2. Maritain explains many Thomistic theses on the basis of the primacy of *esse.* See *Existence and the Existent* (New York: Pantheon Books, 1964), 37–42. That *esse* does not take part in the definition of essence and is really distinct from it is convincingly argued by John F. Wippel, among others. Wippel offers five arguments found in St. Thomas proving the real distinction between *esse* and essence. He does so in forty firmly packed pages, documenting how some of the arguments are repeated throughout St. Thomas's career. There can be little doubt that the real distinction is not just the opinion of St. Thomas, but something he considers a foundational truth. See John F. Wippel, "Essence-*Esse* Composition and the One and the Many," in *The Metaphysical Thought of Thomas Aquinas: From Finite Being to Uncreated Being,* Monographs of the Society for Medieval and Renaissance Philosophy, vol. 1 (Washington, D.C.: The Catholic University of America Press, 2000), 137–76.

3. Jacques Maritain, *The Degrees of Knowledge,* translated by Gerald Phelan (Notre Dame, Indiana: University of Notre Dame Press, 1995), 454–57.

4. Maritain contrasts a philosophy of being with a dialectic of essence; the latter he terms "thumbing through a picture book" in the spirit of Plato, Descartes, or Wolff. See *Existence and the Existent,* 2.

5. Ibid., 2–3.

6. Ibid., 3–4.

7. For a view in opposition to Maritain's, see William E. Carlo, *The Ultimate Reducibility of Essence to Existence in Existential Metaphysics* (The Hague: Martinus Nijhoff, 1966). As Norris Clarke points out in the introduction to Carlo's book, Carlo's understanding of essence and *esse,* while beginning historically in a formulation of a real distinction between *esse* and essence, goes beyond such a formulation: "I suggest that we may finally be led, for the sake of better communication with other philosophers and the avoidance of the almost insuperable ambiguities of the traditional language, to a more modest and less explicit formula something like this: in every finite being there is an intrinsic ontological duality or tension between the perfection of the act of *esse* and a partial negation or limitation of the same act." (Clarke, introduction to *The Ultimate Reducibility,* xiv.) In other words, the limitation of *esse* takes the place of essence. For another

two different orders, and essence is in potency with respect to existence."[8]

The *esse*-essence pair stands in contrast to other act-potency pairs where each pair belongs to the same order, such as faculty and operation or habit and action. In these pairs the act comes out of the reserve of the potency, as it were, and the fulfilment of the potency brings the potency to its correlative act.[9] The ability to do or be, in these cases, becomes the doing or being. But existence and essence are not in the same order such that the perfection of essence in the order of essence would be existence. Essence is ever essence, needing an entirely distinct principle, existence or *esse*, for it to be the essence of something real.

The something real is the subject or the supposit, which differs from both existence and essence. Existence and essence, for Maritain, are only intelligible as principles of the subject, the existent or being that exists. Existing subjects are the single *locus* of metaphysics.[10] Maritain goes so far as to say, "*subjects* occupy all the room there is in the Thomist universe."[11] The true grounding for existentialism is the individual existent subject in its knowability.[12] It is the subject that exercises existence or *esse*, the subject that has an essence, and the subject that acts. This emphasis on the supposit or subject stands in contrast to tendencies that see metaphysical principles like *esse* and essence as reified building blocks or else see *esse* as some kind of quasi-platonic ultra-form.

## II. Metaphysical Principles Applied to Christ

In his Appendix IV to *The Degrees of Knowledge*, Maritain brings these three aspects of metaphysics, *esse*, essence, and supposit, to bear on the

view in opposition to Maritain's, see John D. Caputo, *Heidegger and Aquinas: An Essay in Overcoming Metaphysics* (New York: Fordham University Press), 1982.

8. Maritain, *The Degrees of Knowledge*, 454.

9. Maritain claims that in all act-potency pairs, except for *esse*-essence, the two elements in the pair are in the same order, but it is difficult to see how this is true of such act-potency pairs as form-matter or accident-substance. Form does not come from the reserve of matter the way operation comes from a faculty. Matter is not form's ability the way a faculty is an operation's ability. For a contrasting view where form is considered as elicited from matter, see Lawrence Dewan, "The Importance of Substance," in *Form and Being* (Washington, D.C.: The Catholic University of America Press, 2006), 96–130, especially 120–130.

10. See Maritain, *Existence and the Existent*, 33.

11. Ibid., 62; italics in original.

12. Ibid., 66.

incarnation of the Word.[13] The non-reducibility of essence to *esse* means that there are two modes of individuation. One mode of individuation is completely in the quidditative order, like a body being ensouled or matter being informed. The other mode is existential individuation or subsistence. Subsistence is the individuation of essence with respect to existence, that is to say, *esse*. The humanity of Christ, complete and individuated in the quidditative order, relies on the divine *esse* to be individuated in the existential order. The Word communicates his divine *esse* to the human nature such that the human nature terminates in his Person. It is a condition for the human nature of Christ to be unique and to be in act that the Word possess it as his own. The Word does not take on a human nature that would have *esse* on its own if not assumed, much less human nature with autonomous and proportionate *esse*. However, The Word does take on an integral human nature in the quidditative and natural order.

Maritain's metaphysical analysis of Christ outlined above is consistent with the broad commentarial tradition and several texts from St. Thomas that focus on Christ's single *esse*. Here is a representative sample of St. Thomas's thought on Christ's one *esse* from the *Compendium*:

> Truly it is necessary to confess that those things that pertain to the supposit or hypostasis are only one in Christ: hence if *esse* is taken according as one *esse* is of one supposit, it seems that it must be said that in Christ there is only one *esse*. For it is clear that the divided parts of the singular have proper *esse*, but according as they are considered in a whole, they do not have their own *esse*, but all of them are through the *esse* of the whole. If therefore we consider Christ himself as a certain integral supposit of two natures, his *esse* will be only one, just as he is one supposit.[14]

With this in mind, it is easy to see why St. Thomas's endorsement of a secondary *esse* in Christ in the disputed question *De unione Verbi incarnati* should have been a source of bewilderment to Thomists down through the centuries:

> And therefore just as Christ is one simply because of the unity of the supposit, and two according to which, because of the two natures, thus he has one *esse* simply because of the one eternal *esse* of the eternal supposit. But there is also another *esse*

13. Maritain, *The Degrees of Knowledge*, 454–57.

14. St. Thomas Aquinas, *Compendium theologiae*, lib. 1 cap. 212. All English translations of St. Thomas's Latin are by the author and found at www.corpusthomisticum.org.

of this supposit, not inasmuch it is eternal, but inasmuch as it is made man in time. Which *esse*, even if it is not accidental *esse*—since man is not predicated accidentally of the Son of God, as was said above—it is nevertheless not the principle *esse*, but secondary. But if in Christ there were two supposits, then each supposit would have its own principle *esse*. And thus in Christ there would be two-fold *esse* simply speaking.[15]

There have been many responses to the *esse secundarium* of Christ as explained above by St. Thomas. They range from virtual dismissal, to attempted integrations, to making it the normative key for interpreting all the other texts in which St. Thomas speaks more forcefully of a single *esse* in Christ.[16] Maritain followed for a time Cajetan's opinion, expressed in his *Summa Theologiae* commentary, in thinking that the *De unione* should not be given much regard, and so it originally did not figure into Maritain's metaphysical Christology.[17] Thus, as a first iteration, Maritain favored a strong one *esse* position concerning Christ.

## III. Maritain's Revised Metaphysical Christology with Criticism

Prompted by the criticisms of Fr. H. Diepen in what is, as far as one may judge, an act of genuine intellectual humility,[18] Maritain revised his views; that is, he took back his theological conclusions about the contested point concerning the *esse* of Christ.[19] He did so based on theoretical

15. St. Thomas Aquinas, *De unione verbi incarnati*, a. 4.

16. For information regarding St. Thomas on the *esse* of Christ, the state of the question, an explanation of the conceptual framework, and important secondary sources, see Roger W. Nutt's introduction and notes: Thomas Aquinas, *De unione Verbi incarnati*, Dallas Medieval Texts and Translations, vol. 21 (Leuven: Peeters Publishers, 2015).

17. See Cajetan, *Commentaria in Summa Theologiae Sancti Thomae de Aquino, in Sancti Thomae Aquinatis, Opera Omnia, iussu impensaques*, ed. Leonis XIII P.M., Tom. 11 (Roma: S.C. de Propaganda Fide, 1903), 223–24.

18. See Father H. Diepen, "La critique du Baslisme selon saint Thomas d'Aquin," in *Revue Thomiste* 50, no. 1 (1950): 115. Maritain does not see his position as an appropriation of Fr. Deipen's but something between his and the Dominican commentators: "these texts admit an interpretation bordering on that of Father Deipen, but nevertheless different, and which mediates in a certain way the positions of the eminent Benedictine theologian and those of the great Dominican Commentators." Maritain, *The Degrees of Knowledge*, 464.

19. For a more in-depth explanation of Cajetan's position and Maritain's early dependence on him, see Roger W. Nutt, "Christ's *Esse* and Filiation," in *Redeeming Philosophy: From Metaphysics to Aesthetics*, edited by John J. Conley, SJ (Washington, D.C.: The American Maritain Association, 2014; distributed by The Catholic University of America Press), 118–126.

and textual grounds, with what seems to be an increasing realization of the importance of Christ's humanity.[20] Maritain became convinced of the authenticity and later dating of the *De unione*, which was put in some doubt by Cajetan and others, and was fearful of philosophy unduly leading theology.[21] There is much to say about Maritain's revised position, and it deserves to be read and commented on in full, a task unto itself. For our purposes, at the risk of oversimplification, the focus will be on the central concept Maritain puts forward in his revised account, which is the distinction between *esse* received and *esse* exercised. Applying that distinction, Christ's human nature would receive created *esse* exercised by the supposit of the Word. Here is how Maritain conceives of the exercise of *esse*:

> Finally, we have pointed out that St. Thomas establishes a relation of analogy between the couple essence and *esse* and the couple active potency and operation, and we have stated that it is the supposit or person that *exercises* existence (its own substantial *esse*) and exercises its operations, as well as the accidental *esse* proper to them.[22]

Problems arise on the purely metaphysical level. Maritain's solid principles do not hold unless one takes his analogy above with severe qualifications. The analogy of essence being to *esse* as active potency is to operation rests on a common relation that each couple has to potency and act. But essence and *esse* are as potency and act, each with respect to the supposit, but not directly with respect to each other, because essence and *esse* are not in the "same line": *esse* is the final perfecting principle of a supposit, and so essence in the supposit is perfected by *esse*. This seems to be central to Maritain's metaphysics. Active potency and operation, on the other hand, are as potency and act with respect to each other, because they are in the "same line." Even though the supposit can be said to exercise both *esse* and operations, it exercises them in different ways. The supposit exercises operation by reducing the active potency of the faculty to the act of the operation. But the supposit does not exercise *esse* by reducing essence to *esse* or

20. Maritain says in *On the Grace and Humanity of Christ* (New York: Herder and Herder, 1969), 82–83: "It is an essential exigency of human nature to have a created *esse*, and the human nature of Christ has a created *esse* in addition to the uncreated *esse* of the divine Person." Maritain places the created *esse* of Christ in the context of his more overarching distinction between Christ as *viator* and Christ as *comprehensor*.

21. See Maritain, *The Degrees of Knowledge*, 459.

22. Ibid., 463.

in any way bringing a potential *esse* to an actual *esse*. *Esse* is the most actual of all principles and does not admit in itself of potency.[23]

The term "exercise" seems valid in an analogical sense when speaking of the supposit exercising *esse* because the supposit is the real subject of *esse*, as the supposit is the real subject of its operations. The analogy breaks down, however, when "exercise" is used to imply that there is a first act of *esse* reduced to the second act of *esse* the way the first act of a faculty is reduced to the second act of operation. *Esse* being most actual, there is nothing that stands as act to *esse* as potency. There is nothing to reduce *esse* from first act to second act, not even the supposit. It is not as though a first *esse* lies dormant, as it were, until it is exercised by the supposit. The supposit would then seem to take the place of *esse* as the most actual of all metaphysical principles, and in so doing loses its place as the real field of metaphysics.

In agreement with Maritain's metaphysical position, subsistence is not a third category on the same tier as *esse* and essence. True, subsistence is different from either *esse* or essence; however, the notion of subsistence is still latently contained in a metaphysics of *esse* and essence in that the principles of a subsistent thing are a substantial essence informed by proportionate *esse*. Subsistence is intelligible as the way in which a subject with a substantial essence enjoys its act of existence as its own. To consider subsistence wholly separate from *esse* and essence, to consider it a third principle that is needed in order for *esse* to be exercised, adds an unnecessary layer onto fundamental metaphysical principles. It would be the equivalent of adding a third principle onto act and potency, something that makes act really act.

To explain further, first act and second act are themselves wholly explainable by the notions of act and potency. First act (if second act is absent) is act in one respect and potency in another respect.[24] Being able

23. See *De potentia*, 7, 2, ad 9.

24. Fr. Thomas Joseph White makes use of first act and second act, or primary actuality and secondary actuality, in his *The Incarnate Lord: A Thomistic Study in Christology* (The Catholic University of America Press, 2015), 62–68. White writes: "Primary actuality, for Aquinas, pertains to the substantial being of a thing, its being in act as a certain whole with essential determination.... The second mode of actuality, secondary act, pertains to operations." Ibid., 63. He sees a lack of understanding of this distinction to be at the root of Schleiermacher's and Barth's wanting "to seek to locate the divine-human union in Christ in the human actions of Jesus," (ibid.) instead of in the personal subsistence of the Word made flesh. White favorably appeals to an idea he finds in *The Grace and Humanity of Christ*, that Christ's identity as the Son, a first actuality, is

to see, for example, is act that stands in potency to further act, the very act of seeing. First act and second act do not add a new principle to the act-potency pairing: the distinction between first and second act is an application of the act-potency pairing to faculties and their exercise, for instance. Act as act does not need anything outside itself for it to be act. Act itself is the principle of actuality. Likewise, *esse* needs nothing for it to be *esse*.

At times, that does not seem to be the way that Maritain envisions *esse* in his examination of Christ's secondary *esse*; that is, he seems to envision a first *esse* and second *esse* on the analogy of first act and second act:

> But this *esse* is only *received* by the human nature, it is not exercised by it (since in no case is it the nature, but the supposit, which exercises existence). Nothing human exercises this human *esse*. It is exercised (secondarily) by the pre-existing Divine Person, without entering for all that in any way into the constitution of the *esse personale* of Christ.[25]

This is a difficult passage to reconcile with Maritain's more general metaphysical principles. What would prevent the exercised *esse* of the human nature of Christ from being a principle of its own subsistence regardless of what exercises it? Essence-*esse* compositions subsist. *Esse* is abstracted from an *ens*, so it seems very difficult to hold that something that is not a supposit has *esse* in the sense of act of existence, regardless of the subject of the exercise.

It seems that in Maritain there is a partial forgetfulness of the foundational truth that essence and *esse* are irreducible principles, though he still explicitly affirms it. Because they are irreducible, it is not an inherent contradiction to have a human essence without a proportionate human *esse* in the sense of an act of existence, as long as the human essence is of a supposit—in Christ's case, a divine supposit with a divine *esse*. It is not as though human essence is devoid of meaning without a human act of existence. It

---

related as object to the human knowledge of Christ, a second actuality. In addition, the knowledge of Christ is related to us creatures because it reveals the final good of humanity, the beatific vision. The distinction shows that one can still see the moral importance of a second actuality, Christ's knowledge, without making it the location of the hypostatic union. As a point of clarification, however, it should be noted that even granting that the term "primary actuality" could be applied to a whole substantial being, that is not its ordinary definition, nor how Aquinas usually uses it. For Aquinas, primary actuality, *actus primus*, is some form, whether substantial, (see ST I, q. 76 a. 4, ad 1) or accidental, (see ST I-II, q. 49, a. 3, ad 1) that stands in potential to further act, or secondary actuality. For example, a soul or a habit stands in potential to its operations (see ST I, q. 105, a. 5).

25. Maritain, *The Degrees of Knowledge*, 465.

does not follow that since essence is to *esse* as potency is to act, therefore essence, being potential, is not anything when abstracted from a proportionate correlative *esse*. To be to something as potency does not mean to be nothing but potency. For instance, St. Thomas says that a subject is as potency to accidents: "the subject is compared to an accident as potency to act, for the subject according to the accident is by some manner in act."[26] This does not mean that the subject is pure potency without accidents. It means that the subject receives act in some way from accidents. So, too, does essence receive act from *esse* without essence being pure potency or negation. In the context of the hypostatic union, the human essence of Christ receives act from the divine *esse* of Christ by virtue of the personal union such that the human essence, now in act, has a positive content and intelligibility distinct from the divine *esse*, but without being a subsistent reality. That human act is what St. Thomas means by the term *esse secundarium.*[27]

St. Thomas speaks in the *De unione*, a. 4 of a single divine *esse* of Christ in a suppositał sense of the act of existence, while acknowledging there to be more to Christ's *esse* that this: there is some sort of *esse* by which Christ is man—the act of his humanity as assumed by the Word—and this is not the *esse* by which Christ is simply speaking. The way to understand Christ's secondary *esse* is in terms of the act of the human essence insofar as it is assumed by the Word, a secondary sense of the word *esse*. Christ's human essence is not nothing; it is something, even if this way of being is not suppositał or a *per se* act of existence—hence the term secondary or subordinate *esse*. One need not bifurcate *esse* in the primary sense; one need not separate the act of existence, as Maritain appears to do at times, into a more potential received *esse* for Christ's humanity and a more actual exercise of that *esse* for his divinity.

St. Thomas's use of the term *esse secundarium* in reference to Christ's humanity need not be anachronistically interpreted in the full existential sense of a second act of existence. Many twentieth-century Thomists point out the importance of St. Thomas's use of *esse* in the full sense of act of existence. Yet, *esse* remains an analogical term with different yet related appli-

26. ST I, q. 3, a. 6.

27. For an explanation of the historical circumstances that led St. Thomas to use the term *esse secundarium* to indicate a "full, integral, and real" human nature, see Nutt, "Christ's *Esse*," 126–28.

cations in St. Thomas's texts. There is room for the humanity of Christ precisely as a nature in act by being assumed by a preexisting person, a human nature of a divine person who has one perduring act of existence, but another act by which this person exists in a certain respect, namely, humanly.

## IV. Angling for a Solution?

Maritain wrote a characteristically lengthy footnote in his revised account of metaphysical Christology that does contribute to a more literal understanding of St. Thomas on the *esse* of Christ. This footnote at first seems to make Maritain's position, that the human nature of Christ receives human *esse* but the divine supposit exercises it, a fancy way of saying that Christ's human nature does not subsist in itself, but is that through which the divine supposit subsists.

In this footnote, Maritain draws a subtle yet important distinction. He asks whether the uncreated subsistence of the Word acts as the subsistence for the human nature by "divinely conferring on it the completion which created subsistence, of which this nature is deprived, would confer on it?"[28] Or rather, is it that "the uncreated subsistence *renders useless* the human nature's being perfected or completed by such a completion?"[29] Maritain opts for the latter, and for good reason: the human nature does not subsist. There is no conferral of subsistence on it. Human nature becomes the nature of a divine supposit which subsists. As Maritain explains, a human nature cannot exist without a subsistent being to assume and possess it. The non-conferral of subsistence on Christ's humanity is the explanation fitting for the intimacy and oneness of the hypostatic union. Maritain goes on to explain how the divine subsistence terminates the human nature, because, in his words, "human nature cannot exist without a subsistence which assumes and possesses it" making it "part of itself."[30] While the language of part may need some qualification,[31] the thought behind these words is fairly clear: for a nature to be actual it has to be a nature of a supposit, the supposit subsisting in a nature which does not subsist in itself.

28. *The Degrees of Knowledge*, 466n33.

29. Ibid.; italics in original.

30. Ibid.

31. See ST III, q. 2, a. 4, ad 2. There St. Thomas explains that the composition of Christ is not one of parts.

However, the above explanation is not normative in Maritain's account. He is convinced that some proportionate human *esse* in the sense of act of existence is needed in addition to Christ's human essence for the essence to be real, even if that human essence is denuded of the ability to exercise that act of existence, thus depriving it of human subsistence. He goes on to write:

> On the other hand, the human nature of Christ receives a human and created existence (*esse naturae*) without itself being rendered capable (by subsistence, as in a supposit) of exercising this existence, because it is the eternally pre-existing supposit which, making use of it as a principle *quo* of activity, itself exercises the human and created act of existing proper to the human nature, as it exercises also the human operations accomplished by means of the latter, and the accidental *esse* which are proper to them.

The divine supposit's operative takeover of the human nature that blocks its subsistence is not something that follows from metaphysical principles, even given the unique conditions of the incarnation. The exercise of an operation is not a metaphysical trump card. Human nature is not just a principle by which Christ acts. Granted that Christ's human nature is not that by which he is simply speaking, it is a principle by which he is human. Even if his personhood is not dependent on his human nature the way a human person's is, Christ's human nature is no less his than our human natures are ours. We do not just operate our natures and so make them ours: we are in them. We are in our natures in such a way that our natures cannot have an act of existence parallel to our own, no matter who operates that act of existence, without those natures being separate from ourselves.

Maritain's footnote ends with allusions to the role of Christ's operations and his accidents in trying to understand the exercise of a human *esse*. While these are not completely devoid of explanatory power regarding the *esse* of Christ, it must be pointed out that the immediate result of the Word becoming flesh is not the Word making use of a human nature as a principle of activity, but the Word *being* man with a continuity of the Word's being.[32] Being such has as a consequence a certain instrumentality of the

32. About the "incarnational is," Fr. Thomas Weinandy eloquently writes: "The incarnational 'becoming' must terminate in the extraordinary fact that the Son of God now simply *is* man, and that this 'is' and only this 'is' impregnates the terms of predication, that is 'the Son of God' and 'man' with their full incarnational significance and meaning, for it is this 'is' that establishes their shared ontological unity or oneness. As we shall see, this incarnational 'to be',

human nature. The incarnation is not an exercise or use, but a becoming man. The unity of the Divine Person, not the unity of the source of exercise, is the principle of the union of the divine and human natures.

So the theandric actions of Christ can be misleading if a strict parallel is being drawn between them and the incarnation itself. For instance, St. Thomas says that operation can be twofold in Christ because operation does not carry with it the notion of being distinct from another, and so is not repugnant to the notion of union.[33] Supposit, on the other hand, does carry with it being distinct from another, and so two supposits are repugnant to the notion of union.[34] One could continue the argument and say two *esse*, simply speaking, are repugnant to union as well. If two *esse* are joined by a single exercise, it would seem like it is not a real union, or at least not as strict a union as two natures being joined by being the natures of one person with one act of existence. Besides, the human operation has its own exercise, at least in the sense that it has its own proper form and power.[35] It is used as a conjoined instrument by the Godhead. Operation admits of a diversity in a single subject in a way that *esse* as the act of existence does not.

## V. Conclusion

Maritain is to be applauded both for his fundamental metaphysical principles and for wanting a metaphysical Christology that takes the reality of Christ's humanity seriously while seeing the problems that a two *esse* position would have unless it were modified. Maritain is trying to avoid the two classic pitfalls for orthodox Christology. Simply emphasizing the unity of Christ's being, the singleness of his *esse*, with no further explana-

---

this incarnational 'to exist', this incarnational 'is' is the cornerstone of Aquinas's whole theological enterprise." Thomas G. Weinandy, OFM Cap, "Aquinas: God *IS* Man: The Marvel of the Incarnation," in *Aquinas on Doctrine*, edited by Thomas G. Weinandy, Daniel A. Keating, and John P. Yocum (New York: T&T Clark International, 2004), 69. However, Weinandy sees the question of whether Christ has one *esse* or two as an either-or proposition, not really seeing St. Thomas's position as depending on a heavy qualification and restrictive use of the term *esse* in *esse secundarium*, which would lend itself to a more yes-and-no approach. This leads to inconsistencies within Weinandy's account of Christ's *esse*, which he ultimately sees as being two, despite the quote above. About these inconsistencies, see Victor Salas Jr., "Thomas Aquinas on Christ's *Esse*: A Metaphysics of the Incarnation," in *The Thomist* 70, no. 4 (2006): 594.

33. See ST III, q. 19, a. 1, ad 4.

34. *De unione*, a. 5, ad 6.

35. ST III, q. 19, a. 1.

tion, would leave one wondering where the room is for Christ's humanity and whether it were absorbed by the single divine *esse* in a sort of Monophysitism. Does the humanity of Christ not have a proper act that is not divine act? Positing a second act of existence or *esse* in Christ in the primary sense without qualification leads to two fundamental and irreducible centers in Christ, two supposits, and a sort of Nestorianism. Maritain attempts to solve this problem by saying that Christ's humanity does receive an *esse*, and so avoids Monophysitism, but that *esse* is exercised by the divine supposit of the Word, and so avoids two supposits and Nestorianism. Maritain gives St. Thomas's use of the term *esse secundarium* as a human *esse* in Christ as support of his position. Two questions, however, remain: is *esse* capable of being received by one thing and exercised by another, and is the divine exercise of a human *esse*, were that possible, adequate to the closeness of the hypostatic union? There are good reasons to respond in the negative to both.

Maritain seems to have a good grasp of the problem, the solution to which is perhaps not best expressed as a mix between traditional and intuitive metaphysical language. *Esse* received and *esse* exercised is a distinction that seems to bend metaphysical principles too far. *Esse* does not admit of act-potency distinctions with itself. Even though essence stands to *esse* as potency to act, essence need not have some proportionate modified *esse* for it to be an essence. Essence, if it is an essence of a supposit with *esse*, is actual. The distinction between *esse* received and *esse* exercised also tends toward a Christology where the lack of a properly human subsistence in Christ has more to do with the divine supposit using a human nature than with the human nature being the divine supposit's. Maritain does, however, ask some clarifying questions about the *esse* of Christ that put into relief the crucial issues.

HEATHER M. ERB

# Existents Seeking the Kingdom of God

## *Esse* and the Mystical Ascent in Maritain and Aquinas

### I. Introduction

INSPIRED BY ST. THOMAS'S analogical sense of being, Maritain maintains both the unity and the order among metaphysical, theological, and mystical wisdoms in *Existent and the Existent* (1947), in contrast to both Kierkegaard's disruption of that order, and atheistic existentialism's denial of it. I examine the ways in which versions of Thomist existentialism serve as foundations for topics in Aquinas's mystical theology.[1] For Maritain, metaphysics intersects with mystical theology in yearning for union with ultimate causes, while the principle of existence is said to inform the Thomist theories of human nature, evil, and the spiritual intuition of being. Indeed, it is natural to perceive a link between mystical ascent and metaphysics, since both metaphysics and spirituality seek a unifying vision of reality amidst the sensory multiplicity we experience. Both employ the language of paradox in describing ultimate reality and both affirm the inexhaustible wealth of being against our impoverished grasp of God. Finally, both describe us as inhabiting the horizon of the world of spirit according to the measure of our own existence. In several works across the decades,

1. Maritain, *Distinguish to Unite, or The Degrees of Knowledge*, translated by Gerald B. Phelan, 4th edition (South Bend, Indiana: University of Notre Dame Press, 1995), 13. Originally published in 1932.

Maritain applied his version of existentialism to various aspects of Christian spirituality. I examine key aspects of Maritain's "Thomist existentialism" in contrast to atheist and other non-Thomist existentialisms, comparing his approach to the chief points of intersection between the principle of *esse* (existence) and mystical theology in Aquinas.

Kierkegaard's existentialism, in contrast to Maritain's existentialism, focused on the irreducibility of the subjective dimension of life and on the "ethical" primacy of existence. It involved concepts such as freedom of the individual, authenticity, absurdity, dread, and the denial of fixed essences. Twentieth-century Thomist existentialism, on the other hand, includes several camps. There is Maritain's view, which includes a role for form and essence, known as "thick essence" existentialism, and more radical positions, such as William Carlo's,[2] which stresses the contingent existence of sensible things in relation to God (*Ipsum Esse*) and holds the radical priority of *esse* (the act of being in a thing) to essence and form.

Since metaphysics springs from a desire for union with the source of our being,[3] the notion of existence, even though attained by unaided reason, is foundational to Aquinas's spirituality. Ferreting out the implications of versions of existentialist Thomism for mystical theology is thus useful for evaluating the success of these interpretations as Christian philosophies. In *Existence and the Existent*, Maritain defends his view of Christian existentialism's mystical dimension by appeal to charity as the highest representation of the act of existence and in his discussion of Christian vs. atheistic subjectivity and contemplation. Both earlier and later in his career, Maritain transposed the existentialist themes of solitude and subjectivity into an ecclesial key in *Liturgy and Contemplation* (1960) and in *Prayer and Intelligence* (1922).[4]

After outlining the role of the metaphysical principle of *esse* in Maritain's spirituality, I turn to the mystical theology of Aquinas. Here, existence plays a foundational role in his theory of charity, in that it is in the

2. William Carlo, *The Ultimate Reducibility of Essence to Existence in Existential Metaphysics* (The Hague: Nijhoff, 1966).

3. Maritain, *The Degrees of Knowledge*, 284.

4. In *Prayer and Intelligence*, Maritain states that "In order to advance in the spiritual life and dispose ourselves to receive the grace of contemplation, we must use the means proposed to us by the Church." Jacques and Raïssa Maritain, *Prayer and Intelligence and Selected Essays*, translations by Algar Thorold, Joseph W. Evans, and Julie Kernan (Providence, Rhode Island: Cluny Media, The Thomistic Institute, 2016), 19–20.

intersection of *esse* and love that the transcendence of Aristotle's universe of necessity and finitude becomes apparent. Finally, I explore how various "Thomistic existentialisms" either serve or detract from the tasks of Aquinas's spirituality, a question tied to a proper interpretation of Aquinas's ordering of wisdoms.

## I1. Maritain on Existentialism and Spirituality

### *1. Three Existentialisms*

In *Existence and the Existent* (1947), but even earlier, in the first edition of *The Degrees of Knowledge* (1930) and *A Preface to Metaphysics* (1933), Maritain cleared the path for a Thomist existentialism. By highlighting the role of *esse* in metaphysics, he gained Gilson's praise, despite their differences on the knowledge of being. As his thought on metaphysics and mysticism evolved, Maritain took the view that the subjective experience in which the "intuition of being" is made manifest forms a gateway to metaphysics and, as such, should be studied by the philosopher. The intuition of being also springs from the same "spiritual unconscious" in which the seeds of his "mysticism of the self" dwell. Gradually, Maritain was to leave the classical objective approach to mysticism in search of an unconscious "core" to mystical experiences that would embrace various traditions and religions—until the revival of a more ecclesial and traditional approach in his final work, *On the Church of Christ* (1973).[5]

In *Existence,* Maritain alludes to the role of *esse* in spirituality by noting its role in explaining human freedom[6] and in his meditation on God's act of free creation. In Catholic spirituality, *esse* grounds the Thomist notions of the infinite character of charity and the paradoxical active passivity which characterizes infused contemplation. Maritain focuses, however, on the contrasts between atheistic and Thomist existentialism, also known by

5. See Heather M. Erb, "Natural Mysticism: Gateway or Detour? Aquinas, Maritain, and the Core/Contextualist Debate," in *Redeeming Philosophy: From Metaphysics to Aesthetics,* edited by John J. Conley, SJ (Washington, D.C.: The American Maritain Association, 2014; distributed by The Catholic University of America Press), 23–53.

6. See Maritain, *The Degrees of Knowledge,* 283–85, on a certain "natural spirituality" in which the human soul "bears witness to its proper essence" (283) in morality, art, and metaphysics. He is not speaking here of natural mysticism proper, nor the "supernatural spirituality" given by the Holy Ghost, but rather of a prelude to the life of grace in the self-conscious spiritual soul which culminates in the natural love of God. He says that "the proper activity of the scientist and the philosopher, the mathematician and the geometrician is a sort of spirituality" (283).

him as "existentialist intellectualism."[7] First, he describes and critiques atheistic existentialism and clarifies what he means by *esse*. The act of existing (*l'acte d'exister*), he says, is exercised by all beings—and is "that victorious thrust by which it triumphs over nothingness"[8]—so, *esse* is not the subject of metaphysics (*ens commune*) but that which actuates essence and with it, by God's help, sustains the thing's operations, including those by which it gains glory and union with God. Quoting Aquinas, he notes that it is the act and the perfection of all form and perfection.[9] Further, he distinguishes existentialisms:

> There are two fundamentally different ways of interpreting the word existentialism. One way is to affirm the primacy of existence, but as implying and preserving essences or natures and as manifesting the supreme victory of the intellect and intelligibility. This is what I consider to be authentic existentialism. The other way is to affirm the primacy of existence, but as destroying or abolishing essences or natures and as manifesting the supreme defeat of the intellect and of intelligibility. This is what I consider to be apocryphal existentialism, the current kind which no longer signifies anything at all.[10]

For Maritain, there are three general types of existentialism—the atheist, Christian-Kierkegaardian, and Thomist varieties. To take the first, although Maritain doesn't use the term, sympathizers of atheist existentialism claim a laicized or secular mysticism in their passionate experience of reflecting on human "limit situations" such as the struggle for love, for power, and the confrontation with death. Their thirst for world-transcending meaning is said to annex theological turf by appeal to a supra-rational answer to the mystery of existence (and, in the case of atheist existentialism, by rejecting such an answer but implying the centrality of the question).

The irony of "existential existentialism," he says, is its slide into a detached academic existentialism—a philosophy directed against philosophy itself or a protest of faith caught in a Babylonian captivity.[11] This revolt of the soul destroyed the cry of faith such that "Job has been evacuated, and

7. Maritain, *Existence and the Existent*, translated by Lewis Galantière and Gerald B. Phelan (New York: Image Books, 1947), 50, 57.

8. Ibid., 19.

9. Ibid., 26, quoting *De potentia* q. 7, a. 2, ad 9.

10. Ibid., 3. Maritain includes Kierkegaard and Sartre in the group he calls "apocryphal" existentialists. Kierkegaard's existentialism springs "from a radically irrationalist thought which rejects and sacrifices essences and falls back upon the night of subjectivity" (130–31).

11. Ibid., 132.

only the dunghill is left," Maritain notes, since Minerva "carried off Jacob's ladder to her workshop"[12] when a purely philosophical posture replaced the imprecatory one. This moribund state of existentialism as an academic exercise began with the absurdity of defining man as a "project"—an unsustainable view meant to replace his nature or essence needed for a coherent sense of self-transcendence and ending in an irrational flight of passion and despair.

Despite their differences, Christian existentialists agree on certain points with their atheist counterparts. The recognition of the inadequacy of human life, even the nostalgia for home and for the release given by humility that one sees in modern atheists, such as de Comte-Sponville, verifies the view that atheist existentialism can be a prelude to faith. He laments his atheism, saying, "How one yearns to kneel down in churches! Why deny oneself? ... it is because I would have to believe that God created me."[13] We see moral tragedy alongside the possibility of conversion in Tolstoy's character Prince Andrei in *War and Peace,* in his address as he lay wounded. Noting Andrei's disillusionment with the transience of life exposed through Napoleon's march to immortal fame, Tolstoy says: "He saw above him the remote, lofty, and everlasting sky. He knew it was Napoleon—his hero—but at that moment Napoleon seemed to him such a small, insignificant creature compared with what was passing now between himself and that lofty infinite sky."[14]

This sense of being that had been slumbering within him "suddenly awoke, joyful and youthful, in his soul," and he did not know how to develop what had long existed there.[15] We are reminded of Shakespeare's "sweet uses of adversity"[16] and of Augustine's experience, related in the *Confessions,* that we become aware of the question of being through examining the halls of memory. "Men go to gape at mountain peaks" he says, "or at the boundless tides of the sea ... yet leave themselves unnoticed; they do not

12. Ibid., 132–34.

13. André de Comte-Sponville, *A Small Treatise on the Great Virtues: The Uses of Philosophy in Everyday Life,* translated by Catherine Temerson (New York: Henry Holt and Company, 2001), 148. He argues here that humility is a virtue taught by religion, yet it leads to atheism in the uncomfortable belief that there is no God.

14. Tolstoy, *War and Peace,* translated by Constance Garnett (Barnes and Noble Modern Library Edition: New York, New York, 2002), 3.19.

15. Ibid., 5.10.

16. Shakespeare, *As You Like It,* 2.2.12, in the Duke's speech to his followers, noting the blessings of his banishment to the forest.

marvel at themselves.... What then, am I, my God—what is my true nature? A living thing, taking innumerable forms, quite limitless."[17] Whether the consciousness of being occurs through the experience of suffering, contrast, action, or, as with Augustine, as a record of human desire, existentialism in its various forms involves the acceptance or rejection of the possibility of this plenitude—Maritain would likely agree with this, well put by Augustine—"It is that absolute IS, that true IS ... that I long for; that IS which is in that Jerusalem, which is the Bride of my Lord, where ... there will be a day that passeth not away, but continueth."[18]

But for Maritain, the deficiencies common to non-Thomist existentialisms are, first, their separation of being and intelligibility or divorce of "witness" and "universality,"[19] and, second, their confusion of philosophy and theology. Atheist existentialists make philosophy carry the burden of theology, labouring under modernity's transfer of authority from faith to secular thought. Both rationalism and the despair of reason that spawned existentialism are also non-contemplative. Philosophy's autonomy does not lie in masquerading as theology but in recognizing its place in the hierarchy of wisdoms as guided by theology, which in turn is fed by the streams of mystical theology.[20]

On the other hand, Kierkegaard's Christian existentialism *also* transfers theology's authority and content to philosophy, ending in the struggle between what he calls the Jacob-like or imprecatory posture and the philosophical "Minerva" posture of cause-seeking and theoretical universality.[21] Only in Aquinas is the tension resolved, where being is identified with the full range of intelligibility, reconciling intellect and mystery. Maritain's distinction between the state or conditions in which philosophy is done, and its essence or content, is at work here. While existential anguish may af-

17. Augustine, *Confessions,* 10.8 and 10.16, in *The Confessions of St. Augustine,* translated by John K. Ryan (New York: Doubleday, 1960).

18. Augustine, *Commentary on the Psalms,* 38/39.7, PL 36, 419. See: A. Cleveland Coxe, editor, translator, *Expositions on the Book of Psalms by Saint Augustine,* in Philip Schaff, editor, *Nicene and Post-Nicene Fathers,* First Series, vol. 8 (Peabody, Massachusetts: Hendrickson Publishers, 1995), 114.

19. Unlike Kierkegaard or Sartre, Gerald Phelan, the translator of *Existence and the Existent,* is a good example of "Thomist existentialism," which affirms the primacy of *esse* without side-lining the role of intellect. See his "The Existentialism of St. Thomas," in *G. B. Phelan: Selected Papers,* edited by A. Kirn (Toronto: Pontifical Institute of Mediaeval Studies, 1967), 67–82.

20. Maritain, *Existence and the Existent,* 142–44.

21. Ibid., 130–31.

fect the conditions of the one who philosophizes, Maritain argues that his thinking becomes egoistic if that anguish passes into the philosophical content *per se*.[22] The philosopher's spiritual experience is the nourishing soil of his philosophy but may never formally enter it.[23] Existential anguish is but one of a host of experiences undergone by the philosopher, alongside intellectual joy, a wounding ardour, pity for error, solitude and sweetness, and exaltation of sudden discovery, and even the experience that others despise and reject the truth for being the truth.[24] For Maritain, the light of reason is guided but not altered by affective content.

At this point, we might wish for an explanation of the way in which the passions, will, and intellect influence one another in contemplation, but we will search in vain for one in *Existence*. How exactly contemplation is appetitive in its inception and summit is developed more clearly in Aquinas, where the fear involved in wonder, and even more, the wisdom that informs charity, are far from the existentialists' self-involved passions.

In addition to atheist and academic existentialism, and what he calls Christian existentialism, there is Maritain's "Thomist existentialism." Various paths lead to his famous "intuition of being," based on the judgment of sense. There's the purely intellectual insight into the existence of things, the awakening of wonder in what he calls "a kind of natural grace at the sight of a blade of grass or a windmill, or the sudden perception of the reality of the self."[25] Or, it can be triggered by the inner experience of duration, consciousness that we are selves, or of anguish, or of moral truths, leading to one's bewilderment and joy in being enraptured with being.[26]

He describes how the "primacy of *esse*" informs Thomist theories of human nature, evil, liberty, and mystical ascent.[27] Existence is the principle that establishes a hierarchy in being, he says, by being a participation in *Ipsum Esse*, which sets the standard for human love, in its superabundant "fe-

22. Ibid., 146–49.

23. Ibid., 151.

24. Ibid., 151–52.

25. Ibid., 30. At times, he identifies the deliverances of this intuition with the subject matter of metaphysics (and even its summit), described by Maritain as a product of abstraction: "The intellect may well receive, after the manner of a sudden revelation, a knowledge of that which constitutes the proper object of the third level of abstraction ... at the sight of something or other—a blade of grass, a windmill—the soul may know in an instant that these things do not exist by themselves, and that God exists." *The Degrees of Knowledge*, 296–97.

26. Maritain, *Existence and the Existent*, 31.

27. See ibid., chap. 1.

cundity."[28] A living dog is higher in being than a dead lion, he notes. The power of evil is intelligible in that privation of being is a wound proportionate to the act of existing a thing has.[29] Human freedom is dependent on the sovereign causality of God Whose generosity creates beings with powers to attain their own ends by activating them from within, showing that divine efficient causality is his touchstone for asserting the primacy of *esse*.[30]

Maritain's view that our spiritual growth is grounded on the primacy of existence both in God and man is related to his theory of the "intuition of being," even though the orders of being/nature and discovery remain distinct. Regarding Maritain's "intuition of being" John Wippel notes[31] that Maritain makes the *actus essendi* of things accessible to a pre-philosophical knowledge, so that our knowledge of *esse* as an ontological principle is not attained through metaphysical reasoning.[32] Putting the cart before the horse in this way, and exchanging Aquinas's judgment of separation for a theory of abstraction,[33] courts the danger of univocity in being—rejected by Aquinas and Maritain for its metaphysical and theological immanentism.

Maritain's controversial view that a pre-philosophical intellectual "intuition of being" is a prelude to metaphysics and to later concepts of existence makes the application of his views to spirituality complex. For instance, his intersection of various concepts of existence, the complex reasoning concerning the sources of being, and even religious insight, seem more closely linked than Aquinas's sober metaphysical reasoning and theology of grace would have it. Even greater caution is required in comparing

28. Ibid., 52.

29. See ibid., 48–49.

30. See ibid., 50–51.

31. Wippel gathers textual evidence to distinguish Maritain's theory of the "intuition of being" from Aquinas's views on the concept of existence and the method of attaining the subject of metaphysics. He also traces the evolution of Maritain's views on the concepts of existence. See John Wippel. "Maritain and Aquinas on our Discovery of Being," *Studia Gilsoniana* 3 (2014): 415–43.

32. As Wippel notes, for Aquinas the metaphysical principle of *esse* is not attained by pre-philosophical intuitive experience but only after the subject of metaphysics has been attained.

33. The broad use of abstraction can be applied to our attainment of the subject of metaphysics, says Maritain. See *Existence and the* Existent, 30n14. Wippel warns that his readers might be led into thinking that being is in some way univocal in this view, since here one abstracts being from its differences. See "Maritain and Aquinas on our Discovery of Being," 434n53.

Maritain's novel views in this regard with Aquinas's nexus of metaphysics and spirituality.

## 2. *Maritain on "Esse" and the Spiritual Life*

Maritain's act of existence intersects with spirituality primarily through love and charity, the personal core of our action and the "supreme revelation of existence."[34] Aquinas's existential intellectualism, he says, relates to his ethics regarding human perfection. We do not love "possibles" but rather "that which exists or is destined to exist."[35]

There are two reasons Maritain links *esse* with charity in spiritual ascent. First, the fecundity of *esse* shows itself in the spiritual personality which is free insofar as it gives of itself. The ladder of being parallels the degree to which intellectual appetite is present, where love is understood as self-gift and as mutual indwelling. We can surmise what he means by the fecundity of being in Aquinas. *Esse* is the act of acts, and perfection of perfections,[36] that which is innermost in each and every thing, and that which is deepest in them all, as most formal in respect of all that is in a thing.[37] In itself, *esse* is infinite and not self-limiting,[38] and the hierarchy within being is based on the limitation of *esse*,[39] making *esse* a principle with qualitative degrees between beings.[40] *Esse* is also related to charity for Maritain in that our perfection does not consist in an essence copying an ideal in blueprint fashion but in facing particular and unique situations in a growing union of person with person. In this way, two things happen: First, by love, the wound of knowing the other as an "object" is removed, for the union in

34. Maritain, *Existence and the Existent*, 90.

35. Ibid., 58.

36. See *De potentia* q. 7, a. 2, ad 9.

37. ST I, q. 8, a. 1. See Thomas Aquinas, *Summa Theologica* [hereafter ST], translated by the Fathers of the English Dominican Province (Benzinger Brothers Inc.: New York, New York, 1947).

38. This axiom appears in many places in Aquinas's writings, such as *In 1 Sent.*, d. 43, q. 1, a. 1; *In 1 Sent.*, d. 8, q. 2, a. 1; SCG I, q. 43; ST I, q. 7, a. 1; *Compendium of Theology*, chap. 18. On this topic, see J.-D. Robert, "Le principe: *Actus non limitatur nisi per potentiam subjectivam realiter distinctam*," *Revue philosophique de Louvain* 47 (1949) 44–70.

39. See *In III Sent.*, d. 13, q. 1, a. 2. In this text, Aquinas builds up a hierarchy of the three degrees of realization of *esse*. The first degree is *esse absolutum*, which contains no limitation. In the second degree are the creatures whose *esse* is limited only by the form inasmuch as their essence is pure form. And in the third degree are the creatures in which *esse* is limited by both matter and form because their essence is constituted by both matter and form. Cf. *De ente*, chap. 5.

40. Fran O'Rourke highlights the role of *esse*'s "virtual intensity" in his *Pseudo-Dionysius and the Metaphysics of Aquinas* (Leiden: Brill, 1992), 167–74.

love makes the other another self for us.[41] To the degree that we love the other for God's and his sake, we know the other in his "subjectivity" to a degree.[42] Second, we form with God a "single spiritual superexistence of love."[43]

Yet another sense in which *esse* and mystical ascent are allied for Maritain concerns his emphasis on the soul's passivity in infused contemplation, a theme of *The Degrees of Knowledge.* Reading Thomistic spirituality through the lens of St. John of the Cross,[44] he stresses the non-conceptual nature of infused contemplation, which is the result of charity and infused wisdom, acting in the secret recesses of the soul. Yet, as Bernhard Blankenhorn shows, since Aquinas grounds his theology of the virtues and gifts on the divine missions,[45] his spirituality is not purely apophatic and affective. For "the will's graced act of love realizes the image insofar as the intellect specifies it."[46] Maritain's emphasis on noetic passivity[47] unjustly downplays the role that the human acts of knowledge and love play in mystical ascent in a theology of habits that applies to all believers.[48] It could be interpreted as jeopardizing our status as *imago* by which we share in God's beatitude through our cognitive acts.

41. See Maritain, *Existence and the Existent,* 89–90.

42. Ibid., 91.

43. Ibid., 58–59.

44. The mystical mode of connaturality by which we know God by "suffering divine things" is described by Maritain in terms taken from St. John of the Cross. See, e.g. *The Degrees of Knowledge,* 278n42.

45. Since the Spirit proceeds from both the Father and the Son, "the divine image is attained in the human being according to the word conceived from the knowledge of God and the love derived from it" (ST I, q. 93, a. 8). See Bernhard Blankenhorn, *The Mystery of Union with God: Dionysian Mysticism in Albert the Great and Thomas Aquinas* (Washington, D.C.: The Catholic University of America Press, 2015), 245.

46. Ibid.

47. See, e.g. *The Degrees of Knowledge,* 280ff., where Maritain develops the distinction between the possession of concepts and formulae of faith and their use: "distinct concepts are all silent; they sleep, even as the Apostles did on the Mount of Olives.... [T]he proper light of infused contemplation only comes from the ardor of a love which burns in the night ... [,] an apophatic, or 'negative' contemplation which joins us experimentally to a hidden God who is above all knowledge, *Deo ignoto*" (281). On his treatment of John of the Cross in this regard, see ibid., 360ff.

48. Cf. Blankenhorn, *Mystical Union,* 256. Aquinas, he argues, moved away from Dionysian apophaticism, although he also argues that "the relative primacy of love in union with God distinguishes Aquinas's mysticism from the Areopagite's more intellect-centered approach" (288).

## III. Aquinas's Mystical Theology and The Act of Existence

### 1. Aquinas and Maritain on Mystical Theology

We have seen that Maritain rejects atheist, academic, and Christian existentialisms on the basis of their distortion of the three wisdoms and their rejection of essences. However, we also noted his exchange of modern existential concerns for a more robust role of existence in Aquinas sufficient to ground dimensions of both natural and supernatural spirituality. Aquinas distinguishes the domains of natural, revealed, and mystical theology, while also specifying the type of affectivity contemplation involves. He divides wisdom into that of the philosophers (first philosophy), of revealed theology, and of that given by the Holy Ghost. Following Aristotle, he makes the office of the wise man to order and to judge lesser things in light of a higher cause.[49]

There is the *philosophical* wonder at the First Cause from the summit of the created world, there is *theological* contemplation of God starting from revealed principles, ascending to a simpler contemplation of divine truth, and finally there is *infused contemplation,* or the simple gaze at divine truth through the gifts of the Spirit.[50] Through its meditation on our final end, Sacred Theology helps to effect the ordering of our actions towards that end.[51] Mystical theology, not discussed explicitly by Aquinas, confirms this direction in life, supernaturally elevating all of our efforts towards the highest cause.[52] More wise than philosophy, it not only studies the highest causes—rather, its principles come from them, insofar as Aquinas's spirituality is Trinitarian and sacramental, accepting the friendship with God, possible through a love awakened by grace and a connaturality with

49. See ST I q. 1, a. 6: "thus in the order of building, he who plans the form of the house is called wise and architect, in opposition to the inferior laborers who trim the wood and make ready the stones ... Again, in the order of all human life, the prudent man is called wise, inasmuch as he directs his acts to a fitting end ... Therefore he who considers absolutely the highest cause of the whole universe, namely God, is most of all called wise."

50. These three types of contemplation are dealt with in Heather M. Erb, "*Pati Divina:* Mystical Union in Aquinas," in *Faith, Scholarship and Culture in the Twenty-First Century,* edited by Alice Ramos and Marie George (Washington, D.C.: American Maritain Association; distributed by The Catholic University of America Press, 2002), 80–81.

51. ST I, q. 1, a. 6.

52. Ibid.

respect to divine things.[53] The deeper question, of course, is *how* mystical wisdom informs the natural and revealed orders and *why* human passions are directed, not directing causes, in this pattern.

Yet all contemplation begins and ends in the appetite, because it begins in wonder born of love. A life of contemplation, says Aquinas, is "to cling with our whole mind to the love of God and our neighbor,"[54] and the greatest delight occurs in the act which most befits our nature, directed at God, Who is Love itself.[55] There is no strict divide between forms of contemplation as ways of life—the heights of St. Thomas's theology were climbed in tears, and he was driven to Aristotle to understand his transports of charity or friendship with God.[56] Like Aquinas, Maritain limits the passions' role in metaphysics to the notes of wonder and delight, and the love of wisdom which pushes the intellect to seek universal causes, in contrast to the experiential focus of both Christian and atheist existentialists.

A favorite theme of Maritain is the relation between the "three wisdoms" of philosophy, theology, and mystical theology, as they form a hierarchy in which the dialectic of God's initiative (the "descent") and man's response (the "ascent") displays the Christian spiritual order and secures religion's place in human life.[57] In the soul of the Christian philosopher, mystical contemplation (defined as the life of the theological virtues and Gifts) influences his theology, which in turn influences his metaphysics.[58]

53. See *In De Trin.* q. 2, a. 2, ad 1, on how wisdom adds an "additional note" to science. As the chief of all sciences, wisdom directs all the other sciences. Aquinas cites Aristotle here. Cf. NE 6.7, 1141a18–20; *Metaphysics* 1.2, 983a6; ST I, q. 1, a. 6; SCG I, chap. 1, no. 1. See Armand Maurer, *Faith, Reason and Theology (Questions 1–4 of Aquinas's Commentary on 'De Trinitate' of Boethius)* (Toronto: Pontifical Institute of Mediaeval Studies, 1987), 42. A chaste person knows the virtue of chastity by inclination, even though he might lack a course in moral theology. See ST II-II, q. 45, a. 2. So, in the order of grace, there is connaturality. Through the Holy Spirit, we come to judge events and persons by way of inclination, guided by the mysteries of faith.

54. ST II-II q. 180, a. 1.

55. ST II-II q. 18, a.7 establishes the ways in which contemplation brings delight, according to the operation of contemplation and the object on which it is exercised (God), as well as according to the motive (charity). At ST II-II, q. 180, a. 1, Aquinas examines the interplay between the will and the intellect in contemplation, in general, stating that "everyone delights in obtaining what he loves," referring to our union with God.

56. On his interior life, see Martin Grabmann, *The Interior Life of St. Thomas* (Milwaukee: Bruce Publishing Company, 1951) and Walter Principe, *Thomas Aquinas' Spirituality* [1984 Gilson Lecture] (Marquette: Marquette University Press, 1984), 187–91.

57. Maritain develops the theme of the dialectic of "ascent" and "descent," with the priority being given to the divine descent, as known through the Incarnation, in *Science and Wisdom*, 19ff.

58. Ibid., 25: "And this is not a violent or despotic rule, but a natural and spontaneous movement like that of the tides and the seasons."

Given the life of faith, the three concurrent and synergic wisdoms form a unity in us whose balance depends on "the quickening gift which pours from Pure Act,"[59] leading us to share in God's inner life by a supernatural mode.

While he sees mysticism as a fitting crown (not a *natural* culmination) of metaphysics,[60] he is clear that it is faith (not philosophy) which places in the soul an "unconditional desire for mystical contemplation properly so called."[61] Indeed, if metaphysics demands mystical experience for its completion, grace would be confused with nature, and the gratuity of the divine "descent" would be threatened. Without collapsing the two orders, he maintains both their organic unity in the Christian philosopher and their distinct formal objects and methods. Charity animates the soul in grace, causing it even in this life to love God immediately and through Himself.

For Aquinas, metaphysics and mystical theology are not linked by sharing a method of formal object, but through theology proper, in that mystical theology deals with Christian perfection and the ways that lead to it.[62] Fr. Jordan Aumann gives a fuller definition of mystical theology, saying that it is "*that part of theology which, from the principles of systematic moral theology and the experiential data of religious experience, defines the nature of the supernatural life, formulates the laws of its growth, and explains the process by which souls advance from the beginning of the spiritual life to its full perfection.*"[63]

As such, spirituality concerns not just the supernatural order but the "existential condition of that life in the individual Christian,"[64] and must be expressed in ontological terms. Grace is linked to metaphysics for Aqui-

59. Ibid.

60. Maritain, *The Degrees of Knowledge*, 284–85.

61. Ibid., 295–96. The "supernatural" order is taken by Maritain in the sense of a life of faith lived in sanctifying grace and the theological virtues and Gifts. See ibid., 295n84.

62. All of our acts are governed by the desire for beatitude, but while being as being is the subject of metaphysics, God Himself is the formal motive and object of the theological virtues (ST II-II, q. 4., a. 7), which bear directly on our end. Ultimately, it is by charity that we attain perfection (ST II-II, q. 184, a. 1). Cf. Pierre Pourrat, *Christian Spirituality from the Time of our Lord till the Dawn of the Middle Ages*, translated by W. H. Mitchell and S. P. Jacques (London: Burns, Oates, and Washbourne, 1922), preface (v).

63. Jordan Aumann, "Definition of Spiritual Theology" in his article "Spiritual Theology in the Thomistic Tradition", found at: http://opcentral.org/resources/2013/04/08/jordan-aumann-o-p-spiritual-theology-in-the-thomistic-tradition/

64. Jordan Aumann, *Spiritual Theology* (London: Continuum, 1980), 25. Originally published in French in 1962.

nas by elevating the soul with a "spiritual existence" by which it becomes ordained to God in an elevated way. Beyond our natural being, we become partakers in the divine nature, and our natural and infused virtues come to perfect our powers, so that they operate well.[65]

### 2. Esse *and Mystical Ascent in Aquinas*

If sanctifying grace and *esse* are linked in elevating the soul towards its end, how does this fact relate to the metaphysics of form and *esse* in Aquinas? Etymologically, *esse* is the abstract form of *ens,* and is known as "to be."[66] In an early text,[67] Aquinas presents three meanings of the term *esse,* indicating in *De Potentia*[68] that the second sense is his own innovation: (1) the essence of a thing (signified by the definition); (2) the first act of an essence (*actus essentiae*); or (3) the truth of a proposition. Regarding the second sense, Aquinas says that *esse* is the actuality received by a thing's essence and that essence stands in a relation of potency to *esse,* its act.[69]

In the created order, form plays both a positive and a negative role as the limit principle. Given the Neoplatonic axiom that *esse* as such is infinite and does not diversify itself, Aquinas introduces essence as the principle of diversity.[70] Here, it plays a negative role of limiting and specifying *esse,* so that essence is relative nonbeing as negating created *esse.* Nonbeing here is simply non-identity with created *esse,* not absolute nonbeing. Neither metaphysical principle is a subject; rather, it is the same concrete substance which exists by reason of *esse* and which is what it is by reason of its essence.[71]

In the spiritual life, the interdependence of form and *esse* in metaphysics safeguards against an unreceived, omnipresent act, *Ipsum Esse,* being identified with creatures—in short, pantheism. Indeed, even though *esse*

65. See, e.g., *De veritate* [hereafter DV] q. 27, a. 6, c. See Thomas Aquinas, *Truth,* vol. 2, translated by Robert W. Schmidt, SJ (Chicago: Henry Regnery Company, 1954) 347. Here Aquinas quotes 2 Peter 1.4 on becoming a "partaker of the divine nature."

66. *In De hebdomadibus,* ch. 22. Cf. *In III Sent.* d. 6, q. 2, a. 2: "esse est actus entis...sicut lucere est actus lucentis."

67. *In 1 Sent.,* d. 33, q. 1, a. 1.

68. *De potentia,* q. 7, a. 2, ad 9. Aquinas's qualification there, "quod dico esse," introduces his own view.

69. See *De potentia* q. 7, a. 2, ad 9; *De ente,* chap. 4, nos. 6–7.

70. See, for example, *In De trin.* q. 4, a. 1; *De potentia* q. 3, a. 13, ad 4. The latter text includes an analysis of the "nonbeing" of creatures in relation to God. This is not absolute nonbeing but only the negation of *esse,* as we shall see.

71.Neither principle can exist as a subject on its own. *In III Sent.,* d. 2, q. 2, a. 3.

and grace are more noble in themselves than the soul, they require a being to exist, and created sanctifying grace is the platform of supernatural life, preserving us from pantheism in the absence of secondary causes. Further, grace cannot be the substance of the soul, since it would then be identical with nature—it remains that it is an accident.[72]

### 3. Esse *and* Grace in Aquinas

Aquinas's parallel of the natural and supernatural orders appears in several themes: the parallel role of *esse* and grace; the causation of grace by the sacraments[73]; and the relation of *esse* and charity. First, *esse* and grace. Both are extrinsically and efficiently caused accidents, which have no cause in the subject, are not educed by the principles of the subject, and yet act formally within the soul. Thomas says that God causes them both externally with the help of a mediating form—in the case of a thing's natural *esse*, as he refers to its substantial act of being, the substantial form receives the *esse*; sanctifying grace is a perfecting form united to the soul. Aquinas puts it this way:

> God causes natural being (*esse naturale*) in us by creation, without the mediation of any agent cause, but nevertheless by the mediation of some formal cause, for a natural form is a principle of natural being. And similarly, God causes gratuitous spiritual being (*esse spirituale*) in us without the mediation of any agent, but nevertheless by the mediation of some created form, which is grace.[74]

Further, neither *esse* nor grace subsists in the creature—though more noble than the soul's essence, they are not ontologically prior to it. *Esse* is prior as playing the role of final cause (*De potentia* q. 7, a. 2, ad 10), while grace perfects the soul's essence by grounding the powers informed by the theological virtues and Gifts. If priority for Thomas means "this can be without that, but not vice versa," then neither form nor *esse* can be alone, and both are required for the spiritual life. Any radical existentialism, such as William Carlo's (see section IV.1 below), contradicts the reciprocity of form and existence in Aquinas.

72. Garrigou-Lagrange, *Grace: A Commentary on the Summa Theologica of St. Thomas Aquinas, Ia-IIae q. 109–114*, translated by the Dominican Nuns (St. Louis: B. Herder, 1952), 120ff.

73. See DV q. 27, a. 7, c.

74. DV q. 27, a. 1, ad 3.

### 4. *Causation of Grace by the Sacraments in Aquinas*

A second topic illumining the role of *esse* in mystical ascent is the causation of grace by the sacraments. The question is one of instrumental causes—how does the production of *esse* by creatures which is not proper to their powers occur? A creature can create, in a sense, by producing univocal forms—a kind of self-reproduction; but since existence is the most universal effect, doesn't this require the highest cause (God)?

Aquinas says that the creature is moved by the principal agent and rises above the ability of its own form,[75] so that the effect is conferred by an influx of a higher cause,[76] which is transitory, incomplete, and dynamic in nature, in contrast to the form which possesses it. He likens this process to the power of the carpenter moving through his tools—they have the power to act, and we have the power to cause being as instruments of the First Cause. The transient presence of God in a creature's action making it produce the existence of its effects parallels the workings of actual[77] grace. Aquinas says, "Grace resides instrumentally in the sacraments of the New Law, as the form of a thing designed resides in the instruments of the art designing, according to a process flowing from the agent to the passive object."[78] Instruments are moved by the principal agent, which works of itself—the instrumental power has a being, he says, that "passes from one thing into another, and is incomplete" (ST III, q. 6, a. 4).

He compares the instrumental power of the sacraments to cause grace to a physical voice's ability to transmit the spiritual power of the speaker, since the voice proceeds from a mental concept which affects the hearer: "It is in this way that a spiritual power is in the sacraments, inasmuch as they are ordained by God unto the production of a spiritual effect."[79] Through the sacraments, but not limited to them, God's presence to creatures is of a special mode—as the "known is in the knower and the be-

75. See DV q. 27, a. 4, c., ad 4 and 7. For the other main texts on the twofold action and power of an instrumental cause, see ST III, q. 62, a. 1, ad 2; SCG III, 70; *De potentia* q. 3, a. 7, ad 7; q. 5, a. 1, ad 6; a. 6, ad 4; *In IV Sent.* d. 1, q. 1, a. 4, q. 2.

76. See DV q. 27, a. 7, c. The term "influx" is used to represent the divine causal presence in nature.

77. Vs. sanctifying grace, which is a habit in the soul.

78. Cf. ST I, q. 43, a. 6, ad 4; ST III, q. 6, a. 3.

79. ST III, q. 6, a. 4, ad 1.

loved in the lover"; through knowing and loving, God is received by the rational creature and dwells in them.[80] Thus, *esse* and mystical ascent are also linked through the theological psychology of love, as well as through the parallel qualities of *esse* and grace, as vivifying, particular, and divinely caused.

### 5. Esse, *Love, and Sanctifying Grace in Aquinas*

Maritain linked *esse* and love in *Existence and the Existent,* we saw (I.2 above), through the fecundity of *esse* which reveals itself in us as self-gift and mutual indwelling. This bond can be viewed from the side of God or from the side of man. With God, it is His love that invests things with their being, goodness, and consequent lovableness.[81] With us, it is different. Things' created goodness calls forth *our* response of love, since God "creates goodness in things" as their Cause. Further, He is most lovable as most perfectly existent.

Indeed, all things are lovable in proportion to their perfection in *esse*. And God, as perfect existence, gratuitously extends His love by willing the good for rational agents who are eminently lovable. In this, love becomes charity, which "signifies not only the love of God, but also a certain friendship with him" namely, "a certain reciprocity of love, together with mutual communion." This love consists in a "certain familiar conversation with him,"[82] which will be perfected in the life to come. God's love is not conceptually identical with His existence, but rather the intensity and perfection of His love flows from the fullness of His being. Further, His creative love is flows freely from His absolutely sovereign goodness which makes divine goodness and not its communication to creatures, the ultimate end.[83]

Aquinas also ties *esse* to love in his defense of the view that God cannot hate anything. To hate something means to will evil for it, and since "God's will cannot be inclined to evil … [,] it is impossible that He should hate anything."[84] If God hated something, He would will it not to exist; but

80. ST I q. 4, a. 3.

81. ST I q. 2, a. 2.

82. ST I-II q. 65, a. 5. In his treatment of charity, Aquinas relies on Aristotle's theory of friendship in the *Nicomachean Ethics* but expands it to include the insights of St. Paul. See Romanus Cessario, *The Virtues, or the Examined Life*, 61–96.

83. *De potentia*, q. 4, a. 15, ad 14.

84. SCG I, chap. 96.

God wills goodness to things by making them exist. Thus, He hates nothing. Lesser goods, or evils, are permitted by God in willing greater goods; but these evils are not loved in themselves. Things are lovable to the extent that they possess the perfection of existence, which makes them good; and their existence is a gift from God's love. Aquinas's metaphysics thus has pastoral implications, in that love envelops our existence, acting as its source and eliciting both our gratitude and God's joy.

But how are *esse* and charity linked in the human person? Although always aware of the distinction between the natural and supernatural orders,[85] Maritain contrasts various determinisms with the primacy of *esse* which establishes us in a personal relationship with God through His fecundity of being.[86] Perfecting love, he says, calls us to face "all that is unpredictable, dangerous, dark, demanding, and insensate in love," until our nature is transfigured.[87] Further, *esse* is said to establish our personal relationship with God because loving persons means loving individual existents: "All morality thus hangs upon that which is most existential in the world. For love ... does not deal with possibles or pure essences, [rather] it deals with existents.... And in the last analysis it is because God is the Act of Existing Itself, in His ocean of all perfection, that the love of that which is better than all goodness is that in which man attains the perfection of his being."[88]

Maritain's reverie on love as a corollary of the abundance of existence has similarities to Aquinas's discussions of charity, but the latter specifies its fruits and foundations in a more detailed if equally poetic way. He first notes that the communication (*conversatio*) we have with God in this life flows from our spiritual, not our corporeal, existence, and will be perfected only in the next life.[89] Second, this miraculous friendship is based on the

85. In discussing the relation between metaphysics and mysticism, for example, Maritain warns of the temptation to confuse the orders of nature and grace in the error of thinking that a "divine experience" of the mystical variety is necessitated by the science of metaphysics. See Maritain, *The Degrees of Knowledge*, 295ff. Nonetheless, due to the demands of the analogical reasoning basic to theology, Aquinas often parallels the natural and supernatural orders. See, e.g. DV q. 27, a. 2.

86. Maritain, *Existence and the Existent*, 51–53. Aquinas's "existentialist intellectualism" draws all things into the "fecundity of being" which carries them along "despite themselves in the torrent of divine governance from which nothing can escape" (52).

87. Ibid., 58–59.

88. Ibid., 58.

89. See ST II-II, q. 23, a.1, ad 1.

nature of love itself, as a willing the good for another in himself. By willing the good for rational creatures, God actually wills His own beatitude as their proper end: "God not only loves creatures as an artist might love his work, but also by a communion of friendship ... as a friend loves his friend, to such a degree that he introduces us into the joy of communion, such that our glory and beatitude are precisely those by which God himself is happy."[90] Third, charity is marked by a union of hearts, since it is a proper mark of friendship that one reveal his secrets "and makes, as it were, one heart out of two." In this way, "that which someone reveals to a friend seems not to leave his own heart."[91] Finally, the friendship of charity is active in the procuring of goods for one's friend, as shown by God's most efficacious will.

Further, *esse* and charity are linked in the relative priorities of knowledge and love. Whereas knowledge is an assimilative act ("to be in another is to take on that other's manner of being"[92]), willing is realized in the inclination to the beloved as it exists in itself. So, with things below us, it is nobler to know them, but with things above our nature, it is better to love them—"especially to love God."[93] Things higher than the soul "have a nobler kind of existence in themselves than in the soul."[94]

But while *esse* is linked to charity, it is equally tied to sanctifying grace in Aquinas's theology. Just as the natural existence of the soul is the foundation of its powers and acts, so the soul's spiritual existence, namely, grace, is the basis of its supernatural life of the virtues and Gifts. While grace unites us to God by "assimilation" (providing the form by which we conform ourselves to God through our actions),[95] charity effects our union with Him through the operation of our intellects and wills.[96]

Aquinas explains the relation of grace and charity in terms of the con-

90. *In II Sent.*, d. 26, q. 1, a. 1, ad 2.

91. SCG IV, chap. 21.

92. ST II-II, q. 23, a. 6, c. Here, we find his analysis of the relation of charity to the other theological virtues. See ST I q. 84, a. 1: "Whatever is received is received according to the mode of the receiver"; ST I q. 12, a. 4: "the manner of knowing follows the manner of the nature of the knowing thing."

93. Ibid.

94. Ibid.

95. The process of assimilation is an increasing interiorization of the will of God in our hearts and actions, and an increasing readiness in obeying the movements of the Spirit (although he refers generically to "God"): SCG III, chap. 152, no. 4.

96. *De caritate* q. 2, ad 7, from Saint Thomas Aquinas, *On Charity* (*De Caritate*), translated by Lottie H. Kendzierski, (Milwaukee, Wisconsin: Marquette University Press, 1960), 30.

ditions for obtaining an end, often invoking the parallel of natural and supernatural orders. A triad of form, inclination, and movement appears in various chapters in SCG (and DV. 27.2). In SCG IV, chap. 20–21, the conditions of our beatitude are first, becoming like God by possessing spiritual perfections; second, exercising these perfections; and third, achieving spiritual beatitude. The Holy Ghost, characterized as "love, drive, and motion"[97] governs creation by moving things towards their ends. For us, this means His indwelling presence which renews and cleanses while restoring the "order" of the will.[98]

In SCG III, chap. 150, the motif of movement appears, in his description of God's constant presence to us. He recalls that grace is the help given to us to enjoy the uncreated Good of Himself, as a special mark of his love for man. As the spiritual life of the soul, grace establishes the continual nature of this help, making our response of love a steady movement towards our end: "a thing that is directed toward an end must have a continual relation to it, because the mover continually moves the moved object, until the object comes to its end as a result of the motion. Therefore.... man must continually enjoy this help until he reaches his end."

Against an overly apophatic view of the mystical life, Aquinas argues that charity concerns our dispositions and actions, flowing from an "enduring form, which is, as it were, at rest [in us]," a perfection that remains in us even when we are not acting. A basic metaphysical principle underlies his spirituality of conformity to God—"everything operates in accord with its own form."[99] And Aquinas is insistent that we reach our ultimate end, in a sense, by our own operations (the theological virtues, in this context), with God making this possible by placing something within us which turns us, the beloved,[100] to the love of Himself, so that we become lovers of God.[101]

97. SCG IV, chap. 20, no. 6.

98. SCG IV, chap. 21, no. 11; chap. 22, no. 6.

99. Aquinas applies this argument in SCG III, chap. 150, nos. 5–7, while also distinguishing God's causal, creative love (which causes things to be good) from man's responsive love.

100. Aquinas describes the relation of God and the soul in sanctifying grace as one of a lover (God) whose "main effort inclines, to attract his beloved to the love of Himself" in SCG III, chap. 151, no. 2.

101. SCG III, chap. 151, no. 3. Being a lover of God means a union of wills. He cites Aristotle's notion of shared goods in friendship.

## IV. Varieties of Thomist Existentialism Applied to Aquinas's Spirituality

So far, we have seen a number of ways in which Aquinas's metaphysics is at work in this theory of grace, charity, and the sacraments, and have examined the way in which Maritain contrasts Aquinas's "existential intellectualism" with atheist and non-Thomist views of man. Now, we turn to assess varieties of Thomist existentialism as possible foundations for Aquinas's spirituality.

There are two errors in views on the relation of Aquinas's *esse* to issues in theology in general. The first is held by what some call the "thin essence" camp and consists in collapsing the causality of form or essence into that of *esse* so that form is a mere limit principle, with no causal role except reception of being. In this view, spirituality becomes a radical existentialism without a role for grace as a seat of the virtues and Gifts. Pantheism and other errors attend this view, which can be called "modalist existentialism." A more moderate but equally dangerous view accepts a positive role for form but argues for an actual identification of grace and *esse*, based on their shared extrinsic causality and from the fact that both *esse* and grace join God and creature. Both the "thin essence" view and the more moderate view misconstrue the role of *esse* and form in Aquinas's spirituality by missing their relation in the created order.

### 1. *Radical Existentialist Thomism (William Carlo)*

In *The Ultimate Reducibility of Essence to Existence in Existential Metaphysics*,[102] William Carlo argues that essence or form is a "negative limit principle" in comparison to *esse*, which in itself is infinite and perfect, being identical with God. We can call his view "modal existentialism" in that he views *esse* as all-encompassing and to which all additions are intrinsic. The view that essence is but an intrinsic mode of *esse* is directly related to the attempt to locate a principle of similitude between God and creature and to guarantee the unity of the subject matter of metaphysics. Only by a reduction of metaphysical principles to a unity can the two notions of metaphysics as the science of *ens qua ens* and as knowledge of the First Cause

102. William Carlo, *The Ultimate Reducibility of Essence to Existence in Existential Metaphysics* (The Hague: Nijhoff, 1966).

of Being[103] be reconciled.[104] Thus, the primacy of *esse* translates into the reducibility of the metaphysical principles of form and matter into *esse*.[105] For Carlo, the "finitizing" of *esse* occurs in the act of creation, wherein "essence is the intrinsic limitation of *esse*, the crystallization of existence, bordered by nothingness."[106]

The impact of modalist existentialism on mystical ascent is predictable. It is one thing to collapse all perfections in God into *esse*. It is another to posit *esse* as the sole principle of perfection in creatures; to do so imposes divine simplicity on them, destroys any theory of participation by imaging through grace, and ends in pantheism. Aquinas says, further, that *ens* possesses its own specific meaning which covers act and potency,[107] and *esse* has its own significance aside from "*ens*." For Aquinas, *ens* has four divisions: (1) the real, of reason, and the true;[108] (2) the essential and accidental;[109] (3) substance and accident;[110] and (4) act and potency.[111]

### 2. "Theological" Existentialism (Joyce Little)

In *Toward a Thomist Methodology*,[112] Joyce Little argues that the work done by grace in the supernatural order can be assigned to *esse*, itself already a participation in *Ipsum Esse*. She concludes by saying there is no reason for two extrinsically denominated accidents that both relate the creature to God—effectively blurring the natural and supernatural orders. Her thesis resembles that of transcendental Thomists in drawing so close an analogy between the natural and supernatural orders that the supernatural order collapses into the natural one. Little's logic makes grace redundant, since for her, both a thing's act of existence and sanctifying grace are par-

103. The First Cause of Being is equivalent to the Aristotelian separate substances.

104. Carlo, *The Ultimate Reducibility*, 137.

105. On the question of "reducibility," see ibid., 99–105.

106. Ibid., 103–104.

107. See ST I, q. 77, a. 1, c.; SCG III, chap.7; II, chap. 54, as well as Aquinas's treatment of the divisions of *ens per se* in *In V Meta*. lectio 9, where *ens* is divided into the essential and accidental, substance and accidents and into potency and act. *De ente et essentia* chap.1 begins by dividing *ens per se* into the ten predicaments, on the one hand, and the truth of proposition, on the other.

108. *De ente*, chap. 1.

109. *In V Meta*. lectio 9, no. 885.

110. Ibid.

111. *In V Meta*. lectio 9, no. 889 divides *ens per se* into extramental being, intramental being and act/potency.

112. Joyce Little, *Toward a Thomist Methodology*, Toronto Studies in Theology, no. 34 (Toronto: Edwin Mellen Press, 1988).

ticipations in the fullness of God's being, and creation is the result of God's gratuitous love. In this view, we can say, in the final words of Bernanos's country priest, "*Tout est grâce.*"[113] In short, there is no need for a two-tiered explanation of man's return to God. This view is flawed both metaphysically and theologically.

First and most obviously, it rejects the substance/accident distinction in that while both *esse* and grace are accidents, a thing's substantial *esse* is both ontologically and temporally *prior* to the form of grace in the soul. Grace, says Aquinas, is not a subsistent form and is not properly created in the way in which substances are (they subsist)—yet, he goes on, "the infusion of grace is similar to the notion of creation insofar as grace has no cause in its subject."[114]

Regarding the distinction between substantial *esse* and grace, in several texts Aquinas distinguishes between the formal causality by which grace is caused in the soul and efficient causality. While the primary sense of causing or making is efficient causality, his example for grace is formal: "Something is said to act in two ways: formally, as whiteness makes a wall white; and in this way, an accident can act upon its subject, and so grace acts upon the soul.... In another way, by way of efficient causality, as a painter makes a wall white; and in this way neither grace nor accident acts upon its own subject."[115]

While *esse* is caused efficiently, as a quality, grace is a form making the soul just. While both accidents perfect and actuate their subjects in some way, substantial *esse* has ontological priority by establishing a thing in being, while grace elevates the rational being beyond a vestigial resemblance to God to a relation of active imaging of Him in the infusion of supernatural virtues and Gifts. As he says in *De Ente* 6, accidental forms compose with a subject that is already a complete, actual being—and the latter is naturally prior to any accident which comes to it.

Little's thesis denies the distinction of efficient and formal causality in the acts of creation and redemption; it also entails the view that the loss of grace is impossible. On her view, the being of grace would actually be simultaneous with the created existent—one would be born in grace and

113. Georges Bernanos, *Journal d'un curé de campagne* (Paris: Editions Pon, 1955), 254.

114. *De potentia* q. 3, a. 8, ad 3.

115. *In 2 Sent.*, d. 26, q. 1, a. 2, ad 4. Cf. *In I Sent.*, d. 17, q. 1, a. 1, ad 5; ST I-II, q. 111, a. 2, ad 2; q. 110, a. 2, ad 1. On this, see Barry Brown, *Accidental Being: A Study in the Metaphysics of St. Thomas Aquinas* (Lanham, Maryland: University Press of America, 1986), 147.

possess it in virtue of existing. Finally, her view entails that our natural *esse* would grow, just like supernatural grace and the theological virtues. Just as we grow in grace, so would our substantial being itself grow—a teacher could cause an increase in the substantial being of his or her students in the very act of teaching them.

For Aquinas, charity grows by intensification or quality, and should increase unto death, by taking an ever-deeper root in our will.[116] He balances the language of *habitus* with that of motion and inclination in his descriptions of the life of grace, [117] signaling his view that spiritual growth involves the interplay of stability and growth, stillness and energy, apophatic self-transcendence and cataphatic affirmation, and exercise of our powers towards fulfilment.

Little's view contradicts the distinction between substantial being and the accidental being of knowing and loving as habits. But Aquinas's distinction between the soul's essence and its powers, and his denial of the Lombard's identification of charity in the soul and the Holy Ghost, entails the view that habits, even if infused, are lodged in the soul as their subject, and are thus secondary and posterior to the soul itself. While it is true that the acts of knowing and willing under the direction of grace denote higher participations in the fullness of being, these are secondary to the thing's first act of existence. Neither can there be two substantial beings in a thing without jeopardizing its unity, he says, in relation to Christ's being and the hypostatic union.

## V. Conclusion

Three intersecting paths of inquiry converge to answer the question, "How is the metaphysical principle of existence related to mystical ascent in the thought of Maritain and Aquinas?" First, we asked how Maritain's view of Aquinas's "existentialist intellectualism" differed from atheist and other Christian existentialisms. His focus was on the intersection of *esse* and love stemming from authentic freedom and the proper ordering of wisdoms. Second, we asked how Maritain's description of the role of ex-

116. ST II-II, q. 24, a. 5.

117. Aquinas even parallels the rapidity with which natural motion reaches its end with the intensification of spiritual acts as we approach more closely to God. See ST I-II, q. 35, a. 6; *In Ep. ad Hebr.*, 10.25; ST III, q. 89, a. 2.

istence in spirituality related to Aquinas's own meditations on *esse*'s role in the theology of grace, charity, and the sacraments. This discussion highlighted the theological fruits as gathered from balancing the roles of form and *esse* in mystical ascent. Third, we inquired about the extent to which other "Thomist existentialisms" could be used as foundations for a Thomist spirituality. This inquiry unearthed the problems involved in minimizing form as a metaphysical principle in theology and showed that these interpretations do not serve but rather detract from the character and aims of Aquinas's spirituality.

# IV

# THE ROOTS OF POLITICAL (DIS)ORDER

THOMAS L. MAMMOSER

# A Metaphor Gone Mad

## Jacques Maritain and the Separation of Church and State

NEAR THE END of *Henry VIII,* William Shakespeare wrote a brief dialogue between Lord Chamberlain and the Duke of Suffolk, Henry's brother-in-law. Chamberlain has just left King Henry, who—he says—is full of "sad thoughts and troubles."[1] The issue on Henry's mind, not surprisingly, is marriage. The Duke of Norfolk, also in the scene, asks, "What's the cause?"[2]

Chamberlain responds, "It seems the marriage with his brother's wife has crept too near his conscience,"[3] to which Suffolk, Henry's brother-in-law, slyly replies, "No, his conscience has crept too near another lady."[4]

As Shakespeare dramatized, there is much historical danger in the denial of conscience, that unique human power Cardinal Newman described as "the aboriginal Vicar of Christ in the soul."[5] Among many examples, the Reformation taught us that even small repudiations of conscience at the start can have large repercussions down the road for cultures, for churches, and for nations.

We cannot escape the effects of such denials in our country today. The way church and state are meant to interrelate in America, so protective of

1. William Shakespeare, *Henry VIII,* 2.2.16.

2. Ibid., line 17.

3. Ibid., lines 18–19.

4. Ibid., lines 20–21.

5. John Henry Newman, *Letter to the Duke of Norfolk* (London: Longmans, Green, and Co., 1875), 248

conscience, was once well articulated by our Founders. Unfortunately, we now grapple with a variety of cultural misnomers, not the least of which is "a metaphor gone mad"—the much misunderstood "modern" notion of separation of church and state.

Judicial malfeasance especially has promoted confused perceptions of the necessary dynamic between religion and society, leading to bad laws and misguided mandates—witness the U.S. Department of Health and Human Services mandate on contraceptives, abortifacients, and sterilization—that not only violate a Christian conscience but also denigrate the culture of a free society. And so, guided by Jacques Maritain, it seems opportune to reflect on the foundational wisdom and religious roots upon which this nation, the world's beacon of democracy and protector of freedoms, was built.

Following service as French ambassador to the Vatican after World War II, Maritain was a key drafter of the historic document, *The Universal Declaration of Human Rights,* adopted by the United Nations General Assembly in 1948 and essentially ratified by all the world's countries, including Muslim. The purpose of this document was to extend the basic values of democracy globally. Its Article 18 states that "everyone has the right to freedom of thought, conscience and religion; this right includes the freedom to change his religion or belief and freedom, either alone or in community with others and in public or private, to manifest his religion or belief in teaching, practice, worship and observance."[6]

Maritain was then to spend some years writing and teaching in the United States. He developed a great affection for this country, as evidenced in his gracious book, *Reflections on America* (1958). He thought deeply on church and state matters. As both a European and a Christian philosopher he was especially insightful on the American experiment and church/state separation. One of his more prophetic insights is how mistaken our Founders' meaning of the First Amendment and "separation" might someday come to be. As he wrote shortly after the war,

> The expression "separation between Church and State," which in itself is a misleading expression, does not have the same meaning here and in Europe. In Europe it means that complete isolation which derives from century-old misunderstandings

6. United Nations General Assembly, Article 18, Universal Declaration of Human Rights (December 10, 1948).

and struggles, and which has produced most unfortunate results. Here it means, as a matter of fact—together with a refusal to grant any privilege to one religious denomination in preference to others and to have a State-established religion—a distinction between the State and the Churches which is compatible with good feeling and mutual cooperation. Sharp distinction and actual cooperation, that's a historical treasure.... Please to God that you keep it carefully, and not let your concept of separation veer around to the European one.[7]

## I. The Founders

In recognizing the need for religious freedom, our Constitution is a historical treasure wherein we learn at least two significant things. One is that the Founders did not want to favor, much less establish, a particular Christian denomination. No more the unity of a religio-political body. No more the *republica Christiana* of the Middle Ages. Leave that idea in old Europe.[8] The other is that if we are going to have this freedom, we also better have a way to manage it, not only legally, but also culturally. The Founders believed, as we seem to have forgotten, that freedom is linked to morality, that it requires virtuous behavior, and that religious influence is indispensable for a democracy. John Adams put it this way in a letter to Dr. Benjamin Rush, a fellow signer of the Declaration of Independence: "Religion and virtue are the only foundations, not only of republicanism and of all free government, but of social felicity under all governments and in all combinations of human society."[9]

Religion and virtue? The sentiments may sound old-fashioned, but they should not surprise. Adams was a religious man—a self-confessed "church going animal"[10]—and he put forth a belief and a message of great relevance. Hidden under decades of liberal cant, historical amnesia, and judicial malfeasance, the message is this: there is little hope for democracy without a profound link to religious belief supported by a virtuous body politic. As Adams put it, "The general principles on which the Fathers achieved independence ... were the general principles of Christianity. Now

7. Jacques Maritain, "Christianity and Democracy" (speech, Gettysburg College, February 19, 1950).

8. Jacques Maritain, *Man and the State* (Chicago: University of Chicago Press, 1951), 160.

9. James H. Hutson, *Religion and the Founding of the American Republic* (Washington, D.C.: Library of Congress, 2005), 191.

10. Ibid.

I avow that I then believed (and now believe) that those general principles of Christianity are as eternal and immutable as the existence and attributes of God."[11]

Adams was not unique among the Founders, virtually all of whom supported religious freedom and presumed a certain degree of virtue in the people. They believed they were supporting a system of government that, in Adams' words, "was made only for moral and religious people."[12] As the Founders saw it, the Constitution was both a charter of freedom and a call for political (that is, *responsible*) order. A government "of the people, by the people, and for the people" meant that people must take responsibility for the public order, first by accepting the challenge to live it in a life of virtue, and then by defending it for others.

However much the Founders defended freedom, they recognized it as more than liberation from constraint. They saw it as indispensable to building a new nation—understood not so much as an objective but as a necessary *condition* to achieve something both humane and grand. Freedom, then, would not be something selfish, autocratic, arbitrary, or individualistic. It would not operate in isolation from other values because it was inherently *relational*, typically involving others. In many respects, freedom was contained and structured by values, especially religious values, relating to the common good and public order. As the Russian philosopher Nicholas Berdyaev put it, "There are too many lovers of their own liberty in the world ... and they all deny the liberty of their fellow man."[13]

Moreover, the Founders, unlike our contemporaries, respected the great traditions that supported their beliefs. Adams would write: "In favor of these general principles in philosophy, religion, and government I could fill sheets of quotations from ... philosophers including Locke—not to mention thousands of divines and philosophers of inferior fame."[14] Incipient in these general principles and traditions is what we might call a "new humanism" for America: a vision that, while richly grounded in the

11. John Adams, letter to Thomas Jefferson (June 28, 1813).

12. John Adams, address to the officers of the First Brigade of the Third Division of the Militia of Massachusetts (1798) in *The Works of John Adams, Second President of the United States*, vol. 9 (Boston: Little, Brown and Company 1850–56), 229.

13. Nikolai Berdyaev, *The Fate of Man in the Modern World* (New York: Morehouse Publishing, 1935), 2.

14. John Adams, letter to Thomas Jefferson (June 28, 1813) in *The Works of John Adams, Second President of the United States*, vol. 10 (Boston: Little, Brown and Company 1850–56).

past, carries within it a depth and power to mold a better world. But that world must not be grounded on a prevailing false humanism that flaunts contradiction and contention in the body politic. It will require an authentic humanism that is ennobled and inspired by *caritas in veritate*. As Benedict XVI would write in his last encyclical, "Charity in truth, to which Jesus Christ bore witness by his earthly life and especially by his death and resurrection, is the principal driving force behind the authentic development of every person and of all humanity."[15]

As for the religion of the Founders, whatever its forms, it was Christianity. While respecting the freedom of all citizens, the Founders wished to encourage a nation that would be socially and culturally inspired by the Christian faith. Their task was to respect the religious sympathies of all their fellow citizens, while not preferring one denomination over another—in Maritain's terms, to properly "distinguish Church and state … not to separate but to properly unite them."[16] His well-known books *Integral Humanism* (1936) and *Man and the State* (1951) would foster a significant change by viewing church-state relations as complementary and interactive. Church and state are responsible, in their own ways, both for the human person in his "individuality," as a member of the body politic, and as a "spiritual being" capable "of knowledge and of love."[17]

Maritain's work also provided a groundbreaking intellectual framework for the decree of Vatican II, *Dignitatis Humanae* (Declaration on Religious Liberty), which deals extensively with freedom of conscience. *Dignitatis* emphasizes that "the civil authority, which is committed to the care of the common good in the temporal order, must recognize and look with favor on the religious life of the citizen" (no. 4), and that "in religious matters every form of human coercion should be excluded" (no. 10).[18]

The Founders' response to how church and state, or more appropriately, religion and the body politic, should relate is a pillar of American democracy. The First Amendment elicited enormous admiration from Maritain. He wrote, "The Constitution of this country is deeply rooted in the age-

15. Benedict XVI, Introduction, *Caritas in Veritate* (2009).

16. Jacques Maritain, *Man and the State* (1951; reprinted, Washington, D.C.: The Catholic University Press, 1998), 183.

17. Jacques Maritain, *Scholasticism and Politics*, translated and edited by Mortimer J. Adler (1940; reprinted, Indianapolis, Indiana: Liberty Fund, 2011), 550.

18. Vatican Council II, *Dignitatis Humanae* (1965): no. 2.

old heritage of Christian civilization."[19] He believed the Constitution to be providential because amid religious diversity, it properly distinguished between church and state while protecting their autonomy as well as their unity. It recognized that their constituencies are at one and the same time of both orders. Yes, they are *distinct*. But neither the Founders nor Maritain saw them as *separate* in the way they have come to be understood in this country. Both church and state are concerned with the unity of matter and spirit, of body and soul, that is the unique human person. Metaphorically, they are two sides of one coin. They must respect what is Caesar's ... and what is God's (Matthew 22:21). In concert with the Founders, Maritain believed it is in the best interest of the state to encourage religious practice and expect social and cultural benefits in return. Not the least of these would be a more dynamic unity within the body politic.

The church/state distinction was of special importance to Maritain. He wrote:

> Peerless is the significance, for political philosophy, of the establishment of the American Constitution. This Constitution can be described as an outstanding lay Christian document tinged with the philosophy of the day. The spirit and inspiration of this great political Christian document is basically repugnant to the idea of making human society stand aloof from God and from any religious faith. Thanksgiving and public prayer, the invocation of the name of God at the occasion of any major official gathering, are, in the practical behavior of the nation, a token of this very same spirit and inspiration.[20]

## II. The Misguided Notion of "Separation"

A pressing question today should be: How did we get to our current convoluted, culturally debilitating "separation" notion? More importantly, how do we get beyond it? Some historical facts can help. One is that Thomas Jefferson's famous phrase, "separation of church and state," does not appear in the First Amendment. Nor is it found in the Constitution. Neither mention "separation" or "Church" or "state."

Significantly, during the extensive debates of the 90 Founding Fathers who framed the First Amendment from June 7 to September 25, 1789, not

19. Maritain, *Man and the State*, 183
20. Ibid., 183–84.

one mentioned the phrase "separation of church and state."[21] The key issue for James Madison, who authored the First Amendment, appears to be priority, not separation. "Before any man can be considered as a member of Civil Society," he wrote, "he must be considered as a subject of the Governor of the Universe. We owe duties to each, but duties to God come first in order of preference."[22]

Truth be told, for all his notoriety regarding the "separation" issue, Jefferson never engaged in the First Amendment debates. He was in France at the time the Bill of Rights was passed, and his own views and actions do not support the rigid church/state separation interpretation attributed to him. The "separation" phrase actually appears in a letter Jefferson sent privately 14 years *after* the amendment was passed. The letter was dated 1802 and sent to Connecticut's Danbury Baptist Association to thank them for an earlier greeting and to reaffirm the amendment's language.

For Jefferson and the Baptists, the issue was not the practice of religion. At least 25 different versions of Christianity plus Judaism and Islam abounded at that time. In 1784, Hannah Adams, a cousin of John Adams, found a huge audience for her book, *Alphabetical Compendium of the Various Sects Which Have Appeared in the World from the Beginning of the Christian Era to the Present.*[23] By the Great Awakening of the mid-1800s—called a new "Pentecost" and the "event of the century"—New York City alone had 250 well-attended churches of all persuasions. Historian Philip Schaff quoted an observer who called the United States "by far the most religious and Christian country in the world," proving that an array of churches and faiths can coexist in American society.[24]

The issue then for the Founders was not freedom of religion, which they embraced, but *establishment* of religion. The establishment issue for eighteenth-century America was not advancement of religion, as modern jurisprudence would suggest, but Anglican control.

Three days after Jefferson wrote the Danbury letter, he attended church in the largest congregation in North America at the time. It held its weekly

21. Congressional Records, 1789.

22. James Madison, *Memorial and Remonstrance against Religious Assessments* (1785), para. 1.

23. Hannah Adams, *Alphabetical Compendium of the Various Sects Which Have Appeared in the World from the Beginning of the Christian Era to the Present* (Boston: B. Edes and Sons, no. 42 Cornhill, 1784).

24. Wallace Henly, "Immigration and the 'Whatever' State," *Christian Post*, April 17, 2013.

worship services in the House Chambers of the U.S. Capitol Building. Jefferson approved of paid government musicians to assist at these services and attended them consistently for the next 7 years. He also approved of similar worship services in his own executive branch, both at the Treasury building and the War Office. In fact, "based on extensive research ... with what appears ample justification ... on Sundays during the first years in Washington, 'the state became the church.'"[25]

As for Jefferson's well-known deism, historian Paul Johnson has called him a "closet theologian" who read daily from a multilingual edition of the New Testament.[26] Notwithstanding Jefferson's deism and that of James Madison (both of whom paid homage to the Bible), and Benjamin Franklin's "role model" view of Christ, Christianity in its various Protestant sects was by far the dominant religion in the United States at its founding. So it is clear what "religion" the Founders were protecting. Further supporting this point is the fact that both Jefferson and Franklin, the two most deist Founders, proposed biblical images for the great seal of the United States (themes from the Book of Exodus).

Whatever his ambivalence toward Christianity, Franklin did not appear antagonistic or even indifferent to its tenets. In his earlier years, he became quite enamored with the popular roving preacher, George Whitefield, publishing accounts of Whitefield's appearances in 45 weekly issues of his *Gazette*. "Never did the people show so great a willingness to attend sermons," Franklin reported in the *Gazette*. "Religion is become the subject of most conversations. No books are in request but those of piety."[27] He also saw a strong connection between civic and religious virtue, once writing to his wife: "God is very good to us.... Let us ... show our sense of His goodness to us by continuing to do good to our fellow creatures."[28]

The symbolism of Franklin and Jefferson's actions correspond with the rhetoric of their fellow Founders. Separation was meant to keep government out of religion, but it was not meant to absent religion from public life. Evidently, the wall of separation against religion in 1802 could not be constructed anywhere in the country—not even on government property.

25. Hutson, *Religion and the Founding of the American Republic*, xii.

26. Paul Johnson, *A History of the American People* (New York: HarperCollins Publishers, 1998), 103.

27. Walter Isaacson, *Benjamin Franklin, An American Life* (New York: Simon and Schuster, 2003), 94.

28. Ibid.

## III. The First Amendment

It is appropriate here to briefly review the relevant clause of the First Amendment, which states: "Congress shall make no law respecting an establishment of religion or prohibiting the free exercise thereof." The "establishment" phrase is important because in the 1790s, the new states exhibited exceptional religious diversity, an attribute the Founders respected. The Founders also wished to respect precedent, which meant ensuring religious principles were included in public life, rather than excluded, and protected by the government. Such precedent is reflected in many of the concepts and guarantees of the Northwest Ordinance of 1787, for example, which antedated the First Amendment and was incorporated in the U.S. Constitution and the Bill of Rights. In the Northwest Territory, religious tolerance was overtly proclaimed by enunciating that "religion, morality, and knowledge, being necessary to good government and the happiness of mankind, schools and the means of education shall *forever be encouraged.*"[29]

Historically, the connection between the state and personal religious practice persisted long after the founding period. Justice Joseph Story, in his *Familiar Exposition of the Constitution,* completed in 1840, maintained it was the "general, if not universal sentiment in America ... that Christianity ought to receive encouragement from the state" and that "to level all religions" and "to make it a state policy to hold all in utter indifference, would have created universal disapprobation, if not universal indignation."[30]

In the 1892 case *Church of the Holy Trinity v. United States,* Supreme Court Justice Josiah Brewer wrote that "our laws and our institutions must necessarily be based upon and embody the teachings of the Redeemer of mankind. It is impossible that it should be otherwise; and in this sense and to this extent our civilization and our institutions are emphatically Christian."[31]

During World War II, in a letter to the American bishops, President Franklin Delano Roosevelt said, "We (the United Nations) should seek ... the establishment of an international order in which the spirit of Christ

29. Northwest Ordinance, 1787, art. III; italics added.

30. Joseph Story, *Commentaries on the Constitution of the United States* (Boston: Hilliard, Grey, 1833).

31. Church of the Holy Trinity v. United States (1892).

shall rule the hearts of men and of nations."[32] Several months later, Vice President Henry Wallace declared, "The idea of freedom ... is derived from the Bible with its extraordinary emphasis on the dignity of the individual. Democracy is the only true political expression of Christianity."[33] And in thanksgiving at the end of the war, during the lighting of the White House Christmas tree, President Harry Truman said, "I do not believe there is one problem in this country or in the world today, which could not be settled if approached through the teaching of the Sermon on the Mount."[34]

More recently, Supreme Court Justice Anton Scalia noted in his dissent of *McCreary County v. the American Civil Liberties Union of Kentucky* (2005):

> Our Presidents continue to conclude the Presidential oath with the words "so help me God." Our legislatures, state and national, continue to open their sessions with prayer by official chaplains. The sessions of this Court continue to open with the prayer "God save the United States and this Honorable Court." Invocation of the Almighty by our public figures, at all levels of government, remains commonplace. Our coinage bears the motto "IN GOD WE TRUST." And our Pledge of Allegiance contains the acknowledgement that we are a Nation "under God." As one of our Supreme Court opinions rightly observed, "We are a religious people whose institutions presuppose a Supreme Being."[35]

## IV. The Naked Public Square

As to how we got to our present place as a "naked public square," seriously convoluting the notion of separation and abandoning our religious roots and principles, leading contemporary scholar Philip Hamburger has this to say: "There is much reason to believe that the modern suppositions about the wisdom and influence of Jefferson's words regarding separation have developed largely as part of a twentieth-century myth—an account that has

32. Letter from Franklin Delano Roosevelt to American bishops, *Catholic News*, January 17, 1942.

33. Henry Wallace, "The Price of Free World Victory" (speech before the Free World Association, May 8, 1942).

34. Harry S. Truman, "Address at the Lighting of the National Community Christmas Tree on the White House Grounds" (speech, December 24, 1945).

35. Zorach v. Clauson, 343 U.S. 306, 313 (1952), repeated with approval in Lynch v. Donnelly, 465 U.S. 668, 675 (1984); Marsh, 463 U.S., at 792; Abington Township, supra, at 213. Michael W. McConnell, John H. Garvey, Thomas C. Berg, *Religion and the Constitution*, 3rd edition (New York: Aspen Publishers, 2011), 594.

become popular precisely because it has *seemed* to provide constitutional authority for separation."[36] This is not what the Founders had in mind. In fact, Jefferson had prophetically warned *against* the power of the judiciary to alter the intent of the Founders and the Constitution. He wrote on September 6, 1819, "The Constitution—is a mere thing of wax in the hands of the judiciary, which they may twist and shape into any form they please."[37]

The twisting, of course, eventually happened. Not long after Truman's Christmas message came a Supreme Court decision in *Everson v. Board of Education* (1947) where, for the first time, the court, in dissenting but precedent-setting language, interpreted the "separation" phrase as requiring a sharp separation, not between church and state, but between religion and public life. This decision was a true game-changer because it interpreted the First Amendment not as a limitation on government interference, but rather as a limitation on religious expression and principles. As Justice Wiley Blount Rutledge wrote, the First Amendment's object was to "create a *complete and permanent separation* of the spheres of religious activity and civil authority by comprehensively *forbidding* every form of public aid or support for religion."[38] That court, unlike previous ones, did not reprint Jefferson's Danbury letter. It merely used eight words from the letter and did not give the context of the phrase or mention Jefferson's numerous other statements on the subject. Nor did it mention that previous Supreme Courts had used Jefferson's letter *to preserve* religious principles in public society. In short, the 1947 court was the first to divorce Jefferson's metaphor from its context and then apply it exactly opposite to Jefferson's clearly articulated intent.

Justice Hugo Black's majority opinion reinforced Justice Rutledge, claiming the clause against establishment of religion was intended to erect "a wall between Church and State" that was meant to be kept "high and impregnable."[39] In so doing, it bears pointing out, Justice Black substituted the *judicial* for the *amendment* process.

Game changers are done by key players, and the key player here was

36. Philip Hamburger, *Separation of Church and State* (Cambridge, Massachusetts: Harvard University Press, 2002), 11.

37. Thomas Jefferson to Spencer Roane, September 6, 1819 in *The Works of Thomas Jefferson*, collected and edited by Paul Leicester Ford, Federal Edition, vol. 12 (New York and London: G. P. Putnam's Sons, 1904–1905), 135–38.

38. Everson v. Board of Education (1947).

39. Ibid.

Justice Black. A Baptist from Alabama, Black was a progressive New Dealer who ran for the Senate in 1925 and 1926 by appealing to the "Dry-Protestant-Progressive" voters in the state. He was also a Mason influenced by the anti-Catholic Southern Jurisdiction of Scottish Rite Masons. In the late 1940s, at least seven justices of the Supreme Court belonged to one Masonic organization or another.

Black had also been a member of the Ku Klux Klan and gained some notoriety in 1921 by defending a Klansman against a charge of murdering a Catholic priest. According to Hamburger, "The Klan provided Black with his path to the Senate. In September Black joined the powerful Richard E. Lee Klan No. 1 and promptly became Kladd of the Klavern—the officer who initiated new members with an oath about 'white supremacy' and 'separation of Church and State.'"[40] It was not until 1937 that President Roosevelt disavowed his awareness of Black's former Klan membership and appointed him as Associate Justice of the Supreme Court, much to the horror of many Americans, not least Catholics.

The opinion in *Everson v. Board of Education* would become the dramatically reworked new foundation of constitutional jurisprudence in the United States on the separation of church and state. A year later, *Everson* was reinforced in the *McCollum v. Board of Education* (1948) case. Here, the Supreme Court—with Justice Black again writing the majority opinion—declared that religious instruction on public school premises was contrary to the Constitution. This decision dismayed many Protestants, bringing them to "recognize that they faced a greater threat from secularism and separation than from Catholicism."[41] All of which prompted management theorist Peter Drucker to write, "The way we have handled the problem in the few cases that have come up so far is nothing to be proud of. I am convinced that it is a thoroughly untenable decision on ordinary legal grounds."[42] Drucker's point here is that to rule it unconstitutional for a school district to grant "released time" for religious instruction (because to do so interferes with the religious freedom of an atheist schoolchild) represents an absurdity and is in clear violation of the Constitution's mandate against preventing free exercise. It means the federal government actually

40. Hamburger, *Separation of Church and State*, 426.

41. Ibid., 477.

42. Peter Drucker, "Organized Religion and the American Creed," *Review of Politics* 18, no. 3 (July 1956): 301–302.

controls the question of religion, more specifically the *practice* and *free exercise* of religion, anywhere in the states.

It is not hard to see where this judicial malfeasance leads, contrary to the thinking, practice, and wishes of the Founders and generations of their philosophical disciples. Namely, to an institutionalized, judicially supported bias *against* the practice of religion—and a massive step toward the practical separation of faith from culture in the United States. Yale University professor Lawrence Friedman observed that at present, "religion has politely been shown the door. Indeed many religious parents are disturbed because the schools are now so godless. The schools teach evolution. They ban prayers and Bible reading. They teach nothing about religion. This makes them enemies of religion."[43] As for making schools "neutral," Friedman said it is "strictly speaking, a mirage.... Even science is an ideology. As of 2001, the public schools ignore religion, one of the most powerful social forces in the world."[44]

They also appear to be ignoring what might be called "civil religion." A Harvard and Stanford graduate noted in a *Wall Street Journal* op-ed that the dominant intellectual culture at both schools "provided scant leadership in educating students about the foundation of freedom in the Western world, or even in promoting an understanding of the founding principles of our own nation."[45] As for what this historical amnesia and moral neutrality represent for the public square, Friedman made the compelling observation that it is "the master change in the general culture in the twentieth century: *the triumph of the individual, the exaltation of the self.*"[46]

The ambiguity of all this, especially given the well-defined intent of the First Amendment, is no doubt why Chief Justice William Rehnquist said, "The metaphor of a wall of separation is bad history and worse law. It has made a positive chaos out of court rulings. It should be explicitly abandoned."[47] This is in rather stark contrast to the separationist and secularist position held by Justices Stephen Breyer, Ruth Bader Ginsburg, and David Souter, who claim the establishment clause prevents any government endorsement or support of religious practices.

43. Lawrence M. Friedman, *American Law in the 20th Century* (New Haven, Connecticut: Yale University Press, 2002), 510.

44. Ibid.

45. Paige Rodriguez, letter to *Wall Street Journal Opinion*, March 14, 2012, A12.

46. Friedman, *American Law in the 20th Century*, 516.

47. Wallace v. Jaffree, 472 U.S. 38 (1985).

Predictably, by the late twentieth century the Supreme Court began to interpret the establishment and free exercise clauses so as to actually *restrict* the promotion of religion by the states. Coming full circle from the Founders' intent, for example, Justice Souter, writing for the majority in *Board of Education of Kiryas Joel Village School District v. Grumet* (1994), concluded that "government should not prefer one religion to another, *or religion to irreligion.*"[48] Which means, of course, that religious indifferentism has been taken to a new level in this country: a level of enshrinement and cultural agnosticism. What we have here is our government speaking on religion in a whole new light—namely on the equivalency of believing in God and not believing in God. So much for the perspicacity and intent of the Founders and the First Amendment, so desirous were they to protect religious belief in America.

Maritain refers to this restricting phenomenon as "anthropocentric humanism," representing a one-dimensional despiritualization of the human person and a denial of his inherent religious character. He wrote, "By saying to men, you are gods by your own essence and will, they have soured men. Practically they have left to men no other internal weight than flat egoism and longing for material possessions."[49] Such indifference most certainly represents, he noted, "a *bourgeois liberalism,* whose pretension it is to base everything on the individual considered as a little god, and on his caprice, on the absolute liberty of property, of commerce, and of the pleasures of life, a liberalism which ends with … the hypertrophy and absolute primacy of the State."[50] Which is also to say that the people themselves, the body politic whom the government represents and who are generally religious (the vast majority of Americans believe in God and three-quarters of them declare themselves Christians) should not be concerned as to whether their government is supportive of their deepest beliefs of religion, which is the indispensable "theocentric" activity of the human person and at the core of human society and its political constructs. Apparently, the architects and designers of the Supreme Court building, constructed in 1935, did not foresee such later rulings as *Stone v. Graham* (1980), where the Supreme Court—in egregious irony—ruled it unconstitutional for the state

48. Board of Education of Kiryas Joel Village School District v. Grumet (1994).

49. Jacques Maritain, *Scholasticism and Politics,* 2nd edition (London: Centenary Press, 1945), 667.

50. Jacques Maritain, *True Humanism,* 7th edition (Westport, Connecticut: Greenwood Press, 1970), 107–108.

of Kentucky to permit posting the Ten Commandments in public school rooms. The ruling is particularly flagrant because throughout the Supreme Court building, there are numerous representations of the Ten Commandments and of Moses. Similarly, the architects did not neglect the National Archives, the home of our nation's most important documents, where the entrance features an image of the Ten Commandments engraved in bronze on its floor. Indeed, a simple walking tour of our nation's capital gives ample example, both on parchment and "literally written into the rock, mortar and marble of American history," of the belief that "our Creator is the source of American liberty."[51] Not surprisingly, the Latin words *Laus Deo* ("Praise be to God") appear on the eastern side of our capital's tallest building, the monument dedicated to George Washington.

## V. More Recently: Bible Verses on Banners

A fairly recent example of how constitutional rewiring discourages religious expression involved a Texas public high school cheerleading squad hoisting banners inscribed with biblical verses during football games. The school district received a complaint from the Freedom from Religion Foundation, which argued the banners violated the First Amendment.[52] To banner supporters in (predominately Christian) Texas, the fact that some small degree of religious inspiration found its way onto the high school football field hardly seemed like "establishment," especially given that no specific Christian denomination was mentioned. The Texas law firm representing the cheerleaders argued that the girls' free-speech rights were being violated, and Texas District Court Judge Steve Thomas ruled that the cheerleaders may display banners with Bible verses at football games. The judge determined the banners are constitutionally permissible, noting that no law "prohibits cheerleaders from using religious-themed banners at school sporting events."[53]

51. Newt Gingrich, *Rediscovering God in America,* revised edition (Nashville, Tennessee: Thomas Nelson, 2009), 130–31.

52. Ann Zimmerman, "Bible Verses on Banners Kick Off Texas Conflict," *Wall Street Journal,* October 1, 2012.

53. Bethany Blankley, "Texas Judge Rules Cheerleaders Can Display Bible Verses at School Sporting Events," *Christian Post,* May 9, 2013.

## VI. Maritain on the Constitution

The Texas case marked a small but meaningful step forward for freedom of religious expression. But as Maritain saw so clearly, preserving freedom of conscience and of religion is not strictly or exclusively a legal preservation. *A spirit is also involved.* He would second Alexis de Tocqueville's repeated insistence that the success of the American experiment owes less to the laws than to the culture people create—the widely shared beliefs and habits that constitute the "true and invisible constitution of the republic."[54]

Those shared beliefs go back a long way. An early president of Yale University, Elisha Williams (1694–1755), said religion was the "great cement of civil society" and should be nourished because a high level of rectitude was needed for the successful establishment of a republican government.[55] Williams explained, "Republican government was, above all, self-government and self-government placed higher demands on the average citizen than any other polity."[56] A nation of believers is a nation solidified at a spiritual level—with due respect for religious freedom—and also a more virtuous people, better able to manage both their personal and civic affairs. And thus, said Maritain, "We also understand why civilizations … belonging to the natural order, cannot arrive at their full state and dignity … except in so far as they are elevated in their own order by the influence of those virtues which arise in them, not from what is Caesar's but from what is God's."[57]

In his *On the Philosophy of History* Maritain wrote, "I have long insisted on this point—that as a result of the achievement of grace, as a result of grace [penetrating and] perfecting [and transforming] nature, nature is superelevated in its own order. In my opinion, the temporal common good of the body politic, for instance, will be superelevated in a Christian society. …

[T]he world, as the entire order of nature, is in actual fact in vital connection with the universe of the kingdom of God. Hence it appears that in

54. Alexis de Tocqueville, *Democracy in America* (1835; reprinted, Bantam Classics, 2004), 308.

55. Hutson, *Religion and the Founding of the American Republic*, 60.

56. Ibid., 61.

57. Jacques Maritain, *Scholasticism and Politics*, translated and edited by Mortimer J. Adler (1940; reprinted, New York: Image Books, 1960), 215.

actual fact it is ordained, not only to its own natural ends, but also … to an absolutely supreme end that is supernatural and that is the very end of the kingdom of God."[58]

However abandoned it may seem in today's social and political arenas, the principal of these virtues, from God and in God, is *caritas* … charity. Our earliest forebears spoke to this virtue as foundational. In 1630, John Winthrop, aboard the *Arabella* leading 700 of his fellow Puritans to America, titled his visionary sermon, "A Model of Christian Charity"—one of the finest discourses on Pauline social ethics ever written. In it, Winthrop explained how people within the community should live with one another. He compared the bond between Christians to the love between a mother and child: loving without expecting anything in return. By meeting these requirements, Winthrop believed this body of Puritans were "knit together by the bond of love" and would be blessed by God and impact the world (as they knew it) in a positive manner.[59]

Another great precursor of the Founders was the noted Puritan theologian Jonathan Edwards (1703–1755), a man of "outstanding intellect and sensibility" often called "the first major thinker in American history."[60] Edwards grounded his thought on conceptions of beauty, harmony, and ethical fittingness, and believed in the necessity of charity to the founding of this nation. His scholarly sermons, *Charity and its Fruits*, are an extensive testimony to St. Paul's Epistle to the Corinthians (1 Corinthians 13:1–13). In *A Treatise Concerning the Religious Affections* (1746), Edwards listed in detail the signs by which religious love could be distinguished. The most important was the ability to detect "divine things" by "the beauty of their moral excellency."[61] Echoing Thomas Aquinas's notions of connaturality and "grace perfecting nature," Edwards asserted that from the "sense of spiritual beauty" there arises "all true experimental knowledge of religion and indeed a whole new world of knowledge."[62] Most importantly, from the perspective of conscience, in his celebrated *The Freedom of the Will* (1754),

58. Jacques Maritain, *On the Philosophy of History*, edited by J. W. Evans (New York: Charles Scribner's, 1957), 130–31 in Eduardo J. Echeverria, "Nature and Grace: The Theological Foundations of Jacques Maritain's Public Philosophy," *Journal of Markets and Morality* 4, no. 2 (Fall 2001): 248.

59. John Winthrop, "A Model of Christian Charity" (sermon, 1630; reprinted, New York Historical Society, 1830).

60. Paul Johnson, *History of the American People* (New York: Harper Collins, 1997), 111.

61. Ibid., 112.

62. Ibid.

Edwards insisted conscience must be protected because human beings are free.[63] All must be prayed for. All can choose: we act according to our perceptions and convictions of the good, and God will hold us accountable for our choices.

## VII. Christopher Dawson and Christianizing Culture

A relevant comment here would be from a notable contemporary of Maritain's, Christopher Dawson. Dawson noted that for centuries, Christian civilization was a great ferment of social and intellectual change. Taking responsibility for the world and changing it for the better was an integral part of the Christian cultural ideal. Christianity presented a reality beyond the temporal and provided a force—a *spiritual energy* of love, of goodness, of beauty, of truth, of unity—that was culturally transforming. These energies are "forces of the spirit," not of man's lower nature. They can only come from the mind and from the heart. And they can only come—aided by grace—from generous souls in love with the world, yes, but in love foremost with their Maker.

While Dawson spoke of this creative spiritual force as a thing of the past, he pointed squarely to the challenge facing Christians today: namely, to reawaken among themselves a deep love for all earthly realities and that "missionary character"—the work of transmitting a spiritual energy from one people to another[64]—such that "the world might be fashioned anew according to God's design and reach its fulfillment."[65]

## VIII. Modern Times: "Christian by Inspiration"

As for going forward in these challenging times, Maritain offers further clarification of the church-state issue that not only enriches the intent of our Founders but also provides a marvelous pathway for a pluralistic, religiously inspired nation. That would be his highly relevant distinction between what is "denominationally" Christian and what is "Christian by inspiration."

63. Ibid.

64. Christopher Dawson, *Religion and the Rise of Western Culture* (New York: Doubleday, 1958), 18.

65. Vatican II, *Gaudium et spes* (December 7, 1965): no. 2.

As has been said, the Founders of this country did not want a denominationally Christian nation. But they had both a vision and a missionary character and they wanted a nation that was socially and culturally "inspired" by religion—specifically Christianity.

They implicitly understood the reality grounded in scripture and in natural law—in faith and in reason—that God, not the state, is the end of the human person. The person, having an eternal destiny, transcends the state. God is the prime source of political society, and it is only through a direct and intimate relationship with Him that persons receive the "energies of spiritual and social resurrection" so essential to democracy.[66]

And how do the benefits of religion accrue to the state? It is not primarily by virtue of law or by preferred status, but rather by transmitting the creative energy of a lived Christianity to modern culture. Maritain saw this as a protracted but noble journey led by what he called the "heroism of the plain man" and by "little teams and small flocks" with their political awareness, their personal behavior, and their cultural enlightenment.[67] This is what Maritain meant by the notion of authentic humanism, which must be "Christian by inspiration" or it is not fully human. As he wrote in *The Peasant of the Garonne* (1966):

> It is invariably tiny groups and small flocks that accomplish the great things. Our epoch seems to call for them more than any other.... It is only tiny groups and small flocks that can join together around this thing that escapes technology and mass production: the love of wisdom and intelligence and the confidence of this love to radiate. Its invisible rays carry far.[68]

## IX. Wary of Immediate Success

As for the "long journey," Maritain cautioned against the illusions of Machiavellianism, namely of impatience and immediate success. This is imperative because the journey involves the historical duration of nations and societies. As he wrote in *Man and the State*:

66. Jacques Maritain, *Christianity, Democracy, and the American Ideal: A Jacques Maritain Reader*, edited by James P. Kelly (Manchester, New Hampshire: Sophia Institute Press, 2004), 17.

67. Ibid., xii.

68. Jacques Maritain, *The Peasant of the Garonne* (New York: Holt, Rinehart and Winston, 1966), 249–52.

The duration of the life of a man, or rather the duration of the activity of the prince, of the political man, circumscribes the maximum length of time required by what I call *immediate success.* Now immediate success is success for a man, it is not success for a state or a nation, according to the duration proper to state vicissitudes and nation vicissitudes.[69]

What is required then is that the "small groups" be founded on a sound political philosophy as well as a sound philosophy of history: "They would apply themselves to a political action at *long range,* which instead of hypnotizing itself on the present moment, would reckon on duration and take into account the maturation necessary for an integral humanist renewal of the temporal order.[70]

Not surprisingly, Maritain's hopes were grounded in the timeless message of the Gospel. He wrote:

Christianity cast the net of the Gospel upon the Pagan Empire and the Pagan empire died of it, for there is no quarter given between the evangelical law of the Son of God and the law of the Empire which sets itself up as God. Once man has understood that, in truth of things, politics depends upon morality because its aim is the human good, once he has understood that political life must conform to natural law and, according to specific conditions of its temporal object, even to the law of the Gospel, he sees at the same time that to call for justice and law in politics is to call for a great revolution which will substitute for the power politics of the masters, men, States or nations, the politics of the common good over which the people must watch as the chief interested parties.[71]

Professor Donald Gallagher echoed these thoughts in his introduction to *Christianity and Democracy,* noting Maritain's call for

a single principle of liberation, a single principle of hope, a single principle of peace [that] can stir up the mass of servitude and iniquity and triumph over it, because this principle comes down to us from the creative source of the world, stronger than the world: that brotherly love whose law is promulgated by the Gospel to the scandal of the mighty, and which is, as the Christian well knows, God's own charity, diffused into the hearts of men.[72]

69. Jacques Maritain, *Man and the State* (Chicago: University of Chicago Press, 1951), 57–58.

70. Maritain, *Christianity, Democracy, and the American Ideal,* 41–42.

71. Jacques Maritain, *Christianity and Democracy: The Rights of Man and Natural Law* (San Francisco: Ignatius Press, 2011), 42–43.

72. Donald Gallagher, Introduction to *Christianity and Democracy: The Rights of Man and Natural Law* by Jacques Maritain (San Francisco: Ignatius Press, 2011), 33–34.

This line of reasoning also holds that the social, political, and cultural orders—and economic as well—are not meant to be directly guided by a specific Christian body. But they are, for good or bad, affected by how well Christian believers live up to the tenets of their faith. And the positive law emanating from such a society will reflect these tenets.

As Dawson reminds us:

> every Christian mind is a seed of change so long as it is a living mind, not enervated by custom or ossified by prejudice. A Christian has only to *be* in order to change the world, for in that act of being there is contained all the mystery of supernatural life. It is the function of the Church to sow this divine seed, to produce not merely good men, but spiritual men—that is to say, supermen. In so far as the Church fulfills this function it transmits to the world a continuous stream of spiritual energy. If the salt loses its savor, then indeed the world sinks back into disorder and death, for a despiritualized Christianity is powerless to change anything; it is the most abject of failures since it serves neither the natural or the spiritual order. But the life of the Church never fails, since it possesses an infinite capacity for regeneration. It is the external organ through which the Spirit enters the social process and builds up a new humanity—*populus qui nascetur quem fecit Dominus.* The spirit breathes and they are created and the face of the earth is renewed.[73]

More than ever, the American experiment today requires such an enlightened culture—a Christianized culture reawakened to its history and its founding spirits. Rejecting the agnostic, anthropocentric humanism of recent First Amendment revisionism, Maritain spoke of a "new, theocentric humanism," tasking us all with a deeper faith and respect for our past, so as to pursue a better future.

This grand task of elevating the temporal order should not be understood as an exclusively Christian task. It is a task for all of good heart, Christian or not—as reflected in the Church's teaching at Vatican II, which Maritain saw as "the announcement of a new age."[74] Maritain, an intellectual precursor and defender of the Council, was honored at its closing session by his long-time friend, Pope Paul VI (Giovanni Battista Montini)—who once called Maritain "my teacher."[75] Long before assuming the papacy, Montini had translated Maritain's *Three Reformers* into Italian in

73. Christopher Dawson, *Christianity and the New Age* (Manchester, New Hampshire: Sophia Institute Press, 1988), 103.

74. Maritain, *The Peasant of the Garonne*, 64.

75. Catherine M. A. McCauliff, "Jacques Maritain's Embrace of Religious Pluralism," *Seton Hall Law Review* 41 (2011): 593.

1928. In its Preface, he underlined the importance, even in polemical situations, of always uniting truth and charity. In 1935, he wrote the introduction to the Italian version of Maritain's notable *Integral Humanism*, dealing with the philosophy and culture of society as it relates to a Christian life. Much later, Pope Paul VI cited this book in his first social encyclical, *Populorum Progressio* (1967). Reflecting Maritain's thought, he wrote, "Economics and technology have no meaning except from the human person whom they should serve. And the human person is only truly human in as far as, master of one's own acts and judge of their worth, one is author of one's own advancement, in keeping with the nature which was given to human beings by the Creator."[76]

Maritain warmly embraced Vatican II's historic document, *Gaudium et Spes* (The Church in the Modern World), which recognized that the "mystery of man ... holds true not for Christians only but also for all men of good will in whose hearts grace is active invisibly."[77] As that document avows, "For since Christ died for all, and since all men are in fact called to one and the same destiny, which is divine, we must hold that the Holy Spirit offers to all the possibility of being made partners, in a way known to God, in the Paschal Mystery."[78]

But Maritain also cautioned in *The Peasant of the Garonne* "that the devil marches before the feet of God, and that the new fire, the essential renewal (engendered by the Council) will be an inner renewal."[79] He wrote:

> For the new fire consists of a change of attitude ... that takes place in the deepest recesses of the soul, and has to do, first of all and essentially, not in any way of acting or externally behaving ... nor any tactic to try out on our non-Christian brethren but with a way of seeing them before God, and a way of loving them better, in a deeper and more genuine conformity with the spirit of the Gospel. This inner renewal consists in becoming more fully aware of the dimensions and "weight" of evangelical love, and in completely liberating this love in the soul, so that no final purpose, however lofty, exterior to its own essence, can come to mark out a road for it and restrict it to a particular object.[80]

76. Pope Paul VI, *Populorum Progressio* (On the Development of Peoples) (March 26, 1967): no. 34.

77. Vatican II, *Gaudium et spes* (December 7, 1965): no. 22.

78. Vatican II, *Gaudium et spes* (December 7, 1965): no. 32.

79. Maritain, *The Peasant of the Garonne*, 72–73.

80. Ibid.

I close with these thoughts, given by Maritain at the height of World War II, with Europe in turmoil and the direction of the free world in the balance. He warned, "Not only does the democratic state of mind stem from the inspiration of the Gospel, but it cannot exist without it"[81] because—quoting his mentor Henri Bergson—"democracy is evangelical in essence and . . . its motive power is love."[82]

*"Let us leave the progress as well as the results in the hands of Him who chooses to work by slow influence, and with whom a thousand years are but a single day."*[83]

81. Maritain, *Christianity and Democracy*, 49.

82. Ibid., 36.

83. Robert E. Lee, letter written in response to a speech given by then President Franklin Pierce, dated December 27, 1856.

JOSHUA SCHULZ

# Towards a More Perfect Liberalism

## I. Introduction

AMONG THINKERS INFLUENCED by Jacques Maritain, few are as ideologically disparate as Martha Nussbaum and Alasdair MacIntyre.[1] Nevertheless, both philosophers acknowledge the formative influence of Maritain on the development of their thought, and this essay seeks to investigate that influence.[2]

Each of these thinkers believes that the most important circumstances of justice (to borrow a Humean term) in the contemporary world involve tensions between our affirmation of the universal dignity of persons understood as ends-in-themselves, irreducible ideological and religious pluralism, and the growing recognition that social structures, such as access to globalized markets and caring social networks, are important con-

1. In "Recoiling from Reason" (*The New York Review of Books*, December 7, 1989), her aptly titled review of MacIntyre's *Whose Justice, Which Rationality* (University of Notre Dame Press, 1989), Nussbaum famously brands MacIntyre as an antinomian Augustinian theocrat "in the grip of a world view promulgated by authority rather than by reason," one whose goal is "to justify perpetuating authority at the heart of human life and, indeed, at the heart of human reason."

2. In *After Virtue*, 3rd edition (Notre Dame, Indiana: University of Notre Dame Press: 2007), MacIntyre lists Maritain as a philosopher among those "for whom I have the greatest respect and from whom I have learned the most" (260). Martha Nussbaum cites Maritain as among the first "religious citizens" who "can affirm a pluralistic doctrine ... out of the respect they have for the freedom of the human being" in "Political Objectivity," *New Literary History* 32 (2001): 892, and repeatedly cites him as a model pre-Rawlsian political liberal in her later work. For instance, see "Human Dignity and Political Entitlements," in *Human Dignity and Bioethics: Essays Commissioned by the President's Council on Bioethics* (U.S. Independent Agencies and Commissions, 2008); and "Preface," in *The Fragility of Goodness: Luck and Ethics in Greek Tragedy and Philosophy*, revised edition (Cambridge: Cambridge University Press, 1986), xvii–xix.

version factors in people's ability to achieve well-being.[3] Moreover, in the absence of agreement about the nature of the common good and the justification of human rights—what Maritain called the "democratic charter"—Nussbaum follows Maritain's famous thesis that that it is possible to achieve *de facto* agreement about a concrete set of political entitlements understood as minimum political thresholds required for anyone's pursuit of their comprehensive conception of the good.[4] This charter is of necessity *liberal* (liberty-maximizing), *progressive* (subject to amendment), *partial* and *political* (rather than comprehensive and metaphysically justified). In defending such a charter, Nussbaum and Maritain broke with the dominant liberal tradition of justice grounded in social-contract theory, both by defending the role of "thick" anthropological reflection in the articulation of human flourishing, and by insisting on a constitutive rather than merely instrumental role for the historical deliberations of democratic communities in their articulation of moral and political norms. For his part, though MacIntyre rejects the language of rights and charters, he argues in *Dependent Rational Animals* that the pursuit of any common good will require some agreement about the nature of the end being pursued, including agreement about the status of disparate persons within political communities; that anthropological reflection on the dependent, vulnerable nature of human rationality is essential to an account of political virtue; and that there can be no account of individual flourishing independent of political deliberation about the common goods of particular communities.[5]

Despite these significant overlaps, Nussbaum's version of the Capabilities Approach is in many respects incompatible with the Catholic social

3. "Circumstances of justice" roughly refers to the material, psychological, and social conditions that motivate people to articulate and put into practice a theory of justice. For the Social Contractarians, for example, self-interest, radical equality, and scarcity of shared resources lead to the establishment of the social contract. We will discuss these themes below as they are expressed in Maritain's *Man and the State* (Washington, D.C.: The Catholic University of America Press, 1998).

4. "Well before the Rawlsian idea of 'political liberalism' had currency, Jacques Maritain, one of the architects of the Universal Declaration, maintained that people who differed about metaphysical matters could agree for practical political purposes on a list of human rights." Martha Nussbaum, *Frontiers of Justice: Disability, Nationality, Species Membership* (Cambridge, Massachusetts: Belknap Press, 2006), 305.

5. Consider, for instance, how MacIntyre builds an account of political virtue ("just generosity") and the common good around the necessity of according disabled people political recognition as primary subjects of justice in *Dependent Rational Animals: Why Human Beings Need the Virtues* (Chicago: Open Court, 1999), 140–41.

tradition to which both Maritain and MacIntyre belong.[6] One purpose of this essay is to offer a partial explanation of this incompatibility by contrasting Nussbaum's Rawlsian development of the above ideas with Maritain's development along the lines of Thomistic personalism, aspects of which were later developed more fully by MacIntyre. Accordingly, the first two parts of this essay will broadly sketch how Maritain and Nussbaum developed their accounts of political entitlements, focusing on how their diverging evaluations of the fact-value distinction impacts how they think about democratic deliberation. The final part will illustrate the importance of these differences by considering their responses to some problems common to this family of political theory.[7]

## II. Nussbaum's Capabilities Approach

Nussbaum and Maritain agree that contemporary political theory must start with two assumptions: that all human beings possess equal dignity and that relations among people are marked by irreducible moral and religious pluralism. Likewise, both thinkers argue that an adequate theory of justice must be founded on some account of human "beings and doings" rather than understood as the outcome of an ideal decision procedure. And while they largely agree about how to specify the prerequisites of flourishing, they disagree about their normative implications, which in turn impacts how each thinker interprets the role of democratic practices in the justification of political norms.

Against the Kantian model, which offers a starkly dualistic account of moral worth, Nussbaum argues that many goods constitutive of human flourishing are rooted in our animality.[8] Whereas Kantianism treats personhood as an atemporal, self-sufficient, purely active quality of persons, Nussbaum argues that personhood involves striving, that it matures, peaks, and declines within socially and historically concrete circumstances of care and dependence. Reflection thus reveals that a good human life—a

6. See Joshua Schulz, "The Capabilities Approach and Catholic Social Teaching: An Engagement," *The Journal of Global Ethics* 12, no. 1 (2016): 29–47.

7. Ingrid Robeyns argues for *capabilitarianism* as a family of capability theories. As such, it is possible to have a capability theory that is not politically liberal. Depending on what one means by "politically liberal," Maritain's theory may be such a theory. See Robeyns, "Capabilitarianism," *Journal of Human Development and Capabilities* 17, no. 3 (2016): 397–414.

8. Nussbaum, *Frontiers of Justice*, 132ff.

life "worthy of dignity"—is constituted by a plurality of incommensurable goods ranging from bodily health, mental excellence, social affiliation, and living well with other species.[9]

Against the Aristotelian tradition, however, Nussbaum takes a distinctively Rawlsian approach to such species-based norms.[10] Affirming the fact-value distinction, she argues that insofar as human beings can function in ways which are not worth promoting (e.g., being cruel), we must select among a species' various beings and doings those capabilities that should be promoted.[11] Importantly, however, Nussbaum rejects the use of metaphysical, religious, or thick ethical doctrines as criteria for selecting valuable capabilities. She gives at least two reasons for this. First, in a pluralistic society, narrowly-justified regimes are unlikely to be stable over time.[12] Second, embedding such doctrines in positive law would be "insufficiently respectful of citizens who hold a different view," either directly or indirectly affirming inequalities among citizens.[13] In consequence, she argues, the justification of normative criteria—and *a fortiori* of valuable capabilities—must therefore be conducted on a practical rather than theoretical basis, secured through "overlapping consensus" about which capabilities are prerequisites for a wide variety of comprehensive conceptions of the good life.[14]

Given her "thick" account of the human goods, Nussbaum believes the result of this consensus will be a set of political entitlements taking the

9. See Nussbaum's most recent version of the list of central capabilities in *Creating Capabilities: The Human Development Approach* (Cambridge, Massachuesetts: Belknap Press, 2011), 33–34.

10. In *A Theory of Justice*, revised edition (Cambridge, Massachuessets: Harvard University Press, 1999), 87, Rawls argued that "the natural distribution [of goods] is neither just nor unjust; nor is it unjust that persons are born into society at some particular position. These are simply natural facts. What is just and unjust is the way that institutions deal with these facts," thus grounding claims of justice in society's obligation to rectify morally arbitrary barriers or burdens to achieving a life worthy of dignity. This claim spawned an entire field investigating the relation between luck and justice. For some discussion, see *Responsibility and Distributive Justice*, edited by Carl Knight and Zofia Stemplowska (New York: Oxford University Press, 2011).

11. Nussbaum, *Frontiers of Justice*, 181–82.

12. Nussbaum, *Creating Capabilities*, 89–90.

13. Ibid. These two points reflect the cosmopolitan assumptions that a stable regime must appeal to a wide base of persons for stability, and that metaphysics cannot have this wide appeal. Nussbaum argues that treating any metaphysical position in a privileged way—as 'more rational' than other positions—is at the same time to express negative judgments about large groups of citizens, which destabilizes the state.

14. Ibid., 90ff.

form of a concrete list of effective freedoms, or "capabilities."[15] Because these entitlements are specified "for political purposes only," justifying them requires only that they "either are or can become a part of the many comprehensive doctrines that citizens reasonably hold."[16] Capability entitlements thus constitute a *liberal, partial,* and *political* account of what is required for anyone to pursue a more comprehensive vision of the good life in a pluralistic society.[17] This "politically liberal" account is especially important if one recognizes, as Nussbaum does, a legitimate variety of ways in which human beings can realize the good for our species. It follows that only a liberty-maximizing political arrangement is respectful of or fitting for the wide range of comprehensive conceptions of the good that practical reason makes available as ways of human flourishing.

The first important consequence of this account is that governments must promote capabilities, understood as "spheres of freedom and choice," rather than functioning, since the latter would require people to behave in a certain way.[18] On the other hand, the possession of abstract political freedoms without concrete social, political, or economic means to exercise them is useless.[19] Gaps between capability and functioning thus constitute instances of injustice which generate urgent moral obligations on the part of governments to bring all citizens to minimum thresholds of capability.[20] The account of political obligations in Nussbaum's Capabilities Approach thus differs from standard accounts of human rights, which require states to refrain from injustice but not necessarily to correct injustices caused by non-state agents (such as discriminatory religious structures, markets, or genetic disability), precisely by requiring states to correct inequalities.[21]

15. Ibid., 77–8.

16. Ibid., 90.

17. See Nussbaum, *Frontiers,* 161–64.

18. Nussbaum, *Creating Capabilities,* 25. Although we identify valuable capabilities by their links to valued activities, capabilities themselves are valuable because "options are freedoms, and freedom has intrinsic value" (ibid.). Moreover, promoting capabilities rather than functioning protects pluralism in ways that can be affirmed even by those who do not value the associated functioning (110).

19. Amartya Sen articulated this foundational thesis for the Capability Approach, e.g., in *Development as Freedom* (New York: Random House, 1999).

20. Paul Formosa and Catriona Mackenzie refer to this as the gap between *status* and *achievement* dignity in "Nussbaum, Kant, and the Capabilities Approach to Dignity," *Ethical Theory and Moral Practice* 17 (2014): 880.

21. The means for correcting inequalities range from material provisioning to compulsory autonomy education for girls. See Nussbaum, *Creating Capabilities,* 148, and *Frontiers of Justice,*

Another important consequence of this account is Nussbaum's designation of states as the primary bearers of positive duties to promote capabilities. Various forms of human affiliation structure the delivery of goods, but they do not alter the content or nature of the goods themselves.[22] In fact, given Nussbaum's claims about the negative effects of having dependents on one's well-being, it would seem that only an impersonal state is even capable of providing for the central capabilities without itself suffering the crushing harms she ascribes to human caregivers.[23]

Finally, it is important to note that Nussbaum does not specify the mechanism by which we are to achieve overlapping consensus. Her examples of already-achieved overlapping consensus are wholly derived from American and international case-law.[24] On the other hand, she explicitly rejects the value of cultural and religious practices as sources of moral norms. Because she believes that society is pluralistic all the way down, she argues that "once we understand this point, it is very difficult to think of traditional values as having any normative authority at all: tradition gives us only a conversation, a debate, and we have no choice but to evaluate the different positions within it."[25] Thus, it would seem that the identification and specification of political entitlements occurs primarily at the juridical level and not within the intermediate groups of civil society. Jacques Maritain disputes precisely this point.

## III. Maritain's Communitarian Liberalism

Like Nussbaum, Jacques Maritain argues that the content of the "good" is derived from the "normality of functioning" which follows from some-

185. Also see Nussbaum's *Women and Human Development: The Capabilities Approach* (Cambridge: Cambridge University Press, 2000), especially chapter 4.

22. Nussbaum advocates public salaries for homemakers whose primary work is parenting or caring for disabled family members; reforms to the public sector regarding education that extol family-making as much as economic productivity; family-friendly job design, including extended family leave and flex-time options; and alternative-service replacements for military service. See *Frontiers*, 213–15. I criticized the claim that the mode of delivery does not alter the goods communicated in "care work" in "The Capabilities Approach and Catholic Social Teaching," cited in note 6 above.

23. See "Abortion, Dignity, and the Capabilities Approach," part of the Public Law and Legal Theory Working Paper Series at the Law School of the University of Chicago (2011). Available at < http://www.law.uchicago.edu/academics/publiclaw/index.html>.

24. Ibid.

25. Nussbaum, *Creating Capabilities*, 107; italics added.

thing's essential nature, and thus agrees with Nussbaum that the set of valuable beings is much wider than the Kantian conception of personhood allows.[26] However, whereas the fact-value distinction makes a straightforward inference from species-norms to claims about our moral obligations problematic for Nussbaum, Maritain, in contrast, possesses a teleological metaphysics and a theistic cosmology that privileges human beings among other valuable beings and justifies normative inferences from descriptions of the human essence.

Within Maritain's Aristotelian-Thomistic metaphysics, determining what is natural to a being requires making a qualitative judgment about the operations which properly belong to its essence rather than a quantitative judgment about what a being normally or frequently does. Thus, essential descriptions are functional descriptions from which one can validly infer normative conclusions.[27] Maritain argues that what Nussbaum takes to be a gap between facts and values is in fact merely a qualitative distinction between metaphysical and moral senses of normativity. In the metaphysical sense, any being is "good" if it functions in accord with the ends set by its nature: a good eye is one that sees well. Goodness only takes on a moral character for agents who, through intelligence and will, freely determine which ends they will seek, and thus for whom the seeking of the ends set by their essential nature is choiceworthy rather than necessary.[28]

Moreover, Maritain follows Aquinas in affirming that human beings are by nature ordered to the supernatural end of intellectual and loving union with a personal God whose free offer of grace must be freely accepted for the accomplishment of this end.[29] Deviation from this end thus has over-

26. Maritain writes: "Any kind of thing existing in nature, a plant, a dog, a horse, has its own natural law, that is, the 'normality of its functioning,' the proper way in which, by reason of its specific structure and specific ends, it 'should' achieve fullness of being either in its growth or in its behavior." *Man and the State*, 86–7. Of course, Nussbaum argues that all living things (except fetuses and anencephalic infants) have *equal* value, whereas Maritain does not (see *Frontiers of Justice*, 181–87; *Creating Capabilities*, 161).

27. See MacIntyre, *After Virtue*, 58. Thus, one could claim that sight is the proper function of eyeballs in virtue of their essential structure and role within sensible beings even in the land of the blind, or that procreation is the proper function of sexual organs in virtue of their complementary structure even in the land of the sterile. Indeed, unless talk of "sterility" and "blindness" is parasitic on a teleological understanding of the world, rocks would count as both blind and sterile.

28. Maritain, *Man and the State*, 86–87.

29. Maritain writes: "Human behavior pertains to a particular, privileged order which is irreducible to the general order of the cosmos and tends to a final end superior to the immanent good of the cosmos." Ibid., 87.

tones of personal offense over and above considerations of error or malfunction, just as conformity to this end has overtones of obedience and love. This affects the validity of our moral inferences as well: if my wife tells me to take out the trash, I can validly infer that I ought to do so because my love for her gives me a normative reason to please her in all things tending to her happiness. In short, Maritain argues that human beings differ from other beings in two fundamental ways. First, human beings aim at a qualitatively different end than the immanent ends than other beings, i.e., a supernatural, theistic end. Second, human beings are related to their ends in a qualitatively different way than non-rational beings are related to their ends, i.e., freely, through intellect and will. Together, these characteristics license normative inferences with a moral sense that is not possible (or intelligible) for non-human beings.

However, although he defends the validity of normative inferences from considerations of human nature in these ways, Maritain also argues that we often lack the kind of knowledge necessary for such inferences to be demonstrative. As he writes:

> Natural law is an ideal order relating to human actions . . . which depends on human nature or essence and the unchangeable necessities rooted in it. . . . [But] human situations are something existential. Neither they nor their appropriate regulations are contained in the essence of man. I would say they ask questions of that essence.[30]

And again:

> An angel who knew the human essence in his angelic manner and all the possible existential situations of man would know natural law in the infinity of its extension. But we do not.[31]

The argument seems to be this. We only know the human essence through its operations and dispositions, which are gradually revealed as they are called forth by contingent features of the world. Insofar as some actions, events, social structures, and so on, have the status of future contingents—situations which may be but do not yet exist—we can only come to know the features of human nature called forth by these situations as they are realized in the course of human history. New situations may call forth possibilities of human nature heretofore dormant, existing in us only

30. Ibid., 88.
31. Ibid., 89.

as dispositions to action, and whose compatibility with human flourishing we must now ascertain.[32] Because we have no moral perspective *sub specie aeterni*, our knowledge of the natural law (beyond its first principles) extends only as far as our dynamic knowledge of human nature—and perhaps not even this far, if philosophical reflection usually occurs *after* social change has called forth these dormant dispositions.[33]

This gnoseological element of the natural law has several implications. First, it furnishes Maritain with a multivalent notion of progress in moral philosophy.[34] Morality is quantitatively progressive because we can learn new things, such as the civil and economic rights proper to members of democratic and capitalistic societies, the knowledge of which arose alongside the development of such societies.[35] Qualitatively, changing circumstances and new insights allow us to clarify or correct what was imperfectly or erroneously believed in previous eras. In Maritain's account, the development of moral knowledge is thus similar to the development of scientific knowledge. Just as our scientific knowledge is limited by our current theories and available means of investigation, and sometimes biased or falsified by the viciousness of particular scientists or social structures, so too our moral knowledge can be limited or led astray by error, sin, or social injustice.[36]

Second, Maritain's account entails that our knowledge of natural law is practical before it is theoretical, embodied in "social patterns rather than per-

32. As Maritain writes: "Natural law is coextensive with the whole field of natural moral regulations … [including] natural obligations or rights of which we perhaps have now no idea, and of which men will become aware of in a distant future." *Man and the State*, 89. In our day, for instance, the combination of declining birthrates, aging populations, environmental change, and the movement of the young across national borders to find work has given rise to both globalist and cosmopolitan as well as nationalist and protectionist social structures. Such responses call for sustained moral reflection.

33. The natural law, Maritain concludes, is "an unwritten law," and our knowledge of it "has increased little by little as man's moral conscience has developed." *Man and the State*, 90. For a critical assessment of Maritain on this point, see Gregory Doolan, "Maritain, St. Thomas Aquinas, and the Frist Principles of the Natural Law," in *Reassessing the Liberal State: Reading Maritain's* Man and the State, edited by John Hittinger and Timothy Fuller (Washington, D.C.: The American Maritain Association, 2001; distributed by The Catholic University of America Press), 127–39.

34. Maritain claims that the recognition of a historical and developmental understanding of natural law was not available to Aquinas or the Middle Ages generally, but that these are necessary elements of a comprehensive concept of Natural Law. See *Man and the State*, 92.

35. Writes Maritain: "Human reason has now become aware not only of the rights of man as a human and a civic person, but also of his rights as a social person engaged in the process of production and consumption, especially of his rights as a working person." Ibid., 104.

36. Ibid., 93.

sonal judgments" which are constitutive parts of the common good of society.[37] Insofar as we must creatively and collectively discover which modes of living are most conducive to human flourishing given the social, political, and economic circumstances in which we find ourselves, our knowledge of ends as required (for flourishing) and achievable will change over time. Let us call this Maritain's *principle of epistemic subsidiarity*, i.e., the idea that the data of moral knowledge are generated by the social practices of plain people as they go about the business of everyday living, and that this deposit of knowledge is embodied in the virtues, practices, traditions, and social structures that constitute the common good we call "culture."[38]

Several commentators have suggested that it is in the fruitful tension between these conservative and progressive elements of Maritain's thinking that we find his most enduring insights.[39] For instance, consider this passage from *Man and the State*:

> The body politic also contains in its superior unity the family units, whose essential rights and freedoms are anterior to itself, and a multiplicity of other particular societies which proceed from the free initiative of citizens and which should be as autonomous as possible. Such is the element of pluralism inherent in every truly political society. Family, economic, cultural, education, religious life matter as much as does political life to the very existence and prosperity of the body politic. Every kind of law, from the spontaneous, unformulated group regulations to customary law and to law in the full sense of the term, contributes to the vital order of political society.[40]

Here we find Maritain defending two ideas which are not often thought to be consistent. On the one hand, he articulates the communitarian idea

37. Ibid., 92. Maritain famously infers from this that, "As a matter of fact, those *propria principia* or specific principles of Natural Law are in no way rationally deduced; they play in the practical realm a part *similar* to that of conclusions in the speculative realm. (And they appear as inferred conclusions to the 'after-knowledge' of the philosophers who have to reflect upon and explain the precepts of Natural Law.)" Ibid., 91n11. See also ibid., 9ff.

38. "It is … common inherited experience and the moral and intellectual instincts which constitute a kind of empirical, practical wisdom, much deeper and denser and much nearer the hidden complex dynamism of human life than any artificial construction of wisdom." Ibid., 11. Compare MacIntyre's critique of academic philosophy's distance from the concerns of plain persons, most recently in *Ethics in the Conflicts of Modernity: An Essay on Desire, Practical Reasoning, and Narrative* (Cambridge: Cambridge University Press, 2016), chap. 2.

39. See Brian Stiltner's excellent discussion of Maritain's communitarian liberalism in *Religion and the Common Good: Catholic Contributions to Building Community in a Liberal Society* (Lanham, Maryland: Rowman and Littlefield, 1999), especially 116ff.

40. Maritain, *Man and the State*, 11.

that human beings belong to natural and chosen societies—including familial, scientific, economic, and religious communities—which, as societies of persons, necessarily give rise to practices and bodies of law, some of which possess authority prior to any further political considerations.[41] On the other hand, he also defends the liberal idea that given the inevitable pluralism of political societies, a just body politic will be liberal in its basic structures, i.e., promote the maximum amount of liberty for persons and groups consistent with the flourishing of its intermediate societies and the individuals that comprise them. Nussbaum ultimately rejects the compatibility of these accounts on the grounds that to regard individuals as ends must mean not understanding their welfare as members of groups, whereas Maritain argues that the common good must "flow back" to members such that there is no inherent conflict between the good of individuals and the societies to which they belong.[42]

Maritain's proposal of a democratic charter of rights grows out of the dynamic character of these twin commitments. Persons, he argues, are naturally perfected by society insofar as they need others both to fulfill their deficiencies as well as to realize their excellences: persons need persons as gifts need recipients.[43] A personalist account of the common good thus claims that the social bases of flourishing must be common both to the whole—sustaining a stable and fruitful society—and to its parts *qua* wholes who are constantly transcending themselves, that is, *qua* persons. To achieve this end, the body politic must protect and provide the moral, social, conceptual, and spiritual prerequisites of authentic personal development.[44] Some of these prerequisites already exist in the form of traditions and practices, which Maritain variously describes as "good customs ... great historical remembrances ... civic conscience, political virtues and sense of right and liberty ... unconsciously operative hereditary wisdom," and so on.[45] Since these already-existing goods constitute the mode by

41. See Maritain's *Rights of Man* on the categories of personal, civic, and social rights built on the natural societies to which we belong. Each of these secures freedoms, basic needs, and participatory rights proper to itself, and such rights are natural rather than civic (and so must be respected by states). Cf. Stiltner, *Religion and the Common Good*, 117.

42. Maritain, *The Person and the Common Good*, translated by John Fitzgerald (Notre Dame, Indiana: University of Notre Dame Press, 1966), 51, 63–4.

43. Ibid., 47–48.

44. Ibid., 51–52.

45. Ibid., 52.

which cultures communicate the wisdom, virtues of character, and social structures necessary to convert merely material factors for flourishing into real opportunities for human excellence, the tasks of the body politic must include the conservation of intermediate societies as well as the creation of new conditions for human development. In this second respect then—insofar as he recognizes the rationality and normativity of traditions—Maritain's liberalism differs significantly from Nussbaum's.

However, even this description of the common good is incomplete. While it rightly recognizes that a plurality of traditions and practices can be conducive to flourishing, it does not in itself provide a means for distinguishing those traditions which in fact conduce to flourishing from those that are not. Cruel and barbaric societies develop traditions, social structures, and practices with internally-defined virtues as well. If the common good must be a *bonum honestum*, then we need some further criterion or hierarchy of values with which to judge among them.[46]

Maritain forcefully argues that knowledge of this criterion cannot be acquired from outside our traditions, either through a Platonic grasp of timeless universals or through the imposition of abstract ideals by a sovereign state. The remaining alternative is to identify those conditions in which traditions themselves become critical, reflective, and dynamically self-transcendent. A good tradition, whatever else it is, must be *minimally* dedicated to the development of those personal and political virtues necessary to sustain the search for the good life for man, for only these conditions can convert Maritain's principle of epistemic subsidiarity into good practices (*boni honesti*) generating practical knowledge.[47] A good tradition must promote the virtues necessary for philosophical inquiry into the human good—those that motivate it, such as wonder and curiosity; those that sustain it, such as a culture of patience, respectful dialogue, sustained inquiry, and intellectual courage; and those that protect it, such as the prudent recognition of a catalogue of associated vices, including duplicity, hypocrisy, intellectual servility, and the love of novelty.[48] Indeed, Maritain argues:

46. Ibid., 62–63; Maritain, *Man and the State*, 106–107.

47. See Maritain, "The Moral Rationalization of Political Life," in *Man and the State*, 58–63, and MacIntyre, *After Virtue*, 219.

48. See MacIntyre's similar arguments for the necessity of situating practices within the narrative unity of a life and a tradition in *After Virtue*, chapters 14–16.

> The mistake of bourgeois liberalism has been to conceive democratic society to be a kind of lists or arena in which all the conceptions of the bases of common life, even those most destructive to freedom and law, meet with no more than the pure and simple indifference of the body politic, while they compete before public opinion in a kind of free market of ideas, healthy or poisoned, of political life.[49]

In addition, Maritain argues, a good tradition will articulate a set of institutions and entitlements which structure and sustain these virtues, including a democratic charter of rights stipulating the positive freedoms which are the necessary political pre-conditions of the properly philosophical enterprise which mines good practices for moral knowledge.[50] In contrast, then, to modern liberalism, which advocates state neutrality before all conceptions of the good, Maritain argues that the body politic must be vivified by these commitments, what he calls a *secular faith*—a dogmatic commitment to democratic freedoms, a love of democratic structures which mitigate against secular heretics of various sorts (authoritarians, nationalists, and so forth), and hope in the intermediate social mechanisms by which true moral knowledge is generated over time.[51]

In all, there seem to be seven essential elements of Maritain's "communal liberalism":

1. An account of the human good based on a species-norm
2. An emphasis on the animal, developmental, social, and cultural elements of flourishing neglected by the classical liberal tradition
3. A communitarian and progressive account of practical reason and the development of moral knowledge
4. A personalist and moralized account of the common good (opposed to anti-metaphysical Rawlsian pragmatism)
5. Recognition of a legitimate plurality of social practices and structures conducive to human flourishing

49. Maritain, *Man and the State*, 109–110.

50. See Maritain, *Man and the State*, 114–19. As I understand it, the thrust of Maritain's thought anticipates, in an unclear way, the arguments of MacIntyre with respect to the relations between institutions, virtue, and law in *After Virtue*, 194–95 and 151ff.

51. Maritain *Man and the State*, 110. Maritain identifies as "political heretics" those persons within society who seek to undermine the political presuppositions of the democratic state, including its commitments to "freedom, or against the basic equality of men, or the dignity and rights of the human person, or the moral power of law." Ibid., 114ff.

6. An obligation on the part of the state to respect the independence of civil society and its practices as deposits and laboratories of practical wisdom
7. The need for a democratic charter of positive freedoms justified by practical rather than theoretical agreement

So described, we can identify some important agreements between Maritain and the post-Rawlsian liberalism of Martha Nussbaum. Most importantly, although Maritain differs from Nussbaum in particular in his account of the fact-value distinction, he too is circumspect about drawing direct and particular inference from considerations of human nature or social practices to obligations. Likewise, just as Nussbaum defends the role of "overlapping consensus" in the articulation of norms of social justice, so too does Maritain defend a constructive role for democratic deliberation in the development and articulation of standards of justice. Third, Maritain's personalist account of the common good and socially-embedded description of practical reasoning entails that the body politic has obligations to promote positive freedoms in its members and intermediate societies, a claim which practically if not theoretically dovetails with Nussbaum's account of capabilities as political entitlements.[52] Finally, Maritain's principle of epistemic subsidiarity entails respect for authentic pluralism as a social virtue, since the dynamism created by this pluralism is a spur to genuine progress in moral creativity, reflection, and knowledge.

## IV. Towards a More Perfect Liberalism

So what should contemporary liberalism learn from Maritain's liberalism? Maritain holds that his developmental (*gnoseological*) account of natural law does not necessitate moral progress. Indeed, insofar as practice precedes theory, moral development will be sporadic, and sometimes even regress, as the dominant practices within a culture hew closer to or stray further from the natural law. What Aquinas said of natural theology, Maritain extends to moral knowledge: it can only be imperfectly known by a few (cultures or communities), after a long time, with much admixture of error. However, one difference between theology and morality is that moral errors, at the social level, include genocides (like abortion) and holocausts.

52. See Stiltner, *Religion and the Common Good*, 124ff.

Are we to just accept such moral crises as inevitable negative externalities of the normal process by which we come to knowledge of the moral law, or does the unacceptability of such crises constitute a reason to reject a gnoseological account of natural law on the grounds that condemning such atrocities presupposes moral knowledge which, on the gnoseological account, we cannot possess before we have reflected on (and condemned) atrocities already committed?

Martha Nussbaum seems to accept the first horn of the dilemma. For instance, she argues that "national sovereignty is sufficiently important that military intervention is never justified when a nation has a decent minimum of democratic legitimacy; [and] even when that condition is not fulfilled, it is generally a very bad idea for prudential reasons."[53] According to this argument, our obligation to promote the central capabilities—analogous, I have argued, to Maritain's democratic charter of rights—is a regulative ideal which never generates genuine moral obligations to intervene even in the grossest acts of political evil. The reason is that, at the end of the day, Nussbaum views democratic deliberation as constitutive rather than investigative of the moral law. This entails obvious contradictions, of course. If the evils she counsels us not to intervene in are but "democratic deliberation" by other means, as her argument about "minimum democratic legitimacy" suggests, the same argument should apply, *mutatis mutandis,* to international military intervention.

Maritain, on the other hand, splits the horns of the dilemma. We should neither accept grave moral evils as unavoidable consequences of a *gnoseological* account of natural law, nor reject the *gnoseological* account on the grounds that it cannot provide, prior to the commission of moral evil, grounds for rejecting new instances of evil. He has two reasons, I think, for this claim. First, insofar as he offers an investigative account of the moral law, Maritain can resist the relativism hidden in Nussbaum's claims about national sovereignty without claiming Platonic knowledge of moral truths. Rather, he can defend something like the MacIntyrian account of truth as dialectically successful and so warranted claim of knowledge.[54] For Maritain argues that moral knowledge is an aggregative yet critical tradition of enquiry—one willing to learn from the past, not as a superior community,

53. Nussbaum, *Creating Capabilities,* 121.

54. This is a gross oversimplification. See *Whose Justice? Which Rationality?* (Notre Dame: University of Notre Dame Press, 1988), 366, 398.

but as a wiser one, in virtue of the fact that a living tradition is willing to correct its mistakes and take a stand on their status *as* mistakes. As such, the living tradition of natural law does not face the future with a blank slate, but rather with historically-informed and dialectically-tested principles of moral reasoning capable of providing us with secure starting points for moral reflection even when facing new moral questions.

Maritain thus places himself firmly in a moral and theological tradition running from Pope Leo XIII through MacIntyre, one which holds that the Aristotelian-Thomistic tradition of natural law is necessary but not sufficient for prudential reasoning, relevant but not deterministic in its approach to "new things." This tradition provides us with solid resources for condemning perennial grave moral evils such as genocide, while at the same time being open to what Thomistic ethicists have learned from their engagement with contemporary moral challenges.

The second reason for Maritain's rejection of the above objection to his *gnoseological* account of natural law complements his first. If moral knowledge is investigative and aggregative, as we have argued, then we can ask: In which investigative and living community does this aggregation reside? Who is the ark, floating as it were on the flotsam of history, carrying both our knowledge of the natural law, such as it is, and the story of the stiff-necked people who worked it out, through sin and repentance, in fear and trembling? Who possesses the keys of both experience and authority capable of providing contemporary thinkers with reasonable starting points for reflection? Maritain suggests an answer to that question too—and his respect for the Church is the second reason his is a more perfect liberalism.

JOSHUA D. BRUMFIELD

# Pure Means for Yesterday and Tomorrow

## The Catholic Worker's Embodiment of Maritain's Prophetic Shock-Minorities

### I. Friends Together

THIS ESSAY EXPLORES "the task of professing Christians in this day and age,"[1] that is, the use of pure means to transform society into a place in which persons are aided in their quest for the happiness that does not end. This exploration will be grounded in the mutually enriching thought and examples of Jacques Maritain, on the one hand, and of Dorothy Day, Peter Maurin, and the Catholic Worker movement, on the other. I argue that the Catholic Worker movement provides a Maritainian model of how Christians can transform political society.

It was December 8, 1932, the Feast of the Immaculate Conception. A young woman, about thirty-five years of age, was in Washington, D.C. as a journalist for *Commonweal* to cover a march of unemployed workers. The march stirred up memories of her own engagement in social activism, working and writing alongside communists and socialists, good friends. Just five years prior she had been moved to conversion by the joy of her daughter's birth and entered the Catholic Church, leaving her radical

1. Peter Maurin, "The City of God," *Easy Essays*, http://www.easyessays.org/radicals-of-the-right/. Here Maurin is summarizing what he takes to be Jacques Maritain's notion of pure means as the way to build up both a Christian society and the City of God.

friends and the love of her life for a Church which so often felt like an institution for the privileged, for those in authority. There, in that Church, she found Love Himself. She knew and deeply believed that He and His Gospel, especially in the Sermon on the Mount, held the answer to her deepest questions. Yet, having found Him, she lost her community and felt guilty for abandoning the poor to whom she felt called. And so, on that Feast of the Immaculate Conception, after the march, Dorothy Day visited the Basilica of the National Shrine of the Immaculate Conception and prayed in the crypt. She writes: "There I offered up a special prayer, a prayer which came with tears and with anguish, that some way would open for me to use what talents I possessed for my fellow workers, for the poor."[2] "And when I returned to New York I found Peter Maurin—Peter, the French peasant, whose spirit and ideas will dominate … the rest of my life."[3] Apparently, her prayer was quickly answered.

Peter Maurin, born 1877 in Southern France, was formed by the thought of Charles Péguy and Emmanuel Mounier, of Arthur Penty and Mortimer Adler, of Jacques Maritain and G. K. Chesterton, and by the lives of the saints and the social encyclicals. He eventually immigrated to Canada, and after two years of ultimately unsuccessful homesteading, he moved first to Chicago and then to New York as an undocumented immigrant. "At this time, Peter not only refused to work for pay, accepting only what students chose to donate, but also wore clothing that was donated."[4] He taught French and began writing his so-called "Easy Essays" while developing his vision—a program for going back to the sources to change hearts and minds and thereby to renew the social order.

This program aimed to "blow the dynamite of the church." In one of his Easy Essays he explained:

Writing about the Catholic Church, / a radical writer says: / "Rome will have to do more / than to play a waiting game; / she will have to use / some of the dynamite / inherent in her message." / To blow the dynamite / of a message / is the only way / to make the message dynamic. // If the Catholic Church / is not today / the dominant social dynamic force, / it is because Catholic scholars / have taken the dynamite / of the Church, / and have wrapped it up / in nice phraseology, / placed it in

2. Dorothy Day, *Long Loneliness: The Autobiography of Dorothy Day* (San Francisco: Harper and Row, 1981), 166.

3. Ibid., 166.

4. Mark and Louise Zwick, *The Catholic Worker Movement: Intellectual and Spiritual Origins* (New York: Paulist, 2005), 21.

an hermetic container /and sat on the lid. // It is about time / to blow the lid off / so the Catholic Church /may again become / the dominant social dynamic force.[5]

According to Michael Baxter, "The social theory to which Maurin referred in his essay was dynamic because it possessed an explosive ingredient: Jesus Christ. The image of dynamite jolts the listener/reader into imagining Christ and the Church in temporal rather than in purely spiritual terms. In contrast to standard Catholic social theory, [Maurin's] social theory was, in a word, ecclesial."[6] This ecclesial social theory wasn't merely a theory; Peter and Dorothy shared too sacramental a view of reality to allow the words to be left unaccompanied by actions. They put this theory into action via Peter Maurin's three-fold program, which consisted of Houses of Hospitality to tend to the poor and destitute, farming communes where scholars would work and workers would learn, and round table discussions for the clarification of thought. The coming together of scholars and workers was an important piece of the program. As Maurin explained it:

The scholars must tell the workers /what is wrong /with things as they are. / The scholars must tell the workers / how the thing would be / if they were as they should be. / The scholars must tell the workers / how a path can be made, / from the things as they are / to the things as they should be. / The scholars must collaborate / with the workers / in the making of a path / from the things as they are / to the things / as they should be.[7]

Such a discussion was the context of Jacques Maritain's first visit with the Catholic Worker community in 1934. Shortly thereafter he wrote to Peter Maurin, "Tell Dorothy Day ... how very happy I was to visit her, and how touched at the reception given me by your friends. I wish I could have said all that was in my heart—never was I more vexed by my inability to speak fluent English. It seemed as if I had found again in the Catholic Worker a little of the atmosphere of Péguy's office in the Rue de la Sorbonne. And so much good will, such courage, such generosity."[8] He and his wife Raïssa would visit several times.

5. Peter Maurin, "Blowing the Dynamite," *Easy Essays*, http://www.easyessays.org/blowing-the-dynamite/.

6. Michael Baxter, "'Blowing the Dynamite of the Church': Catholic Radicalism," in *Dorothy Day and the Catholic Worker Movement: Centenary Essays*, edited by William Thorn, Phillip Runkel, and Susan Mountin (Milwaukee, Wisconsin: Marquette University Press), 84.

7. Peter Maurin, "Scholars and Bourgeois," *Easy Essays*, http://www.easyessays.org/scholars-and-bourgeois/.

8. William D. Miller, *Dorothy Day: A Biography* (San Francisco: Harper and Row, 1982), 266.

Lifelong Catholic Worker Stanley Vishnewski explained further the mutual admiration these meetings engendered:

> The philosopher and thinker who had the greatest appeal for the early Catholic Worker was Jacques Maritain. His teaching on the use of 'Pure Means' was one of the cornerstones of the philosophy of the Catholic Worker. His maxim: 'Victory or defeat with pure means is always victory' was imbedded in our way of thinking and our activities. When Maritain came to see the Catholic Worker to give a lecture . . . [t]he place was packed with people and many had to stay outdoors. Maritain would speak for a few minutes in his soft voice and then would wait for Peter, who would translate in a booming voice that I am sure the people outside heard. A critic of the Catholic Worker told Maritain that he thought the weakness of the Catholic Worker Movement lay in the fact that it neglected political action. Maritain thought for a brief second, [then] stated that on the contrary, the Catholic Workers dealt with matters political in the true Aristotelian sense, and that there was a great need for such a work as the Catholic Workers were doing.[9]

The work they were doing, trying to make the Church the dominant social dynamic force, was precisely what Maritain thought democracy needed. For their part, Peter and Dorothy deeply embraced and promoted the thought and writing of both Jacques and Raïssa. Jacques's ideas show up regularly in Peter's Easy Essays. Dorothy made frequent reference to Jacques's work and influence and also wrote glowingly of having read Raïssa's books *We Have been Friends together* and *Adventures in Grace.*[10]

Shortly after both Jacques and Raïssa had died, Dorothy wrote in her column: "I pray not only for those who have died, but to them also. In our November issue, I hope to write about our dear departed, and about the lowliest and the highest among them. Right now, I am praying to Jacques and Raïssa Maritain."[11]

Having established their deep, lasting, and spiritual friendship, we turn to consider some aspects of Jacques Maritain's thought, focusing on those which most deeply influenced the Catholic Worker and contribute to clarifying the importance of pure means and shock minorities.

9. Stanley Vishnewski, *Wings of the Dawn* (New York: The Catholic Worker, 1984), 130–31. Quoted in Zwick and Zwick, *The Catholic Worker Movement*, 181.

10. Cf. Raïssa Maritain, *We Have Been Friends Together and Adventures in Grace: Memoirs*, edited by Michael S. Sherwin and translated by Julie Kernan (South Bend, Indiana: St. Augustine's Press, 2016).

11. Dorothy Day, *On Pilgrimage*– July/August 1973. Accessed at http://www.catholicworker.org/dorothyday/articles/532.html.

## II. Of Means and Shock-Minorities

In the January 1935 edition of the *Catholic Worker,* Peter Maurin published in his "Easy Essay" format a free translation of Maritain's then untranslated *The Temporal Regime and Liberty,* later fully translated into English as *Freedom in the Modern World.* As Maurin read him, Maritain argues that in order to bring the spirit of Integral Humanism[12] into the temporal order, Christians must go back to the roots of the Gospel, seeking a spiritual revolution prior to a social one. "It is not a question of changing the system; it is a question of changing the man who makes the system. It is not the temporal that creates the spiritual, it is the spiritual that creates the temporal environment."[13] Commitment to true radical change requires detachment and generosity and a focus on the change itself rather than its success. Becoming too concerned with success can lead to a betrayal of Christianity. As Maurin explains, "to be engaged in Christian reconstruction and not to do it in a Christian manner would misrepresent it for the sake of making it prevail [and] to so misrepresent it would be the most treacherous way to betray Christianity."[14] What follows from this is Maurin's succinct summary of Maritain's "pure means."[15] Peter explains: "People trying to bring about a Christian reconstruction of the social order, must be made aware of the great temptation to use unchristian means.... 'The pure means are the strongest means.'"[16] Focusing on success rather than conversion leads to an attempt to guarantee success through impure means—the temptation to use power, whether economic, military, or otherwise. Not only is this a betrayal of Christianity, it also will not work. Only pure means—the spiritual means available to the poor—can effectuate a radically Christian

12. "Integral Humanism" names Maritain's attempt to establish the philosophical basis for a personalist theory of democracy by integrating the various aspects of the human person. That is, integral humanism simultaneously recognizes the primacy of the spiritual or supernatural end of each person over the (temporal) common good of the society and maintains the priority of the common good over the individual persons' private temporal good.

13. Peter Maurin, "Pure Means—Ethical Choices," *Houston Catholic Worker* (Houston: Casa Juan Diego, 1995). Accessed at: http://cjd.org/1995/11/01/pure-means-ethical-choices-jacques-and-Raïssa-maritain/.

14. Peter Maurin, "Pure Means—Ethical Choices," *Houston Catholic Worker.*

15. In *Freedom and the Modern World,* Maritain discusses "poor means" and the "Purification of Means." In *Man and the State,* he revisits the "Problem of Means" and sometimes refers to "spiritual means." The Catholic Workers, perhaps due to Maritain's word choice in their presence, tend to prioritize the phrase "pure means." I follow their usage in most of what follows.

16. Peter Maurin, "Pure Means – Ethical Choices," *Houston Catholic Worker.*

reorientation of the temporal order. Anything else may more rapidly bring about social change, but its effects will not be Christian in the end and will do violence to the person.

Maritain's trust in the power of pure, spiritual means came from personal experience. His calls for peace and refusal to take sides in the Spanish Civil War made him many powerful enemies. Reflecting on this, he wrote: "Why is it that unarmed writers, who haven't taken sides with any political camp and who are looking for nothing but truth and peace, appear to them 'more formidable than the enemy in the trenches?' One has to believe that the testimony we are trying to give in favor of justice is troubling the consciences of certain leaders."[17] Maritain's pure means were having an effect; since the victory is ultimately assured, there is no warrant to turn to impure means:

> What we must find out is whether a *political* conception of religion or an *evangelical* concept of religion is to prevail. And on the spiritual level, whatever may be the trials that the world must pass through, those who believe in the Gospel can be absolutely certain to triumph in the end, for it is in behalf of those values most dear to the heart of Christ that they are fighting. We can never accept, nor can the Church ever accept, that extermination is a means for the apostolate, or that adherence to a temporal cause, to a movement of military insurrection, whatever opinion someone might have about it from a political point of view, can ever become a measure of orthodoxy.[18]

Indeed, for Maritain there exists real and concrete Christian responsibilities: "The Christian does not give his soul to the world. But he must go to the world, he must speak to the world, he must be in the world and in the very heart of the world."[19] But, Maurin cautions, this ought not resemble a changing of the masses. After all, "[i]t is not necessary that the majority be changed. Revolutions are the work of the few." A revolution of Christian radicalism need be no different. These few must embody the Christian heroism of the cross exercised in the public square for the transformation of society. Can all this happen? Maurin concludes his Easy Essay version of Maritain's book as follows: "Will a Christian transformation of the social

17. Quoted by Jean-Luc Barré in his *Jacques and Raïssa Maritain: Beggars for Heaven*, translated by Bernard Doering (Notre Dame, Indiana: University of Notre Dame Press, 2005), 334. Barré is quoting from Jacques Maritain's "Rézponse de Jacques Maritain" in *Cahiers Jacques Maritain*, *21* (November, 1990). 54–55. https://gallica.bnf.fr/ark:/12148/bpt6k97699929/f56.image.

18. Quoted by Barré in *Jacques and Raïssa Maritain*, 322.

19. Ibid., 319.

order come to realization in this century? A Christian transformation cannot come about in the same way that other transformations come about. A Christian transformation will be the product of Christian heroism."[20]

In his 1951 book *Man and the State,* published two years after Maurin's death, Jacques Maritain revisits some of these issues, with new emphases. His examination of the essence of the democratic idea and the relation of modern man to modern political society contained therein help to further contextualize the modern problems as he saw them. To understand precisely what it is that the heroism of the Christian few aims to change—the nation? the state? the community? society?—careful distinctions must be made. Maritain explains that communities arise out of nature and the social relations of "given historical situations and environments." Therefore, communities include "regional, and ethnic groups and social classes."[21] Societies, on the other hand, arise out of the reason and will, are shaped by men rather than by the accidents of history, geography, or ethnicity. To speak of "business firms, labor unions, and political parties"[22] is to refer to societies.

Maritain explains: "Now the nation is a community, not a society ... a human community based on the fact of birth and lineage, yet with all the moral connotations of those terms."[23] Therefore, the nation is not the state. The modern history of this confusion, Maritain maintains, has been disastrous. Whereas the nation is a people, a community, the state and the body politic (or political society) are both societies which arise out of human freedom and can make appeals for assent and consent. Nor are the state and political society identical. Political society pertains to the whole, while the State is the topmost part of the political society.[24] In political society law comes up from below through the people and rises to the top, to the State, which, on the other hand, is that part of the whole which is made up of the institutions pertaining to the good of the whole. Therefore, the state is "an instrument in the service of man. Putting man at the service of that instrument is political perversion. The human person as an individual is for the body politic and the body politic is for the human person as a per-

20. Peter Maurin, "Pure Means – Ethical Choices," *Houston Catholic Worker.*
21. Jacques Maritain, *Man and the State* (Chicago: University of Chicago Press, 1979), 3–4.
22. Ibid., 2–4.
23. Ibid., 4–5
24. Ibid., 9–10.

son. But man is by no means for the State. The State is for man."[25] All of this flows from Maritain's personalism and his Thomist notion of the Common Good.[26] This personalism implies that the Christian few ought not to seek the overthrowing of the State but to transform the members of political society, since, in Maurin's summation, "It is not a question of changing the system; it is a question of changing the man who makes the system."[27]

Unfortunately, in place of this properly instrumental view of the state as for man, an absolutist view of the state has been accepted. On the level of the human person, the rise of voluntarism[28] and individualism led to what Walker Percy called the "modern malaise"[29] and to what Charles Taylor describes as "buffered selves."[30] On the societal level, they have led to rival perversions of the State and its relation to man, claiming for the State the sovereignty which belongs to God alone. This sovereignty tends toward totalitarianism and the exercise of the State's self-proclaimed absolute power.[31] Maurin succinctly endorsed Maritain's view against such instrumentalism in an Easy Essay called "Give Me Liberty":

> Patrick Henry said / "Give me liberty or give me death!" / What makes man a man is the right use of liberty. / The rugged individualists / of the Liberty League, / the strong-arm men / of the Fascist State / and the rugged collectivists / of the Communist Party / have not yet learned / the right use of liberty. / Read *Freedom in the Modern World,* / by Jacques Maritain.[32]

In light of the perversion of the State's relation to man, Maritain revisits the problem of means, which is "a twofold problem": first, asking

25. Ibid., 13.

26. For Maritain, this means, "[t]he end of a society [is] the good of the community, of the social body. But if the good of the social body is not understood to be a common good of persons, just as the social body itself is a whole of human persons this conception would lead to errors of a totalitarian type. The common good of the city is neither the mere collection of private goods, nor the proper good of a whole.... It is the good human life of the multitude of persons; it is their communion in good living. It is therefore common to both the whole and the parts into which it flows back and which, in turn, must benefit from it." Maritain, *The Person and the Common Good* (South Bend, Indiana: University of Notre Dame Press, 1973), 50–51.

27. Peter Maurin. "Pure Means – Ethical Choices," *Houston Catholic Worker.*

28. Briefly put, voluntarism, as I here intend it, elevates the individual person's will over the common good and even over human nature as given by God.

29. For example, see Walker Percy, "Diagnosing the Modern Malaise," in *Signposts in a Strange Land* (New York: Picador, 2000), 204–221.

30. For example, see Charles Taylor, *A Secular Age* (Cambridge: Belknap, 2007).

31. Maritain, *Man and the State*, 50–54.

32. Peter Maurin, "Give me Liberty," *Easy Essays,* http://www.easyessays.org/communitarian-personalism/.

how the State should strive toward its proper end and, second, considering by which means the people can "supervise or control the state."[33] Put another way, the current ubiquity of the individualist liberal hegemony indicates the profound dilution of the people's freedom and capacity for self-government by an overreaching state and an apparently biased or bought press. In such a debilitated condition, how might the people reform themselves, the body politic, and the State so that democracy can function as it ought: with the State in service to man as person and to the common good?

The end of political society, contrary to present practices, is not to ensure the material prosperity of individuals, a technological dominance over nature, or "political mastery over men."[34] Rather, explains Maritain, "It is to better the conditions of human life itself, or to procure the common good of the multitude,"[35] which means that the political society is ordered toward developing a civilization and culture which engenders the human development of each member. Some states attempt to achieve this temporal end through a technical rationalization of political life, leading them to adopt Machiavellian means such as power, violence, perfidy, and lawless greed. Maritain admits this approach has an impressive record for garnering immediate success for individuals, though not long-term success for a state or a nation.[36] As impressive as they may be, violence and treachery only serve to dehumanize persons, to break down freedom and conscience. Therefore, they do not work for the common good. Instead impure means place the body politic on the path of self-destruction. Thus, states must adopt a moral rationalization of political life by making use of pure means. The telos of democracy, which is justice and freedom rightly understood, cannot be achieved by means antithetical to that end.

But our concern is more directly the means by which the people can supervise the state. In a democracy, the people supervise the state through regular elections, the peaceful exchange of power, the free press, and citizen-led advocacy groups. However, Maritain maintains these are not enough. Less obvious but more fundamental, the men and women who make up political society must be willing and able habitually to govern

33. Maritain, *Man and the State*, 54.
34. Ibid.
35. Ibid.
36. Ibid., 56–57.

themselves in their daily affairs so that they can develop and maintain the capacity to offer to those in authority the programs, initiatives, and reforms which serve their needs and their good and which thus come from them, from the roots.[37] The capacity of the people to fulfil this responsibility is limited by an overreaching state that lulls people to sleep with welfare programs which handicap and entertainment which anesthetizes. Another means is necessary to awaken the people, what Maritain calls the "means of spiritual warfare."

Spiritual warfare cannot rely on material force but rather reflects the principle act of fortitude, which is not the courage to attack, but that of bearing suffering patiently, courage in enduring.[38] This was precisely the poor means to which Maritain referred in his earlier work *Freedom in the Modern World* and which so influenced and captivated the Catholic Workers' call for pure means. These spiritual means are vital in the struggle "of the people to maintain or gain control over the State" and in the struggle of Christians "to transform civilization by making it actually Christian."[39] They are the existential element which fosters the dynamic political movement that is the lifeblood of a healthy democracy. This activity is generally accomplished by the work of the few, "the prophetic shock minorities."[40] If democracy is government by the people, then the people need prophets to awaken them to "something better than everyone's daily business," to the fact they are *the* people.[41] Maritain suggests Gandhi and Thomas Jefferson as prophets in this sense. We might add Martin Luther King Jr.[42] In light of the historical circumstances surrounding the rise of modern democracy, that is, its connection with liberalism and absolutism, modern democracy needs Christian prophetic minorities to awaken the people to their dignity as persons who are not mere individuals, to the freedom and justice on which legitimate democracy depends, and to the sovereignty of God who alone possesses the transcendent independence and power for such a claim.

37. Ibid., 67–68.
38. Cf. Thomas Aquinas, *Summa theologiae* II-II, q. 123, a. 6.
39. Maritain, *Man and the State*, 70.
40. Ibid., 139.
41. Ibid., 140.
42. Ibid., 141.

## III. The Catholic Worker—a Prophetic Shock Minority

Dorothy, Peter, and the Catholic Worker movement represent just such a prophetic minority. They recognized the importance of consistently going to the roots—to the Liturgy, to the Sermon on the Mount, to the Lord—in order to remain radical in the best sense. Dorothy explained, "If we do not keep indoctrinating, we lose the vision. And if we lose the vision, we become merely philanthropists, doling out palliatives. The vision is this. We are working for 'a new heaven and new *earth*, wherein justice dwelleth.' We are trying to say with action, 'Thy will be done on *earth* as it is in heaven.' We are working for a Christian social order."[43] Maritain would go a step further, stating that "the democratic state of mind … cannot exist without [the inspiration of the Gospel]."[44] Thus, when Dorothy saw the poor and the worker being driven into destitution, when she saw the violence of a system which prioritizes the wealth of the few disintegrating into forms of tyranny, then she recognized the Christian responsibility to wake up political society. Peter Maurin shared this view: "To build up the City of God, / that is to say, / to express the spiritual / in the material / through the use / of pure means, / such is the task / of professing Christians / in this day and age."[45]

Indeed, these prophetic few sought to build up the City of God, to work for a Christian social order within the shell of a liberal social order marked by individualism, acquisitivism, and absolutism. They sought to do so with the purest of means: prayer, penance, and love. Dorothy explained their position well in the June 1940 *The Catholic Worker*: "Instead of gearing ourselves in this country for a gigantic production of death-dealing bombers and men trained to kill, we should be producing food, medical supplies, ambulances, doctors and nurses for the works of mercy, to heal and rebuild a shattered world." She proceeded to narrate a Catholic Worker's defense of Maritain's "Pure Means":

43. Dorothy Day, "Aims and Purposes," in *Modern Spiritual Masters: Writings on Contemplation and Compassion*, edited by Robert Ellsberg (New York: Orbis, 2011), 169; italics in original.

44. Maritain, *Christianity and Democracy* (Freeport, New York: Books for Libraries Press, 1972), 49.

45. Maurin, "The City of God."

> At a meeting of the Catholic Worker when Maritain spoke a few weeks ago, the question was asked: 'What other means are there besides the use of an even greater force than that of the enemy?' Mrs. De Bethune ... spoke up from where she was sitting: "Prayer and penance," she said, recalling what to all should have first come to mind. There had been little mention of it made that evening.[46]

Finally, Dorothy concluded by urging for the use of the poor and pure means of love:

> We are urging what is a seeming impossibility—a training to the use of non-violent means of opposing injustice, servitude and a deprivation of the means of holding fast to the Faith. It is again the Folly of the Cross. But how else is the Word of God to be kept alive in the world? That Word is Love, and we are bidden to love God and to love one another. It is the whole law, it is all of life. Nothing else matters.[47]

In a 1955 article explaining the reasons behind their protest of the air raids and their subsequent arrest, Dorothy went back to Maritain's *True Humanism*. "Jacques Maritain, the French philosopher has written, 'We are turning towards men, to speak and act among them, on the temporal plane, because, by our faith, by our baptism, by our confirmation, tiny as we are, we have the vocation of infusing into the world, wheresoever we are, the sap and savor of Christianity.'"[48] Dorothy and Peter lived to infuse the world with the savor of Christianity. Their lives "stressed the need of building a new society within the shell of the old, 'a society in which it is easier for people to be good,' knowing that when people are good, they are happy."[49]

Just what were the "Pure Means" through which they hoped to build a Christian social order in the shell of the individualistic liberal order? Here I highlight three aspects of the movement which reflect their embodiment of Maritain's principles, respond to the particular call of prophetic minori-

46. Dorothy Day, "Our Stand," *The Catholic Worker*, June 1940, pp. 1 and 4. Accessed at: http://www.catholicworker.org/dorothyday/articles/360.pdf

47. Ibid.

48. Dorothy Day, "Where Are the Poor? They Are in Prisons, Too," *The Catholic Worker*, July–August 1955, pp. 1 and 8. Accessed at: http://www.catholicworker.org/dorothyday/articles/241.html. Dorothy explained, "Just before two p.m. we went to the park and sat down on the benches there, and when the sirens began their warning we continued to sit. That was all there was to it. A number of elaborately uniformed men with much brass, stars and ribbons upon their blue auxiliary police outfits marched upon us and told us to move. When we refused, they announced we were under arrest, and the police van was driven up inside the park, up over the curb, and we were loaded in and driven away."

49. Dorothy Day, *The Long Loneliness*, 170.

ties today, and offer the possibility of blowing the dynamite of the Church's message once again: They are: (1) a withdrawal from technology into community; (2) transcendence of polarized political positions via radically Catholic positions; (3) a commitment to the Mystical Body of Christ lived in the Works of Mercy.

(1) Considering the ubiquity of individualist liberalism, one might describe liberal society as a riptide which grabs persons and pulls them into the deep. We cannot swim against the tide. The message is too pervasive; the tide too strong. We would be swept away. Rather than directly opposing it, escaping a riptide requires swimming perpendicular to the tide, to withdraw from it to rest, to gather one's strength before continuing. This withdrawal is not defeatism, quietism, or escapism. It is withdrawal for action, for awakening the people to be in community with them.

Through their placement of farming communities as a plank of their social theory, their persistent return to the Gospel, their avoidance of the radio and other technologies, Dorothy and Peter bore witness to the importance and power of withdrawal for the sake of waking up.

Many are now drugged into evil indifference by opiates and alcohol, but more often by soft cushions, excessive consumption, and glowing screens. Dorothy and Peter recognized the need to withdraw for continual re-formation. As Dorothy admitted: "The problem is gigantic. There is homelessness, famine, fear, and war, and the threat of war. We live in a time of gigantic evil. It is hopeless to think of combating it by any means than that of sanctity. To think of overcoming such evil by material means, by alleviations, by changes in the social order only—all this is utterly hopeless."[50] Dorothy Day's prophetic minority can both remind us of the need for withdrawal from internet opiates and evil economics in order to be formed in the Mystical Body and at the same time awaken us out of our indifference to the only radical activism which can confront our world, that activism based in sanctity.

(2) Their integration of monastic and liturgical piety with personalist radicalism allows them to transcend the many polarizations of modern society. They do not neatly fit labels. The too common race riots, gender tyranny, capitalist cronyism, school shootings, instances of euthanasia, and attacks on the unborn make it clearer now than it was when Dorothy

50. Dorothy Day as quoted in Miller, *Dorothy Day: A Biography*, 432.

said: "People are just beginning to realize how deep-seated the evil is. This is why we must be Catholic Radicals, we must get down to the roots."[51] Deep rootedness in the dynamism of the Gospel places Catholic workers outside the binary cultural categories and empowers them to bridge the gap, to be a force for unity in a splintering world. Today they can show Christians how to offer a third way to a troubled world and how to find the unity which is the basis of Christian community and mature democracy.

(3) Their commitment to the Mystical Body of Christ lived in the Works of Mercy were the match and wick with which they aimed to blow the Church's dynamite, enabling it to again become the dominant social dynamic force. As Dorothy explained: "We consider the spiritual and corporal Works of Mercy and the following of Christ to be the best revolutionary technique and a means for changing the social order rather than perpetuating it. Did not thousands of monasteries, with their hospitality, change the entire social patterns of their day?"[52]

In a time when one party enforces the tyranny of social liberalism with policies aimed at undermining the family and sequestering religion in the private sphere, while the other doubles down on economic cronyism and military imperialism, and when the poor are robbed of their dignity and responsibility by an indifferent society and a paternalist state, it is naïve to suppose that pious platitudes, multitudinous marches, and political platforms will either fix the social order or save souls. And so, with Jacques Maritain, we ought to place our hope in Christian prophetic minorities to remind us that the Works of Mercy are prerequisites for making the Church once again the dominant social dynamic force. As Dorothy believed:

> There is nothing that we can do but love, and dear God, please enlarge our hearts to love each other, to love our neighbor, to love our enemy as well as our friend.... We are supposed to love as Christ loved.... That was the New commandment. To love to the extent of laying down our lives, dying to ourselves. To accept the least place, to sit back, to ask nothing for ourselves, to serve each other, to lay down our lives for our brothers, this is the strange upside-down teaching of the Gospel.[53]

51. Dorothy Day quoting Peter Maurin in "Peter Maurin 1877–1977," in *The Catholic Worker*, May 1977, pp. 1 and 9. Accessed at: http://www.catholicworker.org/dorothyday/articles/256.html.

52. Dorothy Day, "Catholic Worker Ideas on Hospitality," *The Catholic Worker* May 1940, p. 10. Accessed online at http://dorothyday.catholicworker.org/articles/358.html.

53. Dorothy Day, "Love is the Measure," *The Catholic Worker*, June 1946, p. 2. Accessed online at: http://dorothyday.catholicworker.org/articles/425-plain.htm.

This is the strange upside-down example modeled by Dorothy Day and called for by Maritain's Pure Means. These are the pure means that are the strongest means for starting the right kind, the Christ-kind, of revolution. This is what Day and Maritain still contribute to the transformation of our disintegrated social order.[54]

54. I am grateful to Solidarity Hall Press for permission to adapt for this essay portions of "The Dorothy Option? Dorothy, Benedict, and the Future of the Church," in *Dorothy Day and the Church: Past, Present, and Future.*

ROBERT DELANEY

# Consumerism and Secular Statism

## Two Political Forces Opposing the Person and the Common Good

### I. Introduction

JACQUES MARITAIN'S *The Person and the Common Good* and its foundational metaphysics in *Existence and the Existent* have ever greater relevance in a time of mass immigration, Brexit, American political turmoil, and global terrorism. Both secular statism and its sometime adversary, global consumerism, are in crisis. This essay analyzes both systems and considers what is often thought a quaint but impossible alternative in distributism.[1]

While technology abolishes distance, it has not brought us together when it serves global consumerism or secular statism. Even more than politics, metaphysics is local. Indeed, *locality* is paramount in a society dedicated to the person and the common good. Maritain writes:

> We hold that every materialistic philosophy of man and society [is] blind to the realities of the spirit; responsive only to what belongs to the world of matter, they see in man no more than the shadow of true personality, his material individuality. This alone in man are they able to express. Actually, they jeopardize the person

1. Alasdair MacIntyre's recent *Ethics in the Conflicts of Modernity: An Essay on Desire, Practical Reasoning, and Narrative* discusses how distributism arose from a Thomist critique of both Marxism and Capitalism in the early twentieth century.

either by dissolving it in anarchy or, as inexorably happens under the pressure of political necessities, by subjecting it to the social body as number, economic community, national or racial state.[2]

Two systems that undermine human dignity are consumerism and post-Marxist secular statism. They are the extremes of secular capitalism and globalist socialism.

At first these systems seem polar opposites. Nevertheless, they are plagued by the same disease. Both harm the people involved; both deny that "the person is for the community and the community for the person."[3] Consumerism asserts that community is for the individual, and thus the individual[4] should constitute the community. Secular statism requires that the person be for the community, and so the individual should be subjugated to the community.

## II. Consumerism: The Commodification of Personhood

Consumerism, Maritain writes, comes from "bourgeois liberalism [which is the] ambition to ground everything in the unchecked initiative of the individual, conceived as a little God, and the absolute liberty of property, business and pleasure."[5] Consumerism should not be confused with capitalism. John Paul II condemned the former but endorsed, with qualification, the latter.[6] While consumerism stems from capitalism, capitalism need not devolve into consumerism.[7] Consumerism is "the way of living in which the person, at least in practice, makes consumer goods the object of his heart's desire; that is, they become the source of his identity and the goal toward which his life is oriented."[8] Consumerism can be seen in political ideology. Even though we see ourselves as either "left" or "right," both camps fall into the consumerism of our age. One abandons moral values

2.Jacques Maritain, *The Person and the Common Good*, translated by J. Fitzgerald (Notre Dame, Indiana: University of Notre Dame Press, 1973), 91.

3. Maritain, *The Person and the Common Good*, 85.

4. I use individual and person interchangeably without denying the metaphysical distinction between them.

5. Maritain, *The Person and the Common Good*, 91.

6. Cf. Raymond de Souza, "John Paul II and the Problem of Consumerism," *Religion & Liberty* 9, no. 5 (September and October 1999): 8–10.

7. It is not the scope of this essay to distinguish the difference between the two.

8. Ibid., 8.

for the sake of license, while the other consumes the poor for monetary gain. Both consume for the sake of happiness, yet both become emptier.

Pursuing liberty and happiness is not wrong. But consumerist ideology devolves into having the liberty to gratify any pleasure without regard to moral law. The individual in a consumerist society, instead of learning that he has inalienable rights given by God, is taught the "virtues" of relativism and turns to creating artificial "rights." People claim the "right" to abortion and the "right" to same-sex marriage. The individual becomes the highest good. The consumerists of rights and freedom strip away rights while supposing that they are granting them. They scoff at the person who honors tradition and demonize the person who opposes the majority. Consumerist freedom reduces truth to popular opinion.

In contrast, for Maritain,

> Truths do not depend upon the social community but concern the order of absolute goods of the person as such. The community will never have the right to require[man] to hold as true [one truth] rather than any other [because it] is deemed to be more in conformity with the law of the social group.[9]

Yet the clamoring of consumerism professes to free man but locks him in the cage of his ego. For Maritain, material individuality[10] causes me to "absorb everything into myself and, sacrificing everything to my uniqueness, I am riveted to absolute selfishness and pride."[11] The irony of such consumerism in a democracy is that it ultimately destroys it. Freedom is corrupted into the tyranny of passion; elections are only fair if the consumerist culture wins; religion is subjugated to the secular government. This "freedom" destroys all in its path. Like Plato's "leaky jar," filling one perforated jar from another, it is never filled by the pleasures it seeks.[12]

Consumerism's economic plan equates worth with money or fame. This leads us to deny our inherent dignity in favor of our socio-economic status. Today, worth comes from idolization of the social elites. We follow the moral, social, economic, and fashion codes of those "at the top," because we think this can make us happy. Yet consumerism occludes the

9. Ibid., 74.

10. Ibid., 44.

11. Jacques Maritain, *Existence and the Existent,* translated by J. Galantiere and G. B. Phelan (New York: Pantheon, 1948), 82.

12. Plato, *Gorgias* 493a-d, from *Plato: Complete Works,* edited by J. M. Cooper (Indianapolis, Indiana: Hackett, 1997), 836.

worth of the person *as person*. Often people realize how unhappy glamour and money make them and drift into despondency. The turn to debased pleasures results: most egregiously, sex slavery and pornography and drug addiction. Sadly, we deny the reality of reaching "rock bottom." There is always something to be consumed, even if it is not immediately debased. Whether it be the new tech, new celebrity gossip, or new diet fad, consumerist society distracts us with things irrelevant to our naturally supernatural desire[13] to be happy.

Consumerism makes us believe that only "I" matter. It creates individuals who care only for themselves. Thus, when a political election or new legislation does not favor consumerist individualism, civil unrest ensues. The community is ravaged. The drive to consume products at a low cost and with high efficiency leads businesses to feast on the most vulnerable. Worst of all, consumerism brings about the ignorance of the beauty of the world and of man himself. We consume the world around us rather than marvel at it.

As Maritain writes:

> We shall never know everything there is to know about the tiniest blade of grass or the least ripple in the stream. In the world of existence there are only subjects or *supposita*, and that which emanates from them into being. This is why ours is a world of nature and adventure, filled with events, contingency, chance, and where the course of events is flexible and mutable whereas the laws of essence, [and by it consumability], are necessary.[14]

13. The designation "naturally supernatural" or "trans-natural," is utilized to express our human-and-divine relationship, permeating the course of all human lives and dramatically distinguishing us from the closed-nature of the animals. See Jacques Maritain, *Approaches to God*, translated by P. O'Reilly (New York: Harper, 1954), 111–12: "Nothing is more human than for man to desire naturally things impossible to his nature. It is, indeed, the property of a nature which is not closed up in matter like the nature of physical things, but which is intellectual or infinitized by the spirit. It is the property of a metaphysical nature. Such desires reach for the infinite, because the intellect thirsts for Being and Being is infinite. They are natural, but one may also call them transnatural. [And this desire] ... [i]s not a simple velleity, a superadded desire, a desire of super-erogation. It is born in the very depths of the thirst of our intellect for Being; it is a nostalgia so pro-foundly human that all the wisdom and all the folly of man's behaviour has in it its most secret reason. And because this desire which asks for what is impossible to nature is a desire of nature in its pro-foundest depths, St. Thomas Aquinas asserts that it cannot issue in an absolute impossibility. It is in no wise necessary that it be satisfied, since it asks for what is impossible for nature. But it is necessary that by some means (which is not nature) it be able to be satisfied, since it necessarily emanates from nature." See also Plato, *Symposium* 212a, from *Plato: Complete Works*, edited by J. M. Cooper (Indianapolis, Indiana: Hackett, 1997), 494.

14. Maritain, *The Person and the Common Good*, 74.

Consumerism turns us away from the good of both ourselves and society. Its "freedom" becomes the tyranny of all. As Daniel Schwindt observes: "freedom should not be understood as the arbitrary exercise of the individual's will, but [as] the ability to direct one's will toward a certain end—the good."[15]

Indeed, Maritain writes:

> The common good of civil life is an ultimate end, but an ultimate end in a relative sense and in a certain order. It is lost if it is closed within itself, for, of its very nature, it is intended to favor the higher end of the human person. The human person's vocation to goods which transcend it is embodied in the essence of the common good. To ignore these truths is to sin at the same time, and by the same token, against both the human person and the common good.[16]

Consumerism indulges only in what is pleasurable, believing that man "will be like God" (Gen 3:5) by way of usurpation. In the Beginning that lie led man into sin; it does so today. Consumerism encourages us to step on whomever and whatever in order to consume as much as we can. We do so when we feast off the poor who pay rent for substandard housing, when we hire illegal immigrants to avoid paying fair wages, or when we allow prostitution rings wherever there is a major sporting event.

Yet no one actually enjoys the consumerist society. We dislike its extremes, but we cannot see the threat of the consumerist ideal itself. Maritain spoke prophetically about the political nature of society:

> The tendency towards materialism and atheism inherent in *the city of the individual* appears as one of the absurdities by which it destroys itself. In the political order, the internal dialectic of this tendency, by a similar absurdity, drags it toward dictatorship which is its proper negation. These reflections lead us to believe that the drama of the modern democracies has consisted in the unwitting quest of something good, the city of persons, masked by the error of the city of the individual which, by nature, leads to dreadful liquidation.[17]

This anything-goes liberal consumerism is the forerunner of fascism, not its alternative. As we have learned, the city of the individual has undermined the democratic city of persons of equal worth. The city of the individual leads us to the tyranny of both our own ego and the few who hold

15. Daniel Schwindt, *Catholic Social Teaching: A New Synthesis (Rerum Novarum to Laudato Si')* (McPherson, Kansas: Agnus Dei, 2015), 50.

16. Maritain, *The Person and the Common Good*, 64.

17. Ibid., 104–105.

power. Nonetheless, even though it seems that the goods of democracy are lost, they are not. They can be realized in a new society. But we must first consider the other dreary alternative prevalent today.

## III. Secular Statism

Secular statism sees the person as a collective part of the state, as well might an offspring of Marxist ideology. Secular statism is a response to the abuses of the person that result from a consumeristic/capitalistic culture. While secular statism is correct to respond to consumerism, its response to capitalism aggravates consumerism's wounds; indeed, it actualizes a range of potential disfigurements in the framework of global capitalism. Schwindt observes that "there is no place . . . for the [consumerist] ideology. But at the same time we must be careful to avoid that even greater error, which arose as a false cure for the [consumerist] disease, a cure that was worse than the disease itself, called socialism."[18]

Secular statism's roots lead to the Marx who "held that capitalism involves the domination of the workers (the proletariat) by a minority (the owners, or the bourgeoisie)" and who "opposed the commodification of labor which for him rendered the worker politically as well as economically powerless."[19] In response to the abuses of an individualistic and consumeristic culture, secular statism imposes new restrictions on the person with the aim of strict collectivism. Here I will highlight three of secular statism's ancestral principles in Marxism:

1. The means of production should not be privately owned.
2. Human history is the story of class warfare, and the worker gains more freedom in a revolution that will abolish private property, in that doing so will cause the state no longer to be needed.
3. Marxism advocates this revolution in the current system of ownership to bring about the communist state.[20]

These principles are problematic if only because they worsen the situation. As *Rerum Novarum* taught:

18. Schwindt, *Catholic Social Teaching: A New Synthesis*, 96

19. Donald Goldman, "Distributism and Marxism," *The Hound of Distributism*, edited by R. Aleman (Charlotte, North Carolina: The American Chesterton Society, 2015), 112.

20. Ibid., 112–13.

> But [Marxists'] contentions are so clearly powerless to end the controversy that were they carried into effect the working man himself would be among the first to suffer. They are, moreover, emphatically unjust, for they would rob the lawful possessor, distort the functions of the state, and create utter confusion in the community. To remedy these wrongs the socialists, working on the poor man's envy of the rich, are striving to do away with private property, and contend that individual possessions should become the common property of all, to be administered by the state or municipal bodies.[21]

That "the working man himself would be the first to suffer" is true in a secularist society and surely ironic. After all, the poor man in a consumerist society is just as poor as the poor man in the secular state. The only difference is that instead of the tyranny coming from the few who influence a society, it comes from the state itself. The poor are stripped of what little dignity they do have in the consumerist society; individuality is absorbed into collectivity.[22] The understanding of man as simply a part of collectivity rather than a unique individual is disturbing.

For as Maritain reminds us: "Let us keep in mind this essential point … namely that, if the person of itself requires 'to be part of' society, or 'to be a member of society,' this in no w[ay] means that it must be in a society in the way in which a part is in a whole. On the contrary, the person, as person, requires to be treated as a whole in society."[23] Secular statism proclaims the opposite. The person is simply a part of the whole. If a person is part of a whole, then he is repeatable, common, and to be used for the greater whole. This ideology ignores the dignity of each person.[24] The person becomes a means to an end. Thus it becomes plausible for the weakest in a society to be used for medical experiments to "better the community" or to resort to slave labor for the sake of the many. The poor are made slaves to abolish poverty and people are oppressed to end oppression. This system leaves the person "to the perspective of objectivity … absorbed into everything, and, dissolving into the world." [25]

The irony is that secular statism and consumerism see the person

21. Pope Leo XIII, *Rerum Novarum: Encyclical of Pope Leo XII on Capital and Labor* (Vatican City: Libreria Editrice Vaticana, 2006), no. 4.

22. Cf. C. E. Curran, *Catholic Social Teaching, 1891–Present: A Historical, Theological, and Ethical Analysis* (Washington, D.C.: Georgetown University Press, 2002), 202.

23. Maritain, *The Person and the Common Good*, 53.

24. Ibid., 68.

25. Maritain, *Existence and the Existent*, 82.

through the shared lenses of economism. Economism "is the reduction [of the person] to the economic or material level, on the assumption that if the economy [or state] succeeds, all other social goods will be fulfilled as a result."[26] The person in a secular society is of worth only if he is useful in the economic structure of the state. Otherwise he can be thrown away as unfit. Behind this consumerist façade, "the primary aim of the marshaling is no longer to procure the freedom of expansion of the person but simply the good and maximum production of the economic whole."[27] The secular state supports an atheism which replaces the transcendent with the belief in the state as god.[28] It replaces the godless system of consumerism because "communism makes economics God.... Capitalism denies that economics is subject to a higher moral order. Communism says that economics is morality."[29]

Consider what Maritain says about man in relation to the state:

> Man is constituted a person, made for God and life eternal, before he is constituted a part of the city; and he is constituted a part of the family society before he is constituted part of the political society. This is the origin of those primordial rights which political society must respect and which it may not injure when it requires service of its members.[30]

The intriguing thing about the secular state making economics its god is that it still follows the Maritainian formula. Communist ideology can see the truth that man is first made for the divine before he is made for the state, which is why it replaces God with economics, which allows the state to force the person to submit to the economic Will. The fact that the secular state makes economics a god allows for the high priests of the state to offer human sacrifice to their merciless god.

The secular state's solution to the problem of capitalism makes it worse. It replaces capitalism, a system that is not intrinsically evil, but which often leads to abuses and which is paramount in consumerism, with a system that *is* intrinsically evil, harming the dignity of the human person.[31] What

26. Schwindt, *Catholic Social Teaching*, 98.

27. Maritain, *The Person and the Common Good*, 94.

28. Charles Curran, *Catholic Social Teaching*, 202.

29. Tobias Lanz, *Beyond Capitalism and Socialism: A New Statement of an Old Ideal: A Twenty-First Century Apologia for Social and Economic Sanity* (Norfolk, Virginia: Light in the Darkness, 2008), xix.

30. Maritain, *The Person and the Common Good*, 75.

31. Curran, *Catholic Social Teaching*, 200.

is more dumbfounding is that the secular state does not change any of the secular capitalist problems it aims to fix.[32] Global statism turns out to be fraudulent because

> it does not accept the view that consumption is a trivial thing, to be kept down to the minimum. On the contrary, it adheres to the fundamental belief of [consumerism] that there must be ever more worldly goods to be enjoyed.... The moral seduction of [secular statism] lies in the fact that it repudiates the methodical exploitation of the personal interest motive, of the fleshy appetites, of egoism, which held pride of place in the economic society it has undertaken to supersede; yet that, insofar as it has endorsed this society's pursuit of ever-increasing consumption, it has become ... torn by an inner contradiction.[33]

Outwardly, the secular state does remedy the issues of capitalism[34] but only to take away its positive aspects. These include a place for the market, private property, profit, and entrepreneurship. Not only does it destroy the positive attributes of capitalism, it disallows the expression of our inherent dignity which these positive aspects of capitalism sometimes bring about. At this point it seems that there is no solution to the crisis at hand, and we must choose the lesser of two evils. But I think there is another way.

## IV. Solution: A Look Back and a Step Forward

To find a solution, we must revisit the striking similarities between consumerism and secular statism. They share two problematic themes. The first is that both ideologies take on a secular nature. One says that God does not need to be a part of economics and politics, while the other replaces God with economics. Their second common theme is economism, that is, "the reduction of all social concerns to the economic or material level, on

32. "Like Marxism, capitalism ensures that the bulk of society will be composed of workers laboring for a wage, unlikely to ever become the owners of productive property. Like Marxism, capitalism ensures the bulk of these workers will never have any significant political power, because they will never have the economic independence that will grant them an influence in the political process even remotely similar to that of the owners of productive property. Like Marxism, capitalism ensures that society is strictly defined into two classes, those who control the use of productive property and those who don't. Like Marxism, capitalism ensures that those who belong to the first group have the bulk of the power, including power over those who belong to the second." Goldman, "Distributism and Marxism," 112.

33. Bertrand De Jouvenel, *The Ethics of Redistribution* (Indianapolis, Indiana: Liberty Fund, 1990), 15.

34. As Alasdair Macintyre notes, "secreted within Marxism from the outset is a certain radical individualism." See his *After Virtue* (London: Bloomsbury Academic, 2007), 303.

the assumption that if the economy succeeds, all other social goods will be fulfilled as a result."[35] Economism sees both social concerns and the person from this same vantage point. This is a direct result of destroying the divine relation to man, and it betrays the dignity of the person.

The person's relation to the state must be understood primarily within our relation to God, so that what is fundamental to the political system becomes a relationship of persons identified *as persons*. This statement seems contrary to the understanding of the separation of Church and State, but the opposite is true. The State should view the person in accord with an integral Christian humanism, because the Church reveals the Church and State's natural relation; it *sets* the line, so to speak, and does not *cross* it. It is in the agreement on what man is that the Church and State can understand their own distinction. It is in the agreement that "all men are created equal, that they are endowed by their Creator with certain inalienable Rights" that the separation of Church and State can begin. Both are interconnected because man is a political creature and has a Creator. In this regard, Church and State are necessary if we are to understand our personhood. On these grounds Church and State must recognize man's purpose and goal. About man's end, Maritain writes that "St. Thomas teaches that [man's] perfection consists in charity, and that each [person] is bound to tend towards perfection of love according to his condition and in so far as it is in his power."[36]

If man's end is in charity, then it becomes clearer how the State and the Church bring man to this end. The Church draws him into a closer relationship with Him Who is Love. With the state, clarity is a bit more difficult. First we must see why man has a state although nothing else in nature does. As Aristotle notes, "the real difference between man and other animals is that humans alone have perception of good and evil, just and unjust, and so forth. It is the sharing of a common view in *these* matters that makes a household and a state."[37] If, as Maritain says, morality depends upon love, then the state needs a morality based on love, that is, the willing of the good of the other as other. In this regard, we must understand that the nature of morality depends on the two commandments of Christ: Love your neighbor as yourself and love the Lord your God with all your mind,

35. Schwindt, *Catholic Social* Teaching, 98.

36. Maritain, *Existence and the Existent*, 58–59.

37.Aristotle, *Politics* 1.2, 1253a7–15, from *The Basic Works of Aristotle*, translated by Richard McKeon (New York: Random House, 1941), 1129.

all your heart, and all your soul.[38] The state protects the person by understanding him with regard to love. A political system must promote and sustain the person who realizes that:

> If God exists, then not I, but He is the center; and this time not [only] in relation to a certain particular perspective, like that in which each created subjectivity is the center of the universe it knows, but speaking absolutely, and as transcendent subjectivity to which all subjectivities are referred. At such time I can know both that I am without importance and that my destiny is of highest importance. I can know this without falling into pride, know it without being false to my uniqueness. Because loving the divine Subject more than myself, it is for Him that I love myself, it is to do as He wished that I wish above all else to accomplish my destiny; and because, unimportant as I am in the world, I am important to Him; not only I, but all the other subjectivities whose lovableness is revealed in Him and for Him and which are henceforward, together with me, a we, called to rejoice in His life.[39]

If the state could so understand the person, then man could achieve happiness. Sadly, however, we have no system that even sees this as a goal; we have, rather, two systems that work against this understanding. Consumerism, which claims that "I" am the center of the universe, is brought to tears when it realizes that the universe moves on, with or without the existence of its supposed "center." Secular statism, discounting individuality, claims that the global community is the most important thing—which leads to man fighting his restless heart which is made for more than the global community. We need a politics that makes the common good, which is love, its overarching goal.

Is there a political system that fits these criteria? We dare not underestimate the weight of our sins, and it would be easy to entertain utopian dreams. Nonetheless, we must work to build such a society. The system I propose finds inspiration in Distributism, Catholic Social Teaching, and Maritain's *The Person and the Common Good.* First, this society should adopt Maritain's view:

> The end of a society [is] the good of the community, of the social body. But if the Good of the social body is not understood to be a common good of persons, just as the social body itself is a whole of human persons, this conception would lead to errors of a totalitarian type. The common good of the city is neither the mere

38. Mark 12:30–31, from *The Douay-Rheims New Testament of Our Lord and Savior Jesus Christ.* compiled by Rev. Fr. G. Haydock (Monrovia, California: Catholic Treasures, 1991).

39. Maritain, *Existence and the Existent,* 82–83.

collection of private goods, nor the proper good of a whole which, like the species with respect to its individuals or the hive with respect to its bees, relates the parts to itself alone and sacrifices them to itself. It is the good human life of the multitude of persons; it is their communion in good living. It is therefore common to both the whole and the parts into which it flows back and which, in turn, must benefit from it.[40]

To reach a system that can meet the goals of the common good, we must keep three goals in mind. The first is to create a society that is locally dependent on the members of the community, and thus independent *because* of the local community. The second is to honor the right to private property, so that every person can work to help the community.[41] The third, and most important, is to emphasize the family unit as the most important group in society. These goals do not constitute a manual, nor can we deny the existential and personal nature a society must possess. Each society has unique needs.

To bring about the common good requires that we know the local community and bring it front and center. Localism, indeed, might require that for our own good we sacrifice consumerist commodities to which we are accustomed. This means developing local industries so that we can achieve sustainability. As St. Thomas says of community: "In it should be found everything sufficient for human life ... for it is originally made for living, namely, that men might find sufficiently that from which they might be able to live; but from its existence it comes about that men not only live but that they live well insofar as by the laws of the city human life is ordered to the virtues."[42] This suggests that the community would grow its own crops, build its own furniture, make its own shoes, provide stores run by local people, and harvest its own natural resources, thus minimizing the influence of large scale industries.[43] All this is important for community self-reliance and for a sense of relationship among its members.[44] As Russell Sparks writes:

40. Maritain, *The Person and the Common Good,* 50–51.

41. For an explanation of the difference between the redistribution of property and income, see Bertrand De Jouvenel's *The Ethics of Redistribution.*

42. St. Thomas Aquinas, *Commentary on Aristotle's Politics,* I, lect. 1, n. 31, in *Medieval Political Philosophy: A Sourcebook,* edited by R. Lerner, translated by E. L. Fortin and P. D. O'Neill (New York: Free Press, 1963).

43. Cf. Alonzo Smith, "Distributism and Conventional Economic Theory," *The Chesterton Review* 5, no. 2 (1979): 232.

44. For insights on how to implement the distributist economic system, see John Médaille's *Toward a Truly Free Market.*

> [W]hen … producers see their role as simply providing the necessary goods that [the local community] needs, production has a natural limit. There is no need to persuade people to buy something, because they already know their needs. And the producers themselves will tend to limit their own desire for wealth to what families need in order to survive and to live in a truly human nature."[45]

The beauty of this system is that it can truly provide for the common good, because each person relies on the other; each person matters. If one person becomes sick or is injured, it affects the community as a whole. Each person is interwoven in the community; each receives care in the context of a natural filial relationship.

The importance of locality in the political sphere that sees love as man's end is critical. It can best be achieved in a system that "does not require a high degree of governmental intervention, [nor tries] at every turn to overthrow government. It looks to establish stability by customs and good habits as well as by good government and good laws, all of which encourage local networks of production, exchange, and consumption."[46] When we focus on the local political sphere, supported by a local economy, we can focus on the common good. Government that relies on the local community builds solidarity. Local governance calls for accountability from its politicians and makes citizens more aware of local politics. In a healthy local society, T. S. Eliot wrote, "public affairs would be the business of everybody, or of the great majority."[47] The reliance on a local government also allows the community to solve economic and moral issues in a way that fits community needs. As Maritain observed:

> The same moral case never appears twice in the world. To speak absolutely strictly, precedent does not exist. Each time I find myself in a situation requiring me to do a new thing to bring into an act that is unique in the world, an act which must be in conformity in the world, an act which must be in conformity with the moral law in a manner and under conditions belonging strictly to me alone and which has never arisen before. Useless to thumb through the dictionary of cases of conscience! Moral treatises will of course tell me the universal rule or rules I am bound to apply; they will not tell me how I, the unique I, am to apply them in the unique context in which I am involved.[48]

45. Russel Sparkes, "Chesterton as Economist," *The Hound of Distributism*, 46.

46. William Fahey, "Towards a Description of Distributism," *The Hound of Distributism*, 22.

47. T. S. Eliot, *Christianity and Culture: The Idea of a Christian Society, and, Notes Towards the Definition of Culture* (New York: Harcourt, 1968), 159.

48. Maritain, *Existence and the Existent*, 60.

If this be the case, it only makes sense to have local communities provide solutions to their problems since they can best apply a just solution to a given situation.

To ensure that such a system can come about, every person in the community must own property. Property helps protect the dignity of each person, because "there is nothing like property for casting a protective mantle around the human personality and reminding the other person he has rights."[49] Allowing each person to own a piece of property that he can call his own is instrumental in bringing the local community to fruition. Private property gives man the opportunity to make a livelihood and allows him to use it how he chooses. The person needs a defense against both the abuse of secular statism and the capitalist enslavement of property. "If productive property [is] widely distributed, then more individuals would have the necessary resources to be self-employed."[50] Property allows us to be productive members of society.[51] Moreover, ownership offers the mystical power of man over matter. Man is made man—after the fact that he prays—by the fact that he ploughs, that he builds, that he cuts wood for transport or carves it for an ornament; in short, by the fact that he has this mystical privilege of mastery over the material universe. The one essentially true idea of democracy is the desire to make what is true of man true of a 'man'; that is, if possible, of any man.[52]

The last, but most important, part of this society is the family. For Maritain, society cannot thrive without the gifts which come from persons born of family and locality, so much so that the family society must be constituted prior, not only temporally but hierarchically, to the political society.[53] Because of that, the society that is created must be a "society in which the families composing it are, in a determining number, owners of the land and the means of production as well as themselves the agents of production (that is, the people who by their human energy produce wealth

49. James Canovan and Margaret Canovan, "Chesterton's Politics Today," *The Chesterton Review* 5, no. 2 (1979): 273.

50. Smith, "Distributism and Conventional Economic Theory," 245.

51. Cf. Schwindt, *Catholic Social Teaching*, 42: "Everyone ought to have the opportunity to share in the goods of the earth is a dictate of natural law, but since the best way of achieving the widespread and responsible use of goods does not lie in communal ownership, we choose instead to implement the institution of private property. Private property is a good which is 'super imposed' on top of the universal destination of goods in order to serve it."

52. Smith, "Distributism and Conventional Economic Theory," 238.

53. Maritain, *The Person and the Common Good*, 75.

with the means of production)."[54] The reason the family has to be the most fundamental part of this society, is that if the most local thing in the world, the family, is not the cornerstone of both economics and politics, then a local society will fail. In a society that is based on the development of the person towards his final end, which is love, the family is decisive. The fact that we all have a family is the basis of what we have in common; the family is the center of society. To be sure, it is more difficult in practice than in theory to fashion healthy families. Yet, a society focused on developing the complete person, rather than producing profit, encourages the family to flourish.

The consumerist society and global statism are at best indifferent to the family, and at worst work against it. Consumerism puts career and profit first. Global statism stands ready to mandate how many children one can have. The society that we have explored in this paper sees man as having an allegiance to his family before society. Because of that, everything man does is directed towards his family's well-being and happiness, as sought in a community that has love as its overarching goal. When a person creates a business with his own private property, he does so not for a "desire for wealth [but for] what their families need in order to survive and to live in a truly human manner."[55]

The family is where the generations of tomorrow are taught the first rules about life; it is where the current generation begins its adventure, and where the legacies and lessons of past generations are remembered. The family is where the story of mankind reaches into the next generation ready to embrace the beauty, and terror, that this world offers. The way we treat our own family correlates with how we treat those around us. If we cannot treat our family with hospitality, then we cannot treat immigrants with hospitality. If we cannot spend time with our family to show that they matter to us, then we cannot show the poor that they matter to us. If we cannot speak to those we love with kindness, then we cannot speak to the person we are purchasing lunch from with kindness. It makes sense that a society that has a divorce rate of fifty percent is so broken. A society that disregards family life will disregard the human person. When a society places the family at its center, then love becomes its overarching goal.

Maritain well knew the power of love:

54. Fahey, "Towards a Description of Distributism," in *The Hound of Distributism*, 14.
55. Sparks, "Chesterton as Economist," *The Hound of Distributism*, 46.

By love, finally, is shattered the impossibility of knowing the other except as object. I have emphasized this impossibility ... and noted that it directly concerns the senses and the intellect. To say that union in love makes the being we love another self for us is to say that it makes that being another subjectivity that is ours. To the degree that we truly love ... we acquire an obscure knowledge of the being we love, similar to that which we possess of ourselves; we know that being in his very subjectivity ... by this experience of union. Then he himself is, in a certain degree, cured of his solitude; he can, though still disquieted, rest for a moment in the nest of knowledge that we possess of him as subject.[56]

The only way we can have this love is by first learning how to love our family. It is a training ground for how to love everyone. A society that has as its goal love, and by it happiness, must focus on the family. If we can build a society full of families that know how to love, and thus the meaning of happiness, then we can build a community that can bring us to love each other.

## V. Conclusion

The human person is the reason political societies exist. But what we see today is, as T. S. Eliot noted, the contrary, for "the kind of political theory which has arisen ... is less concerned with human nature, which it is inclined to treat as something which can always be refashioned to fit whatever political form is regarded as most desirable."[57] This is, of course, contrary to the nature of the person.

As Maritain writes:

In the person there are some things—and they are the most important and sacred ones—which transcend political society and draw man in his entirety above political society—the very same whole man who, by reason of another category of things, is in part of political society. By reason of certain relations to common life which concern our whole being, we are a part of the state; but by reason of other relations, things more important than the common life, there are goods and values in us which are neither by nor for the state, which are outside the state.[58]

The two societies that we considered, Consumerism and Secular Statism, wrongly believe all the goods we need can be found in the market or the state. We have to reject those two societies and begin to develop our

56. Maritain, *Existence and the Existent*, 90–99.
57. T. S. Eliot, *Christianity and Culture*, 163–64.
58. Maritain, *The Person and the Common Good*, 73.

own. The society proposed is not perfect, but it can promote the common good for all. What is most important in such a society is the family. The common good is most accessible in the family; it is there that we must start to change our society. The family is our most important work of service. Our work does not demand extraordinary deeds. Rather, it is by doing what seems small deeds that we follow, as St. Teresa of Avila knew, the road of sanctity.

Today's global technological determinism is a far cry from the global village. Notably, it was Marshall McLuhan who wrote of a great distributist:

> Mr. Chesterton has exposed the Christless cynicism of the supposedly iron laws of economics and has shown that history is a road that must often be reconsidered and even retraced. For, if Progress implies a goal, it does not imply that all roads lead to it inevitably. And today, when the goal of Progress is no longer clear, the word is simply an excuse for procrastination.[59]

59. Marshall McLuhan, "G. K. Chesterton: A Practical Mystic," *The Dalhousie Review* 15, no. 4 (1936): 457.

# V

# DISPUTING CULTURAL CONFUSION

JAMES M. JACOBS

# Intensive Subjectivity and the Paradoxical Need for Society

## I. Introduction

THE 2016 ELECTION, and the histrionic reactions it engendered, have led many to comment that American society is facing a crisis. Our government, our institutions, and our very unity as a nation have been brought into question. An antidote for these ills is clearly called for. One such prescription has been offered by Robert George, in his widely disseminated essay outlining the "Five Pillars of a Decent and Dynamic Society."[1] The pre-eminent concern for any thriving society, according to George, is to safeguard the dignity of the person. This indeed is crucial. Yet, even if respect for persons is accepted as foundational, if the nature of personhood is misconstrued, society will fail to flourish; the structures it erects will not conform to the true needs of the persons it is meant to serve.[2] A nominal respect for dignity and rights is not enough; rights must reflect the reality of the human person. I will argue that it is this incongruity

1. Robert George, "Five Pillars of a Decent and Dynamic Society," in *The Thriving Society: On the Social Conditions of Human Flourishing*, edited by James R. Stoner and Harold James (Princeton, New Jersey: Witherspoon Institute, 2015), 1–8.

2. Heinrich Rommen comments, in *The State in Catholic Thought: A Treatise in Political Philosophy* (St. Louis: B. Herder, 1945), 306: "Life is a perpetually changing stream of noble and ignoble impulses, of love and hate, of ardent striving for justice and recurrent betrayal of spiritual values for material advantage. Thus, the actual forms of social life are always in danger of being abused or of becoming obsolete or unfit to reach their objective ends and thus obnoxious to the very end which they ought to serve. It is, therefore, always necessary to measure the actual forms in this historical working by the ideal philosophical end of these social forms."

that is at the source of our contemporary malaise: our notion of rights does not align with the truth of human nature. Jacques Maritain's description of the person illuminates and augments the key insight of George's argument: while contemporary society gives centrality to the person, it does so in a pathological fashion which repudiates the transcendent orientation of the human person to both other persons and to God and so dissolves community. Our contemporary crises can be corrected only by an acceptance of the natural law's insistence on the social nature of human perfection. In the end, it will be clear that persons merit respect not as autonomous atoms; rather, the human person realizes his dignity only in community with other persons.

## II. George's Proposal

We begin from the principle that, for a society to flourish, it must first be *decent*, that is, respectful of the basic dignity of the citizen. Robert George specifies three pillars that are necessary for the development of a decent society: respect for every human person as of equal worth and dignity; the integrity of the family as the constitutive foundation of society and the first school of virtue; an effective system of law which both defends peace and justice and which orders society toward attaining common goods.[3] Thus, any society must acknowledge the interpenetrating spheres of person, family, and *polis* as necessary conditions for moral adequacy.[4] To these pillars, George adds two others which are engines for a *dynamic* society: the universities, which expand the realm of knowledge, and businesses, which expand the wealth and technological capacities of a society.[5]

While I think George is correct in his enumeration of principles, his concision obscures a crucial fact about them for which I will argue: they

3. George, "Five Pillars," in *The Thriving Society*, 1–3.

4. These foundational principles are not new; indeed, Rommen notes that this triad is foundational to the Western Tradition: "Catholic political philosophy distinguishes three essential different circles of human existence, each of which has its own ends, its own rights and duties, and consequently its own organizing and order-producing power. But these circles are not utterly separated. They live in a kind of symbiosis and are equally necessary that man may realize his end." *The State in Catholic Thought*, 376.

5. George, "Five Pillars," in *The Thriving Society*, 4. I would add that these businesses must be based on true human needs and not the commodification of arbitrary desire; see Yves Simon, *Work, Society, and Culture*, edited by Vukan Kuic (New York: Fordham University Press, 1971), esp. 116–42.

are not five disparate principles but are an integrated whole which flow necessarily from an *adequate idea* of the human person. Respect for person, then, is not just first in order of importance; it is first metaphysically, since the other principles are merely immediate conclusions following from the nature of person as the subject for whom society exists. In other words, the relation between the person and the social structures of family and state, on the one hand, and the operations of the mediating institutions of business and education, on the other, are not merely contingent; rather, they exemplify the essential characteristic of personhood as relationally ordered to the attainment of virtue, love, and wisdom in communion with others. Thus, these social institutions are the *necessary means* by which a human being actualizes his capacity for happiness.

Since these pillars mutually entail one another, if the notion of person is erroneous, then the other pillars will be similarly distorted. That is, if we misunderstand the person, we will misunderstand the family and state, and the relation of all three of those to mediating institutions will go similarly astray. The significance of this fact is noted by Roger Scruton in a critical analysis of George's essay. Scruton observes that the notion of *person* has migrated from its origin in philosophy and theology and is now "embedded in the social and political norms of the modern world."[6] He continues, "Precisely because it is so widely accepted as foundational ... the idea of the person has been detached from the history that gave rise to it and presented in purely abstract terms, as a rational construct that is not dependent on any specific experience of community.... [Accordingly,] we find ourselves today with a deeply conflicted idea of the person upon which we nevertheless rely as the premise of our collective decision making." Thus, the modern notion of person, once abstracted from the natural conditions of human flourishing, becomes a cipher upon which each inscribes his own predilections and caprices. It is no wonder, then, that society is in crisis. Scruton's own response to this is to reject the notion of person as an autonomous atom, and to assert the essential social nature of person, especially as reflected in a traditional moral vision based on communal relations.[7] He concludes that virtue can only flourish in communities of

6. Roger Scruton, "The Person and the Parson," in *The Thriving Society*, 38.

7. "The function of the virtues is ... to ensure that our actions stem from our own accountability and self-conception and that they cement the relations of dependency and commitment on which our lives depend." Scruton, "The Person and the Parson," in *The Thriving Society*, 44.

paternal and fraternal correction: "Human beings find their fulfillment in mutual love and self-giving, but they get to this point via a long path of self-development, in which imitation, obedience, and self-control are necessary moments."[8]

## III. Maritain and Intensive Subjectivity

While Scruton's assessment is true, the pragmatic focus on the communal nature of man, even backed up with Scruton's nostalgia, fails to justify *why* man should defer to communal interests. What is necessary is to uncover the essence of man as person, which will elucidate the teleological implications which Scruton implicitly discerns. Maritain's insights are valuable here, for his presentation emphasizes the nature of person in terms of what I would call *intensive subjectivity*. To explicate this term, I would like to cite at length a passage from Maritain's *Existence and the Existent* in which he places personhood in the context of the ladder of being:

> God does not create essences to which he can be imagined as giving a last rub of the sandpaper of subsistence before sending them forth into existence! God creates existent subjects or supposita which subsist in the individual nature that constitutes them and which receive from the creative influx their nature as well as their subsistence, their existence, and their activity. Each of them possesses an essence and pours itself out in action.... In the world of existence there are only subjects or supposita, and that which emanates from them into being. This is why ours is a world of nature and adventure, filled with events, contingency, chance, and where the course of events is flexible and mutable whereas the laws of essence are necessary. We know those subjects, we shall never get through knowing them. We do not know them as subjects, we know them by objectising [*sic*] them.... We know subjects not as subjects, but as objects, and therefore only in such-and-such intelligible aspects....
>
> As we pass progressively to higher degrees in the scale of beings, we deal with subjects of existence or supposita more and more rich in inner complexity, whose individuality is more and more concentrated and integrated, whose action manifests a more and more perfect spontaneity, from the merely transitive activity of inanimate bodies to the occultly immanent activity of vegetable life, the definitely immanent activity of sentient life, and the perfectly immanent activity of the life of the intellect. At this last degree the threshold of free choice is crossed and therewith the threshold of independence properly so-called (however imperfect it be) and of personality. With man, liberty of spontaneity becomes liberty of autonomy,

8. Ibid., 46.

the *suppositum* becomes *persona*, that is, a whole which subsists and exists in virtue of the very subsistence and existence of its spiritual soul, and acts by setting itself its own ends.[9]

Maritain's argument is that while every entity possesses a subjectivity that is radically unique because its singular act of existence brings to reality an essence with distinctive powers, the way in which subjectivity is possessed is not univocal; on the contrary, the radical individuality arising from subjectivity increases in relation to the degree of immanent activity which realizes a proportional ontological uniqueness manifested through that activity. In other words, there is an analogical deepening of intensive subjectivity as one ascends the ladder of being. This reaches its zenith in *supposita* who by virtue of rational powers can intellectually grasp objective truth and concomitantly exercise free choice, thereby granting them control over their activity and so constituting them as subjects in the proper sense. Thus, inanimate substances, whose activity is merely reactive and so determined, exercise subjectivity in a minimal fashion, so that no two atoms of the same element have the same career, but nevertheless behave in an utterly law-like fashion. The life activity of plants and animals, which as immanent is individuated in a more radical fashion, establishes subjectivity in a more intensive mode because life grants true spontaneity to action; yet even that activity, as purely natural and instinctive, does not allow for true self-determination. The apex of subjectivity lies in personhood where freedom empowers subjects in the fullest sense of the term, *supposita* which determine their own acts thereby constituting unique and unrepeatable individuals.

It is this power of self-determination that leads Thomas Aquinas to argue that the person is the "most perfect [substance] in all nature."[10] This perfection, reflecting the principle of intensive subjectivity, is a consequence of the immanent perfections arising from rationality. Rational cognition, which apprehends the necessary truths of being, frees persons from the uncertainty of sensory appearances and the contingency of opinion.

9. Jacques Maritain, *Existence and the Existent*, translated by Lewis Galantiere and Gerald B. Phelan (Garden City, New York: Image Books, 1956), 74–75. This argument is inspired by Thomas's argument in *Summa contra gentiles* 4.11, translated by Anton C. Pegis, James F. Anderson, Vernon J. Bourke, and Charles J. O'Neil (1955; reprinted, Notre Dame, Indiana: University of Notre Dame Press, 1975), 79–90.

10. Thomas Aquinas, *Summa theologiae* I, q. 29, a. 3. Henceforth, ST; all citations taken from the translation by the Fathers of the English Dominican Province (New York: Benzinger, 1948).

Rational appetite, or will, gives persons the ability to choose the true good, thereby freeing them from the tyrannical control of instinctive desires. Because of this knowledge and ability to choose, persons have dominion over their actions: persons, as Thomas says, "are not only made to act, like others; but ... can act of themselves."[11] Because of this dominion over their acts, persons have a unique kind of individuality; they alone exercise choice,[12] which endows them with a moral responsibility for actions. Persons are, therefore, subjects in the complete sense of the term.

Now this notion of dominion might tempt one to think that persons are autonomous. That is, one might believe that our freedom extends not just to freedom of choice, but also to the capacity to determine the very goal of personhood itself. This would make every person an atom defining his own existence; in this, subjectivity would outstrip the human nature that is its foundation. Maritain pre-emptively closes off this potentially disastrous misinterpretation of personal dominion by emphasizing that this freedom is in service to human nature's teleological end. Being able to control our own actions does not mean that we are autonomous atoms. On the contrary, as Maritain insists, the rationality that is the source of dominion only attains perfection in reaching out to other persons in love: "[Perfection] consists in loving ... [;] it consists in the plenitude and refinement of dialogue and union of person with person."[13] Union with others is necessary simply because of the nature of human rationality:[14] the intellect by nature seeks truth; the will by nature seeks to order its love according to the objective worth of the object. But both of these pursuits—growing in wisdom and love—are of necessity intersubjective activities, and so are possible only in communion with others. Wisdom arises from dialogue; love arises in opening the self to others. This teleology has priority over any

11. ST I, q. 29, a. 1.

12. See ST I, q. 83, a. 1; I-II, q. 6, a. 1; and I-II, q. 13, a. 2; cf. SCG II, chaps. 47–48.

13. Maritain, *Existence and the Existent*, 58. For this reason, Robert Spaemann, in *Persons: The Difference between "Someone" and "Something,"* translated by Oliver O'Donovan (Oxford: Oxford University Press, 2007), 27, argues that the very notion of person can arise only in the community of similarly endowed beings: "The difference between the person and its condition, or the king of being it is, is found immediately in the fact that a person so understood can only be thought of in relation to other persons, i.e., in the plurality."

14. I distinguish human rationality here because the other analogical modes of personhood—angelic and divine—as intellectual, but not rational, do not require community in the same way man does. See James M. Jacobs, "The Metaphysical Nature of Personhood and the Need for Analogy," *Heythrop Journal* 49 (July 2018): 707–720.

exercise of subjective dominion, for dominion exists for the sake of this *telos*; as Maritain notes: "Even before the exercise of free choice, the most deeply rooted need of the person is to communicate with *the other* by the union of the intelligence, and with *others* by the affective union."[15]

## IV. The Error of Autonomy

More recently, however, this subordination of personal freedom to man's communal end has been overwhelmed by an outsized notion of subjective dominion. This idea of human freedom tends to view the will not in terms of final causality, that is, as ordered to the good of perfection of human nature through communal interaction, but as a naked efficient cause which has unlimited self-determination. Such an analysis is presented in a recent book by Thomas Pfau. He shows how modern thought, in denying final causality in general, has also denied the teleological order of the will. That teleological orientation has been replaced by an idea of the will as a mere efficient cause, whose efficiency, because it is not ordered to an end, is utterly self-justifying. Lacking an orientation to perfection, personhood is reduced to the brute act of choice itself. Accordingly, personhood has become "a mere heuristic *punctum*, an interchangeable, generic 'self' devoid of all essence and reduced to an indifferent variable, a mere bearer of claim rights exclusively actuated by inscrutable compulsions and desires."[16]

Other scholars have discerned, from a variety of intellectual perspectives, the same problem. For example, Steven B. Smith documents the degeneration of the notion of personhood in modernity in demonstrating how, once the idea of a *telos* by which to evaluate choice has been surrendered, "the idea of the bourgeois, once considered virtually synonymous with the free and responsible individual, [became] associated with a kind of low-minded materialism, moral cowardice, and philistinism."[17] Respect for traditional social relations based on moral values has been replaced

15. Maritain, *Existence and the Existent*, 88; italics in original. Maritain nicely epitomizes the nature of this communion in love (90): "By love, finally, is shattered the impossibility of knowing another except as object. . . . To say the union in love makes the being we love another *ourself* for us is to say that it makes that being another subjectivity for us, another subjectivity that is ours."

16. Thomas Pfau, *Minding the Modern: Human Agency, Intellectual Traditions, and Responsible Knowledge* (Notre Dame, Indiana: University of Notre Dame Press, 2013), 379.

17. Steven B. Smith, *Modernity and Its Discontents: Making and Unmaking the Bourgeois from Machiavelli to Bellow* (New Haven: Yale University Press, 2016), xi.

by resentment against those values specifically because they frustrate the unlimited self-expression demanded by modernity. Smith identifies Machiavelli as the fountainhead of this change, for he insisted that the causal principles of politics were "understood to be not the Aristotelian study of [teleological] ends but efficient cause or the study of means."[18] This Machiavellian will is sheer efficiency acting apart from any standard of goodness; the ability to act takes precedence over any consideration of what one ought to do. This certainly describes the amoral machinations for power in contemporary politics, but these same attitudes are readily identifiable in all modern interpersonal relations where personhood is seen as justifying utterly autonomous self-expression.[19]

In a similar fashion, Charles Taylor describes the rise of our modern secularism and atheism in terms of what he calls the "buffered self," a person whose freedom disconnects him from all natural attachments and objectivizing moral values. Taylor argues that in modernity subjectivity has become disengaged from external defining contexts, leaving only a radical inwardness for each individual. This inwardness has three main facets, each of which exalts the inviolable isolation of subjectivity: a self-responsible independence, a recognized particularity, and an individualism of personal commitment.[20] We can easily see how each of these facets distorts the nature of dominion because it abstracts the person from the necessity of communion. This asocial exercise of dominion then puts the self resolutely at the center of his world, resulting in a pathological subjectivism in which all value is relativized. Taylor describes this situation:

> For the modern, buffered self, the possibility exists of taking a distance from, disengaging from everything outside the mind. My ultimate purposes are those which arise *within me*, the crucial meanings of things are those defined in *my responses* to them.... The buffered self can form the ambition of disengaging from whatever is beyond the boundary [of the ego], and of giving its own autonomous order to its life. The absence of fear can be not just enjoyed but seen as an opportunity for self-control and self-direction.[21]

18. Ibid., 7.

19. That autonomy, when taken seriously, is incompatible with any moral system was pointed out directly and succinctly by Nietzsche, *The Genealogy of Morals*, Second Essay, section II.

20. Charles Taylor, *Sources of the Self: The Making of the Modern Identity* (Cambridge, Massachusetts: Harvard University Press, 1989), 185.

21. Charles Taylor, *A Secular Age* (Cambridge, Massachusetts: Harvard University Press, 2007), 38–39; italics added. Cf. 300–301.

Here, the dominion of personhood has devolved into a kind of perverse sovereignty which entitles one to ignore the world whenever it leads to discomfort. This leads people to simply avoid distressing experiences—society as a mode of communication breaks down. Indeed, since the transcendent no longer impinges on us as a teleological force, the only thing impinging on us is our own desires, and it is up to the individual alone to determine how he should dispose of those desires in a context utterly devoid of social commitment.[22] Taylor will even suggest that because the buffered self is closed off to the other, to the cosmos, and to any sort of transcendent meaning, he can no longer exercise *agape*, that highest expression of humanity; instead, he seeks only the mutual material benefits that accrue from living together.[23] This cloistering of the self from the other ultimately leads to an existential malaise, since the assumption that an individual can generate the meaning of existence purely and solely for oneself really means that all meanings are utterly arbitrary and therefore fragile, and no experience is inherently more meaningful than any other.[24]

There is in fact empirical evidence that the dominion of personhood has degenerated into the isolated sovereignty of the buffered self. In universities, we see it in the need for trigger warnings, safe spaces, and the rise of the unwitting offense of micro-aggression. In politics, we see it in the anti-democratic protests of those who proclaim, "Not my president." The protected sphere of the self, insulated from the challenges of reality, has become the focus of education in our country. The consequences of this have been widely analyzed in a sobering collection of essays called *The State of the American Mind*.[25] These studies document the widespread deleterious effect of privileging the buffered self in education, including astounding ignorance, the loss of civic virtue, narcissistic self-absorption, capricious claims to entitlements, and a willingness to restrict freedom of speech in cases which threaten the self-image in any way.[26] The result is that Amer-

22. Ibid., 135.

23. Ibid., 280–81.

24. Ibid., 307–321, esp. at 309.

25. Mark Bauerlein and Adam Bellow, editors, *The State of the American Mind* (West Conshohocken, Pennsylvania: Templeton Press, 2015). The book sees itself as a follow up to Allen Bloom's seminal 1987 work, *The Closing of the American Mind.*

26. These are the consequence as summarized by the editors in the Foreword, xii. This assessment is confirmed by the 2015 study from the Association of American Colleges and Universities which measured the discrepancy between how recent college graduates assess their own skills as compared to how employers assess their preparedness. For example, in the area

icans now approach the world with little understanding of objective reality and even less ability to empathize with alternative points of view, and so they are incapable of being responsible citizens; they are merely disengaged atoms with wholly parochial outlooks.[27] The damaging effect of this is illustrated by William Deresiewicz in his well-known critique of Ivy League colleges: "Look beneath the façade of seamless well-adjustment, and what you often find are toxic levels of fear, anxiety, and depression, of emptiness and aimlessness and isolation."[28]

The loss of final causality is not just the cause of individual anomie. It also has political implications, for it erodes the ability of individuals to form a meaningful community, as John Courtney Murray foresaw over half a century ago. Murray noted that "the specifying note of political association is its rational deliberative quality, its dependence for its permanent cohesiveness on argument among men.... The distinctive bond of the civil multitude is reason, or more exactly, that exercise of reason which is argument."[29] Indeed, he identifies this public argument as the essence of civilization, for it is by this reasoned argument that we communally discern the truth of the principles which bind us together. He then warns, ominously: "If the public argument dies from disinterest, or subsides into the angry mutterings of polemic, or rises to the shrillness of hysteria, or trails off into positivistic triviality, or gets lost in a morass of semantics, you may be sure that the barbarian is at the gates of the City."[30] Surely this description of

of ethical judgment, 62% of students described themselves as "well prepared" against only 30% of employers; in oral communication it was 62% against 28%; in written communication 65% versus 27%; in critical thinking 66% versus 26%; in problem solving 59% versus 24%. The study is available at http://www.aacu.org/leap/public-opinion-research/2015-survey-results.

27. Bauerlein and Bellow, "Afterword," in *The State of the American Mind*, 240–41. One might raise as an apparent exception to this atomistic buffered self the increasing focus on "identity politics." But this atavistic identification with group identities is just as corrosive to the common good. First, it is not based on a rational understanding of universal human nature, but some arbitrary accident; second, as soon as a society focuses on class interest instead of the common good, it is destined for disintegration. The universality of the rational good is subordinated to less universal immediate individual interests. In the end, this is only the individual writ large because it extrapolates from individuality to a group for the sake of extortionist force.

28. William Deresiewicz, "Don't Send Your Kid to the Ivy League: The nation's top colleges are turning our kids into zombies," *New Republic*, July 21, 2014.

29. John Courtney Murray, SJ, *We Hold These Truths* (New York: Sheed and Ward, 1960), 6–7.

30. Ibid., 11–12. Murray expands on this notion of barbarism: "Barbarism likewise threatens when men cease to talk together according to reasonable laws.... When things like this happen, men cannot be locked together in argument. Conversation becomes merely quarrelsome or querulous. Civility dies with the death of the dialogue." Ibid., 13.

public debate sounds eerily familiar; and surely this is precisely the effect of the buffered selves who increasingly define Western society: unable to argue, afraid to go beyond their own assumptions, and damning as bigotry any assertion to truth other than what they have chosen to believe. These are the barbarians who are eroding civilization, causing the crisis which George and others seek to rectify.

## V. Person and the Common Good

But it is only thus because we have misconstrued the nature of person. The source of all this is the misunderstanding of the dominion of man as efficient causality rather than final causality. Dominion must not be understood as giving us an autonomous sovereignty to define reality apart from all other persons. On the contrary, dominion empowers us to *overcome* our private opinions and personal desires in order to discover the true nature of reality in communion with every other person. Our dominion, paradoxically, makes us utterly dependent on community in order to flourish. The efficacy of the will exists for the sake of its communal finality: to overcome the subjective in favor of the objective. If we do not tend to objectivity, then willing itself is pointless: since every choice would be equally justifiable, none would be any better than another; but if no choice is better, then there would be nothing to motivate choice to begin with.[31] To show how meaning arises in the context of an objectivizing communal end, let us again turn to Maritain, who clearly brings out the priority of man's common good in *The Person and the Common Good*.[32]

The key to Maritain's argument is the famous distinction between man as an individual and as a person which follows from the hylomorphic foundation of his essence: "The human being is caught between two poles; a material pole, which, in reality, does not concern the true person but rather that shadow of personality or what, in the strict sense, is called *individual-*

31. Pfau makes this point: "Far from being concerned with the quasi-fetishistic preservation of their indeterminacy or autonomy, human beings are much more likely to be consumed with the pursuit of specific goals.... Surely, the individual has occasion to prize freedom only insofar as it enables her or him to pursue a specific *telos* to which she or he is either intuitively or deliberately committed." *Minding the Modern*, 296.

32. Jacques Maritain, *The Person and the Common Good*, translated by John J. Fitzgerald (Notre Dame, Indiana: University of Notre Dame Press, 1966).

*ity*, and a spiritual pole, which does concern *true personality*."[33] Individuality, as deriving from matter, "could be described as the narrowness of the ego, forever threatened and forever eager *to grasp for itself*."[34] Matter, as the principle of individuality, separates us, insulates us, and makes us inherently self-interested. Matter, then, is the principle that buffers the self from others; as Maritain comments: "If the development occurs in the direction of material individuality, it will be orientated towards the detestable ego whose law is to grasp or absorb for itself. At the same time personality, as such, will tend to be adulterated and to dissolve. But if the development occurs in the direction of spiritual personality, man will be orientated towards the generous self of the heroes and saints."[35]

This view of man as individual, which is exemplified by the buffered self of modernity, is radically inadequate because it ignores the other pole. The spiritual pole makes man "capable of containing itself thanks to the operations of the intellect and freedom, capable of super-existing by way of knowledge and of love."[36] This "super-existence" arises from reason's openness to the fullness of being in terms of objective truth and absolute goodness: the intellect is perfected in possessing the essences of other beings, while the will moves man to possess the very existence of desired goods.[37] This openness extraverts the person by relating him, not to his own subjectivity, but to the reality of all that is. Accordingly, both of these acts imply a radical decentering of the self, and one's own opinions and desires, in favor of that which is true in itself and good in itself.[38] Thus, it is

33. Ibid., 33; italics in original.

34. Ibid., 37; italics in original.

35. Ibid., 44–45. Maritain often refers to this as the "conquest of freedom"; see *Scholasticism and Politics*, translated by Mortimer J. Adler (Garden City, New York: Image Books, 1960), 117–38.

36. Maritain, *Person and the Common Good*, 40.

37. "The true and the good must therefore add to the concept of being, a relationship of that which perfects. But in any being there are two aspects to be considered, the formal character of its species and the act of being by which it subsists in that species. And so a being can be perfective in two ways. (1) It can be so just according to its specific character. In this way the intellect is perfected by a being, for it perceives the formal character of the being.... It is this mode of perfecting which the true adds to being.... (2) A being is perfective of another not only according to its specific character but also according to the existence which it has in reality. In this fashion the good is perfective." Thomas Aquinas, *De veritate* 21.1, translated by Robert W. Mulligan, SJ, James V. McGlynn, SJ, and Robert W. Schmidt, SJ (Chicago: Henry Regnery, 1954; reprint, Indianapolis: Hackett, 1994).

38. See W. Norris Clarke, SJ, *Person and Being* (Milwaukee, Wisconsin: Marquette University Press, 1993), 36–37.

our intensive subjectivity that enables persons to attain objectivity in value. That objective truth and goodness is attained only by way of opening ourselves to others in real inter-subjectivity. It follows, then, that personhood, although based in the intensive subjectivity, is essentially ordered to inter-subjective perfection. As Maritain explains:

> Personality, therefore, signifies interiority to self. And because it is the spirit in man which takes him, in contrast to the plant and animal, beyond the threshold of independence properly so called, and of interiority to oneself, the subjectivity of the person has nothing in common with the isolated unity, without doors or windows, of the Leibnizian monad. It requires the communications of knowledge and love. By the very fact that each of us is a person and expresses himself to himself, each of us requires communication with *other* and *the others* in the order of knowledge and love. Personality, of its essence, requires a dialogue in which souls really communicate.... The person is directly related to the absolute. For only in the absolute is it able to enjoy its full sufficiency. Its spiritual homeland is the whole universe of the absolute and of those indefectible goods which are as the pathways to the absolute Whole which transcends the world.[39]

Thus, against the modern buffered self, Maritain argues that man's good is inherently communal because of *both* his individuality and his personality. Man has a purely temporal and worldly good, entailed by the material flourishing enabled by communal structures, and for which individual interests are to be subordinated to the good of the community. However, each individual *as person* has an eternal end in the Beatific Vision, which is attained with the communion of saints. From the perspective of this eternal and personal end, society is at the service of the person whose good it serves by providing the occasion for intersubjective communion in the spiritual goods of virtue, wisdom, and love.[40] Thus, he argues:

> The person requires membership in a society in virtue both of its dignity and its needs.... It does so, first, because of its very perfections, as person, and its inner urge to the communications of knowledge and love which require relationship with other persons.... It does so secondly because of its needs or deficiencies, which derive from its material individuality. In this respect, unless it is integrated in a body of social communications, it cannot attain the fullness of its life and ac-

39. Maritain, *Person and the Common Good*, 41–42; italics in original.

40. "The terrestrial common good of such a society is, on the one hand, superior to the proper good of each member but flows back upon each. On the other hand, it sustains in each that movement by which it strives toward its own eternal good and the transcendent Whole; the same movement by which each goes beyond the order in which the common good of the terrestrial city is constituted." Maritain, *Person and the Common Good*, 59.

complishment. Society appears, therefore, to provide the human person with just those conditions of existence and development which it needs.[41]

## VI. Natural Law and the Ethics of Person in Community

While some ethical theories, such as utilitarianism, give precedence to the community over the person, and others, like deontology, privilege the autonomous individual against the community, natural law ethics understands that the good of the person and the common good are interdependent.[42] Accordingly, the teleological ordering of the person to fulfillment of the intellect in truth and the will in love necessitates a community of persons interacting for the sake of mutual perfection.[43] This truth is so fundamental that Thomas recognizes it as a self-evident precept at the basis of natural law, by which all human relations are properly ordered. The primary precepts of the natural law are understood to be self-evident because they are entailed, analytically, by the nature of a human being as a rational animal. Accordingly, most universally as an existent being and in common with all beings, man first seeks to preserve the good of his own existence; secondly, as an animal and in common with other members of the genus animal, man is called on to preserve the good of the species by reproducing.[44] But, as rational, what is specific to human flourishing derives from his rational nature: as persons, "man has a natural inclination to know the truth about God, and to live in

41. Maritain, *Person and the Common Good,* 47–48. Norris Clarke pithily expresses this by saying that man is active because he is simultaneously poor, in need of material sustenance, and rich, endowed with great personal gifts; see *Person and Being,* 10.

42. A good presentation of this interdependence is in the chapter "Precepts, Prudence, and Politics" in Thomas S. Hibbs, *Virtue's Splendor: Wisdom, Prudence and the Human Good* (New York: Fordham University Press, 2001), 86–137.

43. Rommen, in *The State in Catholic Thought,* 42, emphasizes that this substantive understanding of the common good is necessary for understanding the nature of man as a social being: "If social being is not more than is implied in the term 'relations,' then it would only be a nominalist definition of psychological acts of identical character in the individuals, and the classification of social relations would be made from the intensity of these relations or their specific character of love, sympathy, or interestedness.... But the true social being, its form, can be grasped only is we take into consideration the intentional character of these psychological acts and their meaning.... It is the end that defines the community."

44. Thus, while man as person exists for his own sake and therefore has an immortality for himself, animals obtain only a similitude of immortality in the continual reproduction of the species; see *De veritate* 5.3.

society."[45] Thus, it is seen as evident that as rational we must seek communion with other personal beings in order to fulfill the natural inclinations of intellect and will. Moreover, we form relations both with other men and with God, for they fulfill those inclinations in distinct ways. We are called first to live in society, to enter into intercourse with other persons, through which we grow in wisdom and love. But, this participation "flows back" to the benefit of the person,[46] who, by growing in wisdom and love, comes to an appreciation of the highest Truth and highest Good, and so orders himself to the absolute, to God. In this way, the temporal common good of the social order provides the opportunity for man to fulfill his ultimate desire, the communion with God in the Beatific Vision.[47]

These primary precepts of the natural law, however, are exceedingly vague. Therefore, Thomas argues that more detailed secondary precepts can be known as immediate conclusions from these first principles indicating how man justly pursues these ends. These are the precepts of the Decalogue.[48] Crucially, because these are rules of personal morality ordering man to perfection, and because man's perfection is inherently communal, they must simultaneously be principles of social organization. That is, politics is continuous with ethics, for they are founded on the same principles and the same good. The first table identifies justice in relation with God; the second table determines the necessary conditions for just relations in human society: first, respect for authority, then respect for life, the sanctity of the family, and private property.[49]

45. ST I-II, q. 94, a. 2. It might be noted that these are resonant of the two great commandments.

46. See Maritain's conclusion, *Person and the Common Good*, 76: "[The common good] directs itself to persons in a two-fold way: first, in so far as the persons are engaged in the social order, the common good by its essence must flow back over or redistribute itself to them; second, in so far as the persons transcend the social order and are directly ordained to the transcendent Whole, the common good by its essence must favor their progress toward the absolute goods which transcend political society."

47. "Man is a part of and inferior to the political community by reason of the things in and of him which, due as they are to the deficiencies of material individuality, depend in their very essence upon political society and which in turn may be used as means to promote the temporal good of the society.... On the other hand, by reason of the things in and of man, which are derived from the ordination of personality as such to the absolute and which thus depend in their essence on something higher than the political community and so concern properly the supra-temporal accomplishment of the person as person, man excels the political community." Ibid., 73–74.

48. For the Decalogue as the "immediate conclusions" from the self-evident precepts of the natural law, see ST I-II, q. 100, aa. 1, 3, and 11.

49. In ST II-II, q. 122, a. 1, Thomas asserts that the Decalogue, consisting primarily of pre-

What needs to be brought out, though, is that the Decalogue's precepts of justice point us back to Robert George's prescriptions for a decent society. These precepts exemplify clearly how his five pillars are all really derivative from the primacy of the dignity of the person (rightly considered) who is essentially ordained to a common good. This can be demonstrated because human subjectivity only attains perfection in society; consequently, respect for the social realities of family, *polis*, and mediating institutions follows directly from the respect for person.[50]

Let me illustrate this concretely, starting with the need to respect the family. Both the fourth and sixth commandments indicate that family is an inviolable good. Every human person is born into a family in which a child learns the virtues that form the basis for all civic amity.[51] It is in the family that a person first learns to decenter the self, to open himself to correction by authority, and grow into the fullness of being in terms of communion.[52] Indeed, as Heinrich Rommen argues, the family, not the individual, is the foundation for political freedoms: "Inviolability of the home, freedom of the person, freedom of association, of education, all these center on the home and the family far more than on the abstract individual."[53] Moreover, it is because of the central importance of the family for children—and for civilization as a whole—that sexual reproduction must be limited to married couples; out-of-wedlock births are detrimental not just for the individual, but for society as a whole. For this reason, sexual sins are seen as intrinsic violations of rationality, not just in themselves as violations of temperance, but because they disorder society and violate the precepts of justice owed to the child and fellow citizens.

---

cepts about justice, is thus essential for the common good: "Wherefore the first three precepts are about acts of religion, which is the chief part of justice; the fourth precept is about acts of piety, which is the second part of justice; and the six remaining are about justice commonly so called, which is observed among equals." My list obviously recalls the fourth to seventh commandments.

50. A good analysis of the metaphysical and moral unity of person, family, and state, which in turn guarantees the independence of non-governmental mediating institutions is found in Rommen, *The State in Catholic Thought*, 248–55.

51. For an analysis of the essential nature of family, see Gabriel Marcel, "The Mystery of the Family," in *Homo Viator: Introduction to a Metaphysics of Hope*, translated by Emma Craufurd (New York: Harper and Row, 1962), 68–97.

52. On the primacy of marriage for the political community, see Aquinas's *Commentary on Aristotle's "Politics,"* bk 1, lect. 1, no. 17; on the primacy of the good of friendship based in mutual virtue between spouses as a properly human good over reproduction as the good of man's generic animality, see ST Suppl. III, q. 41, a. 1.

53. Rommen, *State in Catholic Thought*, 249n2.

The family, however, is not a perfect society; it gives way to the *polis* as the complete human community.[54] Thus, George's third pillar, law as binding an entire political society, arises of necessity for the sake of the common good. Law is needed, first and negatively, to maintain the tranquility of order by stopping disturbances; second and positively, to stipulate common activity for the sake of mutual perfection.[55] Law, then, continues the decentering of the buffered self by ordering an individual to a common good which transcends personal opinion and desire. But, of course, this law demands obedience and the respect for authority that is commanded in the fourth commandment.

The nature of civil law as authoritatively ordered to the good of persons is well illustrated in Thomas's analysis of the duties of the state in his *De Regimine*.[56] Thomas first specifies that the end of human community is to teach virtue, for a community is formed so that men might live well, and the good life is one lived in accordance with virtue. This notion is mirrored in Thomas's insistence in the treatise on law that *all law* is ordered to the development of virtue,[57] since virtue is the necessary means to attain perfection in wisdom and love. For citizens to attain this maturation in virtue, wisdom, and love, Thomas enumerates the three things a good prince must secure for his community. First, he secures peace, by which the integrity of the person is protected from harm, reflecting the fifth commandment's prohibition on unjust killing. Second, the prince promotes the virtue of justice, by which the rights and duties of citizens and authority are guaranteed so as to enable communal flourishing, reflecting the fourth commandment, and implicitly all the others in terms of rights.[58] Finally, the prince

54. "Out of social acts in their different forms grow friendship in the strict sense, the family as the natural outcome of marital love and the bisexual nature of man, and associations formed for the common aim of worship, of economic cooperation, and of law there the collective aim is the intentional fulfillment of the social acts. But all these natural communities and freely produced associations point to one form of association where all collective aims coincide, where all conflicts between them can be settled: the city-state that embraces all social activities and all coordinated groups, thus establishing moral, social, and economic self-sufficiency and duration. This community is therefore 'perfect.'" Ibid., 24–25.

55. For an analysis of this two-fold purpose of law in terms of substitutive and perfective uses of authority, see Yves R. Simon, *A General Theory of Authority* (Notre Dame, Indiana: University of Notre Dame Press, 1962).

56. Thomas Aquinas, *De regimine principium* I, chaps. 15–16, in *Political Writings*, edited and translated by in R. W. Dyson (Cambridge: Cambridge University Press, 2002), 39–44.

57. ST I-II, q. 92, a. 1 and q. 94, a. 3.

58. On this, see Rommen, *State in Catholic Thought*, 329–33. This argument recalls the

aims to provide a sufficiency of material wealth,[59] for man's flourishing requires leisure, which is the fruit of wealth.[60]

While some might be surprised that a person vowed to poverty like St. Thomas would celebrate material wealth in society,[61] it matches up perfectly with George's last two pillars, those mediating institutions guaranteeing a dynamic society. Indeed, we can also see that they are derived from the seventh and eighth commandments' recognition of the importance of private property and honest inquiry and communication. First, man is ordered to perfection in the realm of knowledge, so universities continually push the boundaries of knowledge forward, and encourage the mutual exchange of truth for the benefit of all. This inquiry requires, above all else, scrupulous honesty, or else it devolves to mere propaganda and indoctrination.[62] But the existence of institutions dedicated to research presumes a certain level of material wealth to support them. Thus, there arises the mediating institution charged with material enrichment: business. Business can only accomplish its goal if private property is respected, for as Thomas points out, stewardship is more effectively exercised when a person has ownership of goods.[63] (Moreover, the ninth and tenth commandment note the importance of accepting the justice of the distribution of private property as a component of social order.[64]) It is important to remember that wealth is never pursued for its own sake, but for the sake of leisure time, in which wisdom and friendship are enjoyed as ends in themselves.

---

priority of legal justice—an acceptance of the need to follow natural law for the sake of the common good—over distributive and commutative justice; see ST II-II, q. 58, a. 6.

59. "The isolated man cannot live an intellectual life, because the satisfaction of the wants of his sensual and vegetative life would wholly occupy all of him. A favorable surrounding, economically an order of organized cooperation, must be created to afford man the intellectual life." Ibid., 25.

60. This, of course, is Aristotle's point (*Metaphysics* 1.1, 981b20–24) which is so edifyingly developed by Josef Pieper in *Leisure, the Basis of Culture*, translated by Gerald Malsbary (South Bend, Indiana: St. Augustine's Press, 1998).

61. See, for example, Christopher A. Franks, *He Became Poor: The Poverty of Christ and Aquinas's Economic Teachings* (Grand Rapids, Iowa: Eerdman's, 2009).

62. That research processes are structured according to the principles of natural law is argued for by Alasdair MacIntyre, "How We Can Learn What *Veritatis Splendor* Has to Teach Us?" in *Veritatis Splendor and the Renewal of Moral Theology*, edited by J. A. DiNoia, OP, Avery Dulles, SJ, and Romanus Cessario, OP (Downer's Grove, Illinois: Midwest Theological Forum, 1999), 73–94.

63. In ST II-II, q. 66, a. 2, Thomas specifies three reasons why property is necessary: it encourages better stewardship of resources; it creates more orderly social relations; and it creates social peace when each is satisfied with his own property (in accord with justice).

64. See ST II-II, q. 118, a. 3, ad 3.

Yet, it is also true that as material beings, societal and personal development is impossible without adequate material wealth.[65]

## VII. Conclusion

George discerns five pillars of a decent and dynamic society; but like the precepts of the natural law, they are really just derivative of the nature of person. Each of these pillars and each of the precepts repudiate the ideology of the buffered self, revealing it to be a false ideology that ineluctably leads to misery. We see this in the crises of modernity, which arise from the fallacy that personal dignity makes man impervious to anything but complete self-determination. The result is a society made up of atoms with nothing to unite them—not truth, not goodness, not happiness.[66] Yet it is the very foundation of natural law that man's teleology requires communion with others: a communion by which we are forced to defer to others for growth in truth; to decenter the self, to objectivize desires for the sake of love; and to attain the happiness that we cannot reach on our own. Thus, the subjectivity that is the basis of man's radical uniqueness only finds perfection in opening itself to other subjects, both human and divine, in the community of persons.

65. We might also note that George does not explicitly mention churches here, but from the time of Augustine they have been recognized as the primary mediating institution by which man is ordered to his eternal end.

66. Maritain critiques this understanding of society as rejecting our spiritual nature: "Materialistic conceptions of the world and life philosophies which do not recognize the spiritual and eternal element in man cannot escape error in their efforts to construct a truly human society because they cannot satisfy the requirements of the person, and, by that very fact, they cannot grasp the nature of society." *Person and the Common Good*, 100–101.

KATHRYN ROMBS

# Thomistic Personalists in Dialogue with Atheists

## Defending the Dignity of the Human Person

### I. The Challenge of a Non-Theistic Defense of Human Dignity

In his address "On Europe's Crisis of Culture," presented in Subiaco, Italy just 18 days before he was elected pope, Cardinal Joseph Ratzinger claims that reason is not "complete in itself" but has a need of a "root outside itself."[1] Reason is not autonomous, he claims, but must consider the roots from which it springs. In the West, reason was rooted in Christian truth. But in the Renaissance and then especially in the Enlightenment, reason sought its independence from faith, and we have never been more enthusiastic than we are today about *ratio* in its technical sense. But technological *ratio* can never answer the question, "To what end?" So it does not provide ethical channeling for its own development. Hence, Ratzinger claims, Enlightenment and post-Enlightenment reason is a limited and distorted version of what reason can be.

A question at the heart of contemporary interest in human rights is whether reason can justify human dignity independently of theological considerations. Ratzinger's view is that, while we once deemed human dignity to be grounded in our being made in the image of God, if we dis-

1. Josef Ratzinger, *Christianity and the Crisis of Cultures* (San Francisco: Ignatius Press, 2006), 38.

avow our Christian roots, it is impossible to continue to justify *rationally* human dignity. He says, "The attempt to manage human affairs disdaining God completely leads us increasingly to the edge of the abyss, to man's ever greater isolation from reality.... We must not lose sight of God, if we do not want human dignity to disappear."[2]

Ratzinger holds a controversial position: the Catholic intellectual might not be able to give a strictly rational argument regarding the ground of human dignity. If he is correct, can we hope to find common ground on this matter when talking with someone who does not believe in God or in human beings being made in God's image? Why is genocide wrong? Why are murder, human trafficking, and slavery violations of human dignity wrong? Ratzinger's position seems to be that Christians might be able to defend that dignity, but that defense will be inspired by Christian revelation. To the extent that the contemporary atheist European or American, bedazzled by scientific rationality, is determined to eschew all remnants of Christian roots from reason, he or she will struggle, Ratzinger claims, to find a philosophical defense for the dignity of the human person.

Ratzinger's position is corroborated by the historical events surrounding the creation of the United Nation's first Human Rights Commission at the end of World War II, as recounted in Thomas Williams' important work on Thomistic personalism, *Who is My Neighbor?: Personalism and the Foundations of Human Rights*. In the wake of the War's devastating violations of human dignity, the Commission, chaired by Eleanor Roosevelt, sought a universally acceptable code of ethics, upon which to form a "bill of rights." The Commission consulted a variety of philosophers, including Jacques Maritain, to support its quest for a rational account of human dignity and consequently of human rights. The Commission desired an account of human dignity that would appeal to people of all nations and creeds. Hence, even though some of the advisors to the Commission were Catholic, they were asked to give a philosophical account of the dignity of the human person without appeal to Christian revelation.

But the advisors were ultimately unable to provide such an account. As Maritain put it: "We agree about the rights but on condition no one asks us why!"[3] The Commission reached agreement about the specific human

2. Ibid., 43.
3. Introduction, in *UNESCO, Human Rights: Comments and Interpretations* (London: Wingate,

rights to be protected but not about how to defend them philosophically. Maritain and his colleagues concluded that it could not be done. Instead, they suggested a view that John Paul II later would adopt, that various cultural, philosophical and religious communities need to provide their own accounts of "the moral bases for the juridic edifice of human rights."[4] Each human community needs its own defense, in light of its own presuppositions and views.

Is this correct? Can no agreement be reached among atheists, Catholics, Protestants, Hindus, Jews, and Muslims, as to a basis for the inherent dignity of the human person? Can Catholics not advocate it without appeal to divine revelation? Catholics stand side by side with atheists, secular humanists, and people of all creeds as they fight for human justice. The question is, can they not come to points of agreement as to why they hold the same assurance regarding human dignity? Recently, Pope Francis has given a more optimistic view. He writes:

> [Defense of the vulnerable] involves the conviction that a human being is always sacred and inviolable, in any situation and at every stage of development. Human beings are ends in themselves and never a means of resolving other problems. Once this conviction disappears, so do solid and lasting foundations for the defense of human rights, which would always be subject to the passing whims of the powers that be. *Reason alone is sufficient* to recognize the inviolable value of each single human life.[5]

Pope Francis claims that human reason alone can disclose the value of human life.

Maritain may have been pessimistic about one rational argument or perspective being a common basis for human dignity and may have concluded that each culture should do its own work to lay out the ethical basis for human rights to its own members. His seminal work, *The Person and the Common Good*, written soon after World War II, does just that. In it, Maritain spells out the basis for human dignity from the vantage point of Thomistic personalism. But could it be that, in this work, he provides the basis for further development toward the goal he pursued, an inter-cultural,

1949), 9. Quoted in Thomas Williams, *Who Is My Neighbor? Personalism and the Foundations of Human Rights* (Washington D.C.: Catholic University of America Press, 2005).

4. John Paul II, Address to the Diplomatic Corps accredited to the Holy See (January 9,1989): no. 7.

5. Pope Francis, *Evangelii Gaudium* (Vatican City: Libreria Vaticana, 2013): no. 213; italics added.

inter-faith perspective concerning the grounds of human dignity? I argue that he does and suggest next steps for progress toward that end.

## II. Maritain's Metaphysics of Human Dignity

Suppose that we approach *Person and the Common Good* with the questions: What grounds human dignity? Can it be established philosophically without appeal to divine revelation? We find that Maritain offers several answers.

He gives eloquent expression to the *Christian* grounds of human dignity, describing humans as made in the image of God, describing the beatific vision as our end, and claiming that we are meant for communion with God. But then, Maritain takes a different tact, defending the superiority of the speculative over the practical intellect. The goal of the practical intellect—and here he echoes Aquinas—is a practical good, a task to be done, while the goal of the speculative intellect is truth to be known, ultimately the subsistent Good itself.[6] Maritain quotes Aquinas: "By the fact that a man contemplates, he directs himself towards the end of contemplation.... The most perfect beatitude resides in the speculative intellect."[7] Maritain recounts that the preeminence of the speculative intellect lies in its high degree of immateriality. He claims: "It binds man to things divine. It is better than life on the human scale. In supernatural contemplation it takes place according to a mode which is itself superhuman.... [I]t makes of the transfigured soul one spirit with God."[8]

Maritain phrases this point in theistic terms, which is consistent with his aim to spell out a Thomistic personalist view; but the point is taken directly from the traditions of Plato and Aristotle, and thus is of pagan origin, lacking influence from the Judeo-Christian tradition. One need only recall the *Phaedo*, in which Socrates claims:

> Don't you think that the person who is likely to succeed in [attaining the true object of knowledge] is the one who approaches each object, as far as possible, with the unaided intellect [,] ... the man who pursues the truth by applying his pure and unadulterated thought to the pure and unadulterated object?[9]

6. Jacques Maritain, *The Person and the Common Good*, translated by John J. Fitzgerald (1947; repr., Notre Dame, Indiana: University of Notre Dame Press, 1966), 25.

7. Ibid., 25–26.

8. Ibid., 26.

9. *Phaedo* 65e, translated by G. M. A. Grube (Indianapolis, Indiana: Hackett, 1977).

And further:

By keeping ourselves uncontaminated by the follies of the body, we shall probably reach the company of others like ourselves and gain direct knowledge of all that is pure and uncontaminated—that is, presumably, of truth [,] … the realm of purity.[10]

For Plato, the human soul's end is contemplation of eternal, immaterial reality. Only a transcendent soul could have as its end this divine *telos*. Hence, for Plato, the human soul is divine. Of course, the sense of "divine" in Plato is at best analogously related to the sense of the "divine" in the Judeo-Christian tradition. Aristotle, too, describes all of nature yearning for the unmoved mover, the good, as its final end in *Metaphysics*, book *lambda*. He describes contemplation as the highest human end in the *Nicomachean Ethics*. Here, contemplation can be rendered as a basis for human dignity via appeal to a pagan philosophy from antiquity. Hence contemplation as man's end, and thereby as a quality that separates him in dignity from other beings, is a possible way of establishing philosophically, and not necessarily theologically, the dignity that belongs to human persons.

Maritain develops this theme by claiming that the moral virtues are at the service of wisdom and are a natural accompaniment of contemplation: "To [contemplation] are ordained the moral virtues.… [W]hen the soul is perfect, the works of the active life must overflow."[11] But again, while Aquinas concurs, this is not an essentially theological claim. It is found, not only in Plato and Aristotle, but also in Plotinus, another philosopher whose philosophy is independent of Christian thought. For Plotinus, moral virtue is necessary for the contemplative life. Moral virtue requires human freedom, and so, too, freedom can be a ground of human dignity. Again, we have the possibility of a non-theological ground of human worth: human persons have the opportunity for moral excellence, entailing another such ground, human freedom, in a way that other animal species do not.

Maritain further pursues a philosophical account of human dignity as he contrasts two aspects of human beings. He writes: "The human being is caught between two poles; a material pole, which, in reality, does not concern the true person but rather the shadow of personality or what, in the strict sense, is called *individuality*, and a spiritual pole, which does con-

10. *Phaedo* 67a.

11. Maritain, *The Person and the Common Good*, 27.

cern *true personality*."[12] As he considers the spiritual aspect of man, could he be considering something that is, in itself, a-religious? Might not people of various creeds, even atheists, assent to this claim that we have spirits? According to Maritain, the human individual—who is individuated by matter—is the human being, considered as a being in the world. But additionally, he says, one can consider the human person with respect to his spiritual nature—another aspect, or "pole" of the human being. Concerning this spiritual aspect, Maritain quotes Aquinas: "The person is that which is most noble and most perfect in all of nature."[13] Regarded as an individual, man is just another fragment of a species, just another part of the universe, "a point in the immense web of cosmic ethnical, historical forces and influences—and bound by their laws. Each is subject to the determinism of the physical world."[14] But regarding the spiritual pole, which is key for the *personhood* of the human being, man emerges as transcendent of the cosmic, historical and political forces: "Our whole being subsists in virtue of the subsistence of the spiritual soul which is in us a principle of creative unity, independence and liberty."[15]

In investigating this spiritual aspect of human beings, Maritain claims that a primary means of disclosing its mystery is love as *eros*. Maritain writes: "the expressions of lovers are unending because their object is ineffable."[16] Lovers love, not certain qualities in their beloved, but the person him- or herself. "We love the deepest, most substantial and hidden, the most existing reality of the beloved being."[17] Love is the key to understanding ourselves as persons. It reveals the infinite possibilities that lie within the soul, the super-abundance of life that makes us more than another member of the species but rather a "reality which, subsisting spiritually, constitutes a universe unto itself, a relatively independent whole within the great whole of the universe."[18] The spiritual component of the human person is, for Maritain, the condition for the possibility of *eros*.

Maritain continues with reflection on human transcendence. He writes: "In short, [a being who bestows itself to another] must be endowed with a

12. Ibid., 33.
13. Ibid., 32.
14. Ibid., 38.
15. Ibid.
16. Ibid., 39.
17. Ibid.
18. Ibid., 40.

spiritual existence, capable of containing itself thanks to the operations of the intellect and freedom, capable of super-existing by way of knowledge and of love."[19] Again, as with the theme of contemplation, human beings are ordered toward an end, and a way of existing, that transcends our material selves. We do not just exist. In Maritain's words, we "super-exist." He writes: "Such a being must exist not only as other things do, but eminently, in self-possession, holding itself in hand, master of itself."[20] Maritain presents a non-theistic view of human beings loving each other for their own sake and possessing themselves in order to give themselves away.

Elaborating on the theme of self-donation, he claims that an essential characteristic of personhood is that, as having a rich interiority signified by our transcendent ends of contemplation and self-donation, we are called to relationality and communion.[21] "Each of us requires communication with others in the order of knowledge and love. Personality, of its essence, requires a dialogue in which souls really communicate."[22] This is a theme that Karol Wojtyla will later develop, that human beings are ordered to interpersonal relationships, that we are called to give ourselves as gifts to others, as expressed in his famous "Law of the Gift." Maritain has given us a foundational metaphysical description of the human person as not truly him or herself until he or she is in a relation of love with others.

## III. Within the Bounds of Reason Alone

Maritain has given us more than enough material with which to develop a philosophy of human dignity that prescinds from the Judeo-Christian tradition. While Ratzinger may be correct that reason is not as such autonomous, the question here becomes: Can we develop an account of human dignity that does not appeal, at least directly, to revelation?

One might begin looking at themes of spirituality that are not specifically Judeo-Christian, since Judeo-Christian monotheism does not "have a corner on" spirituality. One need only recall the various popular secular theories of the soul or spirit ready at hand. Another approach is to consider virtue, morality, and human freedom, as many writers have done. A

19. Ibid.
20. Ibid.
21. Ibid., 41.
22. Ibid., 42.

third approach, as suggested by Pope Francis in his comments from *Evangelii Gaudium* cited above, is never to treat people as mere means to an end. Here, Pope Francis follows Karol Woytyla's approach in *Love and Responsibility.* Wojtyla echoes Kant in claiming that humans are not just a means to an end but should be treated as ends themselves, and that love is tantamount to a respect of this axiom, which Wojtyla calls the "personalistic norm."[23]

What of this Kantian approach? Pope Francis's reference to this norm is not developed in *Evangelii Gaudium,* and so we must refer to Karol Wojtyla's development of it as we consider how a Kantian answer to the question of human dignity fares in the contemporary human rights discussion. Wojtyla employs Kant's "ends and means" terminology in expressing his "personalistic norm," which states that "whenever a person is the object of your activity, remember that you may not treat that person as only the means to an end, as an instrument, but must allow for the fact that he or she, too, has, or at least should have, distinct personal ends"; and again, "the person is the kind of good which does not admit of use and cannot be treated as an object of use and as such the means to an end."[24] This norm in its positive aspect is: "the person is a good towards which the only proper and adequate attitude is love."[25] It is based on Kant's moral imperative: "Act always in such a way that the other person is an end and not merely an instrument of your action."[26]

We might ask: How Kantian is Wojtyla's position? Is it independent of the Christian tradition? Kant's imperative finds its roots in the Christian tradition.[27] It draws on Christ's commandment of love: Do unto others as you would have them do unto you. Wojtyla makes explicit his appeal to Christ's command: "Is the personalistic norm expressed in the duty to behave toward a person in a manner demanded by the essence and value of that person? In light of the Gospel and of the whole tradition of the teachings of revealed morality, it seems that this general content of the personalistic norm can be supplemented by a more concrete content: the content of

23. Karol Wojtyla, *Love the Responsibility* (1983; repr., San Francisco: Ignatius Press, 1993), 41.
24. Ibid., 28, 41.
25. Ibid.
26. Immanuel Kant, *Groundwork of the Metaphysics of Morals,* translated by James W. Ellington (Indianapolis, Indiana: Hackett, 1993), 66–67.
27. Williams, *Who is My Neighbor?* 154.

the commandment of love."[28] And again: "For if Jesus Christ commanded us to love those beings who are persons, then love is the proper form of relating to persons: it is the form of behavior for which we should strive when our behavior has a person as its object."[29] Wojtyla takes his inspiration from the Scriptural commandment, and derives a maxim of reason. He identifies a rational ethical norm that is rooted in Christian revelation.

While there is much merit in this approach, it is important to ask what justifies or grounds the ethical norm of not treating others merely as means, but as ends in themselves. Clearly, for Kant, his imperative is grounded in pure practical reason, independent of all experience. In his view, such an imperative is categorical in that it is "objectively necessary in itself, without reference to another end."[30] The necessity of a categorical imperative is derived from pure reason. As an *a priori* synthetic practical proposition,[31] the second formulation of the categorical imperative is necessary on the authority of reason and independent of experience or culture.[32]

One might have optimism that the grounding of this maxim in reason fits the criteria for which Maritain and the U.N.'s Commission on Human Rights were looking, in that it is independent of faith and appeals only to reason. Moreover, Kant specifically appeals to the categorical imperative having universal applicability and independent of social context (being "hypothetical" and empirical or "impure"). This might be more than enough to inspire some thinkers to develop this line of reasoning.

A possible shortcoming of this approach, however, pertains to the justification of the maxim that "human beings are ends in themselves and never a means of resolving other problems." For the Kantian, this claim is binding due to its grounding in pure practical reason. But most people are not Kantians. For the maxim to have much force for the average contemporary thinker, one would need to persuade him or her of the truth of Kantian ethics. For the non-Kantian, the maxim has much less force; it is reduced to the status of an intuition. "People should be treated as ends in themselves, and never merely as means to an end": this appeals to many people's common sensibilities. It resonates with the moral norms to which many

28. Karol Wojtyla, "The Problem of Catholic Sexual Ethics," in *Person and Community*, 288.
29. Ibid. See also Wojtyla, *Love and Responsibility*, 40.
30. Kant, *Groundwork of the Metaphysics of Morals*, 414.
31. Ibid., 420.
32. Ibid., 429.

people conform. But it falls prey to the same relativism to which all other moral norms are subject. Why this maxim and not another? Nietzsche puts this view well when he describes lambs calling the birds of prey evil and themselves good. Morality, he claims, is born out of this master/slave domination—lambs seeking to justify why the birds should not hunt them. But the birds are quite aware that there is no real morality: moral norms are merely the attempt of the weak to protect themselves against the strong.[33] Why, we might ask ourselves, is the norm "people should be treated as ends in themselves and never merely as means to an end" binding? Might it not just be a function of the weak protecting themselves against the strong? If the modern interlocutor does not see the binding force of pure reason as Kant does, then this maxim becomes relative.

When Karol Wojtyla uses the terms "ends" and "means," he is neither depending on Kantian logic regarding pure reason or *a priori* synthetic judgments, nor is he appealing to the intuition one might have of the legitimacy of this view. Rather, he is adapting Kantian terminology to a realist metaphysics of the human person. As we have seen, Wojtyla is explicit in linking the imperative with the Christian tradition. He draws on Scripture but also on thinkers such as Aquinas, who distinguishes between the rational creature, who should be cared for its own sake, and irrational creatures, which are cared for as being directed to other things.[34] This distinction mirrors closely the difference between an end in itself and a means to an end.[35] As Williams writes, reflecting on Wojtyla's use of Kantian terminology: "Kant's conception of personal autonomy is problematic, since values and moral norms do not have their ultimate source in practical reason but in God."[36] Wojtyla is explicit about seeing the Kantian ethic as grounded in Christian theology. The Kantian approach is one that enjoys favor in the contemporary dialogue concerning human dignity and rights and may prove fruitful. The burden of demonstration, however, is on the personalist, to show what exactly—pure practical reason? God?—grounds the categorical imperative.

While not ruling out the Kantian perspective, we have seen that Mar-

33. Friedrich Nietzsche, *Genealogy of Morals* in *Genealogy of Morals and Ecce Homo*, translated by Walter Kaufmann and R. J. Hollingdale (New York: Random House, 1989), 13.

34. *Summa contra gentiles* III, chap. 112.

35. Williams, *Who is My Neighbor?* 159.

36. Ibid. See also John Paul II, *Veritatis splendor* (Boston: St. Paul Books, 1993): no. 40.

itain does not offer Kantian solutions in *Person and the Common Good.* I would like to suggest another way in which one could develop one's thought to provide a non-theistic account of human dignity. Maritain provides three non-theological grounds for human dignity: first, he considers contemplation as man's end; second, he considers virtue and freedom, which pertain to the human *telos,* since all human goods are subordinated to our highest good; third, he considers love in several senses as our end. It seems to me, without committing to any one of these answers, what they have in common, and what the Thomist or Christian pursuing them might have in common with his or her atheist colleagues, is that we are asking the question, "What is our end?"

Exploring other faith traditions and cultures, is it not the case that many of them identify a human *telos*? The Buddhist, for example, names nirvana as the human end. This end is not theistic but is an end nevertheless. The Hindu, the Muslim, the Aborigine identify various human ends. Cannot it be said, too, that varying strains of atheists and secular humanists identify human ends, whether it be the happiness that comes with co-existence, tolerance, equality, justice, or world peace? While the U.N. Human Rights Commission failed to find a common ground of human rights, it is worth asking whether teleology is at the heart of every divergent answer.

This possible solution has the significant limitation that any talk of a *telos* or end is inherently metaphysical, and thus is not tolerable to contemporary thinkers spanning a wide range, from anti-foundationalist analytic thinkers to deconstructionists to pragmatists. In his *First Principles, Final Ends and Contemporary Philosophical Issues,* Alasdair MacIntyre discusses the conviction "shared both by different, often mutually antagonistic schools of contemporary philosophy and by the culture of modernity at large, that no principle is or can be first."[37] First principles are intimately bound up with the concept of *telos/finis;* in the practical life it is the *telos* which provides the *arche,* the first principle of practical reasoning. But such first principles, and the *telos* or end that is bound up with them, have been "relativized to social contexts and social purposes.... The purposes of each of us are taken to be a matter of our individual temperaments, interests, desires and decisions. This contemporary universe of discourse thus has no

37. Alasdair MacIntyre, *First Principles, Final Ends and Contemporary Philosophical Issues* (Milwaukee, Wisconsin: Marquette University Press, 1990), 6.

place within it for any conception of fixed ends, of ends to be discovered rather than decided upon or invented."[38]

In this intellectual and cultural context, is it not a matter of absurdity to posit anything metaphysical as something that will win widespread agreement? My response is that the question posed by the U.N.'s Human Rights Commission is itself a metaphysical one; the question regarding human dignity, the search for a philosophical basis of human rights, is metaphysical in nature. "Dignity" has little place in what Ratzinger calls "technological ratio" as well as in a variety of the aforementioned schools of thought. "Human" is a word itself fraught with controversy—nothing is more disputed than what it means to be a human being in this age of advancement in artificial intelligence, cloning, and neuroscience. Hence, what grounds human dignity is a question that is a non-starter for many contemporary intellectuals. The answer cannot be expected to be less metaphysical than the question.

The U.N.'s Human Rights Commission asked it nevertheless, motivated by the desire to prevent another world war. And this is a context in which those who might not otherwise be optimistic about such a philosophical position gave their best effort. The Commission's solution was that each tradition must articulate its own expression of the human ground of our dignity. The Jew, armed with his view, the atheist armed with hers, the Thomist Catholic with his, and the Protestant with hers, can stand shoulder to shoulder and defend the human rights that rest on this variety of arguments, specific to the variety of traditions from which they come. But I am suggesting that, while this concession might be necessary, it is still possible that those of various traditions might pursue the question, "Is there a connection between human dignity and the human end?" That we have an end at all, however differently we may describe what this end is, is worth considering as a basis for advancement in terms of a rational defense of human dignity. While variety and difference is still a part of the answer, the common thread of teleology could bring each answer one step closer to cohesion.

It is possible that, once one has granted the question, a solution of this general nature—a solution that functions as a genus, uniting a variety of answers—is possible. Do not all considerations of human dignity have

38. Ibid.

their natural starting point with this very question of whether people have an end? Plato describes our end as contemplation of the immaterial reality; Aristotle describes our end as contemplation of first principles; Plotinus describes the human end as bringing back the divine in man to the divine in the All; Augustine describes us as having a *capex dei*, a capacity for God; Aquinas describes humans as ordered toward the beatific vision. These are just a few examples from non-Christian as well as Christian thinkers in the philosophical tradition. More recently, Viktor Frankl describes us as made for meaning, which can be found, for example, in relationships such as those of marriage and family. Emmanuel Mounier develops a philosophy of human engagement, inseparable from a philosophy of the absolute.[39] Martin Buber claims that we are meant to enter into dialogic relations not just with other humans but with other animate beings, and with the Divine Thou. J. M. E. McTaggart, who describes himself as an atheist personalist, describes the human end in terms of the immortality of the soul, emphasizing the pre-existence of the soul.[40] His position incited the wrath of Martin Luther King Jr., who wrote an essay against McTaggert's personalism, scourging him for his belief in the pre-existence of the soul, among other things.[41] But this only proves my point. Each of these thinkers, the atheists, Christians, and Jews, all proposed some answer to the question, "What is our end?" and found that purpose to be the basis for their defense of human dignity.

Noticing the tradition of teleology that extends to the present time and incentivized by the worthy goal of ending genocide and preventing another world war, the contemporary intellectual might be encouraged to take up a restoration of metaphysics, especially teleology. This is a project that Maritain undertakes in *The Degrees of Knowledge*. He makes the case that, as modern natural science has advanced, our ability to think metaphysically has weakened. He writes:

> Timeless metaphysics no longer suits the modern intellect. Three centuries of empirio-mathematicism have so warped the intellect that it is no longer interest-

39. Emmanuel Mounier, *Personalism* (Notre Dame, Indiana: University of Notre Dame Press, 1952).

40. J. M. E. McTaggart, *Human Immortality and Pre-Existence* (San Bernadino, California: Ulan Press, 2012).

41. See Martin Luther King Jr., "The Personalism of J. M. E. McTaggart Under Criticism," in *The Papers of Martin Luther King Jr.: Rediscovering Precious Values, July 1951–November 1955* (Oakland, California: University of California Press, 2014).

ed in anything but the invention of apparatus to capture phenomena—conceptual nets that give the mind a certain practical dominion over nature.... [T]he modern intellect develops within this lower order of scientific demiurge a kind of manifold and marvelously specialized touch.... But, at the same time, it has wretchedly weakened and disarmed itself in the face of the proper objects of the intellect.[42]

We have become unaccustomed to think in terms of first principles and ends. Nevertheless, he argues, these questions, no matter how neglected, never die. They are "timeless." Human beings will never stop asking questions about what constitutes the human end, what is best for us. Science and technology will never vitiate such metaphysical questions.

Maritain's massive project of rehabilitating metaphysics, as exemplified in *The Degrees of Knowledge,* might find the U.N. Commission's question regarding human dignity as a help in the undertaking. Is it not possible that the desire for a philosophical account of human dignity might help the West rehabilitate metaphysics? Are not pertinent and pressing questions—how to end genocide or slavery, for example—just the starting points we might want to consider in helping us to revisit metaphysics? Emmanuel Mounier, a founder of personalism, also held this as his cherished conviction. Watching our race nearly destroy itself in the two World Wars, he maintained that we should re-think all of our presuppositions until we develop philosophies that will help us end the bloodshed. Hence it is worth at least holding out as a hope that some who oppose the metaphysical and religious traditions might reconsider their opposition in light of what is at stake. Perhaps the desire to end tyranny and violence—one shared by so many people across all lines of culture and creed—could act as the impetus for this much needed rehabilitation, one that would serve to make accessible to we moderns not only personalism but many other rich veins of philosophical thought.

42. Jacques Maritain, *The Degrees of Knowledge or Distinguish to Unite,* translated by Gerald B. Phelan (Notre Dame, Indiana: University of Notre Dame Press, 1995), 3.

FRANCISCO E. PLAZA

# Maritain's Philosophy of Culture

## A Bridge between Metaphysics and Politics

### I. Introduction

IN THE CONTEMPORARY STUDY of metaphysics and political philosophy, it is common to find each pursued in isolation. This was not the case for many of the great thinkers in Western philosophy. Certainly Plato, Aristotle, St. Augustine, and St. Thomas Aquinas (to name a few) developed their political thought in harmony with a foundation laid out by their understanding of being and the human person. This also did not change with modern philosophers, as Hobbes and Marx also developed their own political theories in conjunction with an underlying metaphysical doctrine (even if it amounted to a certain denial of being). With regard to this general point, Maritain is no different: his metaphysics and anthropology serve as the foundational principles for his political theory. If we wish to study how one leads to the other, Maritain's philosophy of culture is particularly useful. It is there that his speculative and practical philosophy bridge the gap between them, shedding light on the greater unity in his thought overall.

Maritain's philosophy of culture may be divided into the following parts: (1) a philosophy of the human person as the author of culture; (2) an analysis of history as the unfolding of human culture; (3) a normative look at what makes a culture good or bad, and; (4) the interaction between culture and the political community. For each part, the primary source for Maritain's philosophy of culture is his *Integral Humanism*. The first part of his philosophy of culture is the anthropological basis (that is, his metaphysics of the human person, which one may also find in his *Existence and the Existent,* with greater detail on human subjectivity). Next, the second and third parts (Maritain's philosophy of history) involves his look at the evolution of Western civilization from the medieval era on, culminating in his analysis and subsequent critique of the modern age. Finally, the fourth part (Maritain's political theory) contains his proposal for a post-modern political age, addressing the modern crisis from the standpoint of an "integral humanism" and the "concrete historical ideal" which flows from it. While the first part is primarily speculative, the last part is primarily practical, with his philosophy of history linking the two in between.

## II. The Human Person as the Author of Culture

Maritain's working definition of culture may be found in his *Religion and Culture,* arguably his fullest treatment of this concept, in which he relates "culture" to "cultivation":

> Cultivating a field means inciting nature by some human labour to produce fruits which nature left to itself would have been incapable of producing, for what nature left to itself alone produces is "wild" vegetation. Such a figure gives us an idea of what culture means in the vocabulary of philosophy, the culture not of an expanse of soil, but of humanity itself. Man being a spirit animating a body of flesh, his nature in itself is a progressive nature. The labour of reason and the virtues is natural in the sense that it is in conformity with the essential inclinations of human nature; it brings into play the essential springs of human nature. It is not natural in the sense that it is supplied ready made by nature; it is an addition to what nature produces by itself and by itself alone.[1]

Here, Maritain emphasizes the creative aspect of man's subjectivity, his actions in the world. Culture is formed as a result of man's creative action, which is natural to him as a rational being. Yet, while culture unfolds according to human nature, it is not natural in the sense that it exists prior to and independently from human creation. Again, Maritain has two major points to make in this respect: first, culture is formed in accord with human nature, which is rational and social; second, while culture is a product of human nature, it requires specifically human action and creativity to come into being. Here the word "nature" has two senses, the first of which is Aristotelian (speaking of human nature, for instance, and referencing culture as

1. Jacques Maritain, *Religion and Culture* (London: Sheed and Ward, 1931), 1.

natural alongside that), the second of which, however, is in a modern light ("nature" as the external, physical universe). Both senses of the word continue to be used colloquially, although the second is arguably more common. While there is an overlap between the two notions, the second, modern conception of "nature" refers more specifically to the material world, unmodified by man. For instance, think of what we call a "nature trail" or "natural preserve." When something is called "natural" in this respect, it is simply thought of as something existing without human intervention. On the other hand, the first sense of "nature" (i.e., the Aristotelian sense) is a broader notion, more closely related to what we would call the essence of a thing. Take, for example, the statement that it is in man's nature to be a political animal. To summarize, then, culture is natural in the first sense but not in the second. It is natural in the first sense as an essential property of human action, but it is not natural in the second sense as it is not something the physical universe could produce left to its own devices. Ultimately, culture is a product of man's spirit; it cannot be reduced to the physical reality of the universe.

To understand the objective dimension of the human person, on the other hand, we refer back to the traditional Boethian definition: "an individual substance with a rational nature."[2] This is the basic starting point in Thomistic anthropology. It acknowledges the finitude of the human being in the universe, as well as his relation to God in the hierarchy of being. While Maritain retains this theocentric understanding of the human person, he emphasizes human subjectivity to an extent that the medievals did not. Individuals discover their own subjectivity through connatural knowledge alongside a *prise de conscience*, a point of self-discovery in which one begins to appreciate one's own subjectivity as subjectivity.[3] Maritain took this to be a key turning point in the shift toward modernity, and one he saw as a positive development, explaining that in this regard we find ourselves

2. Karol Wojtyla, "Thomistic Personalism," in *Person and Community*, translated by Theresa Sandok (New York: Peter Lang, 1993), 167. Boethius's definition for "person," which St. Thomas Aquinas (and Wojtyla) use, is: "*persona est rationalis naturae individua substantia.*" Wojtyla is particularly helpful here in explaining how this forms the "objective dimension" of the human person we refer to in the context of Maritain's anthropology.

3. This term "*prise de conscience*," literally a "beginning of awareness," occurs in several of Maritain's works: "Creative Intuition and Poetic Knowledge," in *Challenges and Renewals* (Notre Dame, Indiana: University of Notre Dame, 1968), 276; *Integral Humanism*, translated by Joseph W. Evans, in vol. 11 of *The Collected Works of Jacques Maritain*, edited by Otto Bird (Notre Dame, Indiana: University of Notre Dame, 1996), 160, 168, 198, 201, 296–99; *On the Philosophy of History*

living in a "reflex age."[4] It is with respect to this development that Maritain argues that the human person is a "universe to himself."[5] Thus, from an objective standpoint, the person is a finite creature; but from a subjective one, the person is infinite. This carries significant political consequence as it establishes a firm basis for human rights and human dignity, insofar as these values flow immediately from the very nature of personhood, so understood. Moreover, there is also a religious dimension to man's subjectivity. Through religion, we acknowledge subjectivity as subjectivity by way of interpersonal love. God's relationship with each person is the perfect model here, for not even we can account fully for our own subjectivity; only God can know us completely. Without God, we are alone, and the full extent of our subjectivity remains forever undisclosed.[6]

## III. History as the Evolution of Culture

Beyond individual human nature, we also come to consider culture through history. Indeed, if history is to be more than a collection of arbitrary facts, it must seek to interpret such facts according to a particular culture and order them in narrative form. We may look back on the Romans, for instance, to try to uncover their cultural milieu and evaluate it from our own cultural standpoint. Thus, in noting the connection between a philosophy of culture and history, Maritain understands "history" itself through the dynamics of culture over time in Western civilization, that is, the unfolding of culture. The philosophical stages in history are defined by cultural differences. His philosophy of history becomes a cultural critique of different historical eras, hoping to understand where we came from and where we are now within our own culture.

History itself can only be understood through a central characteristic that changes through time. As Eric Voegelin put it, "the order of history

(New York: Charles Scribner's Sons, 1957), 69; "Poetic Experience," in *The Review of Politics* 6, no. 4 (1944): 390; *Religion et Culture* (Paris: Desclée de Brouwer, 1946), 30–31.

4. Maritain used this term, "reflex age," in *Freedom in the Modern World*, translated by Richard O'Sullivan, in volume 11 of *The Collected Works of Jacques Maritain*, edited by Otto Bird (Notre Dame, Indiana: University of Notre Dame, 1996), 65. He quoted this same passage in *Integral Humanism*, 226.

5. Jacques Maritain, *Saint Thomas and the Problem of Evil* (Milwaukee: Marquette University, 1942), 9.

6. Jacques Maritain, "The Existent," chap. 3 in *Existence and the Existent* (New York: Random House, 1948).

emerges from the history of order."[7] To even speak of a "medieval" versus "modern" era implies a certain unity within each epoch that allows us to distinguish it from the other. For Maritain, we may explore that unity through the lens of culture. Medieval culture is defined by a theocentric view of man and the universe, whereby the objective dimension of reality is the primary focal point. Modernity, on the other hand, developed around an anthropocentric vision which emphasized subjectivity at the expense of objectivity.

The medieval temptation was to seek God at the expense of self. With this tendency unchecked, the human being came to relegate himself as "nothing" before God. This led to what Maritain called the "problem of grace and freedom," which centered upon the struggle of reconciling the scope of human freedom in light of the efficacy of divine grace.[8] Two paths emerged in response to this, both beginning the transition toward modernity. While one proclaimed itself against humanism from the start, the other intended to champion the person as the highest good. The first of these was the road of anti-humanism in the Protestant reform—"grace without freedom."[9] This pushed the medieval temptation to its logical extreme, accepting the human being as nothing in light of grace, touting "grace alone" as all that mattered. The second path was that of anthropocentric, secular humanism—"freedom without grace."[10] Here, it was the human will which mattered above all else. Both forces are at play in our own time, but it is primarily the second which took hold of the modern project as such. In spite of its intentions, secular humanism would also end in opposition to a true humanism, and this is precisely what led to the crisis of modernity.

## IV. The Problem of Modern Culture

The medieval worldview began to dissolve once man began to feel the pressures of being under so great an order as God's.[11] How could so lowly a creature ascend to these great heights? Man became nothing when placed

7. Eric Voegelin, *Order and History*, 1st vol. in vol. 14 of *The Collected Works of Eric Voegelin*, edited by Maurice P. Hogan (University of Missouri, 2001), 19.

8. See Jacques Maritain, *Integral Humanism*, 161–65.

9. Ibid., 162.

10. Ibid., 165.

11. Ibid., 161.

alongside God and struggled to deal with this reality. Maritain described this phenomenon as man's "horror of being nothing."[12] As a result, man longed to be despised.[13] Yet, this anguish was not meant to last. The shift from theocentricity to anthropocentricity, Maritain explained, was meant as a "rehabilitation"; an attempt at rescuing man from his nothingness.[14]

Maritain placed the beginning of modernity with Descartes, developed further by Rousseau and Kant. All of these, under the banner of rationalism, had raised up "a proud and splendid image of the *personality* of man, inviolable, jealous of his immanence and his autonomy and, last of all, good in essence."[15] In the name of man's "rights" and "autonomy," rationalism condemns any outside intervention into this universe, even if it were to come from God.[16] Yet, in this rage to encompass all of man within the natural realm, what began as exaltation fell into an abyss of despair. Maritain held Darwin and Freud responsible for this fall. Biological evolution and psychoanalysis reduced man to a biological entity determined by his surroundings, much like all else in nature.[17] Human dignity became obsolete, and the individual drowned within the collective. Here, the only hope for man was to establish something greater, something beyond the individual that would be worthy of dignity. There followed the Hegelian shift: a theology of the State.[18] The person as an individual is sacrificed to make way for the ideal man in the abstract collective.

Having illustrated the tragedy of man, Maritain then speaks of the tragedy of culture as a result of the dialectics of anthropocentric humanism. With respect to this dialectic, he identifies three distinct moments in modernity. The first occurs between the sixteenth and seventeenth centuries. In what Maritain calls the "classical" moment, man sought to advance culture in isolation, casting tradition aside in favor of human reason's absolute power.[19] Yet, in spite of man's attempt to abandon his roots, he was able to retain the Christian ideals inherited from the preceding age.[20] The second moment occurs in the eighteenth and nineteenth centuries, in which mod-

12. Ibid.
13. Ibid.
14. Ibid.
15. Ibid.
16. Ibid., 170.
17. Ibid.
18. Ibid., 171.
19. Ibid.
20. Ibid.

ern man came face-to-face with his opposition to God's order, and chose to battle God directly by praising himself.[21] This is the "bourgeois" moment, characterized by its "rationalist optimism."[22] Finally, in the third moment (from the twentieth century on), man comes back to despair. Unable to bear a world according to his own creation, he wages war on himself, seeking to create a new man from the rubble.[23] It is, for Maritain, the "revolutionary" moment of modernity.

Criticizing these three moments, Maritain argues that the first erred in reversing the order of ends.[24] Here, culture's supreme end was itself, and God was merely the means to its possession, in that God gave man the power to reign.[25] The second movement carried this problem forward to an extreme, denying the limitations of nature and seeking instead to have nature conform to man, rather than the reverse.[26] God was no longer a means to the natural end but simply an idea along the way.[27] Lastly, the third movement bows to technology in a desperate attempt to lord over the material realm.[28] Man encounters the harsh reality of nature, submitting himself to inhumanity to continue the ongoing struggle for ultimate dominance. Here, God is an obstacle; "God dies," enabling man to take His place.[29]

This brings us to Maritain's final consideration: the tragedy of God. Abandoning analogy, rationalism sought to arrive at God by its own power.[30] Either God could be sought univocally through human reason, or he could not be found at all. This constituted the split between the Cartesian God and that of Jansenius, where the first discovers God through reason alone and treats Him as a scientific principle, while the second treats God as completely unknown and untouchable save for the action of divine grace.[31] Moreover, as rationalism progressed, God became idealized as

21. Ibid.
22. Ibid.
23. Ibid.
24. Ibid.
25. Ibid., 172.
26. Ibid.
27. Ibid.
28. Ibid.
29. Ibid.
30. Ibid.
31. Ibid. This dichotomy may also be seen above in the "problem of grace and freedom," with rationalism moving into the path of "freedom without grace," and Jansenism going on the opposite path of "grace without freedom."

the perfect architect in a rational order.[32] This culminated in the second moment of the anthropocentric dialectic with Hegel's placement of God as the endpoint of the world's historical unfolding.[33] Finally, in stark contrast to God as the ideal ruler, Nietzsche heralds God's death in the third moment of the dialectic, subsequently calling for an impossible successor: the inhuman superman.[34] This ideal constitutes the heart of contemporary atheism.

## V. The Connection between Culture and Politics

The normative aspect of Maritain's philosophy of culture lies primarily in a return to metaphysical realism and Thomistic anthropology. To put it simply: Maritain's critique of modern culture is that it is anti-humanism masked as humanism, and this is primarily due to the fundamental disconnect between the modern idea of human nature and human nature in reality. Of course, the human will aims at the good by its own nature, and so culture forms the basis of man's attempt to reach the good as a result. If, however, we begin from a flawed vision of human nature, our notion of the human good goes awry, and human culture veers down a wrong path. Political forms arise from these same considerations (that is, of human nature and human good), but also along the same ground: human culture. So with an inhuman form of humanism in modernity, an equally inhuman political order takes shape.

Maritain links culture with civilization, explained as relating to "that same development of the human being considered in an eminent case—I mean to say in the production of the State and civil life of which civilization is, as it were, the prolongation and enlargement. The State and civilization are, at one and the same time, works natural to man and works of reason and virtue."[35] Man's political works, then, are also understood as belonging to human culture, alongside man's other rational and creative endeavors. Maritain ends by saying:

> Let our conclusion be that culture or civilization is the expansion of the peculiarly human life, including not only whatever material development may be necessary

32. Ibid., 173.
33. Ibid.
34. Ibid.
35. Maritain, *Religion and Culture*, 2.

and sufficient to enable us to lead an upright life on this earth, but also and above all moral development, the development of the speculative and practical activities (artistic and ethical) peculiarly worthy of being called a human development.[36]

It must be stressed, as we have begun to note, that part of Maritain's definition for true human culture and civilization involved an actual orientation toward the good, such that culture and civilization must help human life to flourish in an objective sense. Part of Maritain's explanation for culture is that it concerns the temporal good, indeed, the common good. The temporal good, however, is not arbitrarily determined by human will or circumstance. Rather, the temporal good of man is subordinate to the eternal good. Yet, while it is subordinate, the temporal good is not merely extrinsic. There is genuine good in the temporal realm, even as it is teleologically oriented toward the eternal good. Therefore, an integral understanding of culture and politics takes into account their true final end.

## VI. Integral Humanism and the Concrete Historical Ideal

Maritain's view of the modern crisis is that it is primarily anthropological. The secular humanism of modernity is in reality an anti-humanism, because it takes into account one aspect of the human person at the expense of another. Integral humanism, on the contrary, is meant to be a complete humanism, a whole look at the human person in terms of his objectivity (i.e., the metaphysical reality of human nature and his place within the cosmos), and his subjectivity (i.e., man's personal, irreducible dimension). In treating this problem, and again, focusing upon his philosophy of culture as the meeting point, we see the greater unity of Maritain's philosophy in bringing together both his speculative and practical thought.

Maritain's integral humanism is also profoundly important for his political theory itself. Here we see this in his promotion of Christian democracy and the concrete historical ideal, as well as his response to totalitarianism and secularism. Maritain's proposed personalist political order offers a "third path" between totalitarian ideologies (e.g., communism, fascism), and progressive, secular democracies. It seeks to embody within culture the proper anthropological and political principles. There is an objective

36. Ibid, 6.

authority and an understanding of humanity as subject to God together with a respect for liberty and religious pluralism which itself flows from his understanding of the person.

At the core of Maritain's political proposal in response to the modern crisis is the concrete historical ideal. It arises from the middle ground of personalism in a realist framework, as he deals with the reality of where things currently stand in Western civilization (operating under what he called the "historical sky"). When Maritain speaks of the concrete historical ideal, he establishes a contrast between his "ideal" political state and that of a thinker like Marx. Unlike *realpolitik,* Maritain does not deal with the current state of affairs purely in a pragmatic sense, focusing only on immediate consequences; but at the same time, his concrete historical ideal is not the ideal of social engineers and utopians who deal with an *ens rationis.*[37] On the contrary, his concrete historical ideal treats human nature and reality objectively, marking out the direction we must work toward for the sake of the good (in universal terms) as a real potential. This "ideal" good which we aim at does not involve (as with Marx) a change in nature; rather, it considers nature as fixed and objectively real. Practically speaking, Maritain outlines through the concrete historical ideal the principles of a "Christian democracy." As stated, this is a third way between totalitarianism and a purely secular democracy.

Thus, there are two primary elements of Maritain's response to modernity which we have brought together through the nexus of his philosophy of culture: integral humanism and concrete historical ideal. We began with a metaphysics of the human person and conclude with a practical political theory. Integral humanism entails a complete anthropology, that is, the human person both objectively and subjectively considered without a reduction to either one aspect or the other. In other words, integral humanism avoids the extremes of thinking of the human person from a solely subjectivist standpoint (as a being free to determine itself in any way according to his will without being bound by an underlying reality) or a deterministic, objective standpoint (for instance, as a being without personhood, determined by factors outside his control). We have analyzed the pitfalls of modernity, but we need to emphasize the positive aspect of Maritain's thought. Integral humanism maintains the fruits of modern culture's appreciation of

37. Maritain, *Integral Humanism,* 233.

human subjectivity, while retaining a sense of true meaning and goodness grounded on objective reality. We must acknowledge the spiritual dimension of man to have a complete picture of the human person. Man's spiritual dimension grounds his personhood. Objectively, it is ordered toward the eternal, and it serves as the foundation of his subjectivity. Just as man is political by nature, man is also spiritual by nature. The principles of human dignity, grounded upon our personhood, entail necessary consequences for the political order. This allows us to conclude with the concrete historical ideal, which provides us with a political way forward that retains an orientation toward a true common good, while at the same time working under the current historical sky of Western democracy.

ROSE MARY HAYDEN LEMMONS

# Unity and Diversity in Maritain's Stages of Civilization

## Reconsiderations

HISTORY TEACHES US THAT societies need unity in order to function, as Abraham Lincoln reminds us: "A house divided against itself cannot stand."[1] Whence comes this unity? From foundational cultural beliefs about God and the function of government, argues Jacques Maritain.[2] He relies on these beliefs to divide European history into three stages: a sacral stage that conflates Church and State, as in the medieval age; a secular stage that divides church and state and opposes religious belief, as has been occurring since the French Revolution; and, a Christian stage that preserves the church-state distinction while promoting collaboration without compromising the free exercise of religion, as in a future age.[3] Reconsideration of Maritain's arguments not only reveals the usefulness of identifying his religion-state rubric as the hermeneutical key for identifying how cultures, throughout history, vary in promoting unity amidst diversity, but also raises the question of whether the United States,

1. Abraham Lincoln, "Speech at Chicago on 9 July 1858," *Abraham Lincoln's Speeches*, compiled by L. E. Chittenden (New York: B. W. Dodge and Company, 1895), 95.

2. See, for example, Jacques Maritain, *Integral Humanism: Temporal and Spiritual Problems of a New Christendom*, translated by Joseph W. Evans (New York: Charles Scribner's Sons, 1968). *Integral Humanism* consists of lectures first given in 1934, slightly revised in 1946.

3. See ibid., 320–47. This book's subtitle shows Maritain's dedication to a new Christendom. His most concise formulation of these three stages of civilization is in "Church and State," a revision of his 1951 *Man and the State*, published in *Challenges and Renewals: Selected Readings*, edited by Joseph W. Evans and Leo R. Ward (Notre Dame, Indiana: University of Notre Dame Press, 1966) 309–347.

Maritain's vanguard of the third stage, is regressing into the second stage. Other key issues in Maritain's arguments include whether authentic democracy is a Christian artifact required by a new type of non-sacral Christendom, whether evil can triumph over goodness for only a limited time, and whether God is in charge of history. Discussion of these issues occurs throughout the essay's three main sections. The first section focuses on civilization's three stages, the second on the United States and civilization's third stage, and the third on America's current situation.

## I. Three Stages of Civilization

### *1. Civilization's First Stage: Unity through Religious Conformity*

The earliest civilizations were sacral in that social cohesion was won by shared religious beliefs and rites exercised or enforced by government. Sacral civilizations have taken various forms. Sometimes rulers were identified as divine beings as, for instance, were the Egyptian Pharaohs, or as divine agents ruling by God's authority, as did, for instance, the Roman emperors and the French king Charlemagne. Whatever the form, sacral civilizations seek social and political unity through religious conformity. Hence, the 1648 Peace of Westphalia required subjects to adhere to their ruler's faith.

Sacral civilizations charge government with enforcing religious conformity.[4] Hence, religious persecution is not uncommon, e.g., Socrates was executed for impiety in democratic Athens, Christians were persecuted by the emperors of Rome, Catholics by British Queen Elizabeth I, Huguenots by Catholic France in 1572, and Quaker Mary Dyer was executed by Boston Puritans in 1660. In colonial America, some degree of religious establishment was typical. For instance, establishment in colonial Virginia enforced Anglicanism, Church attendance, a tax for the salary of Anglican clergy, and the outlawing of rival religious perspectives. [5] Religious tests for government offices and voting were not uncommon. For instance, Charles Carroll of Carrollton, a signer of the Declaration of Independence, was ineligible

4. See Maritain, "Church and the State," in *Challenges and Renewals*, 319.

5. See G. Alan Tarr, "Church and State in the States," *Washington Law Review* 64 (1989): 73–110, esp. 81.

to vote in his home colony of Maryland because he was a Catholic.[6] In the twenty-first century, Muslim countries enforcing Sharia practice a form of religious establishment.

### 2. *Civilization's Second Stage: Unity through Secularism*

The transition from sacral civilization to secular civilization occurred in the United States in a different way than it did in Europe. While the process of secularization in Europe may be termed *rabid* due to its voracious attacks on religion, the term does not capture the American experience. In the United States, secularization of government began in 1634 when Lord Baltimore founded a religiously tolerant Catholic community in Maryland and in 1636 when dissident Puritan Roger Williams founded a religiously tolerant community in Rhode Island. Further progress in combining a religious society with a non-sectarian government proceeded slowly, with some reversals. For instance, colonial Maryland was quick to welcome large numbers of Puritans, who settled in Annapolis to escape persecution in Anglican Virginia.[7] In 1649, Maryland codified its practice of religious toleration in its Toleration Act. But this act perished when the Puritans established their denomination as Maryland's official church.

The disestablishment revolution received much needed energy with the 1717 publication—and the 1772 reprinting—of a pamphlet, by Congregationalist John Wise, arguing that the natural law could be known directly from the study of human nature and not just from the scriptural study of divine commands.[8] Also influential was the 1771–72 publication of William Blackstone's law books, wherein he argued that British common law was based on natural law as taught by Christian scriptures.[9] These books helped make the case that if moral laws were based on nature, they need not be sustained by the establishment of an official church. The process of disestablishment accelerated with the 1786 passage of Virginia's influential

6. See Alf J. Mapp Jr., *The Faiths of Our Fathers: What America's Founders Really Believed* (New York: Barnes and Nobles, 2006), 131.

7. See "Annapolis History," http://www.city-data.com/us-cities/The-South/Annapolis-History.html.

8. See Benjamin Fletcher Wright Jr., *American Interpretations of Natural Law: A Study in the History of Political Thought* (New York: Russell and Russell Incorporation, 1962), 50n1. First published 1931 by Harvard University Press.

9. Rose Mary Hayden Lemmons, *Ultimate Normative Foundations: The Case for Aquinas's Natural Law* (Lanham, Maryland: Lexington Books, 2011), 409.

Statue for Religious Freedom and the 1791 passage of the Constitution's First Amendment. It was not, however, until 1833 that religion was disestablished in every state.

Key reasons for disestablishment include the rise of various Christian denominations, the establishment's interference with religion, and the desire to prevent any civil authority coming between individuals and God.[10] Also crucial was the belief that natural law morality not only proscribes failing to worship God, killing, lying, committing adultery, and coveting, but is also endorsed by the Ten Commandments. In the States, disestablishment was thus not seen as restraining religious belief but rather as facilitating the exercise of religion. If this were not the case, it would not also be the case, as G. Alan Tarr comments, that even after disestablishment "most state constitutions expressly recognize the existence of God, often admitting the state's dependence on His blessings" with "some state constitutions" acknowledging a duty of religious worship."[11] Disestablishment in the States thus established a non-sectarian government in support of religious free exercise. As a result, although it is an open question whether the US will avoid the stage of rabid secularization, civilization's first stage—the sacral age—ended in the United States without passing through the second stage of rabid secularism.

Europeans were not so lucky. According to Maritain, Europe's sacral age disintegrated into a secularism that was religiously intolerant.[12] Rabid secularization in Europe was the culmination of various cultural and intellectual trends. One of these stretched back to the middle ages with nominalism's denial that things had God-created natures and that words were backed by universals. Nominalism undercut the sacredness of nature and the natural moral law as did early Protestants who sought to facilitate reliance on Scripture and faith alone by rejecting philosophical theology.[13] Accompanying these trends was the gradual development of an empirically based science that nurtured the belief that science could explain everything. The resulting scientism facilitated the popularization of atheistic materialism by Paul Henri Thiry, Baron d'Holbach (1723–89). He not only ran

10. See Tarr, "Church and State in the States," 81.

11. Ibid., 105.

12. See Maritain, "Church and State," in *Challenges and Renewals*, 319–21; *Integral Humanism*, 15.

13. See Maritain, *Integral Humanism*, 103–104. See also Anthony J. Carroll, SJ, "Disenchantment, Rationality and the Modernity of Max Weber," *Forum Philosophicum* 16, no. 1 (2011): 117–37.

a highly influential salon in Paris but also formulated the leading argument for materialism. He argued that unless materialism were true, there could be no regularity in nature.[14] The resulting materialist rationalism attacks not only the possibility of Divine providence, but also free will and the very existence of the soul—as shown, for example, by the works of David Hume, Charles Darwin, and Edward Osbourne Wilson.[15] These trends in philosophy, science, and culture contributed to the rise of materialism, atheism, and an anthropological humanism holding that "human freedom has no other rule or measure than itself."[16] Secular societies built on atheistic materialism and anthropological humanism necessarily fail—as is shown in the next section.

### 3: *The Unsustainability of Secular Civilization*

Maritain argues that secular civilization takes three forms: communistic anti-individualism, bourgeois individualism, and dictatorship.[17] These are self-defeating in so far as they "disregard the human person in one way or another, and, in its place, consider, … the material individual alone."[18]

The ways in which atheistic materialism and anthropological humanism affect society can differ. For instance, Maritain argues that while communism—like Christianity—rejects bourgeois life and proposes social unity and heroic sacrifice,[19] communism—unlike Christianity—also embraces an anti-individualism that reduces persons to a means of production, adopts atheistic anthropocentric humanism, and exercises "radical prejudice against all transcendence."[20] Communist societies thus fail to inculcate the spiritual resources necessary for combating "the self-propagating

14. Paul Henri Thiry and Baron d'Holbach, *The System of Nature: Laws of the Moral and Physical World*, translated by H. D. Robinson (1770/71; repr., Boston: J. P. Mendum, 1889), 88.

15. See David Hume, *Treatise of Human Nature* (Buffalo: Prometheus Books, 1992); Charles Darwin, *The Descent of Man and Selection in Relation to Sex* (New York: D. Appleton and Company, 1897); Edward O. Wilson, *Sociobiology: The Abridged Edition* (Cambridge, Massachusetts: Harvard University Press, 1980).

16. See Maritain, *Integral Humanism*, 107. For a brief critique of scientism and materialist rationalism see my "Modes of Re-enchantment: John Paul II and Familial Love," *Journal of Interdisciplinary Studies* 29 (2017): 91–93.

17. See Jacques Maritain, *The Person and the Common Good*, translated by John J. Fitzgerald (Notre Dame, Indiana: University of Notre Dame Press, 1966), 91. First published 1946.

18. Ibid., 91.

19. See Maritain, *Integral Humanism*, 40.

20. Maritian, *The Person and the Common Good*, 93.

power of money, the selfishness of the monied classes, and the secession of the proletariat raised by Marxism to the mystic principle of the Revolution."[21] This analysis, while conditioned on the exigencies of the 20th century, warns that the masses are susceptible to believing that they are exploited by others and that the overthrow of society and government is the answer. The history of Soviet communism, however, proves not only that communist revolutions produce regimes contrary to human dignity and rights, but also that they are ultimately unsustainable. In the hope of avoiding this fate, China and, perhaps, North Korea are flirting with what I call "communist capitalism," whereby the masses are allowed a very narrow exercise of their entrepreneurial spirit. It remains to be seen whether China and North Korea will continue to evolve along these lines.

A second type of secular society is one that Maritain terms as *bourgeois individualism* in *The Person and the Common Good*[22] and *bourgeois democracy* in *Man and the State*.[23] The bourgeois society is materialistic, egocentric, selfish, and greedy. It enshrines absolute liberty as if every human were "a little god" and the state the means of satisfying every desire.[24] The result is that the state eventually becomes omnipotent and reduces persons to numbers[25]—especially within democracies committed to majoritarian rule. For the bourgeois society lacks a real common good, takes no sides on conceptions of the common life, "even those most destructive to freedom and law … Nineteenth Century bourgeois democracy was *neutral* even with regard to freedom."[26] In other words, Maritain is arguing that the selfish prioritizing of wealth so characteristic of bourgeois democracies destroys concern for the freedom and rights of others. With that destruction, kindness, justice, and even belief in God perish. Furthermore, Maritain argues that the bourgeois mistakenly fear religion in so far as the domain of religion is eternal salvation, not the temporal order of civil life and government.[27] Nevertheless, Maritain also argues that without the Christian

21. Jacques Maritain, *Christianity and Democracy*, translated by Doris C. Anson (New York: Charles Scribner's Sons, 1944), 26.

22. See Maritain, *The Person and the Common Good*, 91.

23. See Jacques Maritain, *Man and the State* (Chicago: University of Chicago Press, 1951), 110.

24. Maritain, *The Person and the Common Good*, 92.

25. See ibid., 92.

26. Maritain, *Man and the State*, 110.

27. The bourgeois feared religion and hence failed to realize that the beliefs necessary for healthy democracies "do not belong to the order of religious creed and eternal life, but to the temporal or secular order of earthly life, of culture or civilization." Ibid., 110.

concern for the liberty and rights of God's children, materialistic societies inevitably disintegrate into fascist, racist, or communist societies.[28] The hedonistic consumerism and uncaring fear of others that have become typical in today's culture are thus a cause for concern.

Maritain's third form of secular society is dictatorial and usually formed in opposition to communism and individualism. In this society, "the multitude becomes conscious of itself and symbolizes its omnipotence unto itself in the person of a Master, the only person … above the 'organized' aggregate of material individualists."[29] As a result, it identifies "the person 'as person' as the enemy"[30]—even while demanding "a total devotion of persons."[31] Third World dictatorships and the fascism of racist Nazi Germany exemplify this form of totalitarianism.

Communism, bourgeois democracy, and dictatorship are Maritain's three archetypes of secular societies. Each reduces political power to coercion. Each assumes materialism and breeds an indifference or hostility towards God. Each promises a refuge for the human heart shorn of its search for God but still seeking meaning. Each denies human equality and imperils the freedom of conscience so indispensable for the common good.[32] Each also violates what Maritain identifies as the first precept of democracy, namely, trusting the people.[33] And each reveals that an all-inclusive secularism inculcates, first, anthropocentric humanism, which is antithetical to the spirituality necessary for pursuing common goods, and second, dysfunctional government lapsing into tyranny. It cannot be otherwise, argues Maritain: an all-inclusive secularism denies the reality of human ontology and cannot sustain the human spirit. For the human person must "win his liberty and his personality" through morality and the prioritization of the spiritual over material individuality.[34] Likewise, society must prioritize generosity, cooperation, and the "life of the spirit and liberty [that] reigns over that of senses and passions."[35] There can be no substitute for the God-centered life. Secularism ultimately deadens the human spir-

28. See ibid., 110.
29. Maritain, *Person and the Common Good*, 94–95.
30. Ibid., 95.
31. Ibid., 96.
32. See Maritain, *Man and State*, 161.
33. See ibid., 143.
34. Maritain, *Person and the Common Good*, 44.
35. Ibid., 45.

it and becomes self-defeating. Ultimately, Maritain saw the modern world as "led by Machiavelli's pessimism to regard unjust force as the essence of politics.... Its ultimate error lay in believing that man is saved by his own strength alone, and that human history is made without God."[36]

Maritain accordingly argues that the secular age is passing away, because he believes that God wills it. A secular world is in need of salvation; and "Christ is the savior of the world" (John 4:42).[37] Thus, human history lurches towards a greater respect for the human person and more humane societies.[38] God works in history to promote a better embodiment of Christian ideals, even if that progress is not linear and marked by regression. As Maritain explains:

> The world ... belongs to God by right of creation; to the devil by right of conquest, because of sin; to Christ by right of victory over the conqueror, because of the Passion. The task of the Christian in the world is to dispute with the devil his domain, to wrest it from him.... The world is saved ... delivered in hope, it is on the march toward the kingdom of God; but it is not holy, it is the Church which is holy.... [A]nd this is why it is treason towards this kingdom not to seek with all one's forces ... a refraction in the world of the Gospel exigencies.[39]

And when evil seems most triumphal as, for instance, when Nazi Germany swept through Europe or communist Russia engulfed much of the world, then, says Maritain, is our moment of choice: "History has launched us in an apocalypse where we are no longer permitted to shut our ears to the Gospel. A choice has to be made. Everything must be staked on hatred or cowardice or love."[40] For Christians, this choice is clear: love demands helping God better this world.

Maritain, prior to 1936 when he published *Integral Humanism,* saw the unfolding of World War Two as the "liquidation ... of the modern world" and the end of civilization's second stage, based on atheistic secularism.[41] The result was a confidence that civilization not only had a third stage but that its development was already in progress. Maritain's confidence was due, on the one hand, to his belief that time and history has a trajectory

36. Maritain, *Christianity and Democracy*, 21.

37. Maritain, *Integral Humanism*, 104.

38. See Jacques Maritain, *Rights of Man and Natural Law*, translated by Doris C. Anson (New York: Charles Scribner's Sons, 1943), 32, 35–36, 38.

39. Maritain, *Integral Humanism*, 108.

40. Maritain, *Christianity and Democracy*, 88.

41. Ibid., 17.

rooted in God's providence: "Time has a meaning and a history … governed by Him from above … by His eternal purposes."[42] This trajectory aims at establishing a new kind of Christendom—a non-sacral one that distinguishes between church and state, respects human dignity and religious liberty, and pursues social justice and civic friendship.[43] Civic friendship is especially important as it is the ultimate unifying cause of community, its "animating form" and "the true cause of civil peace."[44]

On the other hand, his confidence was also due to his discovery of various laws of civilization. One of these laws, he calls "The Law of Two-Fold Contrasting Progress" [45] or "the law of double antagonistic movement."[46] I would propose a combination of these terms: "Adversarial Growth Law." Doing so highlights that "[a]t the very same time that evil seems to grow triumphant, the ferment of justice and the energies of renewal are more or less secretly making headway."[47] Wickedness and goodness grow together as Christ set forth in the parable of the cockle and the wheat.[48] In this antagonistic growth, Maritain sees a relationship in which error helps the truth shine forth more clearly and, as an example, he notes that advances in the psychological understanding of the unconscious was stimulated by the erroneous notions of Freud.[49] More importantly, he uses these laws to explain how one stage of civilization transitions to another: when evil becomes ascendant, there is an undercurrent powered by Judeo-Christianity and classical antiquity that nurtures the continued growth of civilization.[50] These laws suggest that the third stage of civilization would counter the rabid secularization of the second stage by opposing its godless secularism with faith.

42. Jacques Maritain, "Spurious and Genuine Philosophy of History," in *Challenges and Renewals*, 356. Excerpted from *Philosophy of History* (New York: Charles Scribner's Sons, 1957), 29–37.

43. See Maritain, *Integral Humanism*, 6–7, 201.

44. Jacques Maritain, *The Rights of Man and Natural Law*, 36.

45. See Jacques Maritain, "The Law of Two-Fold Contrasting Progress," in *Challenges and Renewals*, 357. Excerpted Maritain, *Philosophy of History*, 43–52.

46. Ibid., 362.

47. Jacques Maritain, *Reflections on America* (New York: Gordian Press, 1975), 190.

48. See Maritain, "Law of Two-Fold Progress," 357. Maritain refers to Matthew 13:29–30.

49. See ibid., 362.

50. See Maritain, *Christianity and Democracy*, 23.

### *4. Civilization's Third Stage: Personalist Democracy and Unity through Christian Persons*

Maritain proposes that the third stage of civilization is one in which political unity thrives in a religiously diverse society: "[t]he unity of religion is not a prerequisite for political unity, and men subscribing to diverse religions or non-religious creeds have to share in and work for the same political or temporary common good."[51] What is necessary is that society's members share a "practical secular faith ... that they similarly revere, perhaps for quite diverse reasons, truth and intelligence, human dignity, freedom, brotherly love, and the absolute value of moral good."[52] This shared practical and secular faith is possible, according to Maritain, because it consists of "a set of practical conclusions or of practical points of convergence" from diverse theoretical justifications.[53] Maritain's proposal of practical convergences anticipates somewhat Rawls's "overlapping consensus"—with one key difference: unlike Rawls, Maritain sees these practical convergences as substantive and rationally necessary moral claims about the nature of the temporal common good as based on objective ethical data.[54] Another point of unification is the realization that, like the self, the other is a subject capable of goodness, of giving himself to another and receiving another self "as gift and giver."[55]

Maritain accordingly stresses that the raison d'être of government in this stage of civilization would be to protect and promote respect for the person through the *temporal* common good. Proper respect for persons enables a civilization to avoid the mistakes of bourgeois individualism, communism, and dictatorship, while organizing human freedom to promote the necessary common goods of social justice and civic friendship. After all, since none can "achieve his fullness alone" [56] and since common

51. Maritain, "Church and State," in *Challenges and Renewals*, 321.

52. Maritain, *Man and the State*, 111.

53. Ibid., 111.

54. Ibid., 80. Cf. John Rawls, *A Theory of Justice* (Cambridge, Massachusetts: Harvard University Press, 1971); and see especially "Justice as Fairness: Political Not Metaphysical," *Philosophy and Public Affairs* 14, no. 3 (Summer 1985): 223–51. For a critique of Rawls, see my *Ultimate Normative Foundations*, 54–58.

55. Jacques Maritain, "The Human Person and Society," in *Challenge and Renewal* edited by Joseph W. Evans and Leo R. Ward (Notre Dame, Indiana: University of Notre Dame Press, 1966), 288. Excerpted from *Scholasticism and Politics* (New York: Macmillan, 1940).

56. Ibid., 292.

goods are "common to the whole and to the parts,"[57] common goods benefit each and all. Temporal common goods recognize human equality[58]—and require democracy. "Democracy," explains Maritain, "is the only way of bringing about a moral realization of politics ... because democracy is a rational organization of freedoms founded upon law."[59] Such a democracy is personalist in its respect for the supra-temporal ends of the human person, while working to promote the temporal common good.[60] This good, according to Maritain, is "a relative though real earthly happiness, a good and livable structure of existence for the whole, a state of justice, of friendship, and of prosperity making possible for each person the fulfillment of his destiny."[61] Accordingly the Christian "asks that the earthly city be ordered so as to effectively recognize the right of its members to existence, to work, and to the growth of their life as persons."[62]

Personalist democracy requires a non-sectarian government respectful of religious liberty. It also requires Christians to be committed to non-sectarian government—and not to the sacral or rabidly secular governments of by-gone ages. Such Christians would keep the distinction between "the things that are Caesar's and those that are God's,"[63] while upholding both a non-sectarian government and a Christian society, by respecting persons and honoring the free exercise of religion.[64] This emphasis on a Christian society stems only partly from Maritain's pre-WWII focus on Europe, when Christianity was the alternative to the secular mainstream culture. It mostly stems from Maritain's eschatological vision of human history ending with a new kind of Christian society that so deeply respects the human person as to be inclusive of diverse religious beliefs and strongly committed to non-sectarian government. After all, Maritain identifies the soul of democracy as the "law of brotherly love and the spiritual dignity of the human person."[65] Love is the hub around which the third stage of civilization turns. And, as Carl Anderson so clearly states: "It is the unique contri-

57. Ibid., 293.
58. See Maritain, *Man and the State*, 161.
59. Ibid., 59, with in-text citation omitted.
60. See Maritain, *Integral Humanism*, 133.
61. Ibid., 133.
62. Ibid., 137.
63. Maritain, *Christianity and Democracy*, 36.
64. See Maritain, *Man and the State*, 175–79.
65. Maritain, *Christianity and Democracy*, 36.

bution of Christianity to have elevated love to the center of human life."[66]

The unifying force of the third stage of civilization is thus the person who is inspired by Christian love to work unselfishly for the establishment and preservation of a non-denominational community with laws and customs that respect the rights and the liberties of all. The result of such Christian activism is *not* the establishment of a sacral civilization that conflates eternity with the temporal world, but rather the establishment of a personalist democracy that welcomes religious expressions of all types. Maritain is confident that such a civilization is possible because he is confident that the Christian understanding of the common good will ultimately prevail. He believes this because "the bearers of this Christian conception will have … enough spiritual energy, enough force and political prudence to practically exhibit to men capable of comprehension that such a conception is in conformity with sound reason and with the common good."[67] As a result, Maritain argues that Christians concerned for the temporal common good will become leaders able to promote those non-sectarian temporal goods and rights that bind citizens together.

### 5. *Personalist Democracy as a Christian Artefact*

Nietzsche famously said, "The democratic movement is the heir of the Christian movement."[68] Maritain would agree: he identifies non-sectarian democracy as a Christian artefact.[69] As such, it is best defended by believers convinced that Christianity requires a non-sectarian, democratic system that respects persons, religious free exercise and human rights, and that promotes the temporal common good.

Christianity excels in inspiring the pursuit of human dignity, liberty, and the common good for several reasons. First, Christianity embeds the Scriptural norm to love others as one loves oneself in the Golden Rule and in the ability of the Golden Rule to suffice universally in practical mat-

66. Carl Anderson, *A Civilization of Love: What Every Catholic Can Do to Transform the World,* (New York: HarperCollins Publishers), 2008.

67. Maritain, *Integral Humanism,* 174.

68. Nietzsche, *Beyond Good and Evil: Prelude to a Philosophy of the Future,* translated with commentary by Walter Kaufmann (New York: Random House, 1966), §202.

69. See Maritain, *Christianity and Democracy,* 37; *Man and the State,* 125. Cf. Steve Bruce, "Did Protestantism Create Democracy?" in *Religion, Democracy and Democratization,* edited by John Anderson (London: Taylor and Francis Group, 2005), 3–20; and John Anderson, "Does God Matter, and If So, Whose God? Religion and Democratization," in *Religion, Democracy and Democratization,* 192–217.

ters—even in the absence of theoretical consent.[70] Universality neither makes the Golden Rule external to diverse local traditions nor imposes on them. Rather, universality emphasizes the insightfulness of local traditions. Second, Christianity inculcates the generosity, familial love, care for the vulnerable, honest work, solidarity, and subsidiarity that are necessary for keeping selfishness at bay, especially when organizing society for posterity. Third, Christianity strenuously defends religious liberty, rights, and non-sectarian governments supportive of religious free exercise. The state, after all, is not a church. A key reason why a Christian civilization would be committed to non-sectarian governments is its commitment to the natural law and to honoring the truths about human dignity and liberty. Fourth, Maritain also emphasizes the commitment to pluralism. Christian civilization, writes Maritain, must practice subsidiarity and be pluralistic in its "administrative and political autonomy" [71] so that smaller communities are granted "the greatest degree of autonomy possible"[72] and tolerance for their religious practices.[73] Subsidiarity and pluralism would thus characterize key institutions whether administrative, political, economic, or social.

Maritain argues that personalist democratic governments need the energy of Christians to accomplish several tasks: improving the common good, bettering the conditions of human life, and promoting justice, civil friendship, subsidiarity, and solidarity. Another task of Christians, according to Maritain, is to speak in ways that revive the unconscious Christian feelings and moral structures embodied in the history of nations due to the on-going influence of the natural law, which Maritain understands in terms of connatural inclinations rather than in terms of concepts abstracted from the intelligibility of nature.[74] So Maritain, although like Aquinas in considering Christianity to fulfill nature, argues that history shows that it was *only* Gospel inspiration that enabled the natural moral law to be sufficiently understood and used to develop personalist democracy: "Only when the

70. For discussion of the Golden Rule's universality, see Jeffrey Wattles, *The Golden Rule* (New York: Oxford University Press, 1996). For the need of the Golden Rule to be embedded in neighborly love to be properly interpreted, see R. Mary Hayden, "The Paradox of Aquinas's Altruism: From Self-Love to Love of Others," *American Catholic Philosophical Association Proceedings* 64 (1989): 77.

71. Maritain, *Integral Humanism*, 163.

72. Ibid., 164.

73. See ibid., 167.

74. See Maritain, *Man and State*, 167 and 91. Cf. Lemmons, *Ultimate Normative Foundations*, 15–20.

Gospel has penetrated to the very depth of human substance will natural law appear in its flower and perfection."[75] Natural law is like a rose bush that requires the sunlight of Christianity to flower into personalist democracy: "democracy can live only on Gospel inspiration."[76] Maritain argues that it is through Gospel inspiration that "the secular conscience has understood the dignity of the people and of the common man."[77] This secular understanding includes believing in human rights, justice, law, and universal fraternity.[78] Belief in fraternity is, for Maritain, the source of compassion and dedication "to make the structure of laws, institutions and customs of this common life a house for brothers to live in."[79]

Only Gospel inspiration can prevent the monstrous errors of the materialistic anthropologies characteristic of civilization's secular stage. Accordingly, the third stage of civilization flourishes when Christianity's role in underpinning personalist democracy becomes explicit and Christianity becomes the state's "all-pervading inspiration."[80] This inspiration is the Church's "moral power with which she vitally influences, penetrates, and quickens, as a spiritual leaven, temporal existence and the inner energies of nature."[81] As such, the role of Christianity is to inspire non-sectarian state officials to respect religious liberty and to advance the temporal common good. It is not, Maritain warns, to return to the monolithic sacral age in which the state wielded religious power.[82] Hence, what Maritain characterizes as Christendom in the third stage of civilization would endorse non-sectarian government and those moral teachings of the natural law that are necessary for the common good.[83] Among the key values to be endorsed by the state is religious liberty.[84] "The cause of freedom and the cause of the Church," writes Maritain, "are one in the defense of man."[85]

The resulting society, argues Maritain in his 1943 *The Rights of Man*

75. Maritain, *Man and the State*, 90.

76. Ibid., 61.

77. Maritain, *Christianity and Democracy*, 48.

78. For an extended treatment of the relationship of Gospel inspiration to secular conscience, see ibid., 42–56.

79. Ibid., 56.

80. Maritain, "Church and State," in *Challenges and Renewals*, 323.

81. Ibid., 325.

82. See ibid., 323.

83. See ibid., 238. By arguing that societal weaknesses allow a state to permit what natural law forbids, Maritain is closely following Aquinas. See ST I-II, q. 92, a.2.

84. See ibid., 342. See also *Man and the State*, 161–62.

85. Ibid., 347.

*and Natural Law*, would have four key characteristics.[86] First, the society would be *personalist* in recognizing that society is temporal and that ultimate human fulfillment is beyond society. It would thus forbid both sacral governments and rabidly secular governments; religious belief and free exercise are to be supported not condemned. Second, the society would be *communal* in its recognition that while the common good enables one to actualize one's potentialities and achieve a degree of fulfillment, it is not reducible to self-gratification as typical of bourgeois democracies. Third, the society would be self-consciously *pluralist* and supportive of the autonomous communities so crucial for human development. Fourth, the society would be "theist or Christian"—presumably by being based on the natural law or Christian revelation. The disjunction is inclusive because Maritain held that natural law virtues (justice, respect for religious liberty, equality, dignity of persons, civic friendship, cooperation in the common good) are also taught by the Gospel. Such a society would hence be tacitly Christian and animated by the desire to fulfill the precept of neighborly love whether known through faith or nature.[87] In such a community, the free exercise of religion would enable Christians—with an eye on eternity—to build a non-sectarian personalist democracy without compromising their beliefs or the church-state distinction.

Maritain also offers some key parameters for a healthy relationship between Church and State. First, he argues that the distinction between church and state is to be respected and that the state is not to be considered superior to the Church.[88] This parameter disestablishes religion while protecting the free exercise of religion, acknowledging a limitation on majoritarian rule, and freely unifying a people under God. This spiritual unification surpasses that provided by the natural law: "Only a faith superior to reason, vivifying the intellectual and affective activities, can assure men a unity founded not on constraint, but on interior assent . . . which nature by itself alone cannot safeguard."[89] For while reason can recognize the unity

86. See Maritain, *The Rights of Man and Natural Law*, 20–24.

87. The integration of natural law and Christian law is possible because both natural law and Christian morality are based on the self-evident obligation to love God and neighbors, according to Thomas Aquinas see (ST I-II, q. 100, a. 3, ad 1). See my "Are the Love Precepts Really Natural Law's Primary Precepts?" *Proceedings of the American Catholic Philosophical Association* 64 (1992): 45–71; and my *Ultimate Normative Foundations*, 133–53, 172–73, 192–94.

88. See Maritain, "Church and State," in *Challenges and Renewals*, 323–31.

89. Maritain, *Integral Humanism*, 160.

of human nature that obliges following the Golden Rule and promoting the temporal common good for minorities as well as for majorities, faith adds that every human is a child of God, made in His image, and redeemed by Christ. Either way, the temporal common good can be known as proper to all, but faith makes fervent the seeking of that good.

Maritain's second parameter is Church-State cooperation in advancing the temporal common good:

> By removing obstacles and opening the doors, the body politic, its free agencies and institutions, would positively facilitate the effort of the apostles of the Gospel to go to the masses and share their life, to assist the social and moral work of the nation, to provide people with leisure worthy of human dignity, and to develop within them the sense of liberty and fraternity."[90]

In keeping with his Thomistic personalism, Maritain argues that cooperation would not be through some "religio-political body" but through persons who are both members of the Church and the State.[91] Maritain adds that the American tradition of distinguishing Church and State while encouraging mutual cooperation is "an historical treasure."[92]

## II. Maritain on the Role of the United States in the Third Stage of Civilization

When Maritain argued for a future third age of civilization in *Integral Humanism*, he was not yet familiar with the American experiment.[93] I suspect that he even identified it as a type of bourgeois democracy—but, then came World War Two and sheltering in the United States. In the late 1950s, Maritain wrote *Reflections on America*. He there identifies the United States as having "inaugurated a really new phase in modern civilization."[94] As such, America is the imperfect vanguard of civilization's last age: "Her true future is somehow clearing the way for a new Christian civilization."[95] This future is unique to her: "if a new Christian civilization ... is to ever come about in human history, it is on American soil that it will find its starting

90. Maritain, "Church and State," in *Challenges and Renewals*, 339.
91. Maritain, *Man and the State*, 160.
92. Maritain, "Church and State," in *Challenges and Renewals*, 343.
93. See Maritain, *Reflections on America*, 174.
94. Ibid., 23.
95. Ibid., 193.

point."[96] Perhaps Maritain was too optimistic about America's future, given the democratic traditions in other Christian countries reporting religious belief to be very important, e.g., over 70% of Brazilians, almost 85% of Filipinos.[97] Maritain, however, based his judgment on the American economy, social life, spirituality, and democracy.

America's economic model, according to Maritain, "renders both capitalism and socialism things of the past."[98] America has humanized industry.[99] The antagonism between capitalists and workers has been overcome through a natural sense of fair play,[100] profit sharing,[101] and "the American ideal of equal opportunity for all and progress in social justice."[102] The key element is organized labor: "one of the most decisive forces in the history of the nation and of mankind."[103] He does, however, criticize this model for lacking an articulation that keeps Americans from communicating its uniqueness and urges Americans to develop an explicit philosophy of economics—and, perhaps, call it "economic humanism."[104]

American society, argues Maritain, expresses and inculcates various Gospel friendly values. For instance, the American passion for constant change expresses an almost "Christian detachment" and "sense of the impermanence of earthly things."[105] Maritain also argues that "deep beneath the anonymous American smile there is a feeling that is evangelical in origin—compassion for man, a desire to make life tolerable" symbolizing "the general, elementary, deep-seated sense of common human pilgrimage and brotherhood."[106] He also points out that America is a nation of immigrants, "bruised souls" perpetually arriving and inculcating compassion "and responsibility toward all those in distress"—and thereby establishing

96. Ibid.,188.

97. See Richard Wike, "Five Ways Americans and Europeans are Different," *Pew Research Center* (April 19, 2016), http://www.pewresearch.org/fact-tank/2016/04/19/5-ways-americans-and-europeans-are-different/

98. Maritain, *Reflections on America*, 101.

99. See ibid., 110.

100. See ibid., 114.

101. See ibid., 109.

102. Ibid., 101.

103. Ibid., 105.

104. Ibid., 113.

105. Ibid., 94.

106. Ibid., 92. Cf. Mother Teresa's analysis of smiling as opening love's door in my *Woman as Prophet in the Home and the World: Interdisciplinary Investigations* (Lanham, Maryland: Lexington Books, 2016), 235–36.

a "trace of Gospel fraternal love" in American spirituality.[107] Maritain also recognizes that Americans are more religious than Europeans[108]—a fact that the Pew Research Center confirmed as still being true in 2014.[109]

American democracy receives high praise from Maritain:

> The American body politic is the only one which was fully and explicitly born of freedom, of the free determination of men to live together and work together at a common task. And in this new political creation, men ... have freely willed to live together in peace, as free men under God, pursuing the same temporal and terrestrial common good.[110]

Herein he stresses several key elements of American democracy: (1) it is based on free consent; (2) it is ordered towards a common life that prioritizes the practical question of how to live together over the theoretical question of how to best live; (3) it acknowledges being under God and the supra-temporal end of persons. In so far as these characteristics presuppose respect for the human person, American democracy is personalist. For Maritain, the unification of these elements make possible a democracy that is non-sectarian in structure but Christian in inspiration. Accordingly, he identifies the U.S. Constitution as "an outstanding lay Christian document."[111]

It is fair to characterize American democracy as inspired by Christianity. First, the country was originally settled by colonists seeking either to establish distinct Christian communities or religiously tolerant societies.[112] Second, the disestablishment of colonial and state religions was sought in order to permit the free exercise of religion.[113] Third, personalist democracy—as developed in the States—embodied natural law's respect for nature, nature's God, and the person, as shown by the Declaration of

107. Maritain, *Reflections on America*, 86–87.

108. See Maritain, *Christianity and Democracy*, 31–34.

109. See Wike, "Five Ways." See Richard Wike, "Five Ways Americans and Europeans are Different," *Pew Research Center* (April 19, 2016), http://www.pewresearch.org/fact-tank/2016/04/19/5-ways-americans-and-europeans-are-different/ See also Laurence R. Iannaccone, "The Consequences of Religious Market Structure: Adam Smith and the Economics of Religion," *Rationality and Society* 3, no. 2 (April 1, 1991): 156–77.

110. Maritain, *Reflections on America*, 168.

111. Maritain, *Man and the State*, 183.

112. See Michael W. McConnell, "The Origins and Historical Understanding of Free Exercise of Religion, *Harvard Law Review* 103, no. 7 (1990): 1409–1517, esp. 1409 and 1422–27; Sanford H. Cobb, *The Rise of Religious Liberty in America: A History* (London: MacMillan Co., 1902).

113. See I.2 section above, "Civilization's Second Stage: Unity through Secularism."

Independence, the Constitution and its Bill of Rights.[114] Personalist democracy was thereby endorsed by the country's founding fathers, whether they were Enlightenment thinkers convinced that every law of nature was intelligible to human reason or religious believers convinced that the natural law is in the Decalogue and that God's grace remains necessary to make fulfillment of the law possible.[115] Natural law thus united American founders and made possible the creation of a country dedicated to freedom and virtue. For it is only through virtue that freedom does not descend into enslavement to disordered desires. The founders argued that virtue was indispensable to American liberty. Consider, for instance, the words of George Washington: "Tis substantially true, that virtue or morality is a necessary spring of popular government. The rule indeed extends with more or less force to every species of free government."[116] Natural law truths are perennial and as non-sectarian retain their ability to unite and encourage those experiencing the emptiness of secular humanism. Nevertheless, as the last section shows, encouragement is not realization, and events in the late-twentieth century have greatly obscured the natural law and impeded further development of civilization's third stage.

Maritain, moreover, argues that, despite having constituent elements of civilization's third stage, the United States has problems that preclude identifying it as having achieved the third stage of civilization. These problems

114. For extensive arguments on this point see Thomas G. West, *The Political Theory of the American Founding: Natural Rights, Public Policy, and the Moral Conditions of Freedom* (Cambridge: Cambridge University Press, 2017). I also argue this point in "Bioethics and the Declaration of Independence: Current Status," *University Faculty for Life 2017 Conference*, Minneapolis, June 2017.

115. See, for instance, John Calvin, *Institutes of the Christian Religion*, edited by John T. McNeill, translated by Ford Lewis Battles (Philadelphia: Westminster Press, 1960), 367–68: "Now that inward law which we have above described as written upon the hearts of all, in a sense asserts the very same things that are to be learned from the two Tables." The like was also argued by John Wise see Wright, *American Interpretations of Natural Law*, 50n1—and by the signer of the Declaration of Independence and Princeton educator John Witherspoon. See Daniel Robinson, "The Scottish Enlightenment and the American Founding," *Monist* 90, no. 2 (2007): 170–81, https://academic.oup.com/monist/article-abstract/90/2/170/998360/The-Scottish-Enlightenment-and-the-American?redirectedFrom=fulltext. Aquinas, likewise, argued that the Decalogue encapsulates natural law (ST I-II, qq. 98–100). For an in-depth discussion of how Aquinas could hold that all are bound by the natural law while also acknowledging the reality of sin and the inadequacy of natural law as a guide for salvation, see my *Ultimate Normative Foundations*, 182–87.

116. George Washington, "Farewell Address" in *The Founders' Constitution*, vol. 1, edited by Philip B. Kurland and Ralph Lerner (Indianapolis: Liberty Fund and the University of Chicago, 1987), 684.

include racism and a need for a spiritual renewal able to oppose naturalism and establish not only "obedience to moral imperatives and the law of God dominate over all other consideration" but also "Christian faith and morality" as the guiding light in "the common consciousness and common behavior."[117] He identifies as a weakness the "lack of sufficiently firm and integrated intellectual certainties" resulting in insecurities about American "idealistic incentives and ... faith in the power of good will and generosity."[118] These insecurities, I argue, arise from being unaware of the religious reasons for disestablishing churches and the crucial roles played by natural law in underwriting the Declaration of Independence and in generating diversity without relativism.[119] Healing American insecurities requires a greater familiarity with history and natural law philosophy. It also requires welcoming religious faith back into what Richard Neuhaus identified as the naked public square.[120] Until then, Americans lack the resources to avoid egocentric materialism and the misguided belief that human dignity is best defended by the rabid secularism of civilization's second stage.

## III. America's Current Situation

Since Maritain's death in 1973, the problems confronting America have grown direr. The sexual revolution, the pill, abortion, and no-fault divorce have precipitated a sea change in attitudes towards promiscuity, marriage, family, and the natural law. For instance, nearly forty percent of all births were non-marital in 2014.[121] Other differences include identity politics and the subjectification of spirituality. Identity politics emphasizes one's race, creed, gender, or economic status as the basis of one's social and political identity rather than one's status as a person "endowed by the Creator with

117. Maritain, *Reflections on America*, 189–90.

118. Ibid., 46–47.

119. For an in-depth look at disestablishment, see McConnell, "The Origins and Historical Understanding," 1409–517; Sanford H. Cobb, *The Rise of Religious Liberty in America: A History* (London: MacMillan Co., 1902). For an in-depth discussion of natural law's influence on the Declaration of Independence and the Revolutionary War, see Forrest McDonald, *Novus Ordo Seculorum: The Intellectual Origins of the Constitution* (Lawrence, Kansas: University Press of Kansas, 1985). For analysis of natural law's diversity without relativism through diverse applications of universal norms, see my *Ultimate Normative Foundations*, 270–73; 351–73.

120. See Richard John Neuhaus, *The Naked Public Square: Religion and Democracy in America* (Grand Rapids, Michigan: Eerdmans, 1988).

121. See Brady E. Hamilton et al, "Births: Final Data for 2014," *National Vital Statistics Reports* 64, no. 12 (December 23, 2015): 1–45, 7.

unalienable rights" as proclaimed by the Declaration of Independence. This emphasis on differences divides a people into antagonistic groups rather than unifying individuals in civic friendship and the pursuit of justice. Spiritual subjectivism emphasizes healing the self and seeking self-sufficiency rather than emphasizing transcending the self and loving God more fully.[122] The popularity of subjective spiritualities has led to more Americans self-identifying as spiritual but not religious, with more of the religiously unaffiliated rejecting belief in God or a universal spirit (up to 33% in 2014, up from 22% in 2007).[123] Overall, the Pew Research Center confirms that the country is becoming less religious.[124] Exacerbating these changes has been the US Supreme Court's hostility towards the free exercise of religion that began in 1990 with its decision in *Smith*.[125] The pervasiveness of these problems threatens to plunge the United States into the secular second stage of civilization.

Nevertheless, there are reasons to hope that these problems will be addressed and that the States will cease regressing into a rabid secularization. One of these reasons is that history confirms Maritain's Adversarial Growth Law, which holds that evil's triumph in this world can never be permanent because there is always an undercurrent of goodness that will eventually become strong enough to overthrow it. For instance, the South's practice of slavery in the eighteenth century was ultimately defeated by the Civil War, by the Thirteenth Amendment, and by a renewed appreciation for the Declaration of Independence's claim that "all men are created equal"—even though slavery had seemed unassailable after the 1854 repeal of the Missouri Compromise and the 1857 Dred Scott decision of the US

122. See Lemmons, "Modes of Re-enchantment," 93–99. Cf. Christopher Patridge, *The Re-enchantment of the West: Volume II Alternative Spiritualities, Sacralization, Popular Culture, and Occulture* (New York: T & T Clark International, 2005), 6–7.

123. See Pew Research Center, *U.S. Public Becoming Less Religious* (3 November 2015): 1–265, esp. 15, 140, http://assets.pewresearch.org/wp-content/uploads/sites/11/2015/11/201.11.03_RLS_II_full_report.pdf. For an in-depth discussion of America's contemporary non-Christian spirituality, see Christopher Patridge, *The Re-enchantment of the West*, 2 vols. (New York: T & T Clark International, 2005); Leon Surette, *The Birth of Modernism: Ezra Pound, T. S. Eliot, W. B. Yeats and the Occult* ( Montreal: McGill-Queen's University Press, 1993); Richard Cavendish, *History of Magic* (New York: Taplinger Publishing Company, 1977); and my "Modes of Re-enchantment," 91–114.

124. Pew Research, *U.S. Public Becoming Less Religious*, 3.

125. See Rose Mary Hayden Lemmons, "Tolerance, Society and the First Amendment: Reconsiderations," *University of St. Thomas Law Journal* 3, no. 1 (2005): 75–91.

Supreme Court.[126] Accordingly, although rabid secularism, subjective spirituality, identity politics, and the sexual revolution's disdain for natural law may appear to be irreversible, the Adversarial Growth Law says otherwise. This is especially the case when one considers that the author of the Adversarial Growth Law is none other than God. In God we must trust, as our coinage urges us.

There are associated reasons for hope. One is that Maritain was right about the American smile: Americans still tend to offer strangers compassion through a smile that recognizes the subjectivity of the other. This recognition of the other as a person is an awareness that others are basically human like oneself, and thereby one's equal. This awareness facilitates following the Golden Rule, heeding the obligations of neighborly love, and acknowledging the need to base government on free consent. This acknowledgement confirms Maritain's insight that governing is a practical matter of figuring out ways to secure basic human rights and advance the common good of equals through a personalist democracy. Personalist democracies honor the right to peacefully pursue happiness as a supra-temporal destiny. They require that all work together to establish a civilization and a government worthy of persons. Maritain is correct in holding that such unification is possible on the practical level, despite diverse convictions, when respect for persons and their basic rights guides policies. Respect, compassion, and practicality are thus essential to fully establish a truly personalist civilization.

There is also hope in the growing numbers of baptized Catholics worldwide, up to 17.7% of the Earth's total population in 2015, a 7.4% increase from 2010.[127] In the US, Americans remain predominately religious. According to a 2014 study by the Pew Research Center, 71% self-identify as Christian, with 76.5% self-identifying as religiously affiliated (albeit down from 83.1% in 2007).[128] Another study from 2015 shows that America is not yet as secular as Europe; among those who consider religion to be *very* important are 53% of Americans; 30% of Poles; 25% of Italians; 20% of Span-

126. See Jason A. Adkins, "Lincoln's Constitution Revisited," *Northern Kentucky Law Review* 36, no. 2 (2009): 211–50, esp. 239–40. For an extensive treatment, see Harry V. Jaffa, *Crisis of the House Divided: An Interpretation of the Issues in the Lincoln-Douglas Debate* (Chicago: The University of Chicago Press, 2009). Originally published 1959.

127. See *Annuarium Statisticum 2015*, https://press.vatican.va/content/salastampa/en/bollenttino/pubblico/2017/04/06/170406e.html.

128. See Pew Research, *U.S. Public Becoming Less Religious*, 11n3 and 17.

iards, Brits, and Germans; and 10% of the French.[129] With these numbers, it seems reasonable to hope that America will rebound from her problems and return to more fully realizing civilization's third stage.

Moreover, there are recent signs that rabid secularism may be weakening in America. The importance of religious belief has increased to 68% in 2014, up from 66% in 2007.[130] As a result, many who experience a crisis of meaning due to adopting one of today's popular subjective spiritualities will encounter a religious believer who can help them find the meaning that only God can provide. The US Supreme Court also seems to be lessening its hostility toward traditional Christianity as evidenced by its 2014 decision that Hobby Lobby would not have to include abortifacients in its health insurance plan to be in compliance with the Affordable Healthcare Act.[131] Other hopeful signs includes the Court's 2017 decision that the Trinity Lutheran Church in Missouri could not be denied state funds it had requested for resurfacing a playground, and the Court's very narrow 2018 decision in favor of the Colorado baker Jack Phillips who had dedicated his creativity to Christ and had refused to create a same sex wedding cake because he believed doing so incompatible with his Christian beliefs. Upcoming cases will further test the Court's commitment to First Amendment rights and determine whether the Court will remedy not only the rabid secularization resulting from its prioritizing anti-establishment concerns over free exercise rights, but also the hostility towards religious believers arising from inconsistencies in its First Amendment jurisprudence.[132]

A closely related reason for hope is the tradition of appealing to the Declaration of Independence for help in crises. The Declaration has been helpful because it identified the country's foundational political philosophy as theistic and based on natural law through its appeals to "nature and nature's God," trust in Divine Providence, and self-evident truths including the equality of human beings and the unalienable rights to life, liberty, and

129. See Wike, "Five Ways." See also Richard Wike, "Five Ways Americans and Europeans are Different," *Pew Research Center* (April 19, 2016), http://www.pewresearch.org/fact-tank/2016/04/19/5-ways-americans-and-europeans-are-different/

130. Pew Research, *U.S. Public Becoming Less Religious*, 11.

131. See https://www.supremecourt.gov/opinions/13pdf/13-354_olp1.pdf.

132. The proper way to interpret the US Constitution is to do so consistently and that it possible only when the anti-establishment provision of the First Amendment is subordinated to its free exercise provision, as I argue in "The Affordable Care Act and Religious Liberty: Principles of Adjudication," in *The Affordable Care Act Decision: Philosophical and Legal Implications*, edited by Fritz Allhoff and Mark Hall (New York: Routledge, 2014), 179–92.

pursuit of happiness. For instance, in the "I Have a Dream" speech of 1963, Martin Luther King Jr. characterized the Declaration as a promissory note of equality and liberty that had not yet been fulfilled. In light of that promise, he proclaimed his dream that "one day this nation will rise up, live out the true meaning of its creed: 'We hold these truths to be self-evident, that all men are created equal' ... that my four little children will one day live in a nation where they will not be judged by the color of their skin but by the content of their character."[133] A hundred years before, in 1863, Lincoln sought to bind the wounds of a nation torn apart by civil war by appealing to the Declaration and characterizing it as a commitment to the proposition that "all men are created equal."[134] And almost a century before that, in 1776, the United States came into existence through the Declaration's argument that governments are established in order to secure the unalienable rights bestowed by nature and nature's God.

These historic appeals to the Declaration in the eighteenth, nineteenth, and twentieth centuries reveal a reliance on an authoritative document that identifies basic American rights and determines the proper interpretation of the Constitution.[135] They also show that the human heart is inspired to adopt its proclamations of equality and unalienable rights as true. The persuasive power of the words "We hold these truths to be self-evident that all men are created equal" is such that Abraham Lincoln describes them as so stirring the heart that even those unconnected with the founding of the country have the confidence to claim that equality—"as though they were blood of the blood, and flesh of the flesh, of the men who wrote that Declaration; *and so they are*."[136]

The self-evidence of human equality under God and the unalienable rights of the Declaration gives hope that Americans in the twenty-first century will retain and strengthen their personalist democracy by remaining faithful to the Constitution's Bill of Rights, especially the First Amend-

133. Martin Luther King Jr., "I Have a Dream Speech," (1963), https://www.archives.gov/files/press/exhibits/dream-speech.pdf

134. Abraham Lincoln, "Gettysburg Address" in *Lincoln's Speeches*, 324.

135. A more in-depth argument about the natural law foundation of the Declaration of Independence and the Constitution's reliance on the Declaration can be found in Adkins's "Lincoln's Constitution Revisited," 211–50.

136. Lincoln, "Speech on 10 July 1858," in *Abraham Lincoln's Speeches*, 112; italics added. Also see his 1861 speech at Independence Hall on February 22: "[The] sentiment in the Declaration of Independence ... gave liberty, not alone to the people of this country, but hope to all the world for all future time." Ibid., 235–36.

ment's guarantee of the free exercise of religion, freedom of speech, a free press, and the right of assembly. By so doing, America will more deeply enter into the third stage of civilization and develop a truly personalist—and religiously diverse—democracy wherein the temporal common good is pursued through church-state collaborations without compromising the distinction between church and state or the free exercise of religion.

## IV. Conclusion

Maritain's division of European civilization into three stages, on the basis of whether church-state relationships are sacral, hostile, or mutually supportive, can be successfully adapted as a religion-state criterion that likewise divides the entire history of civilization into those three stages. This division helpfully analyzes today's challenges of promoting both unity and diversity, while also illuminating the need for increased Christian political activism to develop and secure personalist democracy.

Whether Maritain is also right to identify the third stage as Christendom and civilization's final stage depends on eschatology and the definition of Christendom. Christendom can be defined as sacral geo-political entity with an established Christian Church, as was typical in the American colonies prior to the American Revolution and in Europe prior to the French Revolution. This is not Maritain's definition. Rather, he seems to define Christendom as a personalist non-sectarian democratic political *culture* that respects human dignity and is sustained by Christian activists seeking to collaborate with others interested in establishing the temporal common goods of justice, liberty, subsidiarity, and civic friendship. Such collaboration is possible, first, because Christian activism is based upon universal moral truths embedded both in natural law and the Scriptural precept to love one's neighbors as oneself—whether known through faith or nature.[137] Such collaboration would build the civilization of love sought by Pope John Paul II, and, before him, by Pope Paul VI. Second, collabo-

137. "Thus it is toward the perfection of natural law and Christian law that the pluriform juridic structure of the body politic would be *oriented*, even at those stages of it which would be the most imperfect and the farthest removed from the Christian ethical ideal. The body politic would be directed toward a positive pole that would be integrally Christian, and its different structures would deviate more or less from this pole, according to a measure determined by political wisdom." Maritain, *Integral Humanism*, 167. The integration of natural law and Christian law is possible, because both natural law and Christian morality are based on the self-evident

ration is also possible because a good and loving God is at work in a world already redeemed by Christ.

However, civilization's third stage cannot occur unless the human heart is sufficiently healed to love others and seek truly common goods rather than yielding to spiritual substitutes for God, whether they be egocentric—bourgeois—interests or the twisted seeking for self-transcendence through some form of totalitarianism. Maritain's spiritual analysis of governments enables him to argue that personalist democracy is a tacit Christian artefact ultimately based on the realization that respecting persons and achieving temporal common goods require collaboration between distinct religious and political institutions.[138] His argument takes in the reality of sin and the gifts of Christ to conclude that personalist democracy cannot be sustained without "a genuine living Christianity,"[139] whereby lay Christians—nourished by the Church—seek to establish and maintain non-sectarian personalist democracies that respect the principles of natural law, human rights, autonomous social communities, and religious free exercise as a way of loving their fellow citizens and God. Such a personalist civilization would be truly humane—and a Christian ideal. Its full realization would favor adopting Maritain's view of Christendom as requiring pluralism and non-sectarian government.

Yet, for all his perspicacity, Maritain overlooks his own perceptive extraction of the Adversarial Growth Law from Matthew 13:29–30. This Law predicts that until time ends, there will be no escape from strife and conflicts. Endemic to the human condition are the challenges of government, work, family life, diversity, poverty, hunger, disease, illiteracy, lust, selfishness, laziness, greed, religious indifference, Original Sin, ignorance of Christ and God's merciful love, and difficulties stirred up by the Devil. Given these human realities, ought such a troubled third stage be identified as civilization's final stage?

I think not. Surely, civilization's last stage is the stage in which "Our Fa-

---

obligation to love God and neighbors according to Thomas Aquinas. See ST I-II, q. 100, a. 3, ad 1. For an explication on the foundational role of these love precepts in natural law, see my "Are the Love Precepts Really Natural Law's Primary Precepts?" *Proceedings of the American Catholic Philosophical Association* 66 (1992): 45–71; and, my *Ultimate Normative Foundations*, 133–53, 172–73, 192–94.

138. Maritain discusses the various political truths of Christianity in *Christianity and Democracy*, 44–45, 47–60. For an example of Christianity's love and respect for persons, see the Second Vatican Council document *Dignitatis Humanae* [*Declaration on Religious Liberty*].

139. Maritain, *Christianity and Democracy*, 98.

ther's will is done on earth as it is in heaven." And that means civilization's final stage is one in which the Law of Adversarial Growth no longer applies. According to Revelation 21:1–4, the final stage involves a new Jerusalem descending from heaven in which there is "no more death or mourning, wailing or pain."

Distinguishing Maritain's third stage of civilization from the last one does not diminish his insights into the Adversarial Growth Law, the nature of the temporal common good, the stages of civilization, the United States' rocky venture into civilization's third stage, and the need for Christians to build the civilization of love by supporting personalist and non-sectarian democracies that promote unalienable rights, justice, respect for persons, and civic friendship. Christians, after all, are called to be civilization's salt, "the salt of the earth" (Matthew 5:13).

GREGORY KERR

# A Faustian Bargain

## Jacques Maritain, C. S. Lewis, and the Loss of Reason

> Here are men going afar to marvel at the heights of mountains, the mighty waves of the sea, the long courses of great rivers, the vastness of the ocean, the movements of the stars, yet leaving themselves unnoticed and not seeing it as marvelous that when I spoke of all these things, I did not see them with my eyes.
>
> —St. Augustine[1]

> The mind, even more so than the physical world and bodily organisms, possesses its own dimensions, its structure and internal hierarchy of causalities and values—immaterial though they be. Contemporary idealism, in the last analysis, refuses to recognize that mind has any nature or any structure. It sees it only as a pure movement, a pure freedom. Hence, it never really gets beyond spreading it out, whole and entire, upon a single plane of intellection like a two-dimensional world, infinitely flat.
>
> —Jacques Maritain[2]

1. Augustine, *Confessions*, 2nd edition, translated by Frank J. Sheed (Indianapolis, Indiana: Hackett Publishing, 2006), 197.

2. Jacques Maritain, *Distinguish to Unite or The Degrees of Knowledge*, translated by Gerald B. Phelan (New York: Charles Scribner's Sons, 1959), ix.

## I. The Life of the Mind

Recently, someone recommended that I read an online blog that focused on the disaffection of the millennials towards the Church. One of the solutions that the author offered was this:

> Stop wasting time on the religious mumbo jumbo and get back to the heart of the gospel. If you have to explain your mission and values to the church, it's overly-religious and much too complicated. We're not impressed with the hours you brag about spending behind closed doors wrestling with Christianese words on a paper. We're impressed with actions and service.[3]

Now admitting that perhaps we do not listen to the millennials as much as we should, there is a lot that is troubling here. How did we get to the point where the unchurched know so much more about genuine Christian belief and practice than those who are theologically and spiritually educated? Maybe a clue to the answer lies in what Richard Dawkins tweeted (24 December 2013) about theology: "Again accused of ignorance of theology. But what is there in 'theology' to be ignorant ABOUT? Tell me 1 theological fact & I'll learn it." Even among some believers, there is a deep suspicion that there is little really to know here. And what can be known would be, of course, obvious and plain to everyone. After all, theology and philosophy are not "hard sciences."

The ancient and medieval worlds, to the contrary, believed that truth was difficult. Aristotle told us, "For as bats' eyes are to daylight so is our intellectual eye to those truths which are, in their own nature, the most obvious of all."[4] It is difficult and indeed an achievement to know the truth, for it is more than a collection of ready-made facts. To know something is to "become" it in a way. As Maritain describes it: "In the act of knowing I am identified—spiritually—with another; I, while keeping my actual identity, become immaterially or 'intentionally' the other in so far as it is other."[5] In a sense, while we may talk about having ideas in our mind, it would be more appropriate to say we *are* our ideas and mind. To learn is to

3. Sam Eaton, "59 Percent of Millennials Raised in a Church Have Dropped Out—And They're Trying to Tell Us Why," https://faithit.com/12-reasons-millennials-over-church-sam-eaton/ (accessed by author July 3, 2019).

4. Aristotle, *Metaphysics* 2.1, 993b, cited in C. S. Lewis's *Miracles: A Preliminary Study* (New York: Macmillan, 1960), 39.

5. Jacques Maritain, *Creative Intuition in Art and Poetry* (Princeton, New Jersey: Princeton University Press, 1981), 230.

become different; learning requires us to stretch ourselves. As the proverb attributed to Oliver Wendell Holmes goes, "one's mind, once stretched by a new idea, never regains its original dimensions." For Aristotle, as for Aquinas later, what was vital to acquire, along with the obvious moral virtues, was the development of intellectual virtues, such as wisdom, science and understanding, to make our reason strong. We need these to know reality properly. In the *Nicomachean Ethics,* those who wanted a mathematically certain knowledge of ethics were not even wrong; they were simply uneducated. This was a not a matter of being uninformed; such people were not developed intellectually. Genuine knowledge involved virtue. Like virtues in the moral sphere that perfected one's character, there were virtues in the intellectual sphere that perfected one's mind. And the mind—as Maritain testified in the opening quote above—has a structure that can be perfected or harmed. Developing the health of the mind was much like developing the health of the body; you did not simply feed it facts or numbers to crunch, you stretched and trained it. You made the mind stronger for its intellectual journey. For his education, the escaped prisoner in Plato's Cave had to climb a rugged ascent and it was painful; indeed, he had to be forced to do it and sometimes even dragged! First, it required a conversion and then it required the pain of being blinded by light, a light that was at the source of all prior understanding. It required an adjustment and strengthening of the faculties. Later, it required a willingness to help others in the face of their violent rejection of that help.

One can get a sense of the strength of the minds that St. Thomas taught in the Middle Ages. All one has to do is look over the *Summa Theologica* and then review its beginning and contemplate the significance of the fact that all of this theology was intended for beginners! Beginners were expected to be familiar with, and to think along the lines of, the Scriptures, Aristotle, Plato, Augustine, Boethius and many other thinkers, all for which St. Thomas provides no introduction. In the twenty-five years I have been teaching, I have been required to create many courses and teach many philosophers, and St. Thomas's philosophy stands out for two reasons: first, it is the most difficult to master and, second, it has the power to strengthen my intellectual abilities and to illuminate common sense more powerfully than all the others.

Well, if the beginning student for Aquinas was so informed, why is the contemporary student not expected to be so informed? What happened?

The Age of Reason happened:[6] one was no longer expected to follow any man's tradition but to use one's own reason by oneself. The great irony, I shall argue, was that the degree to which we exalted the life of reason was matched by the degree to which we denigrated it. Thinkers praised the spirit of reason all the while they were claiming that its actual ontological reality was lifeless, mechanical, and insignificant. It was as if in a Faustian bargain we sold our souls in exchange for a masterful knowledge of the physical world. We would increase in our ability to quantify and control the physical dimensions of our world but at the same time lose the ability to know our own souls—the subject who was actually doing all of this.

Jacques Maritain points out this great irony of the Age of Reason in his *Art and Scholasticism*. Those who figured most highly in that age and those that followed denigrated the power or faculty of reason they had sought to extol. Recently, I was struck by a passage in a handsomely republished version of the Scanlon translation of *Art and Scholasticism* that I had read in other translations.[7] There, Maritain asserted that modernity had suppressed and forgotten something critical to the understanding of reason, namely, that it was alive. It was the essential part of human living. It could be trained in the fullness of virtue. Modernity had forgotten that the power of reason could grow and develop and that it could become stronger or weaker, virtuous or vicious. And it is vital that it become strong to attain to the heights of goodness, truth, and beauty. Here is the passage that caught my eye:

> There is, as has been said before, a fundamental incompatibility between *habitus* and egalitarianism. The modern world has a hatred of *habitus* of whatever kind, and a very interesting *History of the Progressive Expulsion of Habitus by the Modern Revolution* might be written. The whole world at the time is agog with excitement about calculating machines, everybody dreaming of method. And Descartes conceives method as an infallible and easy means of bringing to truth "those who have never been to school" and people of quality. Leibniz at last invents a system of

6. I use this term loosely. The popular narrative is increasingly challenged as authors see the seeds of the development that occurred in the renaissance as beginning in the Middle Ages. See Rodney Stark, *Bearing False Witness: Debunking Centuries of Anti-Catholic History* (West Conshohocken, Pennsylvania: Templeton Press, 2016). This also was a major thrust of C. S. Lewis's thought, as Alister McGrath makes evident in his *C. S. Lewis: A Life: Eccentric Genius, Reluctant Prophet* (Carol Stream, Illinois: Tyndale House, 2013).

7. Jacques Maritain, *Art and Scholasticism*. Reprint of the 1933 Sheed & Ward edition (Tacoma, WA: Cluny Media, 2016), 40–49.

logic and a language whose most wonderful characteristic is to make *thinking unnecessary*. We then reach the spiritual acephaly of the age of enlightenment.[8]

But, Maritain continues,

The ancients thought that truth was difficult and beauty was difficult, that the way was narrow; and that to overcome the difficulty and the altitude of the object, it was absolutely necessary to develop in the subject an intrinsic force and elevation: that is to say a *habitus*. The modern conception of method and rules would have seemed to them therefore an outrageous absurdity.[9]

What is most striking here is the phrase, the "altitude of the object." It is foreign to the scientific ear. It suggests something not easily quantified, testable, or controllable in the controlled experiment. It suggests something that is not isomorphic with our ready-at-hand attention, but rather something for which we must change, grow, and become adequate to perceive fully.

Maritain is right on target. Here we will explore three seminal thinkers as examples of this denigration of reason. First, let us attend to the father of modern philosophy, René Descartes. He begins his *Discourse on Method* as if he chose to be an example for Maritain:

Good sense is mankind's most equitably divided endowment, for everyone thinks that he is so abundantly provided with it that even those with the most insatiable appetites and most difficult to please in other ways do not usually want more than they have of this. As it is not likely that everyone is mistaken, this evidence shows that the ability to judge correctly, and to distinguish the true from the false—which is really what is meant by good sense or reason—is the same by nature in all men; and that differences of opinion are not due to differences in intelligence, but merely to the fact that we use different approaches and consider different things.[10]

Passing over the first rather odd argument, we can say that if we subscribe to this Cartesian view, we can know that reason is the same for all men; it does not become "stronger" or "weaker." Differences between people are due to the effort they put into applying the method. Now if Descartes' account were true, we would miss the whole purpose of education for Plato and Maritain. For we will miss the reality that is most central and

8. Ibid., 42; italics in original.

9. Ibid.

10. René Descartes, *Discourse on Method and Meditations*, translated by Laurence J. Lafleur (Indianapolis: Bobbs-Merrill, 1960), 3–4.

alive in us, our reason. In *Education at the Crossroads,* Maritain writes that "the chief task of education is above all to shape man, or to guide the evolving dynamism through which man forms himself as a man... Education needs primarily to know what man is.... Man is a person who holds himself in hand by his intelligence and his will."[11]

Since the acquisition of knowledge becomes a function of a method and especially—if we follow Descartes—a mathematical method, all ideas will be on a level playing field. They will be valued for their clarity rather than their insight. As Maritain claims, the cognitional landscape will be flattened to those ideas that are capable of being conceived clearly. In effect, there will be no higher or lower levels of being. As E.F. Schumacher in his *Guide for the Perplexed* cites Descartes, "Those who seek the direct road to truth, should not bother with any object of which they cannot have a certainty equal to the demonstrations of arithmetic and geometry. Only such objects should engage our attention to the sure and indubitable knowledge of which our mental powers seem to be adequate."[12] In other words, all objects of any "altitude" are suspect. Thus, there is no notion that the mind itself might become more adequate to grasping "higher" truths. The role of *adaequatio,* as described by E. F. Schumacher in his *Guide for the Perplexed,* would be impossible.[13] If I was a young student when my mother wished me to listen to Mozart's *Jupiter* Symphony (her favorite) and all I was adequate for was hearing random notes, well, what could be done? What was then unbearably boring to me could not promise me anything more in the future. It was only after repeated listening that I became adequate truly to hear the melody, the musical phrasing, and harmonic structure of the piece. Only then, could I hear its beauty, force, and power. Many readily understand this strengthening of ability when it comes to musical training. People can, for example, develop an ear for melody and harmony. Why is it, then, that so many think that we cannot strengthen our ability to grasp truths?

Descartes taught us to see the universe as a function of clear and distinct ideas. But if the only way reality can be accessed is through clear and

11. Jacques Maritain, *Education at the Crossroads* (New Haven: Yale University Press, 1943), 1.

12. René Descartes, *Rules for the Direction of the Mind,* translated by E. S. Haldane and G. R. T. Ross, *Encyclopedia Britannica* (Chicago, 1971) as cited by E. F. Schumacher, *Guide for the Perplexed* (New York: Harper & Row, 1977), 8.

13. E. F. Schumacher, *Guide for the Perplexed* (New York: Harper and Row, 1977), 39–60.

distinct ideas, objective reality can never be anything other than a "machine" of some sort. It won't be long before philosophers turn this mechanistic form of knowing upon the knower himself and the soul will disappear as a ghost in its "gears."

## II. The Age of Reason?

All ideas come from sensation or reflection. Let us then suppose the mind to be, as we say, white paper, void of all characters, without any ideas: how comes it to be furnished? Whence comes it by that vast store, which the busy and boundless fancy of man has painted on it with an almost endless variety? Whence has it all the materials of reason and knowledge? To this I answer, in one word, from experience.[14]

These words from the father of British Empiricism, John Locke, are well known. In his *Essay Concerning the Human Understanding,* he rejects innate ideas in favor of a *tabula rasa* or blank slate. Reason is a blank slate open to impressions. It is an empty room to be furnished. Notice that reason is not considered in its power—it must be amazing to accept so much furnishing—but seemingly in its emptiness. What exactly happens when it acquires new pieces of furniture? How does it have this ability to receive ideas? This inquiry leads us to our second thinker.

David Hume follows in the empiricist tradition of Locke. Having, in his *Enquiry Concerning Human Understanding,* exposed causality as an unempirical idea—apparently not a viable piece of furniture—and having exhorting others to burn their metaphysical books,[15] he claims that his very self is no more than a "bundle of impressions."[16] This, of course, implies that his mind or reasoning power is nothing but a bundle of impressions. But the most provocative question comes from his *Dialogues Concerning Natural Religion*: "What peculiar privilege has this little agitation of the

14. John Locke, *An Essay Concerning Human Understanding,* bk II, chap. 1, sec. 2 from *Readings in Epistemology,* edited by Vincent Potter, SJ (Bronx, New York: Fordham University Press, 1986), 73–74.

15. "Commit it then to the flames: for it can contain nothing but sophistry and illusion." David Hume, *Enquiries Concerning Human Understanding and Concerning the Principles of Morals,* 3rd edition (Oxford: Oxford University Press, 1975), 165.

16. David Hume, *A Treatise of Human Nature,* 2nd edition (Oxford: Oxford University Press, 1978), 1.4.6., p. 252–53. Cf: "I may venture to affirm of the rest of mankind, that they are nothing but a bundle or collection of different perceptions." "They are the successive perceptions only, that constitute the mind." Ibid. p. 253.

brain which we call thought, that we must make it the model of the whole universe?"[17] In the *Dialogues Concerning Natural Religion* there are three characters, two of which represent religious thinkers and a third, whose name is Philo, who clearly resembles Hume. What is striking is that Philo, after "dressing down" reason, should still think it appropriate to use his own thought process against his opponents. It is striking, too, that we are given many arguments in the text, for and against God's existence, that seem reasonable enough to be included by Hume. He quite clearly thought *his* thinking here was more than the agitation of the brain (let's say, enough to construct arguments against the believer). Furthermore, if he really did regard reason as merely an agitation of the brain, what should we do? Might we put down the book? Might we say, "Well, I don't know about this thought thing, but it sure seems like hard work!" Why bother? In order to become interested in the project, to become engaged in the arguments, would I not have to think reason is to be preferred over feeling or instinct or intuition? Or whatever default mode the universe caused my mind to be in? In fact, in order to understand and appreciate Hume's philosophy, would I not have to feel in some way that all of the work to understand Hume's reasoning was worth it? Bernard Lonergan, in his seminal work *Insight*, argued that if David Hume's epistemology were correct, he couldn't have come up with it.

Perhaps, I should have listened to Hume when he warned at the beginning of his *Enquiry Concerning the Human Understanding* that I should "Be a philosopher—[that is, a physicalist]; but, amidst all your philosophy, be still a man."[18] He knew that in his philosophy, there were no real men. Indeed, they were but bundles of impressions.

Maybe, he was thinking that "men" rather than "philosophers" did things other than receive sensory impressions and calculate. Maybe men did not need to be men in order to think. After all, in his epistemology, the philosopher's ideas were "atoms" borrowed from the physics of Sir Isaac Newton; like Newton's atoms, they acted under the force of a kind of "gravity." Ultimately, for Hume, reason is not personal at all. It is like a little machine or a little universe of matter.

17. David Hume, *Dialogues Concerning Natural Religion*, edited by Henry D. Aiken (New York: Hafner, 1966), 22.

18. Hume, *Enquiries Concerning Human Understanding*, 9.

## III. Lewis on Modern Naturalism: When Science becomes Philosophy

The third thinker for our consideration is Charles Darwin. In a celebrated passage in his *Autobiography*, he talks about his reasons to think that there is a God. In this discussion of God, we find out what he really thought about the mind of man:

> Another source of conviction in the existence of God, connected with the reason and not with the feelings, impresses me as having much more weight. This follows from the extreme difficulty or rather impossibility of conceiving this immense and wonderful universe, including man with his capacity of looking far backwards and far into futurity, as the result of blind chance or necessity. When thus reflecting I feel compelled to look to a First Cause having an intelligent mind in some degree analogous to that of man; and I deserve to be called a Theist.[19]

Now this oft-quoted section shows that Darwin seems to reason like others in the perennial tradition. Yet a sentence later, and less quoted, comes the following: "But then arises the doubt—can the mind of man, which has, as I fully believe, been developed from a mind as low as that possessed by the lowest animal, be trusted when it draws such grand conclusions?" Darwin continues: "We must not overlook the probability of the constant inculcation in a belief in God on the minds of children producing so strong and perhaps an inherited effect on their brains not yet fully developed, that it would be difficult for them to throw off their belief in God, as for a monkey to throw off its instinctive fear and hatred of a snake."[20]

C. S. Lewis, in his *Miracles: A Preliminary Study*, makes a celebrated argument against naturalism. He argues first that no beliefs caused by subrational mechanisms alone are reasonable, that is worthy of acceptance and belief.[21] We criticize those who have beliefs that are not based upon rational arguments but upon subrational instincts and desires—like Darwin's idea of God in the minds of children. If Darwin was right that this

19. Charles Darwin, *The Autobiography of Charles Darwin*, edited by Nora Barlow (New York: W. W. Norton & Company, 1958), 92–93.

20. This was the one line that Emma Darwin, his wife, wanted deleted from the autobiography, as she thought that he held that all morality was "grown up by evolution." She found it morally repugnant. Charles Darwin, *The Autobiography of Charles Darwin*, 92–93.

21. For example, because once someone has ascertained that Jones thinks that God exists because of wish-fulfilment, a wish to return to the womb, an oceanic feeling and so forth, his belief has been undermined. It is not worthy of rational acceptance.

idea could be fully accounted for by such subrational inculcation, then their beliefs would be suspect. The next premise is that all beliefs that the universe began by a big bang accident alone are beliefs ultimately caused by sub-rational mechanisms. The naturalist or physicalist describes all that happens in the universe as being the result of an accident which by their account is subrational—there is no intelligence present. If these two premises are true it would follow that no belief that the universe began by a big bang accident alone is reasonable.[22] The ultimate cause of this belief is itself subrational. In addition, you cannot get more in the effect (reason) of something than there was its cause (subrational accident). Clearly, Darwin would accept and live by the first premise, believing that a brain descended from the sub-rational brains of the lowest animals cannot produce rational thoughts. He understands his own reasoning—"but then arises the doubt"—as coming from and being infected by sub-rational mechanisms. Lewis might then have asked him, "But why are you not suspicious of your evolutionary musings now? Is not your own naturalistic 'metaphysics' itself a towering example of philosophical speculation?"[23] Why didn't Darwin think it suspect? Might it be because he thought that his *power* of reasoning might not be necessary here? After all, we have a *method*. But, sadly, it is a method that presupposes but does not explicitly and formally acknowledge the existence, veracity, and reliability of a process of reasoning that led to the method's formulation.

Opponents might ask Lewis, given his view of the special nature of reason, why more people don't recognize reason as special? He could reply that since contemporary science is so focused upon physical objects (in a legitimately helpful way for its discipline), it forgets the tremendous power required in reason to know these things. Lewis uses an analogy of reading a book:

> When you are reading a book it is obvious (once you attend to it) that you are using your eyes; but unless your eyes begin to hurt you, or the book is a textbook on optics, you may read all evening without once thinking of eyes. The naturalists have been engaged in thinking about Nature. They have not attended to the fact

22. See Lewis, *Miracles*, chaps. 3 and 4. For an interesting and full analysis of Lewis's argument from reason in the context of the criticisms of Elizabeth Anscombe and others, see Victor Reppert, *C. S. Lewis's Dangerous Idea: In Defense of the Argument from Reason* (Downer's Grove, Illinois: Intervarsity Press, 2003), 45–71.

23. "Naturalism is a prime specimen of that towering speculation" C. S. Lewis, *Miracles*, 22.

that they were *thinking*. The moment one attends to this it is obvious that one's own thinking cannot be merely a natural event.[24]

And Lewis, in *Miracles*, argued that if naturalism were true that everything would be physical and explicable in terms of scientific laws; however, our reasoning cannot simply be an event in the universe that proceeds by mere matter and energy moving according to scientific laws alone. Unlike material objects that arise, change, and decay, reasoning is not just something that happens. We do it! It is not just something that follows biological laws; it knows them and makes judgments about them and sees what is necessary in logical inferences.

Furthermore, moral reasoning is not just a fact about ourselves and our evolutionary heritage. If it were, then a rational judgment of moral obligation or the sense of "I ought" would be the same as "I itch" or "I am going to be sick" or even the same as my "fondness for cheese."[25] But our experience of it comes with a sense of *responsibility for* the free choices we make and is about something about which we can be right or wrong. But scientific inquiry, because it is focused upon the physical alone, cannot take such rational judgments into account. Lewis writes:

It is only when you stand back from particular inquiries and try to form a complete philosophy that you must take it (thinking) into account. For a complete philosophy must get in *all* the facts. In it you turn away from specialized or truncated thought to total thought: and one of the facts total thought must think about is Thinking itself.

Lewis continues:

And since the Sixteenth Century, when Science was born, the minds of men have been increasingly turned outward, to know Nature and to master her. They have been increasingly engaged on those specialized inquiries for which truncated thought is the correct method. It is therefore not in the least astonishing that they should have forgotten the evidence for the Supernatural. The deeply ingrained habit of truncated thought—what we call the "scientific" *habit* of mind—was indeed certain to lead to Naturalism, unless this tendency were continually corrected from some other source. But no other source was at hand, for during the same period men of science were coming to be metaphysically and theologically uneducated.[26]

24. Ibid., 40–41.
25. Ibid., 36 and 38.
26. Ibid., 42. The use of the phrase "scientific *habit* of mind" is appropriate here. Italics added.

In what has been called the scientific revolution, there was the choice by Francis Bacon and Descartes to consider things practically rather than speculatively. It was not a choice to adjust the intellect to become adequate to understand reality but to develop a method that would only focus upon physical things, their measurement and their *practical use*. This left a huge gap in our theoretical understanding of our place and meaningful fit in the cosmos. We stopped considering other sources of knowledge as fully rational.[27]

Even quantum physicist Erwin Schrödinger might have appreciated the problem, for he said that our personalities—which would presumably include our reason—are not even in the scientific picture of the world. He wrote:

> We do not belong to this material word that science constructs for us. We are not in it, we are outside. We are only spectators. The reason why we believe that we are in it, that we belong to the picture, is that our bodies are in the picture. And the reason for this disconcerting situation is just this, that, for the purpose of constructing the picture of the external world, we have used the greatly simplifying device of cutting our own personality out, removing it; hence it is gone, it has evaporated, it is ostensibly not needed.[28]

Schrödinger tells us that the scientific method excises the human person out of the world. This strange notion of what we are is not from a lack of evidence; it is precisely a function of the scientific method itself. As others, such as Thomas Nagel, have well said, it gives us a view from nowhere.[29]

The consequences of making the practical choice of such a method were enormous. There was a time when there were mystics and wise men and women and traditions that could encode and incarnate the higher or difficult truths about truth, goodness, and beauty. But in rejecting Tradition, all people were required to reach the heights by themselves. Lewis asks a haunting question: Is the distinction between wise and simple to disappear because all are now expected to become wise? I suspect not. I suspect that given the leveling out of reason, there now can no longer be

27. Charles Taylor describes this choice well in his *Sources of the Self: The Making of the Modern Identity* (Cambridge: Harvard University Press, 1989), 143–76.

28. Erwin Schrödinger, *Nature and the Greeks and Science and Humanism* (Cambridge: Cambridge University Press, 1964), 95–97.

29. See Thomas Nagel, *The View from Nowhere* (Oxford: Oxford University Press, 1986), 54–57.

a difference between the wise and the unwise; the only difference left is between the informed and uninformed. On the first day of my philosophy classes, I talk about philosophy being the "love of wisdom." I ask students what might wisdom be? Blank stares. It's not their fault.

It's no wonder that we confuse the activities of reason with the functions of the computer. The problem is especially acute in our age of the dominance of the scientific method *as a philosophy* and the dominance of the calculating machine, *par excellence*, the computer. If Nicholas Carr, author of *The Shallows*, is right, our use of the computer and the multitasking that it involves causes an atrophy of our ability to focus, contemplate, and philosophize.[30] While Carr is talking about the brain and its plasticity, these abilities seem like the intellectual virtues of old. By unreflectively interacting with Google and the internet, we are losing our ability to concentrate. For example, Maryanne Wolf (Tufts University psychologist who wrote a book on the neuroscience of reading, *Proust and the Squid*) makes the point that in continually reading online "we sacrifice the facility that makes deep reading possible. We revert to being 'mere decoders of information.' Our ability to make rich mental connections when we read deeply and without distraction remain largely disengaged."[31]

Confusion between information processing and thinking is pervasive. Take, for example, a recent article in the *New York Times Magazine* (February 9, 2017) that featured a transhumanist running for the president of the United States. The transhumanist, Zoltan Istvan, said he did not want to save money for his two daughters' education because he was reluctant to fritter away money on such things. By the time they were in their late teens, it would be possible to upload the informational content of a Harvard degree directly to their brains and at a fraction of what such an education costs today![32] One thinks of movies such as *Transcendence* and *Ex Machina* and the confusion between the power of reasoning and the gathering of data; the former requires *habitus*, the latter does not.

I close with an insight of the novelist David Foster Wallace: "One thing that sets us apart from other animals is the command we have been

30. See Nicholas Carr, *The Shallows: What the Internet is Doing to Our Brains* (New York: Norton, 2011), 122.

31. Ibid.

32. Mark O'Connell, "The Immortality Campaign," in the *New York Times Magazine* (February 9, 2017), https://www.nytimes.com/2017/02/09/magazine/600-miles-in-a-coffin-shaped-bus-campaigning-against-death-itself.html (accessed by author July 7, 2019).

granted over our attention. Learning how to think really means learning how to exercise some control over how and what you think. We cede control over our attention at our own peril."[33] Surely this insight involves a belief that we have a reasoning power that can be strengthened. So how, then, would I respond to the millennial blogger who did not want to spend time explaining mission, values, and the meaning of theological words?

I would address the assumption that despite the command that we are to love God with all our mind, some seem to think that thinking about God and how to serve Him should take no work and effort. It should all be clear and obvious. There is nothing to argue about or struggle to know. Truth is not difficult! Compare this blogger to Augustine. He would have said that for the first thirty years of his life he did not know even himself and that he was a guide to his own destruction. Indeed, his whole life would involve a difficult and rigorous rational inquiry into who he was.

33. David Foster Wallace, Commencement Address, Kenyon College 2005, excerpted from Nicholas Carr, *The Shallows*, 194–95.

# VI

# THE VOICE OF CONSCIENCE

ALICE M. RAMOS

# Shame, Honor, and Conscience

## I. Traditional Shame Culture versus the New Shame Culture. Truth versus Opinion

Attention has recently been focused on the so-called shame culture, seeing in this type of culture a new moral system coming into place. Unlike the moral relativism that was rampant on college campuses thirty years ago, where nothing was judged to be right or wrong, as Allan Bloom argued in *The Closing of the American Mind*, it seems that today students engage in what might be termed moral judgment whenever there is some campus crusade which they feel compelled to support by posting on social media. Those who do not post are noticed and convicted, as it were; those who do post craft their messages with caution, lest they be accused of incorrect thought or violate the norms that have been put in place.[1] This judgmentalism is rampant not only on college campuses. There are many other examples that can be cited such as the case of women journalists who criticized the misogyny of video games and were thereby viciously treated by video gamers who publicly exposed their past faults and so humiliated them; or the Dove campaign, which produced inappropriate negative statements about women's weight and size, thus bringing about body and beauty shaming. What most people would not say in the real world they are now saying on the internet and thus engaging in what has been termed internet violence and cruelty, ruthlessly pointing out people's faults and perhaps waging war on human nature and

1. David Brooks, "The Shame Culture," op-ed page of *The New York Times*, March 15, 2016, located at http://www.nytimes.com/2016/03/15/opinion/the-shame-culture.html?_r=0

its flaws.[2] The omnipresence of media now publicly exposes what was once considered private, and in so doing manifests little or no respect for the excellence of the human person.

My objective in this essay will not be to critique the new shame culture directly but rather to see first how it differs from a traditional shame culture and also guilt culture, and to inquire into the possible reasons behind its development. I take my topic to have both an ethical and political dimension, since it involves not only the words and deeds of human beings as individuals but also the insertion of human beings and their actions within community, even if at times a virtual one. I will secondly explore briefly what contemporary phenomenological thinkers have to say about shame; for them shame is revelatory of the dignity of the human person which should be protected and honored. Thirdly, I will seek the wisdom of Aristotle, Aquinas, and an earlier medieval thinker, Richard of St. Victor, to bring to light the relationship between true shame and conscience and the reasons why this relationship seems absent in our culture today. By way of conclusion, I will discuss the contribution of shame to excellence of character and to a real concern for the self, for the rational nature of man and his dignity—a concern which needs to be recovered and defended.

The notion of a shame culture originated with the American anthropologist Ruth Benedict, who distinguished between the Western guilt culture, whereby an "internalized conviction of sin" makes us aware of being morally good or bad, and Japan's shame culture in which a person's goodness or badness is dictated by what others in the community say about the person.[3] The opposite of shame is honor or what has also been called face. In a shame culture self-respect is contingent on public respect; to lose the esteem of others is therefore a loss of self-esteem and of honor.[4] Unlike the

2. See Chiore Sicha's review of Jon Ronson's *So You've Been Publicly Shamed* (London: Riverhead Books, 2015), in the *Sunday New York Times Book Review*, April 17, 2015. See also Joel Stein, "Tyranny of the Mob," *Time*, August 29, 2016, pp. 27–32.

3. Andy Crouch, "The Return of Shame," in *Christianity Today*, March, 2015, located at http://www.christianitytoday.com/ct/2015/march/andy-crouch-gospel-in-age-of-public-shame .html See Benedict's book *The Chrysanthemum and the Sword: Patterns of Japanese Culture* (Rutland, Vermont and Tokyo, Japan: Charles E. Tuttle Co., 1954).

4. See Simo Knuuttila, "The Emotion of Shame in Medieval Philosophy," *Spazio Filosofico*, no. 5 (2012): 243. In this article Knuuttila starts from a consideration of Gabriele Taylor's book *Pride, Shame, and Guilt: Emotions of Self-Assessment* (Oxford: Clarendon Press, 1985), where according to Knuuttila, Taylor stresses two basic factors of shame: first, that a person is seen by others, by an audience, as it were, to have failed in meeting the demands of the social group of

traditional shame culture's concern with honor, the new shame culture has substituted fame for honor; while fame also regards the public opinion of worth, the traditional ties of community and honor are no longer part of the new shame-fame culture.[5] In a traditional shame culture, people with social and communal ties to the person experiencing shame will try to restore the person's lost face or honor. Relationships within the shame-fame culture are however tenuous. People in this type of culture fear being shamed and thus excluded; they wish to be praised by the community and so form part of it. Moral life in the new shame culture is not based on the continuum of right and wrong but rather on the continuum of inclusion and exclusion.[6]

What readily becomes apparent in present-day shame culture is the emphasis given to external goods, whether it be fame, power, wealth, cosmetic beauty, or the shifting opinions of others. As Alasdair MacIntyre rightly pointed out in *After Virtue*, when external goods become the primary focus of a culture or of a society, the virtues wane. And as virtues are the way to happiness, it should not surprise us that the demise of the virtues, together with the primacy given to external goods and the outer man, as opposed to the cultivation of the inner man, his soul, or spirit, spells unhappiness. The human person's nature is such that he or she cannot be satisfied solely with a plethora of external goods. A society which increases the production of goods destined primarily to sensible pleasures betrays a tendency to goods of a lower rank, that is, goods pertaining to what is merely comfortable, pleasant, or useful; values of a higher rank which are proper to the person, such as the moral good, aesthetic beauty, and the experience of God cannot be produced by artificial or technical means. It is not surprising then that a materialist and consumerist mentality in society reveals an inner unhappiness in that society.[7]

---

which he or she is a part; and second, that the person judges herself adversely, that is, as being somehow debased, not the sort of person she should be. See p. 244 of Knuuttila's article.

5. See Crouch, "The Return of Shame." As Crouch says, "Western culture has become more individualistic over the past generations, as seen in the continuous unraveling of ties to family and local institutions. Bestowing and maintaining honor requires the kind of binding community that Western mobility and personal freedom are practically designed to dissolve. So instead of evolving into a traditional honor-shame culture, large parts of our culture are starting to look something like a postmodern fame-shame culture. Like honor, fame is a public estimation of worth, a powerful currency of status. But fame is bestowed by a broad audience, with only the loosest of bonds to those they acclaim."

6. Brooks, "The Shame Culture."

7. See M. S. Frings, "Introduction to Three Essays by Max Scheler," in *Person and Self-Value: Three Essays* by Max Scheler, edited and partially translated by M. S. Frings (Dordrecht: Mar-

This unhappiness is manifest in those who engage in internet shaming and excluding, where there are few if any norms concerned with the "face" of others and where all too vulnerable people want to feel approved by others and included in the group, a state which constantly needs protection.[8] In order to be accepted and fit in, members of a group will find it necessary to lavishly praise the others in the group, submitting to the power and reputation of those who in a sense police the group. Anxiety levels are high when a group is not duly recognized and respected. Exclusion and disrespect of a group is today tantamount to the ultimate crime or sin.[9] As one journalist puts it: "Everybody is perpetually insecure in a moral system based on inclusion and exclusion. There are no permanent standards, just the shifting judgment of the crowd. It is a culture of oversensitivity, overreaction and frequent moral panics, during which everybody feels compelled to go along."[10] People thus comply with others' feelings and beliefs, accommodating themselves to the group. In this new shame culture, a person's identity is subject to the varying opinions of others; and so in order to avoid the insecurity and anxiety which such a situation creates, it is necessary to rediscover permanent standards of justice and virtue on which to base people's identities and also recover the notion of an ultimate good for the sake of which one acts, regardless of the exclusion and disrespect which they may experience. If permanent standards and an ultimate good are recovered, then exclusion from a group or unpopularity will not make people feel that they *are* bad.[11]

At the moment, however, it would seem that the new shame culture can have destructive effects undermining people's sense of self and acting as an instrument of power and control.[12] People yield to the power of opinion which has the appearance of truth but which in most cases is not true; they also create an image of themselves so that their appearance will provoke

---

tinus Nijhoff, 1987), xxviii–xxix. In speaking of a consumers' society, Hannah Arendt says that "the attitude of consumption spells ruin to everything it touches." See her essay "The Crisis in Culture: Its Social and Its Political Significance," in *Between Past and Future: Six Exercises in Political Thought* (New York: Viking Press, 1961), 211.

8. See Crouch, "The Return of Shame."

9. See Brooks, "The Shame Culture."

10. Ibid.

11. Ibid. This sort of exclusion and feeling has possibly led to suicides due to cyberspace bullying, a form of shaming.

12. Tom Ryan, SM, "Healthy Shame? An Interchange between Elspeth Probyn and Thomas Aquinas," *Australian eJournal of Theology* 12, no. 1 (2008): 10.

the good opinion of others. What dominates then is not truth but opinion, and so people become enslaved by appearance. In speaking of the tyranny of the fear of appearance and opinion, one contemporary theologian has said:

> In their actions [people] are guided no longer by reality but by how the others can be expected to react. Opinion, untruth gains domination. The entire life of a society, political as well as personal decisions, can in this way rest on a dictatorship of untruth: of how things are presented and reported instead of reality itself. An entire society can thus fall from the truth into shared deceit, into a slavery of untruth, of not-being.[13]

It is evident that how people are perceived by others, how they appear before others, and the opinions of others then carry more weight than truth itself. For those who live in a system of deception, their power of perception for what is most essential is darkened, together with the blunting of their moral sense.[14] People thus experience a mundane fear which arises from worldly love, that is, the love whereby we trust in the world as our end, as when we trust in fame or wealth as our end.[15] This is the fear that accompanies the mundane emotion of shame, that is, a shame that is audience oriented.

## II. Contemporary Phenomenological Thought on Shame

Having seen the difference between a traditional shame culture and the new shame culture, in addition to some reasons for the latter and its pitfalls, I would like to turn briefly to what a few contemporary thinkers from

13. Joseph Cardinal Ratzinger, *The Yes of Jesus Christ,* translated by Robert Nowell (New York: The Crossroad Publishing Company, 1991), 86–87. While Ratzinger does not speak of the new shame culture, what he says about the power of opinion and of appearance fits well with what is at stake in a culture where shaming takes place. One might argue that what he says about the image of man created by mass media is applicable to what occurs in social media today. As Ratzinger puts it: "[I]n the society shaped by the mass media this image of man and his world has obtained an oppressive reality. What is shown and 'appears' (on television, for example) is stronger than reality. The 'appearance' of the world in the media is becoming more and more the real governance of the world. Fear of what appears becomes a universal power and damages the courage of the truth." Ibid., 87.

14. See Joseph Cardinal Ratzinger, "Conscience and Truth," 4, in http://www.ewtn.com/library/curia/ratzcons.htm

15. See ST II-II, q. 19, a. 3.

a phenomenological perspective have to say regarding shame. In his essay "Self-Interpreting Animals," Charles Taylor speaks of the experience of shame for wrong-doing but also singles out how we can be shamed or humiliated because we lack a certain property which is essentially attributed to human persons. Being seen by others or by oneself as lacking an essential property or having some degrading property—a lack which accounts for our vulnerability—makes us feel ashamed or humiliated.[16] What is shameful according to Taylor offends our dignity, our goodness as persons, and so upsets the way we present or express ourselves in public. Shame thus seems to be concerned with a certain ugliness, with what degrades or diminishes us, and therefore seems opposed to what is externally grand and beautiful.[17] What may be gleaned from Taylor's interpretation of shame is that there is in the person enduring shame an aspiration to excellence, given the type of being that the person is, but also the experience of disapproval or reproach.

Perhaps one of the better-known interpretations of shame within the phenomenological school is Max Scheler's "The 'Location' of the Feeling of Shame and Man's Way of Existing."[18] Given man's unique position in the universe, belonging both to the spiritual and material realms, transcending the material due to his spirit but nevertheless knowing himself as an embodied spirit, it is in the experience of shame for Scheler that spirit and flesh touch each other in a unique way. Only the human person, who feels and knows himself as a bridge between two orders of being, can be affected by shame. No animal, nor God, can feel shame. As Scheler puts it: "We must feel shame because of our being a continuous movement and a *transition itself* between two orders of being and essence in which one has such equally strong roots that one cannot sever them without losing one's humanity. Ultimately, man feels ashamed of himself and feels shame 'before' God in him."[19] According to this interpretation, shame is never merely a social feeling, that is, a feeling that one has been disapproved of by others, but rather involves a turning to the self such that one is ashamed of

16. See Charles Taylor, "Self-Interpreting Animals," in *Human Agency and Language* (Cambridge: Cambridge University Press, 1985), 53 and 57.

17. See my *Dynamic Transcendentals: Truth, Goodness, and Beauty from a Thomistic Perspective* (Washington, D.C.: The Catholic University of America Press, 2012), 109–110.

18. This essay is found in Max Scheler, *Person and Self-Value: Three Essays*, edited and partially translated by M. S. Frings (Dordrecht: Martinus Nijhoff, 1987), 3–85.

19. Scheler, "The 'Location' of the Feeling of Shame and Man's Way of Existing," in *Person and Self-Value*, 6.

oneself; shame involves an attitude of protecting and preserving the self and his or her value. Moreover, one may feel shame not only for one's own individual self but also for someone else. The self is therefore something of worth which needs protection, especially protection from general notoriety but also from a loss or diminution of its higher value such that it would be pulled down to lower values.

Scheler cites Friedrich Nietzsche as having remarked that "beauty belongs to shame," because as Scheler sees it, authentic shame is built upon a feeling of a positive value of the self, and only positive self-values necessitate protection. When shame is present, the nobler life feels and knows itself in its depth.[20] For Scheler the different forms of shame—shame of the body or the vital feeling of shame and psychic shame or the spiritual feeling of shame—involve the protection of the person from general exposure.[21] Akin to spiritual shame interestingly is reverence, which according to Scheler is described as "a kind of fear whose object enjoys respect, love, and adoration.... The object of reverence is felt and given as the bearer of a high value."[22] Shame, as Scheler sees it, "is 'beautiful' because it is a promise of beauty."[23] Shame hides beauty but also reveals its concealed existence (a beauty that is one's own and thus personal or private). Analogously, reverence, too, enables us to see the deep value of the person and of the world, whereas a lack of reverence toward the person and the world suggests an incapacity to recognize higher values,[24] as we saw above in the

20. See ibid., 37–38.

21. See ibid., 27 and 38. As Scheler says: "The more danger there is through increased notoriety and general publicity, the more shame veils with its protecting cover life's noblest centers. And because the interconnection between shame and individual self-value is one of essence, seeing a person feel shame or modesty is seeing something 'beautiful.' For modesty is *beautiful* by virtue of its aesthetic, symbolic value of the still unknown aspects of beauty 'pre-felt' that shame so eagerly tends to hide. There is a phenomenon here, wonderful beyond all measure. Shame observed renders to one who sees it a feeling of a depth of value which is never given directly and is of a value-dimension different from visible values. In this depth of valueness an infinity of other treasures of value, which gleam magically through, continue to be dormant." In "The 'Location' of the Feeling of Shame," p. 38.

22. Ibid., 26.

23. Ibid., 38.

24. In speaking of reverence, Peter Wust says: "Our soul ... is a secret, and this is the inner chamber of the soul which we are, up to a certain point, obliged to preserve religiously. Reverence for ourselves forbids us to unveil the sanctuary of our souls ... and to do so would be a real profanation and show an unforgivable lack of modesty." Quoted in Gabriel Marcel, *Being and Having*, translated by Katharine Farrer (Westminster, United Kingdom: Dacre Press, 1949), 228. Marcel is of the mind that this reverence and modesty of which Wust speaks have waned in our day and the new culture of shame is evidence of their demise. As Marcel says: "Against this

primacy given to external goods, to lower values, in the new shame culture.

It is interesting to note that Scheler considers the origin of the feeling of shame to belong to "an imbalance and *disharmony in man* between the sense and the claim of spiritual personhood and embodied needs."[25] Scheler cites the fall of the original couple who in eating the fruit perceived themselves in a different way—their eyes were opened, as Genesis puts it—and they were ashamed of their naked bodies. For Scheler, we *must* experience shame because the human essence is linked to a "lived body," and we *can* feel shame because our spiritual personhood is fundamentally independent of the "lived body."[26]

Given Scheler's mention of the fall of man, it seems appropriate here to consider Karol Wojtyla's account of shame. First, like Scheler, Wojtyla also sees in shame a mode of protecting the self so that the person is not objectified or instrumentalized; in this way, for both thinkers, shame protects and reveals the high value of the person. According to Wojtyla, shame is always a tendency to conceal some fact or some state of mind. The need for concealment, which is characteristic of shame, arises precisely because there is in the person an inner life which lends itself to the concealment of facts or values.[27] When the interiority of the person is thus exposed against his will to the view of others, the person will be shamed. The experience of sexual shame, for example, in the need to conceal bodily or sexual values, is for Wojtyla the way to discover the value of the person, that is, the person's objective inalienability and inviolability.[28]

Second, Wojtyla also develops how shame plays a role in the fall of man; this development, as is well known, is found in his theology of the body homilies given early in his pontificate. His interpretation of the fall of man and the origin of shame is like that of Scheler, although more com-

---

modesty [of the spirit], in fact, the most active and most opposite powers of our age have made alliance." In *Being and Having*, 228.

25. Scheler, "The 'Location' of the Feeling of Shame," 5.

26. Ibid.

27. See Karol Wojtyla, *Love and Responsibility* (New York: Farrar, Straus Giroux, 1981), 175. See also 174–82. In his summary of Wojtyla's book, William May says of shame: "According to him shame arises 'when something which of its very nature or in view of its purpose ought to be private passes the bounds of a person's privacy and somehow becomes public' (174). Because the existence of a person is an interior one, revealed only to those to whom one freely chooses to reveal it, a person is naturally shamed or experiences shame when his or her interior is exposed to the view or leer of others." See http://www.christendom-awake.org/pages/may/summaryofl&r. htm

28. See ibid., 178–79.

plete. The couple who have fallen hide themselves from God; their eyes having been opened, they both experience shame and a sense of fear before God. As John Paul II sees it, to the essence of shame always belongs a certain fear.[29] The fall represents man's alienation from the love of the Creator and from God's vision of his creation. Without entering into the different dimensions that the body as expressive of the person has, it suffices to emphasize not only the fear that accompanies shame here but also the new way of seeing that is experienced in shame, for shame limits man's vision and penetrates his very interiority.[30] Because of the fall, man no longer sees as God sees; he no longer participates in the vision that God had of his creation. John Paul II says:

> Man loses the original certainty of the image of God, expressed in his body. He also loses to some extent the sense of his right to participate in the perception of the world, which he enjoyed in the mystery of creation. This right had its foundation in man's *inner self*, in the fact that he himself participated in the divine vision of the world and of his own humanity. This gave him deep peace and joy in living the truth and value of his own body, in all its simplicity, transmitted to him by the Creator in the words: "God saw [that] it was very good" (Gen. 1:31).[31]

We can now summarize what I take to be the important points of these three contemporary thinkers on shame: first, in the experience of shame, the person seems to understand his or her dignity or worth—a dignity that needs to be protected lest we succumb to lower values; second, fear accompanies shame and is of its very essence; third, with the fall of the first man and woman, shame is a new way of seeing or of being seen that does not coincide with the original vision of creation, that is, with God's vision of things as good.

29. See John Paul II, "Real Significance of Original Nakedness," May 14, 1980 General Audience, in *Blessed Are the Pure of Heart* (Boston: St. Paul Editions, 1983), 41.

30. It is important to note here, as does Simo Knuuttila, when referring to Martha Nussbaum's cognitive assessment of Aristotle's passions, that "[a]n emotional reaction [such as shame] involves a distinct mode of seeing things from the point of view of an emotionally sensitive being." In *Emotions in Ancient and Medieval Philosophy* (Oxford: Clarendon Press, 2004), 36.

31. Ibid.; italics added.

## III. Ancient and Medieval Accounts of Shame: Shame and Conscience

Besides contemporary reflections on shame, ancient and medieval thinkers have also considered the emotion of shame in ways that are similar to what has already been stated here but also in an importantly different way which links shame to conscience. I will in what follows be referring primarily to Aristotle, Aquinas, and to Richard of St. Victor.[32] As we have already pointed out, shame regards seeing oneself or being seen by others in a certain light. There is then a mental representation of ourselves and of others which is linked to our experience of emotions: when we imagine ourselves in a positive light, then we experience a pleasant feeling; whereas when we imagine ourselves in a negative light, we experience an unpleasant feeling. This is clear in what Aristotle says:

> Victory is pleasant, not merely to the competitive, but to everyone, for there is produced an appearance (*phantasia*) of superiority and everybody has a more or less keen appetite for that.... Honor and good repute are among the most pleasant things, because they produce the appearance of oneself as possessing the qualities of an excellent man.... A friend is also among the pleasant things, for it is pleasant to love ... and to be loved, for here again an appearance that one is good is produced, a thing desired by all people who are aware of it.[33]

Honor, as noted earlier in this essay, is the opposite of shame; honor, that is, the esteem given by others, makes us appear in a positive light to others and to ourselves. Shame, on the other hand, makes us appear discredited or disgraced. In the experience of shame, according to Aristotle, we are pained due to past, present, or future evil things which involve us in social disgrace. The opinions of others before whom we are ashamed are of importance to us. Aristotle refers to the proverb, "Shame dwells in the eyes," to emphasize the shame experienced "before the eyes of all people" for an action already accomplished.[34] For Aristotle shame arises not from the consequences of an act but rather from the appearance of disgrace.[35] And so it may be said that Aristotle's account of shame is in part audience-

32. My reflections in this part of the essay will be guided in part by the excellent article of Simo Knuuttila, "The Emotion of Shame in Medieval Philosophy," *Spazio Filosofico* 5 (2012): 244–48. See also n. 4 above.

33. *Rhetoric,* edited by W. D. Ross (Oxford: Clarendon Press, 1957), 1.11, 1370b32–1371a20.

34. *Rhetoric* 2.6, 1384a23–1385a13.

35. See *Rhetoric* 2.6, 1384a21–23.

oriented. Such an account is also found in ancient Roman literature, where the experience of the feeling of shame is described in the following way: "I see my self being seen as discredited, when the value that I or others grant that self is not what I would have it be."[36] We see here also what may be termed a discrepancy between the real self, that is, the self in his actions, which manifest who he really is to himself and to others, and an ideal self.[37] While reference to an audience seems generally to characterize the notion of shame in ancient Greek and Roman literature, it is the case that there are instances of shame in which the person sees himself or herself in a disgraced way without necessarily fearing how others see him or her and without therefore fearing their opinions.[38]

In his *Nicomachean Ethics* Aristotle makes clear that shame is not a state of character and so should not be considered a virtue but rather a feeling. Since virtuous persons do not behave shamefully, there is no reason why they should experience shame. According to Aristotle, young people are particularly prone to shame because, given their intense desires, they live according to their emotions and so are inclined to sin. They are however restrained from wrongdoing because of their fear of disgrace which characterizes shame. The virtuous person, on the other hand, as Aristotle says, does nothing to be ashamed of; but if that person did do something base, then he or she would be disposed to feeling shame, which for Aristotle makes shame conditionally good.[39]

Like the Philosopher, Aquinas views shame in a similar light. Since shame is "fear of a base action," it is inconsistent with the perfection of virtue and thus falls short of what virtue is.[40] Aquinas associates shame with the virtue of temperance; because shame entails the avoidance of disgrace, it is considered an integral part of temperance as the vice of intemperance is what is most disgraceful and base. And in so far as other vices may be disgraceful, then shame also would be experienced, making shame pertain

36. Robert Caster, *Emotion, Restraint and Community in Ancient Rome* (Oxford: Oxford University Press, 2005), 29, quoted by Knuuttila, "The Emotion of Shame in Medieval Philosophy," 245.

37. Douglas L. Cairns, *Aidos: The Psychology and Ethics of Honor and Shame in Ancient Greek Literature* (Oxford: Clarendon Press, 1993), 14–26.

38. For Seneca, one judges an action against a judge internal to the mind. See Brad Inwood, *Reading Seneca: Stoic Philosophy at Rome* (Oxford: Clarendon Press, 2005), 342.

39. Aristotle, *Nicomachean Ethics* 4.9.

40. ST II-II, q. 144, a. 1, resp.

to other virtues besides temperance.[41] It is important to note here that for Aquinas shame fosters honesty (*honestas*) or honor by removing what is contrary to honor. Aquinas treats honor as another integral part of temperance, and considers honor as the same as virtue, for honor is due to excellence and man's excellence is determined according to his virtue. While rank, power, and wealth are honored by some people,[42] they are in reality beneath virtue and thus only a help in the practice of virtue and should therefore not be willed for themselves; for both Aristotle and Aquinas it is only the good or the virtuous man that is worthy of honor.[43]

Now in referring to shame as fear of a disgraceful action, Aquinas also points out that there is a disgrace that is penal and consists in the reproach that is heaped on a person, just as "the clarity of glory consists in a person being honored."[44] For Aquinas glory is the effect of honor, since by being praised or honored, a person acquires clarity in the eyes of others. Virtue makes a man honorable and glorious, and so virtue itself is honest and beautiful.[45] Just as honor is due to virtue, reproach, then, is due to vice. Aquinas quotes Aristotle who in the *Rhetoric* says that "a man is less ashamed of those defects which are not the result of any fault of his own."[46] For Aquinas there are two ways in which shame regards fault:

> In one way a man refrains from vicious acts through fear of reproach: in another way a man while doing a disgraceful deed avoids the public eye through fear of reproach. In the former case, according to Gregory of Nyssa (Nemesius, *De Nat. Hom.*, XX), we speak of a person "blushing," in the latter we say that he is "ashamed." Hence he says that "the man who is ashamed acts in secret, but he who blushes fears to be disgraced."[47]

Properly speaking, therefore, shame regards disgrace that is due to a voluntary defect, and so we should be more ashamed of those things of which we are the cause.[48] A virtuous man does not thus fear reproach and,

41. ST II-II, q. 144, a. 1, ad 2.

42. Regarding wealth, Aquinas says, "It is because the excellence of wealth is commonly regarded as making a man deserving of honor, that sometimes the name of honesty is given to external prosperity." ST II-II, q. 145, a. 1, ad 4.

43. ST II-II, q. 145, a. 1, resp. and ad 2.

44. ST II-II, q. 144, a. 2, resp.

45. ST II-II, q. 145, a. 2, resp. and ad 1–2.

46. ST II-II, q. 144, a. 2, ad 1. See *Rhetoric* 2.5, quoted in Aquinas.

47. ST II-II, q. 144, a. 2, resp.

48. ST II-II, q. 144, a. 2, ad 1.

in fact, for the sake of the good he would not even care were he to be disgraced. The more virtuous a man is, the more he despises external things such as the opinions of others and does not therefore fear the reproach of men.[49] While nothing is disgraceful save what is a voluntary fault, man is often ashamed of lacking certain external goods as their lack seems to diminish him in the opinions of others. As Aquinas puts it in juxtaposing honor to reproach and shame: "Though honor is not really due save to virtue alone, yet it regards a certain excellence: and the same applies to reproach, for though it is properly due to sin alone, yet, at least in man's opinion, it regards any kind of defect. Hence a man is ashamed of poverty, disrepute, servitude, and the like."[50] Again, the lack of certain external goods may provoke shame in the man who cares more for these sorts of goods than for virtue; it happens "accidentally," as Aquinas says, that the opinions of others may even make a man ashamed of virtuous deeds.[51]

The virtuous man who cares more for internal goods than for external goods does not, according to Aquinas, experience shame. On the contrary, shame fills the morally good man with horror for whatever is disgraceful; like Aristotle, Aquinas considers shame to be a conditional disposition in those who are virtuous; that is, they would be ashamed of anything that would be disgraceful in them.[52] Aquinas also agrees with Aristotle when he says that the virtuous man not only avoids vice but also avoids the appearance of vice; therefore, the virtuous man not only is good but also appears good.[53]

We turn now to Richard of St. Victor who adds an important element to the ancient and medieval account of shame. In his work entitled *The Twelve Patriarchs*—a treatise that deals with the preparation of the soul for contemplation by redirecting the mind and the will to achieve the quiet and peace needed for contemplation—Richard offers us a tropological

49. Ibid.

50. ST II-II, q. 144, a. 2, ad 2.

51. ST II-II, q. 144, a. 2, ad 3: "Shamefacedness does not regard virtuous deeds as such. Yet it happens accidentally that a man is ashamed of them either because he looks upon them as vicious according to human opinion, or because he is afraid of being marked as presumptuous or hypocritical for doing virtuous deeds."

52. ST II-II, q. 144, a. 4, c. and resp.

53. ST II-II, q. 144, a. 4, ad 2: "It belongs to the virtuous man to avoid not only vice, but also whatever has the semblance of vice, according to 1 Thessalonians 5:22, 'From all appearance of evil refrain yourselves.' The Philosopher, too, says (*Ethic.* 4.9) that the virtuous man should avoid 'not only what is really evil, but also those things that are regarded as evil.'"

interpretation of the significance of the twelve sons and the one daughter of Jacob.[54] True or ordered shame is represented by the daughter whose name is Dina. According to Richard, shame is true when the "hatred of vices precedes and accompanies it."[55] We do not have true shame if our sole concern is for the damage done to our reputation due to our wrongdoing. Mundane shame is oriented outward, that is, toward the opinions of others, while true shame is internalized and regards how one views oneself.[56] But there is still more, since Richard refers to the name Dina, the one daughter of Jacob, as being interpreted by "that judgment." True shame for Richard involves a judgment of conscience whereby one's sinful acts or thoughts are convicted. As he says:

> And so in a marvelous way, when convicted from its own conscience and deservedly cast down by disorder, the mind of everyone at one and the same time delivers a judgment against itself and exacts satisfaction from itself. This is that judgment in which the person who judges and the person who is judged are one and the same: the same, he who condemns and he who is condemned; one and the same, he who punishes and he who is punished.[57]

It is evident from what Richard says here that for him true shame is spiritual, having a reflective structure, in the sense that the one judging is the same as the one judged. This shame then does not seem to be solely an emotion, but rather a spiritual shame whereby the self is the object of one's interior gaze.[58]

Like Aquinas, then, Richard does regard shame as fear of being discredited and being ill thought of for wrong doing, but true shame for him consists in being ashamed for the voluntary fault or sin and not for the infamy.[59] He thus adds an important dimension to the Thomistic account of shame by referring to true shame as a matter of conscience, whereby the subject has an understanding of moral good and evil and thus judges himself against this moral standard; in knowing that his or her action, which is

54. Introduction to Richard of St. Victor, *The Twelve Patriarchs, The Mystical Ark, Book Three of the Trinity*, translated and introduced by Grover A. Zinn (New York: Paulist Press, 1979), 7.

55. Richard of St. Victor, *The Twelve Patriarchs*, chap. 46, p. 102.

56. In this regard, see also Knuuttila, "The Emotion of Shame in Medieval Philosophy," 246–47.

57. Richard of St. Victor, *The Twelve Patriarchs*, chap. 48, p. 104.

58. Again, see Knuuttila, "The Emotion of Shame in Medieval Philosophy," 247. As Knuuttila says: "The self is the object of one's inner sight and of the knowledge of God and the angels."

59. See Richard of St. Victor, *The Twelve Patriarchs*, chap. 46, p. 102.

the fault or sin committed, is not in accord with the standard, the person is ashamed. It is interesting to note however that because we are audience oriented and often regard outward appearance as more important than inner attitude, our shame may be far from the good and ordered shame that Dina represents, that is, shame for sin. As Richard graphically puts it:

> Even perverse men have shame, but if only it were good, if only it were ordered! For if they had good shame, perhaps they would not be perverse. For indeed, if they felt perfectly ashamed, they would not commit sin so easily. What kind of shame do you think it is to feel ashamed of poverty, to feel ashamed of lowliness? . . . those who despise more than follow lowliness, feel more ashamed of filthy clothing than a filthy mind.[60]

True shame for Richard, then, regards sin and moves a person to avoid actions whereby the self is interiorly seen in a negative light and thus we might say as unpleasant.[61] It may be said here that the self thus seen is in disharmony with itself and that this disharmony is unpleasant to the interior gaze. This good or true shame is, according to Richard, a virtue—although not among the higher virtues—which guards the honor of the soul and makes it beautiful, for as he says, Dina or the personification of true shame, is of "admirable beauty and singular form."[62] Let us, then, reiterate what Richard takes to be good shame: Ordered shame is a virtue because it protects the honor of the soul, that is, the excellence of the rational soul which is made in God's image, having within it an understanding of the good; such a virtue safeguards the rational soul's beauty.

We have taken here a step forward, I think, in these past interpretations of shame: from a generally audience oriented account of shame in Aristotle to Aquinas's consideration of shame as fear of a voluntary fault that is disgraceful and where disgrace is penal, consisting in our being reproached by others for our wrong doing, and finally to the distinction between mundane shame, which regards our fear of men and their opinions, and true shame, whereby a man sees himself in a negative light, judges himself for his sin, and fears not men, but God.[63] This last is certainly not the sort of shame

60. Ibid., 102–103. Richard goes on to say, "How many there are today who would be more ashamed to make in a speech a barbarism against the rule of Priscian than to reveal in their discourse a lie against the rule of Christ?"

61. See Knuuttila, "The Emotion of Shame in Medieval Philosophy," 247.

62. Richard of St. Victor, *The Twelve Patriarchs*, chap. 49, p. 106. See also Knuuttila, "The Emotion of Shame in Medieval Philosophy," 247.

63. "No doubt Dina is found within when our conscience is ashamed before God even on

that occurs in the new shame culture. And yet, true shame can enlighten us as to our present-day predicament which regards what we have called here mundane shame and mundane fear, for it turns out that these threaten contemporary man much more than true shame and fear of God do.

I think that Richard of St. Victor's concept of good shame can be associated with *synderesis,* that understanding of good and evil, that permanent moral standard against which the person judges himself or herself, as we saw above. When the person recognizes her sin, which puts her in disharmony with herself, that is, with the truth of her own being, with that orientation to the good that comes from having been created in God's image and likeness, then the person experiences true shame.[64] The notion of synderesis, also known as the "spark of conscience," enables us to know that we have done wrong even if we are overcome by passion or appetite; this spark of conscience has not been extinguished from man, even in his fallen state, although it may be weakened. This weakening takes place for example when the passions confuse the mind and thus prevent it from applying to concrete cases that habitual light of the first moral principles that is synderesis. This light of the first principles is then intercepted at the very moment when the free will makes its choice, but synderesis is never destroyed.[65]

According to St. Jerome, synderesis in Scripture is interpreted as spirit. Aquinas makes use of the metaphysics of Dionysius, a metaphysics of participation, to explain the role of synderesis. Due to the continuity that unites created beings in a hierarchy, what is superior in creatures participates in the perfection of beings that are greater than they; therefore, in what is superior in man, human knowledge participates in the angelic nature which sees truth in an intuitive way, even though in what is inferior in man, human knowledge is dependent on the senses from which it derives its first data. There is then something angelic and immutable about the good and the true in that habit which grasps the first principles. Aquinas thus sees in his teaching on synderesis a confirmation in the expressions

account of its hidden things. That people feel shame on account of God is to have good shamefacedness that is such that undoubtedly pertains to Dina. And so, such shamefacedness is ordered and can in some sense rightly be called human." Richard of St. Victor, *The Twelve Patriarchs,* chap. 49, p. 117.

64. Aquinas says, "[R]emorse of conscience is caused by synderesis protesting against evil." *De veritate,* q. 16, a. 3, sed contra 1. In *The Disputed Questions on Truth,* translated by James V. McGlynn, SJ (Chicago: Henry Regnery Company, 1953). I take this remorse of conscience to be what true shame is.

65. See *De veritate,* q. 16, a. 3, sed contra 1 and resp.

used by St. Jerome, that is, Aquinas refers to synderesis as a spark that has escaped from the divine fire, an eagle that flies above and transcends all other faculties, maintaining in us an orientation to the good.[66] It is not surprising then that synderesis should at times be interpreted by some thinkers as the divine dimension of our being.[67] In stressing the fact that synderesis cannot be extinguished, Aquinas himself refers to the habitual light of the first moral principles as a participated light when he quotes from Psalm 4:7, which says, "'The light of Thy countenance, O Lord, is signed upon us,' so that it shows good things to us."[68]

To return then to Jerome's discussion of synderesis, he says: "And yet we perceive that the conscience (*conscientia*) is itself also thrown aside and driven from its place by some who have no shame or modesty in their faults."[69] Synderesis and true shame are impeded when persons do not live in fear of sin and of God. Synderesis, moreover, is threatened in a society and culture where human subjectivity is forgetful of its own ontological foundation, of that inclination to the true and the good that results from human nature itself, and where the person succumbs rather to "the pressures of social and cultural conformity,"[70] as can be seen in the new shame culture. Consensus and accommodation to groups turn out to be of more importance than truth itself, and so conscience, which represents the presence of truth in the subject himself, is silenced.[71] If man neglects his interiority, his creaturely being with its instilled understanding of the good,

66. *In II Sent.*, dist. 39, q. 3, cited in Philippe Delhaye, *The Christian Conscience*, translated by Charles Underhill Quinn (New York: Desclée Company, 1968), 117.

67. See Marcia Colish, "*Synderesis* and Conscience: Stoicism and Its Medieval Transformations," in *From Knowledge to Beatitude: St. Victor, Twelfth-Century Scholars, and Beyond. Essays in Honor of Grover A. Zinn Jr.*, edited by E. Ann Matter and Lesley Smith (Notre Dame, Indiana: University of Notre Dame Press, 2013), 229–46. Colish sees the Stoic doctrine of synderesis and conscience in terms of the "god within."

68. *De veritate*, q. 16, a. 3, resp.

69. Douglas Kries, "Origen, Plato, and Conscience ('Synderesis') in Jerome's Ezekiel Commentary," *Traditio* 57 (2002): 71. Jerome's passage ends with a verse from Jeremiah which we will give here in a slightly different translation from what appears above: "'The impious man, when he reaches the depths of sin, does not care' (Prov. 18:3). Such people do not have modesty or shame with respect to their faults, and they deserve to hear 'You have the face of a harlot, not knowing to blush [with shame]'" (Jeremiah 3:3). The impious man is one who lacks reverence for the person and the world and of course for God.

70. Joseph Cardinal Ratzinger, "Conscience and Truth," 10, in http://www.ewtn.com/library/curia/ratzcons.htm

71. Ratzinger says, "A man of conscience is one who never acquires tolerance, well-being, success, public standing, and approval on the part of prevailing opinion, at the expense of truth." "Conscience and Truth," 6.

then he becomes "deaf to the internal promptings of truth."[72] This neglect seems to be at issue when St. Jerome speaks of conscience as thrown aside by those who have no shame for their faults and so no shame before God. While synderesis provides us with immediate knowledge of the first principles of the moral order, this natural capacity which we have within us can either be strengthened or weakened by habituation. And so a sort of connaturality between the human person and the true good is essential, a connaturality which is developed in the person through the cultivation of the virtues.[73] With each choice, as Augustine says, man fashions his own self, that is, he builds his moral interior for good or for ill.[74]

## IV. Conclusion

As we have seen, shame is not merely dependent on the judgments of others, since it arises rather from that inner moral standard or natural capacity of the mind called synderesis whereby we recognize that we are at odds with ourselves, at odds with our natural inclination to the true and the good. Such an interpretation of shame seems to contradict the generalizations made by Ruth Benedict regarding the differences between a shame culture and a guilt culture.[75] Moreover, shame does not express simply a concern for the consequences of our actions, nor is it solely the fear of ill-repute, but regards the intrinsic character of our actions,[76] such that we are ashamed of what is morally ugly, of that which is not in consonance with our rational nature and our dignity as persons. It is no wonder then that for both Aristotle and St. Thomas persons with the proper habituation seek to do the honorable good or the *bonum honestum*, what is morally beautiful or *kalon*, and thus reject the morally ugly or the *aischron*, as that which would be shameful. In Aristotle shame also has a role in the concern for self as a rational agent, in that concern for the best part of man. The virtuous person does the good for its own sake and thus values most of all the expression of rational agency in his or her virtuous actions, whereas the

72. Joseph Cardinal Ratzinger, "Conscience and Truth," 11.

73. See John Paul II, *The Splendor of Truth* (Boston: St. Paul Books & Media, 1993), no. 64.

74. See Augustine, *In Ps.* 45, 3, *PL* 36, 515C, quoted in Philippe Delhaye, *The Christian Conscience*, translated by Charles Underhill Quinn (New York: Desclée Company, 1968), 97.

75. See n. 3 above.

76. See Cairns, *Aidos: The Psychology and Ethics of Honor and Shame in Ancient Greek Literature*, 430–31.

vicious person is at odds or at variance with himself or herself, pursuing pleasures at hand, and so does not have a permanently stable character. The concern for self in Aristotle is called *philautia* or love of self; the man who has ordered self-love seeks to be true to himself as a rational agent. In Aquinas proper self-love involves not only the submission of our lower powers and desires to reason but also the submission of reason to God.

Perhaps indirectly the new shame culture might make us more aware of our interiority and our dignity and less concerned about appearances and others' opinions which so readily can enslave us, as we see in the undermining of conscience and freedom today. The new shame culture also brings to our attention a new moral system, if so it may be called, which is unacceptably heteronomous, relying crudely on public opinion,[77] and thus contrary to the dignity of the human person, who is capable of self-determination and self-mastery. Aquinas holds, as we saw, that man has through his nature and reason a participation in the divine Reason that directs the universe,[78] a participation found in conscience which includes the perception of the principles of morality or synderesis. As we also saw, synderesis needs to be strengthened through virtue so that we recognize true goods from apparent goods and so that our conduct is indeed in harmony with the orientation to the true and the good of our rational nature.

77. See Bernard Williams, *Shame and Necessity* (Berkeley, California: University of California Press, 1993), 97.

78. See Delhaye, *The Christian Conscience*, 86. See also John Paul II, *The Splendor of Truth*, no. 41, where man's authentic moral autonomy means the acceptance of God's law and where emphasis is given to theonomy or participated theonomy, that is, "man's free obedience to God's law effectively implies that human reason and human will participate in God's wisdom and providence."

NIKOLAJ ZUNIC

# Conscience and Responsibility

## Maritain *contra* Arendt

### I. Introduction

OUR KNOWLEDGE OF good and evil is traditionally understood to be anchored in a moral sense or power called "conscience." Conscience is the source of our insight into the goodness of human actions, and it enables us to recognize evil whenever it appears, especially in ourselves. So central is conscience to our moral sensibility that to lack it, either in part or entirely, would be considered a radical diminution of our humanity, making us less than fully human. This prospect raises an important philosophical question: is it possible to extinguish the voice of conscience? Can conscience be eliminated or silenced sufficiently so that a human being can no longer tell the difference between good and evil? It is this question concerning the possibility of stifling conscience that I first wish to address in this essay. Related to it is the question of one's responsibility for an impaired conscience. Even if one were unable to discriminate between good and evil, it might still be possible to blame the one so blinded for his blindness.

The question of moral responsibility, therefore, is one that is distinct from and yet accompanies that of conscience. What responsibility does one have to act ethically in this world? Furthermore, what is the source and nature of such a responsibility? In this essay, I wish to show that the phenomenon of responsibility is one that applies even to conscience itself, insofar as a human being could be said to be held responsible to form properly his or her own conscience. In other words, human beings are responsible to themselves to nurture, sustain and be attentive to their own conscience.

Why are the topics of conscience and responsibility worthy of attention today? Our world displays many instances of human conduct that seem to lack a proper awareness of moral truth. We see ample evidence of immoral behavior, which makes us question the existence of conscience. Such evidence includes, but is not limited to, the atrocities committed in acts of genocide (for example, Rwanda and Bosnia), the widespread acceptance of abortion, and the rejection of truth and reason in our post-modern and post-Christian civilization. At the same time the category of responsibility has become a prominent one in modern philosophical and political discourse. The invocation of responsibility reminds us that we are accountable for our actions, that our freedom is not unrestricted, and that we have a duty to act morally. Some examples in this regard include the truism in the political order that ignorance of the law does not excuse one from being held accountable for one's actions; that parents are expected to care for and educate their children and can be prosecuted under the law if they neglect to do so; and that generally in ordinary human interaction there is the unwritten and tacit expectation that human beings acknowledge reality and speak the truth, that is, to borrow Robert Sokolowski's phrase, that human persons live up to their calling as "agents of truth."[1] One could argue that what is happening is that at the very moment when moral conscience seems to be radically compromised in our societies, a call to a deeper kind of moral responsibility is being sounded. To express this insight in colloquial terms, precisely when morality is finally thought to be overthrown through an absolutized freedom, the natural moral law responds with a stern reprimand: "Not so fast! You thought you could get away with forsaking your conscience, but I am here to remind you that this is just not going to happen!" The category of responsibility is in many ways a sign that we are indelibly and inescapably moral beings and that whenever we attempt to deny this truth we will be judged accordingly.

I will be examining the related ideas of moral conscience and responsibility by delving into some of the writings of Jacques Maritain. But I wish also to offer an alternative account to the Thomistic one by also looking at the thought of Hannah Arendt, whose major works focus on the responsibility of a citizen to stand up against the evil of totalitarian political

1. See Robert Sokolowski, *Phenomenology of the Human Person* (Cambridge: Cambridge University Press, 2008).

regimes. In her provocative report on evil, *Eichmann in Jerusalem*, Arendt argues that evil arises from thoughtlessness and good from thoughtfulness. I will argue that Arendt is mistaken to hold that good and evil should be understood in terms of thought (or the lack thereof) and that Maritain is on the right track when he explains good and evil in reference to his theory of the virtues, especially prudence.

## II. Maritain on Conscience

The concept of conscience arose with the discovery and promotion of a universal moral law. Conscience, in short, goes hand in hand with the natural law. The natural law is the idea that morality inheres in the nature of things, particularly human nature, and that moral truths are not reducible to any specific culture, epoch, ideology, or religion. Any human being can become moral by coming to know what good and evil are, because they inhere in the kind of being which human persons are. We see this way of thinking in the ancient Stoic insistence on the universal moral precepts as embedded in the natural law.[2] St. Paul, influenced by the Stoics, wrote about this inner moral conscience which allows us to know what the good is and thus to will it. Conscience is important in Paul's writings because it opens the door for all people, not only Jews, to come to know God's law. He writes in the *Letter to the Romans*: "For when the Gentiles who do not have the law by nature (*phusei*) observe the prescriptions of the law, they are a law for themselves even though they do not have the law. They show that the demands of the law are written in their hearts, while their conscience (*syneidesis*) also bears witness and their conflicting thoughts accuse or even defend them" (Rom. 2:14–15).[3]

In his book *The Law of God*, Rémi Brague mentions that this idea of conscience is not found elsewhere among Jews. Brague writes: "The notion of a knowledge of the law through the force of the conscience alone is foreign to the rabbis. Moreover, Judaism is ill at ease with the idea of conscience: according to Yeshayahu Leibowitz, it is a pagan idea that has no place in Judaism."[4] It is only through the law of Moses that Jews can

2. On this topic of the natural law in ancient Stoicism, see Brad Inwood, *Reading Seneca: Stoic Philosophy at Rome* (Oxford: Clarendon Press, 2005), chap. 8, pp. 224–48.

3. Translation from *The New American Bible*.

4. Rémi Brague, *The Law of God: The Philosophical History of an Idea*, translated by Lydia G. Cochrane (Chicago: The University of Chicago Press, 2007), 89.

come to know God's will. The situation is similar in Islam. Muslims believe that one needs to learn how to act from a revealed book, the Qu'ran. There is no innate sense of good and evil for Muslims. Rather, they receive all their moral knowledge from the Qu'ran, and those who have not read this book or are not exposed to its teachings are therefore ignorant of God's law.[5]

It is clear that the Christian and philosophical conceptions of conscience are at odds with certain non-Christian religious beliefs concerning the human being's capacity to know moral and divine truth insofar as conscience is presented as a moral knowledge that is universally possessed. The sectarianism and particularism of the Judaic and Islamic traditions, as well as the modern secular counterpart of ethical relativism, contradict this doctrine of conscience. They instead place the emphasis on the contingent, empirical exposure to specific doctrines and cultural influences. According to this particularistic model, morality is local, not universal, embedded in cultural, social, and religious mores. One learns morality in a contingent way from one's surroundings and from one's education, not by listening to a source of moral guidance which all human beings possess.

We have described conscience as moral knowledge, that is, a knowledge of good and evil, of the distinction between praiseworthy and blameworthy acts. What kind of knowledge is this? Jacques Maritain is clear that conscience belongs to the moral sphere and as such is oriented towards

5. Ignaz Goldziher, in his *Introduction to Islamic Theology and Law* (translated by Andras and Ruth Hamori [Princeton: Princeton University Press, 1981]) counters the suggestion that there is no such phenomenon corresponding to conscience in Islam. It is true that there is no *word* or *term* in Arabic for "conscience," but the reality that underpins the word is still present in Islam, says Goldziher. He cites the *Forty Traditions* of al-Nawawi to prove his point (p. 17), not the Qu'ran. No. 27 states the following: "Question your heart [literally ask your heart for a *fatwa*, a legal opinion]. Virtue is that which brings heart and soul tranquility, and sin is that which throws perturbation into the soul and makes the heart flutter, no matter what people may say"; "Lay your hand on your chest and question your heart. Whatever disquiets your heart you should keep from doing." In conclusion, Goldziher offers the unsubstantiated judgement: "According to Islamic tradition, Adam imparted the same teaching to his children before his death, concluding with 'as I approached the forbidden tree I felt a perturbation in my heart,' which is as much as saying 'my conscience troubled me'" (pp. 17–18). It is not conclusively shown by Goldziher that this appeal to the heart in some Islamic texts is synonymous with our concept of conscience. Another probable interpretation of these statements suggests that the heart serves as a kind of "barometer" of virtue and not a source of moral insight. In other words, when one is virtuous the heart is experienced as calm and peaceful, and when one is not virtuous the heart is in a chaotic and disturbed state. But this does not mean that it is *from* the heart that one derives one's understanding of good and evil.

action, not knowing for its own sake.[6] It is a species of practical reason whose end is the deed. Aquinas famously distinguishes between synderesis and conscience.[7] Synderesis is the disposition or habit of the first principle of practical reason. The first principle of practical reason is founded on the notion of the good and can be expressed in the proposition: "The good is what all things desire." Synderesis is nothing other than the human being's rational and natural inclination towards the good. Conscience is distinguished from synderesis in the respect that conscience is an act that follows from synderesis or this natural inclination towards the good. However, we must understand this notion of "act" correctly. The act of conscience is not the deed itself—what is executed by means of the will—but is an act of judgement; as such, it is an intellectual and rational act, albeit practical because it is ordained towards action.

Aquinas tells us that there are three senses of conscience.[8] They are to be understood as three types of application of our knowledge of the first principle of practical reason to our acts. The first sense of conscience is to make us aware of our acts, of what we are doing or have done. We are "conscious," aware, attentive to our actions; we bear witness to them. The second sense of conscience is the judgement of our acts before we execute them. We deliberate whether we should perform or not perform a specific action. In this sense conscience precedes our actions and provides the moral motive for the action, telling us whether it is good to perform the action. The third sense of conscience is the practical intellect's evaluation of our action once it has been performed. We judge our act after its occurrence. Conscience in this third sense approves the act as praiseworthy or denounces it as blameworthy. In each of these three cases or instances of conscience, the same structure obtains: moral knowledge is being applied to our actions. It is clear that conscience does not produce the action itself, but bestows the intellectual component on the act, providing the cognitive interpretation of the act.

Jacques Maritain reiterates this Thomistic view that conscience in-

6. "La conscience qui s'éveille à la vie morale éprouve avant tout l'impératif fondamontal de la raison pratique: 'étant donné que tu es homme, agis en homme!'" Francesco Viola, "La conaissance de la loi naturelle dans la pensée de Jacques Maritain," *Nova et vetera* 1984 (3): 218. See also Pierre-Antoine Belley, *Connaître par le coeur. La connaissance par connaturalité dans les oeuvres de Jacques Maritain* (Paris: Téqui, 2005).

7. See Thomas Aquinas, *Summa theologiae* (ST) I, q. 79, aa. 12 and 13.

8. See ST I, q. 79, a. 13.

heres in a judgement of practical reason. He writes that the judgement of conscience is a "speculativo-practical judgement."[9] This terminology is distinctively Maritainian. He makes a distinction between speculatively-practical knowledge and practically-practical knowledge.[10] This distinction is based on different modes of defining and conceptualizing, that is, the different ways of constructing concepts. Maritain explains the distinction in the following way: "In the speculatively-practical sciences, the concepts preserve their naked value of abstraction and intelligibility: while in the practically-practical sciences they incorporate a train of concrete overtones that tune in with the dynamic currents through which action comes into existence."[11] When we consider the domain of human action, that is, the way in which practical reason engages with human acts, we can distinguish various layers or grades of abstraction, some more remote from the act itself and some closer to it. Speculatively-practical knowledge preserves a certain theoretical aspect in its conceptualization and as such is at a certain distance removed from the act itself. On the other hand, the practically-practical knowledge is less removed from the act, being more intimately wedded to it, and thus evokes more of the practical side of the act, rather than its theoretical aspect. These two distinct kinds of knowledge are both geared towards action, but they do so in different ways, one being more theoretical and the other more practical.

Conscience is, therefore, a speculatively-practical judgment because its focus on action emphasizes the cognitive and intellectual dimension of the act.[12] On the other hand, the chief archetype of practically-practical knowledge is the virtue of prudence—*phronesis*—which is the perfected

9. Jacques Maritain, *La loi naturelle ou loi non-écrite,* edited by Georges Brazzola (Fribourg: Éditions universitaires, 1986), 68: "En d'autres termes, le jugement de conscience est un jugement *speculativo-pratique,* car on n'a pas tout a fait quitté avec lui le règne de l'universel, la loi n'a été qu'incomplètement particularisée."

10. See Jacques Maritain, *Science and Wisdom,* translated by Bernard Wall (London: Geoffrey Bles, 1940), 138–40.

11. Ibid., 139.

12. In the posthumously published notes on natural law, *La loi naturelle ou loi non-écrite,* Maritain goes so far as to state that the natural law depends on reason, not on the will (pp. 105–118), so strongly does he emphasize the cognitive or intellectual dimension of morality. Lawrence Dewan, OP, criticizes Maritain for this view, suggesting that St. Thomas always includes the will as part of the natural law alongside the intellect. See his *Wisdom, Law and Virtue: Essays in Thomistic Ethics* (New York: Fordham University Press, 2007), 559. Dewan's criticism, it seems to me, misunderstands Maritain's point, namely, that reason is the source of moral insight, although not the sole source of the moral life, since without the will there could be no moral actions. Maritain does not diverge from an orthodox reading of Aquinas's theory of the moral life.

practical reason which issues in concrete acts in specific situations. The distinction between conscience and prudence is a tricky one, as many believe them to be synonymous. They do share many similarities, such as they both involve the application of general principles to a particular act. However, as Ralph McInerny emphasizes, they are not identical.[13] According to Aquinas in *Quaestio disputata de veritate* (*Disputed Questions on Truth*), we need to distinguish the judgement of conscience from the judgement of free choice. McInerny writes:

> The judgement of conscience, Thomas says, is purely cognitive whereas the judgement of free choice consists in the application of knowledge to affections or appetite. The judgment of conscience is purely cognitive, that of free choice is not. I take this to mean that the judgement of choice reveals our moral character in a way that the judgement of conscience does not. My choices reveal my character, the condition of my appetite, whereas the judgement of conscience reveals my cognitive ability to see that a given act is forbidden, commanded or permitted.[14]

To be sure, conscience resides in pure cognition; its very essence lies in practical reason's grasp of what one ought to do and what kinds of actions one ought to refrain from performing. Prudence, by contrast, is the virtue of choosing an act and as such it more intimately engages free will. Prudence aims at practical truth, which is the morally good act, the act to be done. The only way that prudence can achieve practical truth *in deed* is if the will is properly ordered to the good by being educated in virtue. The appetites and desires must be virtuously channeled toward the good which is the result of a proper kind of moral training. The rectitude of the will is thus a necessary counterpart to the virtue of prudence, as the practical reason's ability to choose morally good acts must be carried forward by a will that desires the same end or good.

The distinction between conscience and prudence can be further clarified by two different ways in which the "good" is apprehended by the human subject. Conscience grasps the good *as known to be good*, whereas prudence approaches the good *as good*. In the former case, conscience simply knows the good as something to be done; in the latter case, prudence apprehends the good as something desirable, worthy of being done. The concept of "the good as good" suggests that the good tugs at and attracts

13. See Ralph McInerny, "Prudence and Conscience," *The Thomist* 38, no. 2 (April 1974): 291–305.

14. Ibid., 300.

the will, rather than simply being known to be good. By means of the virtues, especially prudence, the will desires the good—Maritain would say that one *loves* the good—and is thus directly geared towards it in act. Truly virtuous persons do not deliberate extensively on what they should do but act straightaway from a rightly ordained will. Moral acts occur seemingly spontaneously for virtuous people. To be clear, the rectitude of the moral act with respect to the absence of a dithering mind has to do with the *end* of the moral act, that is, that to which the act is ultimately ordained. One does not deliberate about the ends of human action, as these are fixed and not open to change. However, as the Aristotelian-Thomistic tradition stresses, one does deliberate on the *means* to the end, that is, on what precisely one should do to achieve the end or goal of the moral life. For someone to deliberate about *what one should do as an end* (*telos*) exhibits a deep confusion and even corruption in both intellect and will. Such a person supposes that the moral life in its ultimate trajectory is open to incessant change and that there are no established givens in the moral life. If we dig deeper here the chief issue under discussion is what it means to be good. To be a morally upright person is it sufficient to simply know what good is without doing it? Or is performing a good deed the very essence of moral goodness? But even this may be deficient, for a person could perform a deed reluctantly or against his will. There is thus a third possibility: perhaps moral goodness inheres in a good deed being performed by a person who has a virtuous character and who thus desires to perform such good deeds. The moral tradition of Aristotle and Aquinas certainly holds that it is this third option that is the essence of genuine moral goodness in human acts.

We need to admit, therefore, that conscience is no guarantee for morally good acts. As Ralph McInerny puts it: "To have cognitive knowledge of what I ought to do here and now is not a function of, is not dependent upon, being related to the good known as good. A bad man can have a correct conscience. The correctness of conscience does not of itself guarantee that action and choice will be in accord with it."[15] Knowledge of the good is insufficient to produce good deeds. In fact, this is a very common moral defect in those—most of us—who have not achieved complete virtue, a condition in which people have a properly formed conscience and yet violate it in their choices and actions, such as in cases of incontinence or

15. Ibid., 303.

weakness of will (*akrasia*). Conscience is a necessary, but insufficient condition for morally good acts. However, at the same time it would be a rarity to have a fully and properly formed conscience. One might argue that most moral problems are due to the conscience not being properly formed or to being corrupted in some sense. Maritain writes:

> *Moral conscience* can be pure and right with a defective or imperfect knowledge of natural law, since the imperfection itself of this knowledge, in our view, is not voluntary, even if it is due either to ignorance or to harshness, moreover, it being well understood that there may be deviations, perversions, due either to intellectual errors or to false convictions, about which St. Thomas speaks, or to a hardening of conscience caused by the passions or perverse habits.[16]

How is it possible to have a defective knowledge of natural law or even to have it wiped out of a man's heart? Aquinas addresses this point in *Summa theologiae* I-IIa, q. 94, a. 6. He argues that the general precepts of the natural law, those belonging to *synderesis*, cannot be abolished from men's hearts. However, the secondary precepts can. These are the more particular precepts that follow from the general ones. They include the precepts of self-preservation, procreation and the education of children, and the end of knowing truth. These secondary precepts can be erased from the hearts of men either because of bad arguments or because of depraved customs and corrupt habits. People's knowledge of right and wrong can be corrupted by bad teaching and a bad society. One's social and political environment can mislead one into holding ideas that conflict with the natural law. This can happen, for example, when legislators pass laws which conflict with the natural law. As Aquinas writes: "Some lawmakers have made statutes opposed to these precepts, and such statutes are wicked."[17]

In his *On the Philosophy of History*, Maritain discusses the law of progress of moral conscience, which he considers to be the most important law

16. Maritain, *La loi naturelle ou loi non-écrite*, 194–95: "La *conscience morale* peut être pure et droite avec une *connaissance défectueuse* ou imparfaite de la loi naturelle, puisque l'imperfection même de cette connaissance dans la perspective qui est la nôtre, n'est pas volontaire, même si elle est due soit à l'ignorance, soit à la rudesse, étant bien entendu par ailleurs quil peut y avoir des déviations, des perversions, dues soit aux erreurs intellectuelles ou aux fausses convictions dont parle saint Thomas, soit à l'endurcissement de la conscience causé par les passions et les habitudes perverses." My translation.

17. Thomas Aquinas, ST I-II, q. 94, a. 6. English translation is from Thomas Aquinas, *Treatise on Law. The Complete Text*, translated by Alfred J. Freddoso (South Bend, Indiana: St. Augustine's Press, 2009), 48.

in the philosophy of history.[18] Here he makes an interesting distinction between moral conscience and particular moral laws. He writes: "In its essence and even in its value, the rectitude and purity of moral conscience are independent of the explicit knowledge of all particular moral laws."[19] Maritain is alluding to the Thomistic distinction between primary and secondary precepts of the natural law, the former which is inviolable and the latter which can be modified and even corrupted. Our knowledge of the natural law—what Maritain calls the "gnoseological" aspect[20]—develops and progresses through human history. Practices and customs that were once widely considered to be permissible are today rejected. Maritain cites slavery in this regard: in the ancient world it was accepted as normal, but now it is condemned. However, despite this development in our knowledge of the natural law, slavery is still practiced in certain quarters of the globe. As Maritain writes:

> Take, for instance, the notion of slavery. We are now aware that slavery is contrary to the dignity of the human person. And yet there are totalitarian States which enslave the human being. But, nevertheless, they would not like to acknowledge this fact—that's why propaganda is so necessary—because there is a common awareness in mankind today that slavery is contrary to the dignity of man.[21]

Even though the gnoseological dimension of the natural law has progressed in history, people still violate the natural law. Maritain makes this clear:

> Allow me to stress that I am not pointing to any progress in human moral behaviour (or to any progress in the purity and sanctity of conscience, for Abraham, again, was a very great saint, with an absolutely pure heart). I am pointing to a progress of moral conscience as to the knowledge of the particular precepts of natural law. This progress in knowledge can take place at the same time as a worsening in the conduct of a number of men.[22]

Let us clarify Maritain's basic ideas here. First, he asserts that moral conscience is something sacrosanct and is distinct from particular moral

18. See Jacques Maritain, *On the Philosophy of History*, edited by Joseph W. Evans (Clifton, New Jersey: Augustus M. Kelley, 1973), 104–111.

19. Maritain, *On the Philosophy of History*, 104.

20. See Jacques Maritain, *Natural Law: Reflections on Theory and Practice*, edited by William Sweet (South Bend, Indiana: St. Augustine Press, 2001), 32–38.

21. Maritain, *On the Philosophy of History*, 106.

22. Ibid., 105–106.

laws. Somebody can be "pure of heart," that is, completely obedient to his or her conscience, and yet be at odds with particular moral laws. The paragon case is Abraham, who was prepared to sacrifice his son, in accord with the prevailing cultural norms permitting child sacrifice, but was stopped by God at the last moment, and who, by obeying God's command in good conscience, acted against the laws of his society.[23] Second, Maritain is convinced that the natural law progresses and that human beings come to know the natural law progressively. We know more about the natural law today than our forebears did two thousand years ago. Third, despite this progress of our knowledge of the natural law, human behavior is not necessarily improved. Although our knowledge of the natural law is greater today than in the past, human beings continue to behave just as immorally as our ancestors did. Fourth, this suggests that moral conscience can be improved with the progress in the gnoseological aspect of the natural law. Those people who follow their conscience today will behave more in line with the dictates of the natural law than our ancestors did. Once we grasp Maritain's teachings on conscience and the natural law, we can understand why he holds that "history progresses both in the direction of good and in the direction of evil."[24] He does not adhere to a rosy picture of human progress that envisions it as only moving in the direction of the good. History is symptomatic of human fallenness, and evil will be part of the human condition until the end of time.

23. For a commentary on the meaning of Abraham's attempt to sacrifice Isaac, see Joseph Ratzinger, *The God of Jesus Christ: Meditations on the Triune God*, translated by Brian McNeil (San Francisco: Ignatius Press, 2008), 54–55: "A misunderstood theology has left many people with a completely false image, the image of a cruel God who demands the blood of His own Son. They have read out of the Cross the image of Job's friends and have turned their backs on this God in horror. But the opposite is true! The biblical God demands no human sacrifices. When He appears in the course of the history of religion, human sacrifice ceases. Before Abraham can slaughter Isaac, God speaks and stops him; the ram takes the place of the child. The cult of Yahweh begins when the sacrifice of the firstborn, which was demanded by the ancestral religion of Abraham, is replaced by his obedience and his faith—the external substitute, the ram, is only the expression of this deeper reality, which is not a replacement, but rather looks ahead to the future fulfillment. For the God of Israel, human sacrifice is an abomination; Moloch, the god of human sacrifices, is the embodiment of the false god who is opposed by faith in Yahweh. For the God of Israel, it is not the death of a man, but his life that is the act of worship. Irenaeus of Lyons expressed this in the wonderful formula: "*Gloria Dei homo vivens*" (The living man is the glorification of God.) And this is the kind of 'human sacrifice,' of worship, that God demands."

24. Maritain, *On the Philosophy of History*, 43.

## III. Arendt on Responsibility

Maritain helps us to see how we can develop and progress as a civilization and yet succumb to barbarism and savagery. This is something that perplexed many a thinker in the twentieth century. How could a civilized Europe descend into the chaos of two world wars? The German political thinker Hannah Arendt spent most of her career pondering totalitarianism and the type of evil that the Nazis perpetrated. The remainder of my essay examines some of Arendt's thoughts on what brings people to commit evil acts in repressive political regimes. Her book *Eichmann in Jerusalem* is a fascinating study of Adolf Eichmann, who was in charge of executing the Final Solution (i.e., the extermination of the Jews) during World War II.[25] Arendt covered the Eichmann trial in Jerusalem as a journalist for *The New Yorker* magazine. She was profoundly interested in understanding Eichmann's motives and how he was capable of such heinous acts. Eichmann was ambitious, yet quite unremarkable in his accomplishments. Arendt describes him as ordinary, and she emphasizes that he was not a monster, contrary to what many would suppose. The psychiatrists who interviewed him described him as very normal, perhaps more normal than the psychiatrists themselves.[26] Thus the kind of evil that Arendt was witnessing at the trial was not a monstrous, radical evil, but an evil that presented itself in its ordinariness. She labelled that kind of evil *banal*, suggesting it to be commonplace. However, there was one characteristic of the defendant that stood out for Arendt: Eichmann did not think. She discerned in him the absence of original thought. In his speech he repeated hackneyed phrases and clichés. His language was robotic and stunted. Because of how he communicated, Arendt inferred that Eichmann must be a thoughtless, unreflective human being. This certainly makes sense when we consider that Eichmann's defense at his trial was that he was merely following orders and

25. Hannah Arendt, *Eichmann in Jerusalem. A Report on the Banality of Evil* (New York: Penguin, 2006).

26. "Half a dozen psychiatrists had certified him as 'normal'—'More normal, at any rate, than I am after having examined him,' one of them was said to have exclaimed, while another had found that his whole psychological outlook, his attitude toward his wife and children, mother and father, brothers, sisters, and friends, was 'not only normal but most desirable'—and finally the minister who had paid regular visits to him in prison after the Supreme Court had finished hearing his appeal reassured everybody by declaring Eichmann to be 'a man with very positive ideas.'" Ibid., 25–26.

thus not questioning what he was told. Such conduct is representative of someone who does not think for himself.

Nonetheless, for Arendt this thoughtlessness was a prime ingredient in the kind of evil that was committed during World War II. For her, evil is caused by the absence of thinking. She explains her view in her book *The Life of the Mind*:

> It was this absence of thinking—which is so ordinary an experience in our everyday life, where we have hardly the time, let alone the inclination, to *stop* and think—that awakened my interest. Is evil-doing ... possible in default of not just "base motives" ... but of any motives whatever, of any particular prompting of interest or volition? Is wickedness, however we may define it, this being "determined to prove a villain," *not* a necessary condition for evil-doing? Might the problem of good and evil, our faculty for telling right from wrong, be connected with our faculty of thought?[27]

How are we to make sense of Arendt's suggestion that evil is linked to thoughtlessness? To do this we need to investigate her concept of thinking.

Arendt understands the activity of thinking in the same way that Socrates and Plato define it, namely, as a silent, inner dialogue which is conducted between me and myself.[28] Plato famously described thinking as an interior conversation that one has with oneself.[29] This view suggests that the external dialogue between people in the public sphere is the primary context for the coming to be of thinking. In other words, the interior dialogue of the mind is derived or generated from the exterior, public dialogue that human persons have with each other. Thus thinking is defined in reference to society, as a kind of reaction or response to public discourse. Furthermore, thinking presupposes a view that the human person is really a divided self. There are, in a manner of speaking, two persons in one, in the sense that I am conducting a dialogue with myself. In this way I am both the initiator of the conversation as well as the respondent; both the speaker and the listener.

The key idea for us to consider is Arendt's view of society and the public sphere. Thinking is an activity that is derived from public exchanges

27. Hannah Arendt, *The Life of the Mind* (New York: Harcourt, 1971), 4–5.

28. See ibid., 185–87.

29. Plato, *Theaetetus*, 190a: "[W]hen the mind is thinking, it is simply talking to itself, asking questions and answering them, and saying yes or no.... So I should describe thinking as discourse." Translated by F. M. Cornford, in *The Collected Dialogues of Plato*, edited by Edith Hamilton and Huntington Cairns (Princeton: Princeton University Press, 1989), 895–96.

among persons. When one enters into thinking, one is removing oneself from society, backing away from it in order to assess it. Thinking is the power by which we are disengaged from society. When we think we enter into an interior sphere of activity of the mind and so withdraw from the public sphere. It is a movement from exteriority to interiority. On the other hand, common sense, as Arendt understands it, is the faculty by which we are included in society.[30] It connotes what we have in common with other citizens, bringing about some kind of social cohesion. However, this social cohesiveness and inclusion in the world is not absolute; the problem with the world of appearances in society is that lies, errors, and untruths can manifest themselves. When people engage in public dialogue, they are not always truthful in their assertions, and it is precisely this possibility of untruth that jeopardizes the human person's participation in the public sphere. Because society is not completely virtuous, we cannot always be immersed in it through common sense. We are, therefore, forced to retreat from society and take refuge in thinking, which allows us to scrutinize society and to make sense of it.

Thought always questions itself in an ongoing, ceaseless process, according to Arendt. It never simply accepts propositions and statements as true. She refers to Kant's claim that thought has a "natural aversion" against accepting its own results as "solid axioms."[31] What this means is that thinking does not provide us with doctrines or knowledge or propositions—that is not its proper nature. Thinking, in other words, does not tell us what to do; it does not prescribe a specific course of action. In this sense, thinking is contrasted with knowing. One can have people who are very knowledgeable but do not think, and conversely, people who think but who are not very knowledgeable—like Socrates, who claimed to be ig-

30. "The only character of the world by which to gauge its reality is its being common to us all, and common sense occupies such a high rank in the hierarchy of political qualities because it is the one sense that fits into reality as a whole our five strictly individual senses and the strictly particular data they perceive. It is by virtue of common sense that the other sense perceptions are known to disclose reality and are not merely felt as irritations of our nerves or resistance sensations of our bodies. A noticeable decrease in common sense in any given community and a noticeable increase in superstition and gullibility are therefore almost infallible signs of alienation from the world." Hannah Arendt, *The Human Condition* (Chicago: The University of Chicago Press, 1958), 208–209.

31. Hannah Arendt, *Responsibility and Judgment*, edited by Jerome Kohn (New York: Schocken Books, 2003), 167.

norant yet thought a great deal.[32] Since thinking is not about knowing, it is an activity that anybody can do, not just the well-educated. It does not matter if one has read many books and been schooled in the best institutions; thinking is a truly universal activity. But if thinking does not tell us what to do, then how does it make us moral? For Arendt, the effect of thinking is that it disrupts human action. She writes: "For thinking's chief characteristic is that it interrupts all doing, all ordinary activities no matter what they happen to be."[33] It ruptures the process of acting and forces human beings to reflect. It inculcates a certain disposition toward society, one in which a person is detached from it, not wholly immersed in it, and is thus able to evaluate it. For only if one is able to step back from one's activities can one understand them. Being completely immersed in the world results in a certain mental blindness of the meaning of what one is doing.[34]

What is clear in Arendt's writings is that society has an ambiguous meaning. On the one hand, society is tainted and fallible. One should never give one's entire consent to society, as in the phenomenon of Group-Think, by accepting uncritically everything from one's social surroundings. Thinking is what enables the human being to break away from society. The way thinking does this is to focus on "invisible" objects, things that do not appear in the world, such as moral concepts like justice or truth, or religious ideas like God and salvation. Society is the realm of appearances, so when thinking proposes invisible realities, things that do not fit into society, the people who think become outsiders. On the other hand, belonging to society is crucial to human well-being and to the flourishing of justice. We need to live and work with others to build a common world. The establishment of a common world is the chief aim of politics.

Arendt is careful to distinguish between society and the public sphere. Society, as stated, has a rather negative meaning for Arendt. Its main characteristic is that of conformism.[35] This tendency can lead into unsavory directions, as in the conformity of citizens in a collectivist or totalitarian regime. The public sphere, however, is the space of genuine human action

32. See ibid., 173–75.

33. Ibid., 164.

34. This doctrine of stepping back from one's actions in order to understand them is a typical philosophical stance. It is reminiscent of what Edmund Husserl calls the *phenomenological reduction* or *epoché*, the mental act of detaching oneself from one's acts in order to understand them.

35. See Arendt, *The Human Condition*, 38–49.

and interaction. Action for Arendt is executed in and through speech. We communicate with each other in the public sphere, and these verbal exchanges constitute the heart of political activity. It is precisely in reference to the political order that responsibility rears its head. According to Arendt, responsibility is a political reality. Responsibility is a disposition on the part of the person towards the world, one in which the person is receptive of the givenness and the goodness of the life of interpersonal belonging. One is grateful and appreciative of the common world in which people live. This gratitude inspires human beings to leave the intimacy of their private lives and to engage with each other in complete freedom in the public domain for the sake of creating a just political order. In many ways, responsibility is motivated by the attempt to overcome the condition of isolation and loneliness so widespread today. One of Arendt's principal insights was that modernity established the conditions of loneliness that produced the unique forms of political totalitarianism in the twentieth century.[36]

Responsibility cannot be divorced from thinking, which occupies the core of Arendt's understanding of conscience. What is this connection between responsibility and thinking? As noted, thinking is an inner dialogue that one has with oneself. Its structure is derived or borrowed from the public sphere. As such, thinking is an echo or palimpsest of the original interpersonal relations that obtain in the public world. It is this inner dialogical voice of one's thinking that is the ground of one's responsibility. How so? Arendt argues that responsibility's first moment is one's responsibility to oneself. German citizens who refused to participate in the Nazi regime were trying to be true to themselves. Their consciences forbade them to participate in the murderous activities of their government, not by articulating specific decrees, but by aiming to preserve the integrity of interpersonal reality. To reject one's conscience would be tantamount to violating the social and political orders as mirrored in one's own thinking. As for those who did participate in the evil of the Third Reich, like Adolf Eichmann, they are still responsible for their actions. A common refrain from such individuals after the war was that they were merely following orders. This excuse was meant to exonerate them of any personal guilt. Arendt was most perturbed by this aspect of Hitler's totalitarianism, namely, that all the acts done in its name were legal. Eichmann stated that he was mere-

36. See Hannah Arendt, *The Origins of Totalitarianism* (New York: Harcourt, 1976).

ly obeying the law, which for Arendt meant that he was obeying Hitler's orders. She was eventually able to find an adequate explanation for why obeying Nazi laws was wrong: obedience has no place in morality and politics.[37] As moral and political beings, we are not supposed to obey others; each one of us is responsible to act from our own freedom. Arendt writes:

> The reason, however, that we can hold these new criminals, who never committed a crime out of their own initiative, nevertheless responsible for what they did is that there is no such thing as obedience in political and moral matters.... Much would be gained if we could eliminate this pernicious word "obedience" from our vocabulary of moral and political thought.[38]

As moral and political beings, we are all equal and free; no person is superior to any other. It is an abrogation of one's responsibility merely to obey the laws of one's society or the leader of one's government. We are responsible for our actions because of the very structure and nature of the common world constituted by the public sphere which is the hallmark of human thought.

## IV. Conclusion: Maritain contra Arendt

Arendt's analysis of personal responsibility in the context of political dictatorship is intriguing, yet ultimately flawed. She locates responsibility in the activity of thinking which, in her view, is the bedrock of morality. However, this theory has two main deficiencies.

First, Arendt's political thought lacks a proper metaphysical foundation. On her view, the political order is an end in itself; there is nothing beyond it, nothing transcendent to politics. Responsibility is therefore a mere temporal or worldly phenomenon; what beckons to action is human society and nothing more. But Maritain's vision of the common good is much more encompassing. He argues that God, the supernatural common good, must be regarded as the foundation of the terrestrial common good, otherwise we could not explain the distinctive kind of relation that obtains between persons and the common good.[39] For Maritain, the person

37. See Arendt, *Responsibility and Judgment*, 47–48.

38. Ibid., 48.

39. "[T]he common good of the city or of civilization—an essentially human common good in which the whole of man is engaged—does not preserve its true nature unless it respects that which surpasses it, unless it is subordinated, not as a pure means, but as an infravalent end,

as person is a whole, rather than a part, as the individual is. As such the person is a "mirror" of the whole common good, insofar as the common good is communicated by the person and is received back to the person in his wholeness.[40] We are responsible to one another and to the common good because of the metaphysical nature of personhood, what Maritain describes as the subsistence of the spiritual soul communicated to the composite (that is, the union of body and soul). The true basis of responsibility, I would argue, is not adequately explored and uncovered in Arendt's thought due to her prejudices against metaphysics—despite, ironically, her emphasis on thinking.[41] In *The Life of the Mind,* Arendt puts on full display her view of metaphysical and theological thinking. She essentially accepts the Nietzschean and Heideggerian theories that we have entered a new phase of civilization in which the super sensory realities expressed in metaphysics and theology are no longer plausible.[42] Therefore, to speak of God, eternity, being and truth in the modern world is to utter gibberish. We cannot understand these words, so foreign are the realities which they now represent. Hence Arendt frames her entire political philosophy in terms of action and decries the older philosophies which were steeped in contemplation. There is a clear absence of metaphysics in Arendt's writings and consequently an inability to locate the source of political morality in anything higher or deeper than temporal human interaction.

The second problem with Arendt's musings has to do with her understanding of morality. As a disciple of Immanuel Kant, her moral theory is rooted in reason which is the faculty of thought. As a consequence there is no positive content to her moral code. When one asks, "What am I to do?" Arendt responds: "Think!" But this is a command that is empty of cognitive content. Thinking by itself does not tell a person what he ought to do. A cursory glance at the history of modern moral philosophy is quite telling on this point, as there is a tendency among modern philosophers to promote theories of individual rights and freedoms understood in negative terms—what Isaiah Berlin calls "negative liberty"—these being the freedom of non-interference, and a reluctance to defend any prescriptive

---

to the order of eternal goods and the supra-temporal values from which human life is suspended." Jacques Maritain, *The Person and the Common Good,* translated by John J. Fitzgerald (Notre Dame, Indiana: University of Notre Dame Press, 1966), 62.

40. See Maritain, *The Person and the Common Good,* 49.

41. For her negative view of metaphysics, see Arendt, *The Human Condition,* 17–21.

42. See Arendt, *The Life of the Mind,* 8–14.

moral code, that is, a "positive liberty." In other words—and we see this everywhere today—people are inclined to assert freedom from oppression and authority but are agnostic when it comes to saying anything about how somebody should live. This leaves an enormous vacuum in our moral lives. Essentially, people are supposed to choose how they wish to live without any intrusion from external sources. But now the question arises: How is a person's moral conscience to be formed when doing so requires experience and instruction, that is, receiving input and direction from teachers, the world, and *a fortiori* God? At bottom, there is no criterion of *right* choosing, of making the correct decision, in Arendt's philosophy. After all, if I am tasked with deciding for myself what I should do, on what basis are my decisions to be judged to be good? Is it enough that they are chosen by me and not imposed heteronomously? Such a moral theory is unable to articulate the ground of moral goodness or, conversely, evil.

Arendt also overlooks the role that the will plays in action. Maritain never ceases to repeat the Thomist principle that morality aims at actions, not knowledge. Practical reason, in the form of conscience, can tell us *what to do*, but it cannot *do it*. It needs the will to make decisions. The moral virtues guided by prudence are required to make moral choices. Yet all our choices are oriented towards the good which provides both the content and the motive of our actions. The true good, the highest good, is beatitude, the union with God arrived at through love. Arendt is unable to articulate why somebody would act morally, other than by relying on Kantian deontological ethics. Thought by itself cannot explain why somebody is moral or responsible; reason does not constitute the source of ethics. Why not? Because I can reflect on what I should do and come to know what I should do, but still not do it. The Aristotelian-Thomistic tradition, which Maritain upholds, argues that ethics has to do with *actions*, not merely with *thoughts* or *knowledge*. In this way, then, the role of the will, as the executive authority in human actions, is paramount. Maritain asserts that the moral act is the product of both a reason and will which have been formed by the virtues so that the good which is the end of the act is deeply desired and even loved by the person. It is precisely the good—the moral object of our acts—which informs and effectively channels our desires. Morality depends on the movement of the will towards the good, which attracts and directs the will, as Maritain explains:

There are objective norms of morality, there are duties and rules, because the measure of reason is the formal constitutive element of human morality. However, I neither apply them, nor apply them well, unless they are embodied in the ends which actually attract my desire and in the actual movement of my will.[43]

This moral theory underscores that the moral good can only be apprehended by the will, not the intellect, as something that pulls at the will, and thus leads the person to action. Without this love of the good, morality is empty. It is not enough to know what is good; one must also do it.

43. Jacques Maritain, *Existence and the Existent*, translated by Lewis Galantiere and Gerald B. Phelan (Mahwah, New Jersey: Paulist Press, 2015), 44–45.

MARY KATERINA MASEK, RSM

# Enraptured with Being

## Preconscious and Connatural Habits as Sources of Conscience

### I. Introduction

In *Existence and the Existent*, Jacques Maritain asserts: "If the poet can be called a seer, the philosopher is no less entitled to the name, though in his own way. He may at times be the victim of some bewilderment; but at other times he will know the joy of discovery." Maritain further explains how a philosopher is a seer: "he will owe both bewilderment and joy to the fact that he remains enraptured with being."[1] A philosopher is able to "see" or understand being in a particular way. All philosophical knowledge flows from this source. The phrase "enraptured with being" evokes St. Thomas Aquinas's doctrine of being, which is fundamental to Maritain's thought. The significant factor for understanding the sources of conscience is that within the apprehension of being is the concomitant primal understanding of goodness. Aquinas, in *Quaestiones disputatae de veritate* q. 21, a. 1, considers the relation between being and good and argues that good adds something conceptually to being.[2] He writes:

> A being is perfective of another not only according to its specific character but also according to the existence which it has in reality. In this fashion the good is perfective; for the good is in things, as the Philosopher says. Inasmuch as one being by reason of its act of existing is such as to perfect and complete another, it stands

1. Jacques Maritain, *Existence and the Existent: An Essay on Christian Existentialism*, translated by Lewis Galantiere and Gerald B. Phelan (New York: Pantheon Books, 1948), 22.

2. According to Aquinas, good does not limit being but rather indicates a perfective relation.

to that other as an end. And hence it is that all who rightly define *good* put in its notion something about its status as an end.[3]

The relation between being and good further pertains to Aquinas's understanding of *adequatio,* in which there is a kind of natural correspondence between the human intellect and all created things.[4] This correspondence is a kind of measurement of natural understanding and love, which Maritain develops.[5] Thus, the human intellect cannot naturally understand angels or God in Himself. However, the human intellect can understand other persons or creatures. The human intellect is naturally aware of the truth and goodness of other beings and itself, as well as of their respective deficiencies. In other words, the intellect is implicitly aware of the imperfection of its objects and of itself, and due to this awareness, it understands obscurely that there is perfection. Through discursive reason and conscience, one also comes to understand and know that a right moral order exists.

The purpose of this essay is to explore Maritain's development of one aspect of connatural knowledge, which exists between the apprehension of goodness and the discursive reason in conscience to provide a clear view of how Maritain considers sources of conscience. Particularly of interest is what the human being "does" with his primal understanding of good. The premise from which the essay develops is that one may form good or bad habits of reason from a basic understanding of a good, which may influence one's choice positively or negatively. As mentioned, the understanding of a right moral order occurs because of conscience. Prior to exploring conscience, this essay explores three foundational areas for Maritain: the preconscious, connatural knowledge, and judgments made at the dawn of human awareness. Finally, moral knowledge, due to conscience, is considered. The significant influences of these aspects of the intellect exist at pro-

3. Aquinas, *Questiones disputatae de veritate* q. 21, a. 1, c. from *Le Questioni Disputate: Testo Latino dell'Edizione Leonina e Traduzione Italiana,* vols. 1 and 2, *La Verità,* translated by Roberto Coggi (Bologna: PDUL Edizioni Studio Domenicano, 1992).

4. I focus on a single aspect of Maritain's thought while presuming that the reader understands the richness of Aquinas's epistemology. For a fuller account, see my "The Light of Natural Divine Illumination in the Knowledge of Natural Law according to St. Thomas Aquinas," Ph.D. diss, Pontifical University of the Holy Cross (Rome: EDUSC, 2017), chapter 4.

5. See Maritain, *Existence and the Existent,* 35–37. In Aquinas, knowledge is measured by the existence of the thing. This existing thing is measured by the First Cause, God. Maritain extends this to love "by which the lover tends inwardly towards union with the beloved . . . and thus loses itself in the reality of the beloved." Maritain notes on p. 40, that this wording is taken from the English translation of *Les Degrès du Savoir,* translated by Gerald B. Phelan (New York: Charles Scribner's Sons, 1959), 452–53.

found depths in the human person moving toward moral understanding and knowledge. Maritain re-presents essential arguments of Aquinas regarding natural understanding.[6] These arguments of Aquinas further lead to moral understanding. The first consideration is Maritain's treatment of the preconscious.

## II. The Preconscious

In "The Preconscious Life of the Intellect," chapter three of *Creative Intuition in Art and Poetry,* Maritain draws the reader to the mysterious depths of the human intellect:

> Far beneath the sunlit surface thronged with explicit concepts and judgments, words and expressed resolutions or movements of the will, are the sources of knowledge and creativity, of love and supra-sensuous desires, hidden in the primordial translucid night of the intimate vitality of the soul. Thus it is that we must recognize the existence of [a] preconscious which pertains to the spiritual powers of the human soul and to the inner abyss of personal freedom, and of the personal thirst and striving for knowing and seeing, grasping and expressing.[7]

Maritain explores the capacity which enables every human being both to understand reality and to have profound values. He develops this capacity regarding art. In order to consider, however, intellectual sources of conscience, this essay focuses on capacities at the foundation of reason. These capacities are also significant for Maritain's distinction between being an individual and being a person. The individual focuses on his or her own ego or self, whereas the person is generous, "like the heroes or the saints." Drawing on Aristotle and Aquinas, Maritain develops his thought on the ability of the intellect to understand naturally through induction.[8] This ability exists prior to reason and yet does not imply a range of rationality that is pre-rational.[9]

6. Maritain re-presents this argument as a counterpoint to various twentieth-century existentialists. See *Existence and the Existent,* 24–25. Here I simply explore his notions of human understanding.

7. Jacques Maritain, "The Preconscious Life of the Intellect," in *Creative Intuition in Art and Poetry* (New York: Pantheon Books, 1953), 94.

8. Aristotle, *Posterior Analytics* 2.19, 100a11–13, in *The Basic Works of Aristotle,* edited by Richard McKeon (New York: Random House, 2001).

9. Stephen L. Brock, "Natural Inclination and the Intelligibility of the Good in Thomistic Natural Law" in *Vera Lex New Series* 6 (2005): 60. Such a pre-rational notion could give rise to arguments for an understanding of good that is prior to the apprehension of the intellect. Brock

For Maritain, the preconscious is not discursive in the same way as conscience.[10] As a result, the free-flow of inducted natural notions cannot be the only source for the discursive judgment of conscience. Yet, personal dispositions and habits of thought are formed in many ways prior to rational moral thought, and they may, as already mentioned, directly or indirectly influence moral reasoning.[11] Thus, it is necessary to consider the preconscious as one of the sources of conscience, as one may form or de-form his or her conscience according to such dispositions without immediate awareness of such effects.[12] Maritain describes the preconscious and its relation to moral reason as follows:

> Reason does not only consist of its conscious logical tools and manifestations, nor does the will consist only of its deliberate conscious determinations. . . . [W]e must recognize the existence of an unconscious or preconscious which pertains to the spiritual powers of the human soul and to the inner abyss of personal freedom.[13]

In another place in the same essay, he elaborates:

---

notes arguments from Finnis and Grisez which indicate that natural inclinations provide data in which goods are first grasped before any judgment that they are good is made. In these cases, there is an assumption that the natural inclinations are pre-rational, existing independently of reason's apprehension of their objects as good. Thus, apprehension would somehow follow on them. Brock discounts this idea. However, my interest at this point is not in natural inclinations but the aspect of reason which influences and is influenced by sense knowledge, referred to by George Klubertanz in his *Discursive Power: Sources and Doctrine of the 'Vis Cogitativa' according to St. Thomas Aquinas* (Saint Louis, Missouri: The Modern Schoolman, 1952), 240. Maritain seems refer to this aspect of the intellect when he speaks of the "range of reason," which Aquinas assigns to the governance of the cogitative power.

10. Cf DV, q. 17, a. 1 c., where Aquinas writes of the "judgment of conscience." A judgment is a conclusion to premises and is known. A judgment can be unpacked to reveal the underlying premises. However, Maritain's image of the 'translucid night' is an appropriate descriptor of the preconscious as the region in which the human being understands many things obscurely, and more immediately. This "region," is filled with sources of understanding, which may be drawn forth into discursivity. It is therefore, not discursive, in the same way as the "judgment of conscience."

11. See Maritain, *Existence and Existents*, 51. (See also note 3 above). Maritain refers to the syllogistic form of human reasoning in the note on p. 52: "In the second syllogism it is the existential disposition of the subject in the free affirmation of his unique self which decides the question." This disposition is grounded in habits which are formed and based in the preconscious.

12. Such lack of awareness does not occur in the first deforming choice for Aquinas. Rather, one "lacks awareness" because of consistent choices made against a certain knowledge that an action is wrong. See DV, q. 17, a. 1, ad 4. "Thus, it sometimes happens that the judgment of free choice goes astray, but not the judgment of conscience...one errs in choice and not in conscience. Rather, he acts against conscience and is said to do this with an evil conscience, in so far as the deed does not agree with the judgment based on knowledge."

13. Jacques Maritain, *Creative Intuition*, 94.

> [R]eason possesses a life both deeper and less conscious than its articulate logical life. For reason indeed does not only articulate, connect, and infer, it also *sees*; and reason's intuitive grasping, *intuitus rationis*, is the primary act and function of that one and single power which is called intellect or reason. In other words, there is not only logical reason, but also, and prior to it, intuitive reason.[14]

The *intuitus rationis* is vital. What the human person does with such primal intuitions may have either positive or negative effects on the work of conscience. For example, one may make a "more-or-less" free choice at one time, which results in a particular approach to a later choice because of a person's dispositions.[15] An examination of such dispositions to choose is important for good moral reasoning with a healthy conscience. Maritain elaborates on this subtle yet powerful aspect of making a choice by introducing the concept of connatural knowledge.

## III. Connatural Knowledge and the Preconscious

According to Maritain, connatural knowledge consists of two domains: moral science and the ability to know virtue intuitively. He defines moral science as the conceptual and rational knowledge of virtues "which produces in us a merely intellectual conformity with the truths involved."[16] He describes the second domain of connatural knowledge, the intuitive, as knowledge in which "through union or inclination, connaturality or congeniality, the intellect [is] at play not alone, but together with affective inclinations and the dispositions of the will, which is guided and directed by them."[17] Here he seems to suggest that the will is guided by affective incli-

14. Ibid. Maritain refers to Aquinas's aspect of reason called *intellectus*.

15. "Where a habit receives dispositively, *per modum habitus*, then what is received is, as it were, connatural with the receiver." Vivian Boland, *St. Thomas Aquinas* (New York: Bloomsbury, 2007), 167. Boland refers to DV, q. 20, a. 2, c., in which Aquinas also writes that one habit which becomes connatural in the intellect is the direction of its acts. Thus, the intellect may become disposed to choose in a certain way. An example might be a person who struggles with Aristotle's *akrasia* or weakness of will regarding food. While striving to diet, if such a person is presented with a dessert, the dieter knows what is better to do but often takes the dessert. Doing so can form habits which can make later choices to resist more difficult.

16. Jacques Maritain, "On Knowledge through Connaturality," in *The Range of Reason* (New York: Charles Scribner's Sons, 1952), 23.

17. Ibid., 23.

nations alone.[18] This, however, is a misreading of his position.[19] Rather, he considers connaturality, so to speak, in full natural operation.[20]

Intuitive connatural knowledge may be considered in two ways: first, the intellect is truly working together with inclinations[21] founded on the understanding of a good; second, the natural inclinations may not be founded on understanding the good, intellectively, but founded instead in sensible experience. The second way suggests that the senses guide human choice.[22] However, were one to consider inclinations in the latter way, one would not be sure of the rectitude of reason. Unfortunately, many operate with this latter perspective. To give a clear understanding of what Maritain argues, I will consider these two ways of looking at intellect and inclinations by turning to three Thomists: J. Budziszewski, Wojciech Giertych, and Stephen Brock. J. Budziszewski refers to connaturality as that in which "certain aspects of second nature—acquired habits or habitual graces—cooperate with our nature in the sense of *completing or perfecting it*."[23] Wojciech Giertych refers to a *quasi-habitus* which is "experienced as 'connatural,' but does not necessarily incline to that which is objectively in accord with human nature."[24] One can see from these views that "connatural knowledge" may be perceived either positively or negatively. Maritain's own view is closer to Budziszewski's idea. Thus, connatural knowledge may

18. See Marco D'Avenia, *La Conoscenza per Connaturalità in San Tommaso D'Aquino* (Bologna: PDUL, 1992), 17–26. The purpose of Maritain's arguments on connatural knowledge is to break through the limits which Kant imposed on reason. D'Avenia traces the importance of various thinkers in breaking through the Kantian doctrine. Maritain uses the notion of connatural knowledge through inclination to form a structure of analogy to suggest how the intellect operates in ways that extend beyond discursive rational knowledge to promote a more organic understanding of thought.

19. Maritain seeks a way to free the post-Kantian world to consider reality from a more Thomist viewpoint.

20. A clarification may be helpful. Maritain uses "connaturality" in analogous forms to promote an understanding of mystical knowledge. I consider connatural knowledge as a source of conscience.

21. See Daniel Westberg, *Right Practical Reason: Aristotle, Action and Prudence in Aquinas* (Oxford: Clarendon Press, 2002), 131. Westberg shows that this concurrence between the intellect and will occurs from apprehension to execution.

22. An example of the second way may occur when we allow our passions to sway us.

23. J. Budziszewski, "The Natural, the Connatural, and the Unnatural," a paper presented at the conference "St. Thomas and the Natural Law," Jacques Maritain Center, University of Notre Dame, Notre Dame, Indiana, July 2004. Italics added.

24. Wojciech Giertych, "Philosophical Anthropology: The Foundation of Certitude in Ethics," 7. This paper was presented at the St. John Vianney Theological Institute in Denver, Colorado February 23, 2016.

be likened to Aristotle's "undemonstrated sayings" of one's elders.[25] Such sayings are a source of wisdom which aid in understanding and potential actions; they lead to a perfection of human nature. Such sayings are not intended to cause confusion. An example of such a saying would be "haste makes waste." If one rushes through an action, one may have to re-do it. When we rush we often waste time and effort. Life seems to verify Maritain's understanding of the "intellect at play together with the inclinations and the will."

When one considers "natural inclination," in and of itself, he or she may have difficulty. Stephen Brock argues that rational natural inclinations are aspects of the *rational* appetite. He makes the important clarification that the natural inclinations are not inclined to the good until such a good is understood,[26] implying that natural inclinations are clearly related to the power of the intellect, not simply "some aspect of human nature in general." In an alternate way, Wojciech Giertych explores how natural inclinations from nature may be *mis*-read as connatural. Giertych thus brings into focus ways that natural inclinations may mislead one when mistakenly considered as rational. According to Giertych, a *quasi-habitus* can be seen as resulting from a *sense* judgment of the cogitative power and may be experienced as "connatural."[27] Such a *quasi-habitus* may affect practical knowledge positively or negatively.[28] If a *quasi-habitus* of the senses is understood to be connatural to right reason, one may think that one "must" act, for example, in what is really an unnatural way. This understanding runs the risk of disregarding a right conscience. Giertych connects Aquinas' account of a *quasi-habitus* to various unnatural actions done by many today who consider these actions as 'right.'

To address any ambiguity that may be seen in Maritain's position on connatural knowledge, I turn briefly to consider the position of Aquinas on natural understanding. Doing so will help to clarify aspects of human

25. Aristotle, *Nicomachean Ethics* 6.11, 1143b11.

26. See Brock, "Intelligibility of the Good," 61.

27. A *quasi-habitus* is "something like" a habit, but Aquinas would not define it as habit. It is an early phase of what later becomes a disposition and then a habit.

28. Giertych gives an example of a "positive" effect. A pianist moved by his artistic sense will strike the keys correctly. A "negative" example is someone who has an inclination toward something which is not in accord with human nature, such as eating soil. See Aquinas, ST I-II, q. 31, a. 7. Brock would speak of natural inclinations in the negative realm (which lead one to unnatural acts) as non-rational natural inclinations or simply inclinations of the sensitive power. These would not lead to a greater likeness to God.

knowledge undergirding Maritain's work. Then I will return to the topic of the *quasi-habitus.*

## IV. Aquinas on Natural Understanding

According to Aquinas, three aspects of the intellect, significant for Maritain's preconscious, are the agent intellect, the *habitus principiorum,* and *synderesis.* Aquinas, in a simple overview, draws from Aristotle's famous "battle in rout" passage, in which he describes the process through which the intellect comes to grasp universal truths as being "like a rout in battle stopped by first one man making a stand and then another, until the original formation has been restored."[29] Maritain corroborates, in *Existence and the Existent,* that the human intellect grasps universals through induction, then compares and judges between the universals to reach simple propositions. Here, initially, the intellect understands the fundamental universal of *ens* or being, then truth, goodness, and beauty. As further universals are drawn upon, the intellect compares them with former ones and makes judgments; propositions are formed, and deductive reason begins. The speculative and practical intellect further compare the universals and simple propositions, depending on whether the end is a truth or an action. Conclusions are then drawn from such comparisons. For the sake of brevity, concepts are drawn; from these operations, the intellectual virtue of prudence develops. Therein the appetite is intrinsically present, and knowledge and action occur.[30]

At this point it is crucial to address how a good is understood. For Aquinas, *synderesis* "incites to good and murmurs at evil."[31] *Synderesis* responds to all goods.[32] The important aspect of this response is that all

29. *Posterior Analytics* 2.19, 100a10–13.

30. "The second point of doctrine, dominating the whole theory of the virtue of prudence in particular, concerns the judgment of the moral conscience and the manner in which, at the heart of concrete existence, the appetite enters into the regulation of the moral act by the reason." Maritain, *Existence and the Existent,* 50.

31. ST I, q. 79, a. 12, c.

32. "Synderesis does not denote higher or lower reason, but something that refers commonly to both. For in the very habit of the universal principles of law there are contained certain things which pertain to the eternal norms of conduct, such as, that God must be obeyed; and there are some that pertain to lower norms, such as, that we must live according to reason. However, synderesis is said to refer to these unchangeable things in one way, and higher reason in another... A thing is also said to be unchangeable because of the necessity of a truth, although the truth may concern things which according to their nature can change. Thus the truth: every

goods that are truly perfective reflect universal goodness to the human being. Aquinas traces such universal goodness to God. All perfective goods reflect the One Good, God Himself, but in varying ways. *Synderesis* is the primordial attraction in the human being, through goodness, to God; it begins inchoately through natural goods.[33] All who respond through *synderesis* must also reason about such goods and how one is drawn to them in order to discern what one is attracted to and whether this attraction moves toward or away from God. Unfortunately, we may not always understand such goods as reflecting God. With regard to our response to a good, some may respond simply to aspects of a good that are "useful" and others to aspects that are "delectable." Neither of these goods are necessarily perfective; hence they do not lead toward the final end toward which *synderesis* inchoately awakens one. The distinction between those goods that are useful or delectable, on the one hand, and those that are perfective on the other, is between goods that satisfy and goods that perfect.[34] A *bonum honestum*, a perfective good, leads us to become more virtuous and thus leads us most directly to greater likeness to the First Good. For this reason, Brock designates the good that rational natural inclinations tend toward as "perfective." One does not understand perfective goods "through" inclination.[35] Rather, human beings are inclined to goods only after they understand the good in some way.[36]

Multiple influences in society draw one to varying types of goods. One's understanding of such goods can lead away from a virtuous understanding. A particular response to such influences may form various *quasi-habitus*, either positive or negative. On the one hand, if one acts according to a neg-

whole is greater than its part, is unchangeably true even in changeable things. Synderesis is said to refer to unchangeable things in this way." DV, q. 16, a. 1, ad 9.

33. What is unchangeable in natural goods reflects the immutable Good in some way to the intellect.

34. Gahl writes: "how can one distinguish … the natural inclinations, which are aimed at *bona honesta*, from the inclinations of feelings and emotions? [P]ractical reason understand[ing] an object as good...primarily sees that object as possessing a teleological relationship of perfection with oneself, not just of satisfaction (in the broadest sense) of oneself. True, all perfection provides some sort of satisfaction, but not vice versa." Robert Gahl, "Practical Reason in the Foundation of Natural Law according to Grisez, Finnis and Boyle" (Ph.D. diss., Athenaeum Romanum Sanctae Crucis, 1994), 134.

35. Brock, "Intelligibility of the Good," 66. For Brock, the natural inclinations *follow upon* the understanding of something as good.

36. The reader should distinguish understanding from knowledge. One may understand that something is good or bad yet not be able to articulate why. When one knows, one can articulate reasons.

ative *quasi-habitus*, dispositions not according to nature may be formed, resulting in addictions. If, on the other hand, one acts according to a positive *quasi-habitus*, one may form a disposition according to nature which would result in a good habit.

In order to trace a sure path toward conscience, that is, right thinking about moral choices, persons attend to the formation of right dispositions and habits of thought which lead to right thinking. The result of such formation will be a healthy conscience which makes right judgments. In contrast, the result of forming bad habits is an erroneous conscience to some degree, which requires that one strive to reform one's thinking. In order to accomplish such an alteration, the formation of new, good habits is necessary. For Aquinas, such re-formation is not easy. Habits are difficult, though not impossible, to change.[37]

## V. Judgments at the Dawn of Moral Awareness

According to Aquinas, early judgments are conclusions of comparisons of universals. Examples might be: "food is good," "my mother is a being," "my mother is not I." As understanding and knowledge develop, judgments become increasingly precise and complex. They may become premises for further conclusions. These judgments apply to all rational judgments, which Maritain refers to as "created liberty."[38] There is a relation between what is created and uncreated that becomes particularly apparent in acts of conscience which are truly free, that is, one chooses a good without being fettered by bad habits.[39] Freedom from bad habits can be attained with the aid of grace.

Maritain maintains that apprehension and judgment occur simultaneously. In some ways apprehension and judgment may appear to occur this way; but Brock's interpretation holds that a good must first be under-

37. See ST I-II, q. 49, a. 2, ad 3.

38. "The suppositum...is a problem, or rather the highest and most awesome mystery, with which the sciences which 'lisp of things divine' have to deal, namely, the problem of the relation between the liberty of the created existent and the eternal purposes of uncreated Liberty... already in the natural order, the question of the relation between these two liberties arises." Maritain, *Existence and the Existent*, 85.

39. See ibid., 94. He speaks of such a choice as choosing in union with the divine unshatterable activation. The human being has the capacity to shatter such activations due to created freedom.

stood[40] before a judgment can be made based on one's rational natural inclinations. However, once this good is understood, other apprehensions and judgments can occur *almost* simultaneously due to habits and dispositions.

## VI. Moral Understanding and Conscience: The Flexible and Delicate Instrument

For Maritain, there is no moral life without the personal judgment of conscience.[41] An elucidation of moral understanding is not simple. Morality is exceedingly complex as each human person uniquely regards how his or her conscience operates. Such complexity is not due to some aspect of the intellect that is particularly intricate. Rather, the paths of conscience and choice can be complex owing to three aspects which face the human person. These aspects are: (1) how well the conscience is formed; (2) the practical understanding of a contingent situation; (3) habits of thought and choice which exist in the one who decides or chooses. For Maritain, the conscience is a delicate and flexible instrument.[42] His position accords with general experience:

> The same moral case never appears twice in the world. To speak absolutely strictly, precedent does not exist. Each time I find myself in a situation requiring me to do a new thing, to bring into existence an act that is unique in the world, an act which must be in accord with the moral law in a manner and under conditions belonging strictly to me alone and which have never arisen before.[43]

Every human action is unique. To act in a way which is perfective, interior clarity is required. Such clarity may exist at times or remain bound in obscurity at other times. According to Maritain, natural law and various rules can be helpful, but they cannot take the place of the work behind the judgment of conscience. He writes:

40. See Brock, "Intelligibility of the Good," 65.

41. "When St. Thomas teaches us, with regard to the universe of ethics as a whole, and in connection with the life of the practical reason and the mere moral virtues, that there is no exercise of the virtues without the personal judgment of prudence, and more generally that there is no moral life without the personal judgment of conscience, he teaches us thereby that in every authentically moral act, man, in order to apply and in applying the law, must embody and grasp the universal in his own singular existence, where he is alone face to face with God." Maritain, *Existence and the Existent*, 59.

42. See ibid., 60.

43. Ibid., 51.

Useless to thumb through the dictionary of cases of conscience! Moral treatises will of course tell me the universal rule or rules I am bound to apply; they will not tell me how I, the unique I, am to apply them in the unique context in which I am involved.[44]

A fascinating interaction occurs between the pre-conscious, connatural knowledge, rational deliberation, and the will in what is understood as the judgment of conscience. Conscience in itself is razor-sharp, always attentive to truth and goodness. Yet, behind or beneath the reasoning which occurs is the pre-conscious or its effects. For Maritain, "the motives which reason deliberates upon do not play the decisive role of [a] moral option but [rather] that unforeseeable impulse of one's inscrutable subjectivity."[45]

It seems that a certain kind of *habitus* can be operative when one faces a moral choice. Such a *habitus* is, for the intellect and will, a repeated action which becomes second-nature. This *habitus* can be well or ill-disposed to what Aquinas speaks of as sensible habits and dispositions which he calls passions.

Conscience cannot ever be second-nature. Each act requires deliberation before a free choice is made. When conscience acts in its full nobility, the person grows in real freedom. Each act of conscience is a full consent of the will to go beyond any structure of safety one may have enjoyed within rules established by an ideology. This consent of the will is to do "the right thing," no matter what the cost. As Blessed John Henry Newman stated in his "Toast to the Conscience," in its full nobility, conscience acts as a "primordial vicar of God."[46] It speaks within the depths of the human being habituated to understanding and discriminating between goods that are lesser or greater for reaching self-perfection. It rings out in the depths of one who is attentive and vigilant about all of the voices which can lead one away from true freedom.

44. Ibid.

45. Ibid., 53.

46. John Henry Newman, *Grammar of Assent* (New York: Image, 1955), 101. See also Kevin Brendan Fagan, "A Toast to Conscience: Freedom of Conscience in John Henry Newman" (Ph.D. diss., University of Dallas, 1977).

## VIII. Conclusion

Many exist in slavery to immoral choices. Perhaps, in some cases, one may have understood a perfective good and chosen an alternate way because it was easier. A *quasi-habitus* could have been formed in such a case founded on a sensible good rather than a rational good. We can hope that such choices for sensible goods can be changed by working to will something which is truly good.[47] How does one make such a change? Each day, one is called to "turn away from apparent goods and learn to do true goods."[48] The smallest turn from a habit which entraps one in a lesser kind of perfection leads to the reward of a stronger hope and greater confidence. One forms new habits of self-control. One begins to form dispositions and habits that lead to prudence and wisdom. Right reason in habits can lead to rectitude in action. Attention to these habits, formed from preconscious awareness, is vital to growth in the right formation of conscience and a greater practice of real virtue, not only for persons but for entire societies.

Courage and perseverance are required to change such ingrained habits. Striving to make small changes may bring more success in the long run than attempting sweeping changes. Such work brings a greater subjective awareness of oneself *as person* and a greater objective awareness of one's relation to the common good.[49] Maritain considers the development of the person through the perspective of subjectivity. He writes:

47. "It should be noted here that man must realize through his will that of which his nature is but the sketch...man must become what he is. And this he must do at a sorrowful cost and with formidable risks. He himself, in the moral order, must win his liberty and his personality... if the development occurs in the direction of spiritual personality, man will be oriented towards the generous self of the heroes and saints." Jacques Maritain, *The Person and the Common Good*, translated by John J. Fitzgerald (Notre Dame, Indiana: Notre Dame University Press, 1985), 44.

48. Aquinas, *Commentary on Aristotle's Nicomachean Ethics*, lect. 11, cap. 9, no. 375., translated C. I. Litzinger, OP (Chicago: Henry Regnery, 1964). Aristotle develops the notion of the apparent good and the *bonum honestum* in his *Nicomachean Ethics*. In this section of his commentary, St. Thomas refers to Aristotle's incontinent man and how he must strive to act rightly. "Turning away from the apparent good toward the true good" is one way that a reader may think of this passage of Aquinas.

49. "The common good is not only a system of advantages and utilities but also a rectitude of life, an end, good in itself...a *bonum honestum*. For, on the one hand, to assure the existence of the multitude is something morally good in itself; on the other hand, the existence, thus assured, must be the just and morally good existence of the community. Only on condition that it is according to justice and moral goodness is the common good...the good of a people and a city." Maritain, *The Person and the Common Good*, 53.

The person is a substance whose substantial form is a spiritual soul; a substance which lives a life that is not merely biological and instinctive, but is also a life of intellect and will. It is a very simple-minded error to believe that subjectivity possesses no intelligible structure.[50]

Intelligible structures formed in the person's subjectivity assist or detract from one's growth as person. Maritain emphasizes in *The Person and the Common Good* that one purpose for right moral reasoning and willed action is the formation of a just society. If a society is not founded on rightly-formed conscience, it becomes "a mob of gangsters and murderers."[51]

Reflection on one's actions and motives is crucial for re-forming societies. If we discover that we have turned away from upright action, we can take heart. If one works to turn away from apparent goods and to turn to true goods, one can succeed with the help of wise mentors. Growth in virtue acts like leaven in a society, providing strength and confidence for future generations.[52]

50. Maritain, *Existence and the Existent*, 81.

51. Maritain, *The Person and the Common Good*, 53.

52. Reading today's headlines, one might be forgiven for concluding that we live in a morally degenerate society, one tending rapidly toward Maritain's "mob of gangsters and murderers." But we need not despair. We can work to counter this moral decline by striving to become virtuous ourselves. Growth in virtue, like the light and warmth of a fire, cannot help but be seen and felt by those who live around us. In this way, the virtues of any generation, like seeds planted in good soil—to change metaphors—might be expected to produce a bountiful harvest of virtues in future generations, thus preventing society from degenerating into Maritain's frightful "mob." Needless to say, all of this is the fruit only of great hope and perseverance.

# About the Authors

STEPHEN L. BROCK is Ordinary Professor of Medieval Philosophy at the Pontifical University of the Holy Cross in Rome. His most recent book is *The Philosophy of Saint Thomas Aquinas: A Sketch* (Wipf and Stock, 2015).

JOSHUA D. BRUMFIELD holds the Sue Canizaro Chair of Theology at the University of Holy Cross in New Orleans and is a founding board member of *The Newman Idea*. He has published articles on Dorothy Day and Joseph Ratzinger, and his first book, *The Benedict Proposal: Church as Creative Minority*, is forthcoming from Pickwick. He resides in New Orleans with his wife and four children.

JOHN J. CONLEY, SJ, holds the Henry J. Knott Chair in Philosophy and Theology at Loyola University Maryland. A specialist in modern French philosophy, he has published *The Suspicion of Virtue: Women Philosophers in Neoclassical France* (Cornell University Press, 2002), *Jacqueline Pascal: A Rule for Children* (University of Chicago Press, 2003), *Adoration and Annihilation: The Convent Philosophy of Port-Royal* (University of Notre Dame Press, 2009), and *The Other Pascals: The Philosophy of Jacqueline Pascal, Gilberte Pascal Perier, and Marguerite Perier* (University of Notre Dame Press, 2019).

ROBERT DELANEY studies theology at the University of Holy Cross. His interests include the philosophy of Jacques Maritain and the theology of Joseph Ratzinger. He is currently working on his Master's thesis, "The Gift of Hope in iGen's Meaningless Culture." In it he offers a Christian alternative to today's nihilistic and therapeutic culture. He is looking forward to doctoral studies.

HEATHER M. ERB teaches philosophy at Lock Haven University of Pennsylvania, the Great Books in the Ignatius-Angelicum Liberal Studies Program, and is an Associate Professor of Philosophy at Our Lady Seat of Wisdom College. Her publications focus on the nexus of metaphysics and mystical theology in Aquinas and his interpreters, as well as on issues in Catholicism and culture. Her book, *The Path of Spiritual Happiness*, examines the philosophy of happiness as developed by Aristotle, St. Thomas, and Josef Pieper.

JOHN FROULA is an Assistant Professor of Theology at the Saint Paul Seminary School of Divinity, in Saint Paul, Minnesota. He received his Ph.D. from Ave Maria University. He has published articles about Christology and Spiritual Theology in *The Thomist, The Josephinum Journal of Theology, The Heythrop Journal, The Downside Review*, and in several anthologies, as well as an annotated translation of the Christological section of Hugh of Saint Victor's *De Sacramentis.*

JAMES JACOBS is Professor of Philosophy and Assistant Academic Dean at Notre Dame Seminary in New Orleans. He is currently Vice-President of the American Maritain Association and edited the 2015 AMA volume, *A Piercing Light: Beauty, Faith, and Human Transcendence.*

GREGORY J. KERR is Associate Professor of Philosophy at DeSales University in Center Valley, Pennsylvania. He received his B.A. and M.A. in philosophy from Boston College and his Ph.D. from Fordham University, where he did his dissertation on *Maritain's Receptive Intuition and the Benefits of Art.* He is a former editor of the *Maritain Notebook*, the official newsletter of the American Maritain Association. He has published articles on Maritain's views on aesthetics, epistemology, ethics, love, and education in volumes in the AMA's series and elsewhere. Currently, he is finishing a volume that explores the very different and often conflicting ways humans know. He is married to Cindy and they have four sons and three grandchildren.

ROSE MARY HAYDEN LEMMONS is an associate professor of philosophy and an affiliate of both Catholic Studies and Family Studies at the University of St. Thomas in St. Paul, Minnesota. She is also a special issue editor for *Studia Gilsoniana: A Journal in Classical Philosophy*, the President of University Faculty for Life, the founding president of the Society for Thomistic Personalism, and an Advisory Board Member for the Saint John Paul II Institute in Houston Texas. She has published on the person, love, Thomistic natural law, American jurisprudence, religious liberty, bioethics, the family, personalist feminism, and John Paul II. Her publications include *Ultimate Normative Foundations: The Case for Aquinas's Personalist Natural Law* (2011, 2017), the edited anthology *Woman as Prophet in the Home and the World* (2016), and four entries in the *New Catholic Encyclopedia Supplement 2012–2013*.

THOMAS L. MAMMOSER has a B.A. in philosophy from the University of Notre Dame (1960) and pursued graduate studies at both the University of Chicago and Loyola University. For many years he was director of corporate communications for Walgreens. His staff's publications won numerous regional, national, and international awards. Mammoser also developed the acclaimed *One-on-One* mentoring program that pairs young professional adult mentors with Chicago's inner-city youth. He now serves on the Midtown Educational Foundation's board of honorary directors. Over the years, he has taught and lectured at the University of Santa Croce in Rome on communications, culture, and the church. In 2014 he completed a well-received book entitled *The Evangelical Roots of Democracy*, emphasizing the respect shown by America's early leaders for Christianity and religion. He now writes on subjects related to the Christianization of culture.

MARY KATERINA MASEK, RSM, is a professor of philosophy at Benedictine University in Mesa, Arizona. She completed her doctoral work at the Pontifical University of the Holy Cross in Rome, in 2014, specializing in the thought of St. Thomas Aquinas on Natural Divine Illumination in Natural Law.

MARK MOES completed an M.A. in philosophical theology at the Aquinas Institute of Theology and a doctorate in philosophy at the University of Notre Dame. He is currently Professor of Philosophy at Grand Valley State University in Michigan, specializing in Ancient Philosophy. He is author of *Plato's Dialogue Form and the Care of the Soul* and articles on ancient philosophy and philosophy of medicine. He is currently doing research on two connected projects: (1) a book on Plato's *Republic*, and (2) a book on the whole corpus of the published writings of Alasdair MacIntyre.

FRANCISCO PLAZA is a doctoral candidate in Philosophy at the University of St. Thomas (Houston). His dissertation centers on Jacques Maritain's analysis of culture and how it applies to politics in the modern West. In 2017, his article "Subjectivity and the *Prise de Conscience* in Jacques Maritain" was published by the American Maritain Association in *Engaging the Times: The Witness of Thomism,* edited by Joshua Schulz. Plaza focuses primarily on political theory, ethics, and the culture of modernity.

HANNAH WOLDUM RAGUSA is an instructor of philosophy, theology, and religion at Saint Leo University and an instructor of philosophy at Prince George's Community College. She is currently a doctoral student in philosophy at the Catholic University of America. Her article, "Beholding the Beauty of Being: Artistic Creativity in the Thomistic Tradition," appeared in the Spring 2017 volume of *Logos: A Journal of Catholic Thought and Culture.*

ALICE RAMOS is Professor of Philosophy at St. John's University in Queens, New York. Her publications include *Dynamic Transcendentals: Truth, Goodness, and Beauty from a Thomistic Perspective* (The Catholic University of America Press, 2012), two edited volumes of the American Maritain Association entitled *Beauty, Art, and the Polis* (2000) and *Faith, Scholarship, and Culture in the 21st Century* (co-edited with Marie I. George, 2002), *Signum: De la semiótica universal a la metafísica del signo* (EUNSA, 1987), and over sixty articles in areas such as Thomistic metaphysics and ethics, aesthetics, and Christian anthropology. She is presently editing a volume of fifteen essays entitled *Beauty and the Good: Recovering the Classical Tradition from Plato to Duns Scotus,* which will be published in 2020 by The Catholic University of America Press. Ramos is the recipient of grants for scholarly work both in the United States and in Europe. She is also a past president of the American Maritain Association (2002–2004) and has served several terms on the executive council of the American Catholic Philosophical Association as well as on the executive committee of the Metaphysical Society of America.

KATHRYN ROMBS, PH.D., is an instructor of philosophy at the University of Dallas. She is currently living for two years with her husband and six children in Rome. She is also the founder and president of a Catholic mothers' ministry, Mighty Is Her Call, Inc.

JOSHUA SCHULZ is an Associate Professor of Philosophy at DeSales University, Pennsylvania. In addition to writing about ethics and political philosophy, he enjoys hobby farming, playing board games, and reading science fiction.

DENIS SCRANDIS began his love of Maritain and the Aristotelian-Thomistic philosophy more than half a century ago when he found his vocation reading Maritain's *Preface to Metaphysics*. Although his undergraduate school (CCNY) could not nurture his development, subjection to Enlightenment thinking convinced him of its sterility before he came to understand its historic role undermining Western civilization. He remains convinced that Maritain is a beacon illuminating the path to truth and fullness of being in thought and in life.

ELEONORE STUMP is the Robert J. Henle Professor of Philosophy at Saint Louis University. She is also Honorary Professor at Wuhan University and at the Logos Institute, St Andrews, and a Professorial Fellow at Australian Catholic University. She has published extensively in philosophy of religion, contemporary metaphysics, and medieval philosophy. Her books include *Aquinas* (2003), *Wandering in Darkness: Narrative and the Problem of Suffering* (2010), and *Atonement* (2018). She has given the Gifford Lectures at Aberdeen (2003), the Wilde lectures at Oxford (2006), the Stewart lectures at Princeton (2009), and the Stanton lectures at Cambridge (2018). She is past president of the Society of Christian Philosophers, the American Catholic Philosophical Association, and the American Philosophical Association, Central Division; and she is a member of the American Academy of Arts and Sciences.

NIKOLAJ ZUNIC is Associate Professor in the Department of Philosophy at St. Jerome's University, Waterloo, Ontario, Canada. His scholarly work focuses on the philosophy of human nature and ethics as well as topics in modern and contemporary philosophy. He serves as the Vice-President of the Canadian Jacques Maritain Association and is the editor of the academic journal *Études maritainiennes—Maritain Studies*. He is the editor of *Distinctions of Being: Philosophical Approaches to Reality* (2013), an American Maritain Association publication.

# Index

# PUBLICATIONS OF THE AMERICAN MARITAIN ASSOCIATION

1. *Jacques Maritain: The Man and His Metaphysics*
Edited by John F. X. Knasas, 1988
ISBN 978-0-268-01205-2, (out of print)
Distributed by the University of Notre Dame Press

2. *Freedom in the Modern World: Jacques Maritain, Yves R. Simon, Mortimer J. Adler*
Edited by Michael D. Torre, 1989, Second Printing, 1990
ISBN 978-0-268-00978-6
Distributed by the University of Notre Dame Press

3. *From Twilight to Dawn: The Cultural Vision of Jacques Maritain*
Edited by Peter A. Redpath, 1990
ISBN 978-0-268-00979-3
Distributed by the University of Notre Dame Press

4. *The Future of Thomism*
Edited by Deal W. Hudson and Dennis Wm. Moran, 1992
ISBN 978-0-268-00986-1
Distributed by the University of Notre Dame Press

5. *Jacques Maritain and the Jews*
Edited by Robert Royal, 1994
ISBN 978-0-268-01193-2
Distributed by the University of Notre Dame Press

6. *Freedom, Virtue, and the Common Good*
Edited by Curtis L. Hancock and Anthony O. Simon, 1995
ISBN 978-0-268-00991-0
Distributed by the University of Notre Dame Press

7. *Postmodernism and Christian Philosophy*
Edited by Roman T. Ciapolo, 1997
ISBN 978-0-8132-0881-7
Distributed by The Catholic University of America Press

8. *The Common Things: Essays on Thomism and Education*
Edited by Daniel McInerny, 1999
ISBN 978-0-9669226-0-8
Distributed by The Catholic University of America Press

9. *The Failure of Modernism: The Cartesian Legacy and Contemporary Pluralism*
Edited by Brendan Sweetman, 1999
ISBN 978-0-9669226-1-5
Distributed by The Catholic University of America Press

10. *Beauty, Art, and the Polis*
Edited by Alice Ramos, 2000
ISBN 978-0-9669226-2-2
Distributed by The Catholic University of America Press

11. *Reassessing the Liberal State: Reading Maritain's Man and the State*
Edited by Timothy Fuller and John P. Hittinger, 2001
ISBN 978-0-9669226-3-9
Distributed by The Catholic University of America Press

12. *Faith, Scholarship, and Culture in the 21st Century*
Edited by Alice Ramos and Marie I. George, 2002
ISBN 978-0-9669226-5-3
Distributed by The Catholic University of America Press

13. *Jacques Maritain and the Many Ways of Knowing*
Edited by Douglas A. Ollivant, 2002
ISBN 978-0-9669226-4-6
Distributed by The Catholic University of America Press

14. *Truth Matters: Essays in Honor of Jacques Maritain*

Edited by John G. Trapani, Jr., 2004

ISBN 978-0-9669226-6-0
Distributed by The Catholic University of America Press

15. *The Human Person and a Culture of Freedom*

Edited by Peter A. Pagan Aguiar and Terese Auer, OP, 2009

ISBN 978-0-9669226-7-7
Distributed by The Catholic University of America Press

16. *Maritain and America*

Edited by Christopher M. Cullen, SJ and
Joseph Allan Clair, 2009

ISBN 978-0-9669226-8-4
Distributed by The Catholic University of America Press

17. *The Renewal of Civilization:*
*Essays in Honor of Jacques Maritain*

Edited by Gavin T. Colvert, 2010

ISBN 978-0-9669226-9-1
Distributed by The Catholic University of America Press

18. *The Vocation of the Catholic Philosopher:*
*From Maritain to John Paul II*

Edited by John P. Hittinger, 2010

ISBN 978-0-9827119-0-3
Distributed by The Catholic University of America Press

19. *Reading the Cosmos: Nature, Science, and Wisdom*

Edited by Giuseppe Butera, 2011

ISBN 978-0-9827119-1-0
Distributed by The Catholic University of America Press

20. *Distinctions of Being: Philosophical Approaches to Reality*

Edited by Nikolaj Zunic, 2013

ISBN 978-0-9827119-2-7
Distributed by The Catholic University of America Press

21. *Love and Friendship: Maritain and the Tradition*

Edited by Montague Brown, 2013

ISBN 978-0-9827119-3-4
Distributed by The Catholic University of America Press

22. *Aquinas and Maritain on Evil: Mystery and Metaphysics*
Edited by James G. Hanink, 2013
ISBN 978-0-9827119-4-1
Distributed by The Catholic University of America Press

23. *Human Nature, Contemplation, and the Political Order: Essays Inspired by Jacques Maritain's* Scholasticism and Politics
Edited by Peter Karl Koritansky, 2014
ISBN 978-0-9827119-5-8
Distributed by The Catholic University of America Press

24. *Redeeming Philosophy: From Metaphysics to Aesthetics*
Edited by John J. Conley, SJ, 2014
ISBN 978-0-9827119-6-5
Distributed by The Catholic University of America Press

25. *A Piercing Light: Beauty, Faith, and Human Transcendence*
Edited by James M. Jacobs, 2015
ISBN 978-0-9827-1197-2
Distributed by The Catholic University of America Press

26. *The Wisdom of Youth: Essays Inspired by the Early Work of Jacques and Raïssa Maritain*
Edited by Travis Dumsday, 2016
ISBN 978-0-9827119-8-9
Distributed by The Catholic University of America Press

27. *Engaging the Times: The Witness of Thomism*
Edited by Joshua Schulz, 2017
ISBN 978-0-9827119-9-6
Distributed by The Catholic University of America Press

28. *The Things that Matter: Essays Inspired by the Later Work of Jacques Maritain*
Edited by Heidi M. Giebel, 2018
ISBN 9780997220506
Distributed by The Catholic University of America Press